PICTURE PERCEPTION IN ANIMALS

Picture perception in animals

edited by

Joël Fagot

Centre National de la Recherche Scientifique, Marseille

Published in 2000 by Psychology Press Ltd
27 Church Road, Hove, East Sussex, BN3 2FA

www.psypress.co.uk

Simultaneously published in the USA and Canada
by Taylor & Francis Inc
325 Chestnut Street, Suite 800, Philadelphia, PA 19106

Psychology Press is part of the Taylor & Francis Group

British Library Cataloguing in Publication Data
A catalogue record for this book is available from the British Library

Library of Congress Cataloging-in-Publication Data

Picture perception in animals / Joël Fagot.
     p. cm.
   Includes bibliographical references (p.).
     ISBN 1-84169-156-9 (alk. paper)
     1. Animal psychology. 2. Perception in animals.
     3. Picture perception. 4. Psychology,
   Comparative. I. Fagot, Joël, 1960-

   QL785 .P49 2000
   156'.214--dc21

                                                    00-050497

Cover design by Jim Wilkie
Printed and bound in the UK by Biddles Ltd., Guildford and King's Lynn

Contents*

* This book was first published as a special issue of the journal *Cahiers de Psychologie Cognitive/Current Psychology of Cognition* (Vol. 18, 1999, n° 5-6).

List of contributors

James R. Anderson, Department of Psychology, University of Stirling
Stirling FK9 4LA, Scotland

Christopher I. Baker, Center for the Neural Bases of Cognition
Carnegie Mellon University - 115, Mellon Institute
Pittsburgh, PA 15213, USA

Irving Biederman, Hedco Neuroscience Building, MC 2520
University of South California, Los Angeles, CA 900089-2520, USA

Ruth Campbell, Department of Human Communication Science
University College London, Chandler House
Wakefield Street, London WC1N 1PG, England

Robert G. Cook, Department of Psychology, Tufts University
Medford, MA 02155, USA

Juan D. Delius, Allgemeine Psychologie, Universität Konstanz
78457 Konstanz, Germany

Delphine Dépy, Centre de Recherches en Neurosciences Cognitives, CNRS
31 chemin Joseph Aiguier, 13402 Marseille cedex 20, France

Jan B. Deręgowski, University of Aberdeen, Department of Psychology
William Guild Building, Old Aberdeen AB24 2UB, Scotland

Winand H. Dittrich, Department of Psychology, University of Hertfordshire
Hatfield AL10 9AB, England

Jacky Emmerton, Department of Psychological Sciences, Purdue University
1364 Psychological Sciences Building
West Lafayette, IN 47907-1364, USA

Joël Fagot, Centre de Recherches en Neurosciences Cognitives, CNRS
31 chemin Joseph Aiguier, 13402 Marseille cedex 20, France

Wolfgang Hörster, Allgemeine Psychologie, Universität Konstanz
78457 Konstanz, Germany

Dr. Ludwig Huber, Institute of Zoology, University of Vienna
Althanstrasse 14, 1090 Vienna, Austria

Ralph Jäger, Allgemeine Psychologie, Universität Konstanz
78457 Konstanz, Germany

Jeffrey S. Katz, Department of Psychology, Auburn University
Auburn, AL 36849, USA

Debbie M. Kelly, Department of Psychology, P220
Biological Sciences Building, Edmonton, Alberta T6G 2E9, Canada

Jun H. Kim, Department of Psychology, University of Washington
Seattle, WA 98105, USA

Stephen E. G. Lea, Psychology Department, University of Exeter
Exeter, EX4 4QG, England

Erika N. Lorincz, School of Psychology, University of St Andrews
St Andrews, KY16 9JU, Scotland

Julio C. Martinez Trujillo, Cognitive Neuroscience Laboratory
Department of Cognitive Neurology, University of Tuebingen
Auf der Morgenstelle 15, 72076 Tuebingen, Germany

Julie Martin-Malivel, Centre de Recherches en Neurosciences Cognitives
CNRS, 31 chemin Joseph Aiguier, 13402 Marseille cedex 20, France

Joachim Ostheim, Allgemeine Psychologie, Universität Konstanz
78457 Konstanz, Germany

Olivier Pascalis, Department of Psychology, The University of Sheffield
Sheffield S10 2TP, England

Jessie J. Peissig, Department of Psychology, University of Iowa
Iowa City, IA 52242, USA

David I. Perret, School of Psychology, University of St Andrews
St Andrews, KY16 9JU, Scotland

Odile Petit, CNRS, Laboratoire d'Ethologie des Primates
7 rue de l'Université, 67 000 Strasbourg, France

Sheri Reid, Department of Psychology, University of Alberta
Edmonton, Alberta T6G 2E9, Canada

Marcia L. Spetch, Department of Psychology, University of Alberta
Edmonton, AB T6G 2E9, Canada

Stephen Treue, Cognitive Neuroscience Laboratory
Department of Cognitive Neurology, University of Tuebingen
Auf der Morgenstelle 15, 72076 Tuebingen, Germany

Edward. A. Wasserman, Department of Psychology, University of Iowa
Iowa City, IA 52242, USA

Shigeru Watanabe, Department of Psychology, Keio University
Mita 2-15-45, Minato-Ku, Tokyo, Japan

Donald M. Wilkie, Department of Psychology
The University of British Columbia, Vancouver, BC V6T 1Z4, Canada

Michael E. Young, Department of Psychology, Southern Illinois University
Carbondale, IL 62901, USA

Acknowledgements

This volume is the result of convergent efforts from a large scientific community, and there are many people I wish to thank. In particular, I would like to express my deep gratitude to the authors who have immediately perceived the real originality and interest of this volume, and have enthusiastically agreed to write a chapter for it. I am also very grateful to many colleagues who devoted their time to review early versions of selected chapters. They include James R. Anderson, Ramesh S. Bhatt, Claude Bonnet, Muriel Boucart, Raymond Bruyer, Josep Call, Ken Cheng, Dominique Domken, Michèle Fabre-Thorpe, Gregor Fetterman, Kazuo Fujita, Gordon G. Gallup Jr., Charles R. Hamilton, William D. Hopkins, Shoji Itakura, Iver Iversen, Masako Jitsumori, Donald F. Kendrick, Kieran Lee, Jack Loomis, Guillaume Masson, Lisa A. Parr, Patrick Péruch, Camille-Aimé Possamaï, Alexé Riehle, William A. Roberts, Herbert Roitblat, Etienne Save, David Sheinberg, Roger K. Thomas, Roger K. R. Thompson, Betty A. Vermeire, David A. Washburn, and Tony Wright.

Preface

One of the most striking abilities animals share with humans is the capacity to recognize visual objects: to quickly and efficiently respond to them in an appropriate manner. Given its biological importance, object recognition has been (and remains) intensively studied in the fields of comparative psychology and cognitive neuroscience. The aim of this volume is to contribute to the domain of object recognition in a unique way by addressing the question: "How do animals perceive pictures of realistic objects?". For 35 years, visual recognition has been investigated by presenting to animals pictorial stimuli, such as color slides of social or non-social objects, or scenes. For some authors, pictorial stimuli are simply considered to be complex stimuli, sharing some dimensions with the real objects that they depict, such as color or luminance variations. For other authors, pictorial stimuli are considered to be ecologically valid and "realistic" stimuli, because they represent real objects or scenes existing in nature. For these authors, presentation of pictorial stimuli is therefore considered to be an efficient way to investigate how real objects are perceived and conceptualized.

Although pictures have commonly been used to study cognitive abilities in animals, very few researches have questioned the realistic nature of pictures, and the validity of pictorial representations for studying the processing of objects or scenes existing in the real world. To my knowledge, this volume is the first attempt to synthetically address these issues. In the context of this volume, researchers from various fields of comparative psychology and cognitive neuroscience were invited to contribute a chapter on the topic of picture perception, in order to present a comprehensive overview of what is currently known about how animals perceive and process pictures. The resulting volume contains a total of 14 chapters. These chapters touch on the high points in this area by asking questions such as: Can animals recognize visual objects or scenes on pictures despite variations in viewpoint? (Peissig et al., Watanabe); to what extent do birds recognize the real world from its 2D representation? (Wilkie, Spetch et al.); what can be inferred from the psychophysical and neuroscientific literature on bird's vision? (Delius et al., Huber); can animals demonstrate transfer of learning from picture to objects or vice versa? (Delius et al., Fagot et al.); how do animals perceive pictures of faces? (Pascalis et al., Huber); can monkeys extract gaze information from pictures? (Lorincz et al.); what does the literature on concept formation in animals tell us about picture perception? (Cook et al., Delius et al., Fagot et al.); what do birds see in moving video images? (Lea and Dittrich); what are the neural bases of visual scene representation in animals? (Treue and Martinez Trujillo); what is the effect of selective attention on scene perception? (Treue and Martinez Trujillo); and how do monkeys and apes perceive their image in a mirror? (Anderson). The 14th chapter (by J. B. Deręgowski) serves as a bridge between the animal and human literature on picture perception. It questions the processing of pictures by humans, by focussing on inter-cultural differences.

Although not exhaustive, it is expected that the tour offered in this volume will convey a clear sense of the progress that has been made in the field of picture perception and will underline the risks, limits, and advantages of presenting pictures to animals. That tour is expected to be of major interest to those working in the field of comparative cognition – including developmental psychologists – as well as to anthropologists, psychologists, or neuroscientists, who study the processing of real objects through the convenient use of pictures.

Joël Fagot

June 2000

Picture-object recognition in pigeons

Juan D. Delius,[1] Jacky Emmerton,[2] Wolfgang Hörster,[1]

Ralph Jäger,[1] and Joachim Ostheim[1]

1. Universität Konstanz, Konstanz, Germany
2. Purdue University, West Lafayette, IN, USA

Abstract. Photo-, computo-, and videographic pictures have been popular stimuli in experimental studies on the cognitive capacities of pigeons. Most authors have simply considered them as complex stimuli but some authors have talked about them as being natural stimuli. More popular accounts of these studies have mostly assumed that the pigeons were recognising the equivalencies between the pictures presented and the objects or scenes that were represented on them. We argue that this assumption may often not be warranted because picture technology is adjusted to fool human vision but not pigeon vision. Mammalian and avian visual systems have a long divergent evolutionary history. Anatomical, physiological, and behavioural investigations indicate that colour, depth, flicker, movement and other aspects of vision are probably sufficiently different from humans in pigeons and other birds, enough for pictures to appear to them quite different from reality. We review a number of studies in pigeons and chickens that were concerned with the cross-recognition of real objects or scenes and pictures thereof. The conclusion is that these animals are capable of some gross transfer of recognition between pictures and reality and vice-versa but that when the behavioural tasks require more complex or refined discriminations this transfer generally brakes down.

Key words: Pictures, objects, cross-recognition, stimulus discrimination, pigeons, chickens, avian vision.

Correspondence should be sent to Juan D. Delius, Allgemeine Psychologie, Universität Konstanz, 78457 Konstanz, Germany (e-mail: juan.delius@uni-konstanz.de).

INTRODUCTION

With the arrival of the so-called cognitive revolution in the field of animal behaviour, the use of quite complex pictures as discriminatory stimuli in learning experiments has become widespread. The domestic pigeon (*Columba livia*), a laboratory species known to be a proficient learner and thought to have excellent vision, has been a popular subject of experiments in which such pictures are used. Several hundred papers published during the last few decades report results obtained in pigeons with complex photographic or computographic stimuli. There are also a number of publications on domestic chickens (*Gallus gallus*). This species has been a popular subject in more ethologically-oriented experiments involving videographic stimuli (for a review, see D'Eath, 1998); we shall mention some of these studies later. A few studies with pictures have been carried out on other avians, such as budgerigars (*Melopsittacus undulatus;* Trillmich, 1976; Brown & Dooling, 1992), bluejays (*Cyanocitta cristata*; Pietrewicz & Kamil, 1979; Bond & Kamil, 1998), zebrafinches (*Taenopyygia guttata*; Bischof, 1980; Adret, 1997), Bengalese finches (*Lonchura striata*; Watanabe, Yamashita, & Wakita, 1993), and tree sparrows (*Spizella sp.*; Hebrard, 1978). Since real rather than pictorial objects, conspecifics, and scenes will be relevant later, it is also worth mentioning that although there have been only a few studies using such discriminanda with pigeons (Cumming, 1966; Verhave, 1966), quite a number have presented real items to chickens and some other bird species. This research has been mainly concerned with the study of learning by imprinting (Bolhuis, 1996). Readers will also want to consult the several other thematically cognate papers in this journal issue.

Photographs

The use of complex pictures in learning experiments with pigeons really started in 1964, when Herrnstein and Loveland first trained pigeons to distinguish pictures containing humans from ones that did not. They then showed that pigeons could transfer this ability to other pictures that did or did not include human figures. These authors projected a collection of 80 randomly ordered colour transparencies onto a small screen. The collection included a great variety of scenes, half of which showed a human figure and half of which did not. Hungry pigeons saw the screen through a transparent pecking key. Several responses to any stimulus showing a human yielded a grain reward. Responses to any stimulus without a human failed to produce a reward. After about 700 trials, the pigeons responded more frequently to the pictures with humans than to ones without. They were then exposed to a collection of 80 human and non-human transparencies that they had not previously seen. The pigeons immediately preferred to peck at the novel pictures showing a person or people rather than those not showing anyone. They thus demonstrated that they could apply the categorisation principle they had learned with one set of pictures to another novel set of pictures. With analogous methods, it has been shown that pigeons can learn to classify many other categories shown in photographs. Such categorisation experiments have involved discriminating pictures of trees from pictures of non-trees, pictures of fish from underwater pictures lacking fish, pictures of water from pictures without water, even pictures of a particular person from pictures of other people, or pictures of a particular scene from pictures of another scene (Herrnstein, Loveland, & Cable, 1976; Honig & Stewart, 1989; Herrnstein, 1990). Pigeons' capacity to categorise extends not only to photographs representing natural objects and scenes, such as they might come across in their normal environment, but also to computographs of rather artificial scenes such as impressionist and cubist paintings (Watanabe, Sakamoto, & Wakita, 1995).

Which features pigeons attend to when categorising such complex pictures is not at all certain. Surprisingly, Greene (1984) found that pigeons able to discriminate pictures containing humans from those not containing humans relied predominantly on unidentified features of the background, rather than on the presence or absence of a human. Only when Edwards and Honig (1987) carefully used a collection of pairs of pictures in which one picture always showed a person against a given background and the other picture showed exactly the same background without a person, did the pigeons learn to rely on the presence or absence of the human as the discriminatory feature. Fersen and Lea (1990) showed that when classifying a set of photographs of buildings, only some of their pigeons could be trained to combine additively all five dichotomous features intended by the experimenters. The five features were architecture (public bar, university building), orientation (vertical, oblique), view (from below, from above), distance (near, far), and light (sunny, cloudy). Several pigeons only attended to some of these features and only a few pigeons to all five of them.

Computographs

Wright, Cook, Rivera, Sands, and Delius (1988) used colour computographic pictures of objects such as a bee, a camel, an accordion, a screwdriver, a book, and a windmill to train individual pigeons on the so-called matching-to-sample task. These cartoon-like stimuli were presented on a computer monitor, and pecks on them were detected by a touch-sensitive screen. On a given trial of the training procedure a sample picture of, say, the bee was shown first on the middle of the screen. After the pigeon had pecked the sample stimulus, two comparison stimuli were presented left and right of the sample. In our example, one comparison picture was that of the bee again and the other was, say, the book. The pigeon was rewarded for pecking the matching picture of the bee with a few seeds delivered next to the picture, and penalised with time out for pecking the non-matching picture of the book. For training, stimulus triplets were randomly assembled from 152 different pictures. When the pigeons had learned to respond to these training triplets at a rate of 75% correct after about 6500 trials, they were confronted with 20 stimulus triplets constructed from 40 pictures of objects they had never seen before (mouse, artichoke, whistle, and so on). On this transfer test they performed at an 80% correct level, indicating that they had learned to respond to an identity relation between pictures, independently of what particular objects were depicted. Pigeons who were trained on 4 triplets based on only 2 different pictures learned the matching task faster, requiring only about 1200 trials to reach the 75% correct criterion. But they only reached a 55% correct response rate on the transfer test with novel pictures. This group clearly had not really learned the identity rule. Macphail and Reilly (1989), who used a large number of photographic slides, and Todd and Mackintosh (1990), who used a large collection of computographic pictures, employed a successive rather than a simultaneous variant of the matching-to-sample procedure. In fact, the task for the pigeons in both of these studies was more one of picture familiarity/novelty discrimination than of identity/oddity discrimination. These authors showed that pigeons were capable of detecting the novelty or familiarity of a very large number of pictorial stimuli. This is something the birds can only have done by combining a large number of features to decide whether, overall, a picture was one they had or had not seen before.

Attitudes

In these studies and in many others of their kind, investigators in the behaviourist tradition mainly regard the pictures they use as plain stimuli. They are purportedly not at all concerned with the issue of whether the pigeons perceive the pictures as representations of the objects or scenes they depict. In spite of the fact that they promoted the cognitive revolution in the field of animal behaviour, neo-behaviourists have remained highly sceptical about the variables and mental processes involved. Some authors do talk of photographs that depict real objects, and of scenes as being natural stimuli, as if to distinguish them from the simpler abstract geometrical designs (triangles, circles, crosses, bars) traditionally used in earlier times. But beyond that, some authors seem to assume that what pigeons see in such natural pictures must be much the same as what we humans see in them, that is, natural scenes. Secondary sources, such as popular books or newspaper articles, are even more apt to make this assumption. They often suggest, based for example on the findings of Herrnstein et al. (1976), that pigeons have been shown capable of learning to recognise a particular person from other people, regardless of the view and the context in which these people were presented. In fact, all that has been strictly shown by these authors is that some pigeons learned to recognise certain pictures as worth pecking for food and certain other pictures as not worth pecking. On which characteristics of the pictures this discriminative behaviour was based remains largely undetermined.

The problem at its extreme is that, much as in humans, it is not easy to discover what the subjective experiences of pigeons are when they look at pictures. But the question that can potentially be answered is whether pigeons are prepared to view pictures as standing for, or as being equivalents of, the objects or scenes that they depict. Remember that in humans, equating pictures with objects is by no means a trivial process and it might indeed only arise through fairly specific experiences. Very young children have trouble with this equating process, possibly because their visual apparatus is not yet fully developed (Slater, Rose, & Morrison, 1984). Individuals with poor spatial-visual abilities may persistently have trouble with pictorial representations such as geographic maps or technical drawings of real scenes and objects (Potegal, 1982). Human adults who live in cultures that are not regularly exposed to pictorial representations often have difficulty equating pictures with the objects or scenes they depict (Der̨egowski, 1989). Even people who are visually intelligent and pictorially conversant occasionally fail to recognise familiar objects or scenes on photographic, cinematographic, computographic, or videographic pictures. However, even with the best pictorial technology, humans never have more than transient problems deciding whether they are viewing real things or depictions of them. The simple fact is that pictorial images lack, or misrepresent to various degrees, a number of sensory cues that normally support the recognition of real things. Leaving aside stereoscopic pictures, which are difficult to employ with animals, this has to do firstly with the inevitable two-dimensionality of pictures and the three-dimensionality of objects and scenes. Secondly, it has also to do with the inherent technical shortcomings of pictures in depicting even the purely two-dimensional properties of objects and scenes (restricted spatial and temporal resolution, poor luminous and chromatic replication, unnatural size/distance correspondence, constrained spatial extent, artifactual surface reflections, etc.).

Evolution

Technological advances are intended to minimise these defects of pictures but naturally only with the perceptual apparatus of human clients in mind. When pictures are used with animals, there is a propensity among researchers to ignore the fact that the visual functions of species, breeds, and even individuals may differ as a consequence of their differing phylogenetic and ontogenetic histories. In fact, concerning the mistaken equation of pigeon and human vision, one must remember that these species stem from two different reptile clades, the therapsids and the theropods, which went separate evolutionary ways some 310 million years ago (Kumar & Hedges, 1998). Mammals arose from the former about 250 million years ago and birds from the latter about 150 million years ago. A succession of geoecological scenarios steered the two lineages along quite different evolutionary pathways (Ahlberg & Milner, 1994; Feduccia, 1996). For a long time, reptiles dominated almost all niches accessible to cold-blooded vertebrates. The ancestral mammalian stock stayed mainly terrestrial but managed to spread into the nocturnal habitat thanks to homeothermy. Their nocturnal habits diminished the demands on the visual system and increased demands on their forebrain-based olfactory system. The early birds remained diurnal but moved instead into the aerial niche. Perhaps due to the need to out-compete the reptilian pterosaurs, which were also diurnal and aerial, these early birds similarly developed warm-bloodedness (Ruben, 1995). When the reptile lineages were badly decimated right at the end of the Cretaceous period (68 million years ago) by a cold phase brought about by the impact of a large meteorite, the climatically better buffered avians and mammals largely took over. The birds continued to be selected for a predominantly diurnal-aerial habitat that demanded ever more performance from their fundamentally reptilian, midbrain-based visual system. Some mammalian lineages, however, began to move into the diurnal-terrestrial habitats left vacant by the saurian mass extinction. The increased visual demands on them led to the expansion of a forebrain-based, mammalian visual system. Humans naturally descend from one of these diurnal lineages. The upshot of all this prehistory is that human and pigeon vision share some functional similarities which are less the product of homologies due to common ancestry than the result of convergences due to their only recently shared diurnality (Delius, Siemann, Emmerton, & Xia, 1999).

Pigeons are highly visual animals, as are nearly all birds, including even those secondarily turned somewhat nocturnal, for example, owls and nightjars. The sophistication of the pigeon's visual system is signalled anatomically by their relatively large eyes, which are each about 1 ml in volume. Beyond that fact, gross estimates suggest that about one third of the pigeon's nervous system, with its 2.5 ml volume and approximately 10^9 neurons, is mainly engaged in visual functions. This provides the pigeon with a visual-neural network involving perhaps some 10^{11} synaptic connections and, which, in principle, equips them with information-processing capacities sufficient for the most sophisticated picture and object perception conceivable (Delius et al., 1999). However, with due respect to the earlier phylogenetic arguments it is important to stress that, though it is the best studied species, the pigeon cannot stand as a representative for all avian species. This caveat is true even for the not-so-unrelated, but meanwhile rather terrestrial, chicken. Comparative data, although rather limited, suggest that the divergence of visual anatomy and physiology among birds is indeed considerable (Martin, 1993; D'Eath, 1998; Güntürkün, 1991). Even within the domestic pigeon it may not be wise to assume too readily that the various artificially selected breeds (homing, carneaux, strasser, fantail, etc.) are entirely equal in their visual anatomy or functions (Jahnke, 1984).

PIGEON VISION

In line with the fact that, geologically speaking, the visual systems of pigeons and humans diverged for a long time and only converged for a short time, the vision of pigeons differs from our own in very many respects. But not all the differences are directly relevant to the question of whether pigeons recognise the equivalence between real natural scenes and artificial pictures. In this brief overview we only focus on the aspects that clarify the latter issue.

Depth vision

Pigeons differ from us in the fact that their eyes are placed laterally in the head. Each eye has a visual field of about 170 degrees, but when both eyes are at rest, the overlapping binocular field of view is only about 20 degrees wide (Nalbach, Wolf-Oberhollenzer, & Remy, 1993). This means that pigeons mainly view their surroundings monocularly. They then fixate with their central monocular foveae, achieving this with head movements and eye movements, the latter being largely independent for each eye. Some head and eye movements, however, routinely serve to maintain relatively stable retinal images while the pigeon walks about (Wohlschläger, Jäger, & Delius, 1993). The foveae are characterised by locally high densities of cones and retinal neurons. Monocular viewing is naturally devoid of stereoscopic vision, which depends on the disparities between the retinal images of two eyes viewing the same scene. The fact that the eyes of pigeons are placed closer together than ours reduces the magnitude of the inter-retinal mismatches on which they can rely. This relative emphasis on monocular vision might be thought to contribute to pigeons perceiving two-dimensional pictures and three-dimensional scenes as equivalent. However, it has been shown that when pigeons approach, fixate, and peck at objects and pictures from a range of about 30 cm (Goodale, 1983), as they are often expected to do in experimental settings, they can exhibit true binocular stereoscopy (McFadden, 1993). This is undoubtedly aided in part by the fact that, as they prepare to and then actually peck, pigeons regularly increase the size of the binocular field overlap to almost 40 degrees by means of convergent eye movements (Bloch, Leimeignan, & Martinoya, 1987; Wohlschläger, Jäger, & Delius, 1993). The deftness with which pigeons can rapidly pick up even small food items from variable locations suggests that they can indeed precisely assess the depth of targets (Siemann & Delius, 1992). Incidentally, the convergence effort itself may also be used by pigeons for non-stereoscopic depth gauging (Martinoya, LeHouezec, & Bloch, 1988). Because of their pronounced locomotor and neck mobility, pigeons can also easily bring items of interest into their stereoscopic range. Stereoscopy is connected with the presence of fairly large, specialized areas in the dorsoposterior region of the retinae. These so-called red areas have high densities of cones and associated neurons and they project binocularly into the visual field surrounding the tip of the beak. Within the red area of each retina, there is a smaller area dorsalis with a particularly high retinal element density. This area dorsalis, although not associated with a retinal depression, obviously functions as a binocular fovea (Galifret, 1968). Pigeons tend to attend preferentially to small visual features when they peck (Jenkins & Sainsbury, 1970; Lindenblatt & Delius, 1988). This is consistent with the reduced extent of the high-resolution binocular field but possibly also relates to pigeons' reluctance to swallow larger items. The pigeon's eye shape is such that at accommodative rest, the lower half of the visual field is somewhat myopic while the upper field is emmetropic (Fitzke, Hayes, Hodos, Holden, & Low, 1985). However, the accommodation power of pigeons' eyes is considerable, about 10 dioptres, and the two eyes can accommodate independently (Schaeffel, 1994). The clear innermost portion of the nictitating membrane that is drawn over the eyes during pecks may contribute to close-range accommodation because it has an optical magnifying effect (Ostheim, Krug, & Schlotter, 1999). It is also probable that a partial lid closure during pecking, in interplay with the pupil, acts as an aperture-limiting device that augments the depth of focus (Ostheim, 1997a, b). Contrary to an earlier belief that pigeons close their eyes as they peck, it is now clear that they continue seeing throughout this motion (Hörster, 1997; Hörster, Krumm, & Mohr, 1999).

Apart from stereoscopy, there are several other mechanisms that can provide visual depth information without requiring binocular image overlap. Those we can expect to play an important role in pigeons because of their body and head mobility depend on successive monocular image disparities, that is, on position and movement parallax effects. Direct proof that pigeons use optic flow fields is still lacking. But there is at least indirect evidence that rotating stimulus arrays that, to us, appear to expand or contract (i.e., stimulation that mimics looming or receding scenes) can induce the corresponding illusions in pigeons (Martinoya & Delius, 1990; see also Frost, Wylie, & Wang, 1994; Sun & Frost, 1998, for neural correlates). Other depth cues are potentially provided by occlusion patterns, perspective size, texture gradients, shading patterns, and accommodation efforts. The extent to which pigeons utilise these depth cues is still uncertain. Generally we would be inclined to assume that they do so in their natural environment because, at the high speeds at which pigeons fly through cluttered spaces, monocular information about visual depth must be essential for safe navigation. Some studies have already addressed the question of whether pigeons can discriminate pictorial or computer-generated stimuli on the basis of one or other of these cues. To date, pigeons have treated occluded figures as equivalent to incomplete shapes, rather than completing the occluded parts. However, these studies have only been limited to two-dimensional pictures of geometric shapes or cartoon figures (Cerella, 1980; Sekuler, Lee, & Shettleworth, 1996).

Pigeons have also been tested for their ability to distinguish pictures of objects from similar pictures in which depth cues based on either shading or perspective have been removed or manipulated (Reid & Spetch, 1998). Pecks towards a picture that contained both types of depth cues, as solid objects do, were rewarded, whereas the choice of a picture in which one or the other depth cue was lacking was not rewarded. The birds were able to make these discriminations and to transfer them to novel stimulus displays. They also discriminated pictures of three-dimensional objects (e.g., a cube with shading and perspective cues) from a two-dimensional shape of similar aspect (e.g., a uniformly shaded square). Since the stimuli were displayed on a computer monitor, they were all physically two-dimensional, but this study does suggest that birds might be able to utilise some depth cues, even in pictorial representations. Pecking preferences for variously shaded three- and two-dimensional stimuli indicate that naturalistic shading patterns also act as a three-dimensionality cue for neonate domestic chickens (Dawkins, 1969; Hershberger, 1970). Pigeons probably have little difficulty distinguishing the two-dimensionality of pictures and the three-dimensionality of real scenes and objects. Additionally, when they actually peck at stimuli, pigeons can assess the flatness or solidness of these stimuli through tactile (haptic) cues (Schall & Delius, 1991).

Colour vision

The retina of pigeons is, like our own, equipped with rod (twilight vision) and cone (daylight vision) photoreceptors. However, pigeon cones come in two easily identifiable varieties, double cones and single cones. Furthermore, there are five morphologically distinguishable cone types (Emmerton, 1983a). The principal cone of the double variety is characterised by a highly refractive glycogen ellipsoid that fills the neck of its outer segment. The accessory cone adheres tightly to it except for its outer segment. Most if not all pigeon cones include a so-called coloured oil droplet at the base of the photopigment-bearing outer segments. All light entering these segments passes through the oil droplets. They contain lipid-dissolved carotenoid pigments and occur in red, orange, yellow, pale yellow, colourless, and clear varieties. Microspectrophotometry has revealed that the oil droplets act as long-wavelength light pass filters with differing short-wave cut-off flanks (Bowmaker, 1977). The same technique has also been used to show that, apart from the rhodopsin contained in the free oil-droplet rods, there are at least three different cone pigments with absorption maxima in the red, green, and blue regions of the spectrum. Further evidence indicates the presence of a photopigment peaking in the violet region of the spectrum (Varela, Palacios, & Goldsmith, 1993). Electroretinographic and behavioural spectral sensitivity measurements have shown that, besides a main sensitivity maximum in the spectral region visible to humans, there is a secondary maximum in the near-ultraviolet region which is not visible to humans (Remy & Emmerton, 1989). The ocular media of pigeons, including the lens and certain oil droplets, are fully transparent to near-ultraviolet light, and pigeons are not only capable of visual shape discrimination in this wavelength range (Emmerton, 1983b), but also exhibit good wavelength discrimination down to at least 360 nm (Emmerton & Delius, 1980). The presence of an additional ultraviolet absorbing photopigment is thus probable in pigeons. Recently, pigeons were found to exhibit a higher visual near-infrared sensitivity than humans, but nothing is yet known about its physiological basis or its functional consequences (Ostheim, 1998).

Combinations of the various photopigments and oil-droplets in different cones yield cones with differing effective action spectra (Bowmaker, 1977). Furthermore there are regional differences in the spectral cutoffs of the different oil droplets, and in the frequency of the cones with different oil-droplet/photopigment combinations. In the red area of the retina (the dorso-temporal quadrant of the retina projecting into the lower frontal field of view; Galifret, 1968), where the cones contain mostly red and orange oil droplets, there are at least six different cone types. In the remainder of the retina, the yellow area, where the cones chiefly bear yellow oil droplets, there are at least five cone types (Emmerton, 1983a). The small fovea centralis located within this yellow area is also rich in cones containing red and orange oil droplets; it may be like a red area in terms of its cone types.

The two major retinal areas are associated with different spectral sensitivities, with the yellow field exhibiting a relatively higher sensitivity for shorter wavelengths than the red field (Remy & Emmerton, 1989). Beyond this, it is likely that the colour perception differs between the two areas (Delius, Jahnke-Funk, & Hawker, 1981). More generally the colour vision of pigeons, as one would expect from the numbers of the different cone types, is quite complex. One of the functions that partially characterises the performance of colour vision systems is the wavelength discrimination function. At each light wavelength, this function shows the smallest wavelength difference that the species can discriminate behaviourally. The curve of human trichromats has two minima that lie very roughly at the points where the absorption spectra of their red-, green-, and blue-absorbing cones overlap. Human dichromats display only one minimum that lies between their blue and longer-wave-length cone absorption spectra (usually they lack either the green-absorbing or the red-absorbing cones: Neitz & Neitz, 1998). The wave-length discrimination function of a pigeon for frontally presented spectral stimuli exhibits four minima, suggesting that its vision is pentachromatic and based on cones with five different effective absorption spectra (Emmerton & Delius, 1980; Varela, Palacios, & Goldsmith, 1993). This would mean that, while all hues that humans see can fit into a three-dimensional space (usually presented collapsed into a two-dimensional colour triangle), the hues a pigeon can see requires a five-dimensional space. More practically speaking, whereas three basic colours are sufficient to mix all hues humans can see (the principle on which colour photography, computography, and videography are based), five different basic colours would probably be needed to do the same for pigeons. Though the rules of colour mixing have not yet been fully determined for pigeons or for any other bird species, the results available so far suggest the presence of an at least tetrachromatic colour vision (Jitsumori, 1976; Palacios & Varela, 1992).

The differentiation of the retina of pigeons may also be related to their sensitivity to the polarisation plane of light. Evidence concerning this sensitivity in pigeons reported some time ago (Kreithen & Keeton, 1974; Delius, Perchard, & Emmerton, 1976) has recently been challenged (Coemans, Vos, & Nuboer, 1990), but there is much evidence of the presence of polarisation sensitivity in various other bird species (Able & Able, 1997). The polarisation of sky light, which is undoubtedly used by these birds for navigational purposes, happens to be maximal in the ultraviolet range. Delius et al. (1976) suggested that polarisation sensitivity in pigeons may be restricted to the yellow area of the retina and be connected with its higher ultraviolet sensitivity. In the case of pictures, this area may enhance the perception of surface reflections that tend to be strongly polarised. Burkhardt (1989) showed in turn that many natural objects likely to be of interest to birds (plumages, berries, etc.) are ultravioletly coloured.

Other factors

As in all non-mammalian vertebrates, the optic nerves of birds cross over almost totally into the contralateral side of the brain (Bagnoli, Porciatti, Fontanesi, & Sebastiani, 1987). Information from the two eyes is kept largely separate in the two contralateral brain hemispheres throughout the visual system areas, the interhemispheric commissures in pigeons being of small calibre (Güntürkün, 1991). Behavioural evidence shows that pigeons display some degree of hemispheric specialization, with pecking, for example, being predominantly controlled visually by the left hemisphere, that is, by the right eye (Güntürkün, Emmerton, & Delius, 1989; Güntürkün, Hellman, Melsbach, & Prior, 1998). These birds also have some difficulty with interhemispheric (interocular) transfer of visual information. Having learned a visual task when seeing with one eye, pigeons often cannot master it well when they are tested with the other eye. They have less trouble when viewing stimuli in the frontal, normally binocular visual fields than when viewing them in the lateral, monocular visual fields (Remy & Watanabe, 1993). Pigeons also exhibit information transfer asymmetries when viewing with just one eye. Visual discrimination tasks learned with stimuli presented in the frontal field are poorly performed when the stimuli are subsequently presented in the lateral field of the same eye. The transfer of performance is markedly better in the other direction (Mallin & Delius, 1983; Remy & Emmerton, 1991; Roberts, Phelps, Macuda, Brodbeck, & Russ, 1996). But pigeons nevertheless have a relatively hard time discriminating stimuli presented laterally when they have to respond by pecking a key viewed frontally (Güntürkün et al., 1989). This is probably related to the fact that there is partial separation of the projections of the red (binocular) and yellow (monocular) areas of the retina into a tecto-thalamo-telencephalic pathway and a thalamo-telencephalic pathway (Remy & Güntürkün, 1991; Güntürkün, 1999).

The detection and or increment thresholds for various visual variables have been determined psychophysically for the frontal visual field of pigeons. The threshold for brightness and size is about 10% of a given magnitude, for tilt it is about 10 degrees, for acuity it is about 0.1 degrees of visual angle, and for movement it is about 5 degrees of visual angle per sec. These values are generally worse than those determined for humans. But note that they have usually been obtained with successive stimulus presentation methods. Successive discrimination paradigms are likely to be affected by pigeons' less durable short-term memory compared to humans (Wright, 1989). In cases where measurements with simultaneous presentation techniques are available, the thresholds obtained are markedly better (brightness: Hodos, 1993; size: Schwabl & Delius, 1984; movement: Martinoya & Delius, 1990). Incidentally, acuity is definitely better for lateral viewing than for frontal viewing (Hahmann & Güntürkün, 1993). In general, animal psychophysical measurements are known to improve when the measurement techniques are carefully adapted to a given species' propensities and peculiarities. There is still much to be done in this respect with pigeons. Visual flicker fusion frequency, a temporal resolution index, has been found to be considerably higher in pigeons (reaching about 150 cycles per sec at high luminance levels; Powell & Smith, 1968) than in humans.

Recognition of visual stimuli depends mainly on the interaction of several parameters. This brings up the question of how well pigeons can cope with the so-called constancy or invariance aspects of picture and scenes. Concerning size/distance constancy, i.e., recognition of a stimulus as large or small independently of whether it is close by or far away, the pigeon's abilities may be somewhat limited (McFadden, 1993). Regarding size invariance, i.e., recognising a silhouette shape regardless of its size, pigeons seem to be even more limited (Lombardi & Delius, 1990; Cerella 1990). But for orientation invariance i.e., the recognition of silhouette shapes independently of their orientation, pigeon performance is excellent (Delius & Hollard, 1995; Jitsumori & Ohkubo, 1996). Silhouette shapes presented in differing contrasts and colours are reasonably well recognised as equivalent. Outlines of silhouette shapes and silhouette shapes of structured/shaded drawings of objects are easily recognised, but outline tracings of the latter are not (Lombardi & Delius, 1989; Cook, Wright, & Kendrick, 1987). Complex movements of simple stimuli are well discriminated by pigeons, perhaps in agreement by the ubiquitous motion sensitivity of their visual neurons (Emmerton, 1986; Dittrich & Lea, 1993; Frost, Wylie, & Wang, 1994). Pigeons derive motion-in-depth information from two-dimensional optical flow displays (Martinoya & Delius, 1990). It may also be that, contrary to earlier opinions (Cerella, 1990), pigeons recode successively-presented, two-dimensional pictures of objects or scenes viewed from different angles into a unified three-dimensional memory representation (Spetch, Kelly, & Lechelt 1998; Cook & Katz, 1999).

PICTURE/OBJECT EQUIVALENCE

Let us return to the question of whether for pigeons, two-dimensional pictures actually represent the three-dimensional objects and scenes they depict.

Objects

Some of the first experiments concerning this question were of a mixed behaviouristic-ethological nature. When pigeons that peck a key for a food reward are exposed to a reduction in the reinforcement ratio per response, or to long intervals between rewards, these frustrating events usually induce aggression. If the experimental pigeons are provided with a live pigeon or a stuffed model in their training chamber, they attack it by pecking it. They have also been reported to attack their reflection in a mirror, life-size colour photographs, black and white silhouettes, and even line drawings of a pigeon. The attacks on the last three were recorded using an electric switch (Looney & Cohen, 1974).

Whether pecking attacks on these images did or did not occur partly depended on the pigeons' previous experience with live or stuffed targets. Generally, readiness to attack decreased as less and less realistic images or pictures were used. Unexpectedly, however, the pigeons pecked the upper parts of the pictures when they were shown upside down: normally pigeons attack by pecking the head of live or stuffed targets. Ramirez and Delius (1978) found that, compared with live pigeons, colour pictures were quite ineffective as targets of such schedule-induced aggression. Moreover, they found that marked individual differences in aggressiveness exhibited by a number of experimental pigeons vis-à-vis live target pigeons were not apparent when the photographic targets were used. In a variety of bird species, mirror images have been found in field experiments to elicit transitory displays, mostly of an aggressive kind but sometimes also courtship-related (Smith & Hosking, 1955; Tinbergen, 1959). Rapid waning of these responses is the rule, however, presumably because of the various limitations that mirror images have as social partners (limited frame, impenetrability, mimicking property). However, socially isolated, possibly mirror-imprinted birds, including pigeons, may persistently seek out their mirror-image and produce social displays to it (personal observation).

Cabe (1976) trained pigeons to discriminate two three-dimensional objects, a rectangular white block and a white cross. The stimuli were presented in succession behind a transparent pecking key and against a dark grey background. Pecking was food-rewarded when one object was presented, but no reward was given for any responses made when the other object was shown. When the pigeons discriminated the objects well they were tested in transfer trials, using black and white photographs, line drawings or white-on-black silhouettes of these objects. The transfer tests demonstrated that the photographs and the silhouettes, but not the drawings, were treated as equivalent to the objects they were supposed to represent. But since the birds could easily learn to discriminate any of the pictures from the objects they represented, the equivalence was not total. Lumsden (1977) trained pigeons to discriminate a rewarded target object of a particular shape presented in a standard oblique orientation from two other similarly sized but differently shaped non-rewarded distractor objects when these objects were shown successively behind a transparent pecking key. Once the pigeons had learned the discrimination, they were tested on extinction tests for response generalisation to the target object presented at different orientations, to cut-out black and white photographs, and to cut-out line drawings of the object at the corresponding orientations. The generalisation response rates were about the same with the object and with the photographs but were lower on the drawings. However, when pigeons were trained on the harder task of discriminating the above target object shown in two symmetric oblique orientations, and were again tested with the object and the photographs, the generalisation rates on the photographs were quite low.

Spheres

Delius (1992) trained two groups of pigeons to categorise up to 72 small three-dimensional, diversely coloured objects according to the somewhat abstract physical property of being spherical or non-spherical. A series of different object triplets mounted on small metal plates attached to an automated conveyor chain were successively presented. Each triplet consisted either of two spheres and one non-sphere or of one sphere and two non-spheres. The pecking-grasping responses to the objects, which provided haptic stimulation, were sensed by piezo-ceramics positioned beneath each set of object-plates when the chain had moved a triplet into place. The apparatus was controlled by a micro-computer. If a bird grasped a spherical shape, it received a reward of several seeds, whereas if it pecked a non-spherical object, a period of darkness followed. The animals learned the discrimination task, reaching the 85% correct criterion very quickly (within 150 trials), probably because of the realism of the stimuli, which offered tactile as well as visual cues. Familiar training objects were thereafter readily discriminated by the pigeons, even when they were presented on novel background plates. Several tests with sets of new spherical and non-spherical objects showed that the birds generalised their categorisation by discriminating at a 75% level or better. The test objects, incidentally, were routinely added to the repertoire of training objects so that, together with some other new objects that were introduced, the pigeons ended up discriminating a total of up to 260 objects. Only when a test set consisted of novel transparent spherical and non-spherical objects, all of which included non-spherical opaque intrusions, did the pigeons fail to show a performance transfer. However, after some training with these objects, even they were correctly classified as spherical and non-spherical. Other tests revealed that the pigeons would also categorise objects on a relative basis without any special training, meaning that when presented with non-spherical objects only, they would preferentially choose those which human observers also judged to be the most spherical ones.

The pigeons were also tested with photographic pictures of spherical and non-spherical objects pasted onto stimulus plates. Tests with a total of up to 54 colour photographs yielded an average correct discrimination rate of 69%. Tests with up to 36 black and white photographs yielded a significantly better average score of 79%. In fact, a test with 18 black and white pictures of spheres and non-spheres drawn by an artist yielded a better result (71% correct) than tests with colour photographs. The average discrimination score during comparable tests with 36 real objects was 84%, which was significantly better than that achieved with the black and white photographs. Delius (1992) interpreted these results as suggesting that pigeons could transfer a categorising discrimination behaviour learned purely on the basis of real objects to pictures of objects, although only with a decline in performance. The reason for this decrement was seen in the fact that, when the birds classified the real spheres and non-spheres, they could benefit from the visually available stereoscopic and parallax cues. Their attention to these depth cues was possibly enhanced by the additional availability of haptic cues. Neither depth nor haptic cues were available when the birds discriminated the pictures. Colour photographs were thought to have yielded the worst results because, by being suited to human trichromatic colour vision within the blue to red range, they probably presented a false colour representation for the pigeons with their ultraviolet to infrared, pentachromatic vision. These false colours probably also disturbed the three-dimensionality cues which photographs retain, such as shading and texture gradients. The latter may have been more veridical in the black and white pictures and even in the black and white drawings than in the colour pictures. The idea that colour photographs are deficient pictures of reality is backed by another experiment. Pigeons exhibit an excellent discriminatory behaviour when they feed on milo grains mixed with stone grit, and they needed virtually no training for this task (Jäger, 1990). However, when they were required to operantly discriminate slides that were back-projected onto pecking keys and either showed milo grains on a stone grit background or the latter background without grains, pigeons could not satisfactorily master this discrimination, even after lengthy training (Jäger, 1995).

Photographs

Note that the experiment by Delius (1992) showed that categorical discrimination of sphericity and non-sphericity established with real objects was transferred, albeit with some decline, to pictorial representations of the objects. However, the author did not examine whether pigeons could achieve the opposite task, that is, learn to categorise pictures representing spherical and non-spherical objects and then transfer that competence to the classification of real objects. Watanabe (1993) trained pigeons to discriminate four kinds of edible seeds and grains (corn, pea, wheat, and buckwheat) and four kinds of junk (stone, twig, screw-nut, and paper clip). These items were placed in small containers fixed to an automated conveyer-belt device and presented to pigeons behind a transparent, vertically arranged pecking key. There were three groups of pigeons: one learned to discriminate between the grain and the junk, with responses to the grain being rewarded with food, and no reward for responses to the junk; the second learned the same discrimination, but with the junk rewarded and the grains not rewarded; and the third learned to discriminate two grains plus two junk items from the other two grains and junk items. When tested with photographic colour prints of the objects, instead of the objects themselves, the first two groups showed substantial transfer, but the last group did quite poorly. Another set of three groups of pigeons learned to discriminate the pictures first and were then tested with the objects. They showed a very similar pattern of transfer. These results suggested that for pigeons, photographs convey sufficient information about real objects to allow for general categorical cross-recognition of objects, but that they do not carry sufficient information to allow for a precise identification of a particular individual object. However, Watanabe also trained pigeons to discriminate real corn kernels from real stones and found that they transferred the discrimination to other grains and junk objects rather well. But when other pigeons were trained on colour slides of the same kernels of corn and the same stones, there was virtually no transfer to the other grain and junk objects (Watanabe, Lea, & Dittrich, 1993). This suggests that photographic pictures can only supply a fraction of the visual cues that real objects are capable of conveying to pigeons.

More recently, Watanabe (1997) trained pigeons to discriminate between four different kinds of edible seeds and grains (corn, safflower, wheat, and soya) and four kinds of non-edible junk (stone, twig, screw-

nut, and paper staple). One group of pigeons learned the grain/junk discrimination, the other the object/picture discrimination. They were then
tested with new kinds of seeds (buckwheat, red bean) and new kinds of
junk (resistor, paper clip). Both groups showed good generalisation of
discrimination to these novel objects. In a second test the objects were
displayed horizontally rather than vertically. The transfer was good, that
is, the pigeons showed invariance with respect to orientation changes.
On the third test, all objects were painted matt black and the photographs were of these blackened objects. The transfer was good in the
object/picture group, but was very poor in the grain/junk group, indicating that the pigeons could discriminate between flat and solid stimuli
despite a degradation of cues, but could not maintain an object-class
discrimination under these conditions. Finally, the subjects of the object/
picture group were retrained with either the right or the left eye seeing.
Discrimination performance was good with both eyes. Interestingly, lesions of the ectostriatal end-projection of the tecto-thalamo-telencephalic
visual pathway (Güntürkün, 1991), were found to impair substantially
the grain/junk discrimination, but had less effect on the object/picture
discrimination. Watanabe argued that the dissociation could not be due
to a simple difference in task difficulty because both were initially
learned equally fast. However, the blackening results suggest that there
may nevertheless have been a more subtle difference in task difficulty.

Locations

There has been a great deal of interest in the transfer from real locations to pictures of the same locations, or vice versa, in connection with
the role visual locality cues play in the near-range orientation of
pigeons. Earlier studies claimed that pigeons with experience of real
localities were at an advantage when they learned to discriminate colour
photographs of these localities, compared to pigeons that lacked such
experience, but these studies were not well controlled or were not reported in sufficient detail (Wilkie, Willson, & Kardal, 1989; Kendrick,
1992; Wilkie, Willson, & MacDonald, 1992). We summarise the results
of two relatively recent, better-designed studies on this topic. Cole and
Honig (1994) trained pigeons to discriminate between pictures showing
two ends of a room and then put them in the real room and rewarded
them for choosing one end of the room rather than the other. One group

of pigeons (congruent) was rewarded for entering the end that had been rewarded during training. The other group (incongruent) was rewarded for entering the unrewarded end. The first group learned the real room task significantly faster than the second one. However, a further control group of pigeons that was first trained to discriminate pictures unrelated to the room learned the room task as fast as the birds in the congruent group. In other words, the incongruent picture training seems to have slowed down the real-room learning task, rather than the congruent picture training having facilitated it. A different set of pigeons was trained first with the real room task and then tested with the picture task. Here the congruent and incongruent groups showed no difference in performance. Thus, there was apparently some sort of weak transfer from pictures to objects but not from objects to pictures. Dawkins, Guilford, Braithwaite, and Krebs (1996) worked with two groups of pigeons. While the birds were held in wire-mesh cages at six different viewpoints, they were pre-exposed to views of a common's medow or a sports field. The pigeons were highly unlikely to have seen these locations before. Both groups were then trained to discriminate 55 different colour slides taken at the relevant sports field from another 55 colour slides taken at an unrelated public park. The slides were back-projected in random order on a screen located some inches behind a transparent pecking key, and responses to the sports field pictures were rewarded. There was no significant difference in the number of sessions the pigeons in either group needed to reach a predefined discrimination criterion, nor was there a difference in transfer performance when they were tested with 40 new slides of both locations. This means that the pigeons who had been pre-exposed to the real sports field made no use of that experience while discriminating between the pictures of that field and the park. This is probably due to the fact that they did not recognise the equivalence between the photographs and the real scenes. But an alternative explanation is that simple pre-exposure to one of the stimuli does not facilitate its discrimination from other stimuli. With quite simple visual stimuli, there is evidence that mere pre-exposure does not always facilitate subsequent discrimination by pigeons. Indeed, in some cases it even retards it (Channel & Hall, 1981).

In a kind of follow-up study, Dawkins and Woodington (1997) had two groups of chickens learned to discriminate pairs of chicken-sized junk objects on the basis of their colour or shape. The objects were presented either close by (about 15 cm) or further away (120 cm). The results revealed that the chickens performed better under the close condition than under the far condition, regardless of group, although the colour group performed better overall. When the objects were replaced with colour prints showing these objects in natural size, there was substantial transfer in the colour group but rather little in the shape group. The authors accordingly concluded that the pigeons' failure in the earlier experiment may not have been due so much to the false colours in the slides, but rather to the fact that the slide pictures were small and close by, whereas the real scenes were big and further away. They did not see this as being a size/distance inconsistency, a factor that might be suspected as important given the limited size invariance and better size/ distance constancy pigeons exhibit when recognising simple shapes (Lombardi & Delius, 1990; Cerella, 1990; McFadden, 1993). Instead, they considered it to be a potential lateral/frontal viewing inconsistency problem connected with the fact that chickens and pigeons have the habit of looking at more distant items laterally (monocularly) and at nearer objects frontally (binocularly). The recognition of individual birds apparently only occurs after visual inspection from close up (Dawkins, 1995).

Mimicry

Avian predators are a major selective factor in the evolution of the shapes, colours, and movements of insects. Most insect predators hunt using visual cues. Insects have evolved a number of defensive ploys, including the so-called Batesian mimicry. Several wasp species have distinct markings and colours, and birds learn to avoid capturing them once they have been stung. Some fly species, themselves inoffensive, have evolved a morphology that mimics the shape, marking, and colouring of these wasps. In some species this mimicry is very precise; in others it is less exact. It is clear that in the former case, bird predators may be fooled into avoiding the mimics, but what about the latter? The degree of precision in the mimicry has traditionally been assessed by human observers, but our vision may differ from that of avian predators, in the sense that imperfect mimics to us may in fact be quite good mimics to birds. Dittrich, Gilbert, Green, McGregor, and Grewcock (1993) had pigeons learn to discriminate pictures of model wasps and pictures of flies that were definitely non-mimics. Once the pigeons had learned to make this discrimination, they were given tests with pictures of fly species that were good, medium, and poor wasp mimics. The pigeons were found to judge the mimicry of the various flies in much the same way as humans do, so the authors concluded that the imperfect mimics were indeed exactly that. Cuthill and Bennet (1993), however, drew attention to the fact that photographic colour slides are adjusted to trichromatic, red-to-blue human colour vision, and that there is evidence that pigeon colour vision is tetra- if not pentachromatic, extending from red to ultra-violet, the latter being a light quality that cannot at all be reproduced in slides. Upon this critique Green, Gentle, Peake, Scudamore, McGregor, Gilbert, and Dittrich (1999) partially repeated their experiment using dead specimens of wasps and flies as stimuli. The pigeons viewed the specimens through a pecking key that was transparent to both "visible" and ultraviolet light. They obtained much the same results as in the first study: pigeons considered flies classified as medium mimics by humans to be visually intermediate between model wasps and non-mimicking flies. Yet to be determined is whether pigeons would show precise trans-fer between real insects and pictures of them, and vice versa. There is also the more general point that it is not certain whether actual insectivo-rous predators, presumably flycatcher species, have a colour vision that is comparable to granivorous pigeons, although this was implicitly assumed in the above study. The available evidence suggests that colour vision in different avian species probably differs considerably (Varela et al., 1993), although ultraviolet sensitivity appears to be widespread among birds (Chen & Goldsmith, 1986). Whereas humans perceive dead insects as equivalent to live ones, this might not be the case for birds, since at least some of the mimicry probably relies more on similarity of movement than on similarity of shape and colour. Flycatchers are more likely to capture their prey when it is moving than when it is at rest (Srygley & Ellington, 1999).

Videographs

There are only a few studies on whether pigeons recognise video-graphed sequences as equivalent to live moving scenes. Ryan and Lea (1994) found that pigeons do not respond to video sequences of conspe-cifics as they do to live birds, since they tend to show avoidance rather than approach to video images. Rather than relying on pigeons' natural responses to video images, Jitsumori, Natori, and Okuyama (1999) trained their birds to discriminate videographed scenes. The pigeons were first trained to distinguish moving videographs of two different conspecifics displaying different types of action (key pecking and circling). Transfer tests to novel scenes that included a new bird as well as a new movement pattern (pacing) suggested that the particular type of activity the birds had seen in the training sequences was the most salient feature of the video scenes. However, when specifically trained to do so, the pigeons could also learn to base their discrimination on either the particular behavioural activity, or the specific bird shown in the video. They then transferred their discrimination ability to scenes of a different bird showing the same activity as in training phases, where activity was the relevant feature, and to a different activity performed by the same bird as in the training, when the specific individual was relevant.

In another test, static frames from the videographs used in the latter type of training were presented. Not only did the birds continue to discriminate specific pigeons when they had been trained to recognize particular conspecifics, but also and more surprisingly, they discriminated static images of particular activities. Also, rather revealingly, the direction (either normal or reversed) in which the moving video scenes were played had no effect on their ability to discriminate the scenes. Although Jitsumori et al. concluded that pigeons can learn to recognize either specific individual birds or their patterns of activity in video images, they warn us that pigeons still might not see the video images as showng proper birds in normal motion. Rather, they may perceive the images as a series of stroboscopically presented, false colour frames. At no point did this study attempt to examine whether there was any cross-recognition from pigeon pictures to real pigeons or vice versa.

It is important to note here that videos normally operate at 25 or 30 frames per second, well below the temporal fusion frequency of pigeons. (Some special, but more expensive equipment can operate at higher frequencies, see Watanabe & Furuya, 1997.) Incidentally, the high temporal resolution of pigeons might also impair their perception when real objects and scenes are illuminated with certain fluorescent lamps that flicker at 50 or 60 Hz. More studies with animation have been performed on chickens. An early study attempted to use cinematographic pictures (16 frames per sec) of moving stick insects but found that chicks were unresponsive to them, even though they were responsive to real stick insects. With elegant experiments, including one showing that chicks would respond to continuously but not to intermittently illuminated shadows of moving stick insects, the same study made it seem quite likely that the unresponsiveness was chiefly due to the low temporal resolution of the cinematographic display, good enough for humans but too poor for chickens (Robinson, 1966). More recent video-graphic experiments on chickens have been thoroughly reviewed by D'Eath (1998), but let us mention some of them. Keeling and Hurnik (1993) found that chicks would feed more if they were shown a video of a hen feeding than if they were not. But this facilitative effect can also be obtained with quite primitive mechanical hen surrogates (Turner, 1965). McQuoid and Galef (1993) reported that chicks that saw a video of a hen feeding from a particular coloured bowl, later preferred that bowl to another bowl from which they had not seen her feeding. But the authors did not check whether the chicks recognised a hen in the video images or just responded to something that nodded into the bowl in question. Evans and Marler (1991) showed that cockerels would give alarm calls in response to an aerial predator model when either real hens or videos of hens were presented. However, to a lesser extent, real bob-white quail or videos of the same quail also had this effect. The fact that live individuals of two species of quite different appearance were capa-ble of yielding the facilitative effect suggests that the videos may also have provided only coarse similarity to the live actors.

D'Eath and Dawkins (1996) showed that chickens feed more readily and closer to live, familiar flock mates than to live, unfamiliar conspe-cifics. The chickens did not exhibit this discrimination, however, when colour videos of familiar or unfamiliar conspecifics were substituted for live companions, even though they did respond with avoidance behav-iour to videos showing hens displaying threat postures. Related to this latter finding is the fact that pigeons have been found to display fear and aggressive responses merely to an approaching wooden stick (Ramirez & Delius, 1986). Using colour slides, Bradshaw and Dawkins (1993) obtained no evidence of recognition, by experimental chickens, of indi-viduals actually discriminated in real life. Patterson-Kane, Nicol, Foster, and Temple (1997) trained three groups of chickens with food rewards in a Y-shaped maze to discriminate red and green coloured cards, a brown live chicken from no chicken, and a white live chicken from no chicken. When videos of these stimuli were presented after training, there was good transfer with the colour card group, some transfer with the brown chicken group, but no transfer with the white chicken group. In another experiment, two groups of chickens were trained either to discriminate a real brown chicken from a brown basket-ball, or to discriminate videos of these objects. The first group learned very fast, but the second learned quite slowly. When the groups were tested with videos and objects, respectively, the first group showed no generalisation and the second showed some. Coinciding with what D'Eath (1998) concluded after a more comprehensive review, this small sample of studies is already enough to claim that for chickens and pigeons, videos at best only very partially represent the objects they de-pict. Videos may enable some cross-recognition when the discrimination tasks are comparatively easy, or when the response used to assess re-cognition is normally triggered by fairly unspecific real stimuli. Inciden-tally, D'Eath pointed out that when live subjects are involved, the noises and vocalisations they produce must also be considered. The videos used in the relevant studies have often not reproduced these sounds. Even when acoustic stimuli were included, it is questionable whether the video soundtrack replicated them with sufficient accuracy for birds, as these animals generally have an extended low frequency sensitivity (down to fractions of a cycle per sec) compared to humans (Delius & Emmerton, 1978; Kreithen & Quine, 1979; Necker, 1983). Ordinary audio technology does not reproduce these infra-sound frequencies.

CONCLUSIONS

Our general conclusion must be that pigeons and chickens are capa-ble of recognising at least some equivalence between photographic, videographic, or computographic pictures and the objects or scenes the pictures represent. But at the same time, it must be concluded that this equivalence is seriously limited, in such a way that when a behavioural task requires a relatively precise correspondence, then artificial pictures cannot be substituted for the real thing. This is in many ways what in-formed common sense would lead one to suspect. Pictorial technology, whether photo-, cinemato-, video-, or computographic, is designed with the peculiarities of comparatively less-sophisticated, human vision in mind, and even then with technical and economic constraints very much in the foreground. After all, although we ourselves recognise a lot of objects and scenes in such pictures, our performance is by no means anywhere near perfect. Even the most perfect, outlandishly priced imita-tion that virtual reality technology can presently offer (for example, simulators for pilot training) cannot fully fool humans into believing that they are truly looking at the real world. Our research grant institutions are disappointingly, but understandably, hesitant to support the development of anything like a simulator optimally adapted to the requirements of pigeons or chickens, whatever its exact specifications might be. In the meantime, researchers have to settle for the cheaper, off-the-shelf pictorial technology that is designed for humans and is poor on three dimensionality. Under these circumstances, scientists cannot hope to satisfactorily fool pigeons, chickens, and other birds, given the overall superiority of avian vision. In any case, birds as necessarily less-pampered realists may not be as dumb and willing as we are to engage in the make-belief of virtual worlds.

ACKNOWLEDGEMENTS

We would like to thank the Deutsche Forschungsgemeinschaft for supporting our research over many years. J.E. was a visiting professor in Konstanz while on sabbatical from Purdue. J.D.D. is grateful to Prof. I. Morgado-Bernal for sabbatical hospitality at the Departmento de Psicobiología, Universitat Autónoma de Barcelona, Spain. We thank Dr. Martina Siemann for her critical reading of an earlier draft.

REFERENCES

Able, K. P., & Able, M. A. (1997). Development of sunset orientation in a migratory bird: no calibration by the magnetic field. *Animal Behaviour, 53,* 363-368.

Adret, P. (1997). Discrimination of video images by zebra finches (*Taeniopygia guttata*): direct evidence from song performance. *Journal of Comparative Psychology, 111,* 115-125.

Ahlberg, P. E., & Milner, A. R. (1994). The origin and early diversification of tetrapods. *Nature, 368,* 507-514.

Bagnoli, P., Porciatti, V., Fontanesi, G., & Sebastiani, L. (1987). Morphological and functional changes in the retinotectal system of the pigeon during the early posthatching period. *Journal of Comparative Neurology, 256,* 400-411.

Bischof, H. J. (1980). Reaktionen von Zebrafinkenmännchen auf zweidimensionale Attrappen: Einfluß von Reizqualität und Prägung. *Journal für Ornithologie, 121,* 288-290.

Bloch, S., Leimeignan, M., & Martinoya, C. (1987). Coordinated vergence for frontal fixation, but independent movements for lateral viewing, in the pigeon. In J. K. O'Reagen & A. Levi-Schoen (Eds.), *Eye movements: from physiology to cognition* (pp. 47-56). Amsterdam: Elsevier.

Bolhuis, J. J. (1996). Development of perceptual mechanisms in birds: predispositions and imprinting. In C. F. Moss & S. J. Shettleworth (Eds.), *Neuroethological studies of cognitive and perceptual processes* (pp. 84-112). Boulder, CO: Westview.

Bond, A. A., & Kamil, A. C. (1998). Apostatic selection by blue jays produces balanced polymorphism in virtual prey. *Nature, 395,* 594-596.

Bowmaker, J. K. (1977). The visual pigments, oil droplets and spectral sensitivity of the pigeon. *Vision Research, 17,* 1129-1138.

Bradshaw, R. H., & Dawkins, M. S. (1993). Slides of conspecifics as representatives of real animals in laying hens (*Gallus domesticus*). *Behavioural Processes, 28,* 165-172.

Brown, S. D., & Dooling, R. J. (1992). Perception of conspecific faces by budgerigars (*Melopsittacus undulatus*). Natural faces. *Journal of Comparative Psychology, 106,* 203-216.

Burckhardt, D. (1989). UV vision: a bird's eye view of feathers. *Journal of Comparative Physiology A, 164,* 787-796.

Cabe, P. A. (1976). Transfer of discrimination from solid objects to pictures by pigeons: A test of theoretical models of pictorial perception. *Perception and Psychophysics, 19,* 545- 550.

Cerella, J. (1980). The pigeon's analysis of pictures. *Pattern Recognition, 12,* 1-6.

Cerella, J. (1990). Shape constancy in the pigeon: the perspective transformations decomposed. In M. L. Commons, S. M. Kosslyn, R. J. Herrnstein, & D. B. Mumford (Eds.), *Pattern recognition and concepts in animals, people and machines* (pp. 145-163). Hillsdale, NJ: Erlbaum.

Channel, S., & Hall, G. (1981). Facilitation and retardation of discrimination learning after exposure to the stimuli. *Journal of Experimental Psychology: Animal Behavior Processes, 7,* 437-446.

Chen, D. M., & Goldsmith, T. H. (1986). Four spectral classes of cone in the retina of birds. *Journal of Comparative Physiology, 141,* 47-52.

Coemans, M. A. J. M., Vos, J. J., & Nuboer, J. F. W. (1990). No evidence for polarization sensitivity in the pigeon. *Naturwissenschaften, 77,* 138-142.

Cole, P. D., & Honig, W. K. (1994). Transfer of a discrimination by pigeons (*Columba livia*) between pictured locations and the represented environments. *Journal of Comparative Psychology, 108,* 189-198.

Cook, R. G., & Katz, J. S. (1999). Dynamic object perception by pigeons. *Journal of Experimental Psychology: Animal Behavior Processes, 25,* 194-211.

Cook, R. G., Wright, A. A., & Kendrick, D. F. (1987). Visual categorization in pigeons. In M. L. Commons, S. M. Kosslyn, & R. J. Herrnstein (Eds.),

Pattern recognition and concepts in animals, people, and machines (pp. 187-214). Hillsdale, NJ: Erlbaum.

Cumming, W. W. (1966). A bird's eye glimpse of men and machines. In R. Ulrich, T. Stachnik, & J. Mabry (Eds.), *Control of human behavior* (pp. 246-256). Glenview, IL: Scott Foresman.

Cuthill, I. C., & Bennet, A. T. D. (1993). Mimicry and the eye of the beholder. *Proceedings of the Royal Society London, B, 253,* 203-204.

Dawkins, M. S. (1995). How do hens view other hens? The use of lateral and binocular visual fields in social recognition. *Behaviour, 132,* 591-606.

Dawkins, M. S., Guilford, T., Braithwaite, V. A., & Krebs, J. R. (1996). Discrimination and recognition of photographs of places by homing pigeons. *Behavioural Processes, 36,* 27-38.

Dawkins, M. S., & Woodington, A. (1997). Distance and the presentation of visual stimuli to birds. *Animal Behaviour, 54,* 1019-1025.

Dawkins, R. (1969). The ontogeny of a pecking preference. *Zeitschrift für Tierpsychologie, 25,* 170-186.

D'Eath, R. B. (1998). Can video images imitate real stimuli in animal behaviour experiments? *Biological Reviews, 73,* 267-292.

D'Eath, R. B., & Dawkins, M. S. (1996). Laying hens do not discriminate between video images of conspecifics. *Animal Behaviour, 52,* 903-912.

Delius, J. D. (1992). Categorical discrimination of objects and pictures by pigeons. *Animal Learning and Behavior, 20,* 301-311.

Delius, J. D., & Emmerton, J. (1978). Sensory mechanism related to homing in pigeons. In K. Schmidt-Koenig & W. T. Keeton (Eds.), *Animal migration, navigation and homing* (pp. 35-41). Berlin: Springer.

Delius, J. D., & Hollard, V.D. (1995). Orientation invariance in pattern recognition by pigeons (*Columba livia*) and humans (*Homo sapiens*). *Journal of Comparative Psychology, 109,* 278-290.

Delius, J. D., Jahnke-Funk, E., & Hawker, A. (1981). Stimulus display geometry and colour discrimination learning by pigeons. *Current Psychological Research, 1,* 203-214.

Delius, J. D., Perchard, R. J., & Emmerton, J. (1976). Polarized light discrimination by pigeons and an electroretinographic correlate. *Journal of Comparative and Physiological Psychology, 90,* 560-571.

Delius, J. D., Siemann, M., Emmerton, J., & Xia, L. (1999). Cognitions of birds as products of evolved brains. In G. Roth & M. F. Wullimann (Eds.), *Brain evolution and behaviour.* Heidelberg: Spektrum (in press).

Deregowski, J. B. (1989). Real space and represented space: cross-cultural perspectives. *Behavioral and Brain Sciences, 12,* 51-119.

Dittrich, W. H., & Lea, E. G. (1993). Motion as a natural category for pigeons: generalization and a feature positive effect. *Journal of the Experimental Analysis of Behavior, 59,* 115-129.

Dittrich, W., Gilbert, F. S., Green, P. R., McGregor, P. K., & Grewcock, D. (1993). Imperfect mimicry: a pigeon's perspective. *Proceedings of the Royal Society London, B, 251,* 195-200.

Edwards, C. A., & Honig, W. K. (1987). Memorization and "feature selection" in the acquisition of natural concepts in pigeons. *Learning and Motivation, 18,* 235-260.

Emmerton, J. (1983a). Vision. In M. Abs (Ed.), *Physiology and behaviour of the pigeon* (pp. 245-266). London: Academic Press.

Emmerton, J. (1983b). Pattern discrimination in the near-ultraviolet by pigeons. *Perception and Psychophysics, 34,* 555-559.

Emmerton, J. (1986). The pigeon's discrimination of movement patterns (Lissajous figures and contour dependent rotational invariance). *Perception, 15,* 573-599.

Emmerton, J., & Delius, J. D. (1980). Wavelength discrimination in the visible and ultraviolet spectrum by pigeons. *Journal of Comparative Physiology, 141,* 47-52.

Evans, C. S., & Marler, P. (1991). On the use of video images in birds: audience effects on alarm calling. *Animal Behaviour, 41,* 17-26.

Feduccia, A. (1996). *The origin and evolution of birds.* New Haven, CT: Yale University Press.

Fersen, L., von, & Lea, S. E. G. (1990). Category discrimination by pigeons using five polymorphous features. *Journal of the Experimental Analysis of Behavior, 54,* 69-84.

Fitzke, F. W., Hayes, B. P., Hodos, W., Holden, A. L., & Low, J. C. (1985). Refractive sectors in the visual field of the pigeon eye. *Journal of Physiology, 369,* 33-44.

Frost, B. J., Wylie, D. R., & Wang, Y. C. (1994). The analysis of motion in the visual system of birds. In P. R. Green & M. N. O. Davies (Eds.), *Perception and motor control in birds* (pp. 248-269). Berlin: Springer.

Galifret, Y. (1968). Les diverses aires fonctionnelles de la rétine du pigeon. *Zeitschrift für Zellforschung, 86,* 535-545.

Goodale, M. A. (1983). Visually guided pecking in the pigeon (*Columba livia*). *Brain, Behavior and Evolution, 22,* 22-41.

Green, P. R., Gentle, L., Peake, T. M., Scudamore, R. A., McGregor, P. K., Gilbert, F., & Dittrich, W. H. (1999). Conditioning pigeons to discriminate naturally lit insect specimens. *Behavioural Processes, 46,* 97-102.

Greene, S. L. (1984). Feature memorization in pigeon concept formation. In M. L. Commons, R. J. Herrnstein, & A. R. Wagner (Eds.), *Quantitative analyses of behavior: Discrimination processes* (Vol. 4, pp. 209-229). Cambridge, MA: Ballinger.

Güntürkün, O. (1991). The functional organization of the avian visual system. In R. J. Andrew (Ed.), *Neural and behavioural plasticity: The use of the domestic chick as a model* (pp. 92-105). Oxford: Oxford University Press.

Güntürkün, O. (1999). Sensory physiology: Vision. In G. C. Whithrow (Ed.), *Sturkie's avian physiology.* Orlando, FL: Academic Press (in press).

Güntürkün, O., Emmerton, J., & Delius, J. D. (1989). Neural asymmetries and visual behaviour in birds. In H. C. Lüttgau & R. Necker (Eds.), *Biological signal processing.* Weinheim: VCH Verlag.

Güntürkün, O., Hellmann, B., Melsbach, G., & Prior, H. (1998). Asymmetries of representation in the visual system of pigeons. *Neuroreport, 9,* 4127-4130.

Hahmann, U., & Güntürkün, O. (1993). The visual acuity for the lateral field of the pigeon (*Columba livia*). *Vision Research, 33,* 1659-1664.

Hebrard, J. J. (1978). Habitat selection in two species of *Spizella*: a concurrent laboratory and field study. *Auk, 95,* 404-410.

Herrnstein, R. J. (1990). Levels of stimulus control: a functional approach. *Cognition, 37,* 133-166.

Herrnstein, R. J., & Loveland, D. H. (1964). Complex visual concept in the pigeon. *Science, 146,* 549-551.

Herrnstein, R. J., Loveland, D. H., & Cable, C. (1976). Natural concepts in pigeons. *Journal of Experimental Psychology: Animal Behavior Processes, 2,* 285-302.

Hershberger, W. (1970). Attached-shadow orientation perceived as depth by chickens reared in an environment illuminated from below. *Journal of Comparative and Physiological Psychology, 73,* 403-411.

Hodos, W. (1993). The visual capabilities of birds. In H. P. Zeigler & H. J. Bischof (Eds.), *Vision, brain, and behavior in birds* (pp. 63-76). Cambridge, MA: MIT Press.

Honig, W. K., & Stewart, K. E. (1989). Pigeons can discriminate locations presented in pictures. *Journal for Experimental Analysis of Behavior, 50,* 541-551.

Hörster, W. (1997). Modelle einer "einfachen" Bewegung und ihrer Steurung: Das Pickverhalten der Taube. *Neuroforum, 97,* 3-7.

Hörster, W., Krumm, E., & Mohr, C. (1999). Pecking behaviour in pigeons: a higly variable movement pattern (submitted).

Jäger, R. (1990). Visuomotor feeding perturbations after lateral telencephalic lesions in pigeons. *Behavioural Brain Research, 40,* 73-80.

Jäger, R. (1995). Pigeons failure to discriminate grains from grit on pictures. Unpublished results.

Jahnke, H.-J. (1984). Binocular visual field differences among various breeds of pigeons. *Bird Behaviour, 5,* 96-102.

Jenkins, H. M., & Sainsbury, R. S. (1970). Discrimination learning with the distinctive feature on positive or negative trials. In D. I. Mostofsky (Ed.), *Attention: Contemporary theory and analysis.* New York: Appleton Century Crofts.

Jitsumori, M. (1976). Colour mixing in pigeons. *Japanese Psychological Research, 18,* 126-135.

Jitsumori, M., Natori, M., & Okuyama, K. (1999). Recognition of moving video images of conspecifics by pigeons: Effects on individuals, static and dynamic motion cues, and movement. *Animal Learning and Behavior, 27,* 303-315.

Jitsumori, M., & Ohkubo, O. (1996). Orientation discrimination and categorization of photographs of natural objects by pigeons. *Behavioural Processes, 38,* 205-226.

Keeling, L. J., & Hurnik, J. F. (1993). Chicken show socially facilitated feeding behaviour in response to a video image of a conspecific. *Applied Animal Behaviour Science, 36,* 223-231.

Kendrick, D. F. (1992). Pigeon concept of experienced and non-experienced real world locations: discrimination and generalisation across seasonal variation. In W. K. Honig & J. G. Fetterman (Eds.), *Cognitive aspects of stimulus control* (pp. 113-134). Hillsdale, NJ: Erlbaum.

Kreithen, M. L., & Keeton, W. T. (1974). Polarization plane detection by pigeons. *Journal of Comparative Physiology, 89,* 83-92.

Kreithen, M. L., & Quine, D. B. (1979). Infrasound detection by the homing pigeon: a behavioral audiogram. *Journal of Comparative Physiology A, 129,* 1-4.

Kumar, S., & Hedges, B. (1998). A molecular time scale for vertebrate evolution. *Nature, 392,* 917-920.

Lindenblatt, U., & Delius, J. D. (1988). Preventing a feature positive effect in pigeons. *American Journal of Psychology, 101,* 193-206.

Lombardi, C. M., & Delius, J. D. (1989). Pattern recognition invariance in pigeons: outline, color and contrast. *International Journal of Comparative Psychology, 2,* 83-102.

Lombardi, C. M., & Delius, J.D. (1990). Size invariance in visual pattern recognition by pigeons. In M. L. Commons, S. M. Kosslyn, R. J. Herrnstein, & D. B. Mumford (Eds.), *Pattern recognition and concepts in animals, people and machines* (pp.41-65). Hillsdale, NJ: Erlbaum.

Looney, T. A., & Cohen, P. S. (1974). Pictorial target control of schedule-induced attack in white carneaux pigeons. *Journal of Experimental Analysis of Behavior, 21,* 571-584.

Lumsden, E. A. (1977). Generalization of an operant response to photographs and drawings/silhouettes of a three-dimensional object at various orientations. *Bulletin of the Psychonomic Society, 10,* 405-407.

Macphail, E. M., & Reilly, S. (1989). Rapid acquisition of a novelty versus familiarity concept by pigeons (*Columba livia*). *Journal of Experimental Psychology: Animal Behavior Processes, 15,* 242-252.

Mallin, H. D., & Delius, J. D. (1983). Inter- and intraocular transfer of color discriminations with mandibulation as an operant in the head-fixed pigeon. *Behaviour Analysis Letters, 3,* 297-309.

Martin, G. R. (1993). Producing the image. In H. P. Zeigler & H. J. Bischof (Eds.), *Vision, brain, and behavior in birds* (pp. 5-24). Cambridge, MA: MIT Press.

Martinoya, C., & Delius, J. D. (1990). Perception of rotating spiral patterns by pigeons. *Biological Cybernetics, 63,* 127-134.

Martinoya, C., LeHouezec, J., & Bloch, S. (1988). Depth resolution in the pigeon. *Journal of Comparative Physiology, A, 163,* 33-42.

McFadden, S. A. (1993). Constructing the three-dimensional image. In H. P. Zeigler & H. J. Bischof (Eds.), *Vision, brain, and behavior in birds* (pp. 47-61). Cambridge, MA: MIT Press.

McQuoid, L. M., & Galef, B. G. (1993). Social stimuli influencing feeding behaviour of Burmese red junglefowl: a video analysis. *Animal Behaviour, 23,* 13-22.

Nalbach, H. O., Wolf-Oberhollenzer, F., & Remy, M. (1993). Exploring the image. In H. P. Zeigler & H. J. Bischof (Eds.), *Vision, brain, and behavior in birds* (pp. 25-46). Cambridge, MA: MIT Press.

Necker, R. (1983). Hearing. In M. Abs (Ed.), *Physiology and behaviour of the pigeon* (pp. 193-219). London: Academic Press.

Neitz, M., & Neitz, J. (1998). Molecular genetics and the biological basis of color vision. In W. G. K. Backhaus, R. Kliegl, & J. S. Werner (Eds.), *Color vision* (pp. 101-119). Berlin: de Gruyter.

Ostheim, J. (1997a). The eye-closing response of pecking pigeons. *Netherlands Journal of Zoology, 47,* 457-475.

Ostheim, J. (1997b). Visual sensation during pecking in pigeons. *European Journal of Morphology, 35* (4), 269-276.

Ostheim, J. (1998). Infrared sensitivity in pigeons (unpublished manuscript).

Ostheim, J., Krug, I., & Schlotter, B. (1999). A depth of focus controlling function of eyelid slits in pecking pigeons. (manuscript submitted).

Palacios, A. G., & Varela, F. J. (1992). Color mixing in the pigeon (*Columba livia*). Psychophysical determination in the middle, short and near-UV wavelength ranges. *Vision Research, 32,* 1947-1953.

Patterson-Kane, E., Nicol, C. J., Foster, T. M., & Temple, W. (1997). Limited perception of video-images by domestic hens. *Animal Behaviour, 53,* 951-963.

Pietrewicz, A. T., & Kamil, A. C. (1979). Search image formation in the blue jay (*Cyanocitta cristata*). *Science, 204,* 1332-1333.

Potegal, M. (1982). *Spatial abilities, development and physiological foundations.* San Diego, CA: Academic Press.

Powell, R. W., & Smith, J. C. (1968). Critical flicker fusion thresholds as a function of very small pulse to cycle fractions. *Psychological Record, 18,* 35-40.

Ramirez, J. M., & Delius, J. D. (1978). La projección de diapositivas y su ineficacia en la inducción de agressión por programas de refuerzo en la paloma. *Revista de Psicología General y Applicada, 33,* 993-1010.

Ramirez, J. M., & Delius, J. D. (1986). The assessment of individual "aggressiveness" in pigeons by a variety of means. *Aggressive Behaviour, 12,* 13-20.

Reid, S. L., & Spetch, M. L. (1998). Perception of pictorial depth cues by pigeons. *Psychonomic Bulletin and Review, 5,* 698-704.

Remy, M., & Emmerton, J. (1989). Behavioural spectral sensitivities of different retinal areas in pigeons. *Behavioral Neuroscience, 103,* 170-177.

Remy, M., & Emmerton, J. (1991). Directional dependence of intraocular transfer of stimulus detection in pigeons (*Columba livia*). *Behavioral Neuroscience, 105,* 647-652.

Remy, M., & Güntürkün, O. (1991). Retinal afferents of the tectum opticum and the nucleus opticus principalis thalami in the pigeon. *Journal of Comparative Neurology, 305,* 57-70.

Remy, M., & Watanabe, S. (1993). Two eyes and one world: studies of inter-ocular and intraocular transfer in birds. In H. P. Zeigler & H. J. Bischoff (Eds.), *Vision, brain, and behavior in birds* (pp. 333-350). Cambridge, MA: MIT Press.

Robinson, M. H. (1966). *Antipredator adaptations in stick- and leaf-mimicking insects.* Ph. D. thesis. University of Oxford, England.

Roberts, W. A., Phelps, M. T., Macuda, T., Brodbeck, D. R., & Russ, T. (1996). Intraocular transfer and simultaneous processing of stimuli presented in different fields of the pigeon. *Behavioral Neuroscience, 110,* 290-299.

Ruben, J. (1995). The evolution of endothermy in mammals and birds: from physiology to fossils. *Annual Review of Physiology, 57,* 69-95.

Ryan, C. M. E. & Lea, S. E. G. (1994). Images of conspecifics as categories to be discriminated by pigeons and chickens: slides, video tapes, stuffed birds and live birds. *Behavioural Processes, 33,* 155-176.

Schaeffel, F. (1994). Functional accommodation in birds. In M. N. O. Davies & P. R. Green (Eds.), *Perception and motor control in birds* (pp. 35-53). Berlin: Springer.

Schall, U., & Delius, J. D. (1991). Grasping in the pigeon: control through sound and vibration feedback mediated by the nucleus basalis. *Physiology and Behavior, 50,* 983-988.

Schwabl, U., & Delius, J. D. (1984). Visual length discrimination in the pigeon. *Bird Behaviour, 5,* 118-121.

Sekuler, A. B., Lee, J. A. J., & Shettleworth, S. J. (1996). Pigeons do not complete partly occluded figures. *Perception, 25,* 1109-1120.

Siemann, M., & Delius, J. D. (1992). Variability of forage pecking in pigeons. *Ethology, 92,* 29-50.

Slater, A., Rose, D., & Morrison, V. (1984). Newborn infants' perception of similarities and differences between two- and three-dimensional stimuli. *British Journal of Developmental Psychology, 2,* 287-294.

Smith, S., & Hosking, E. (1955). *Birds fighting.* London: Faber & Faber.

Spetch, M. L., Kelly, D. B., & Lechelt, D. P. (1998). Encoding of spatial information in images of an outdoor scene by pigeons and humans. *Animal Learning and Behavior, 26,* 85-102.

Srygley, R. B., & Ellington, C. P. (1999). Discrimination of flying mimetic, passion-vine butterflies Heliconius. *Proceedings of the Royal Society London B* (in press).

Sun, H., & Frost, B. J. (1998). Computation of different optical variables of looming objects in pigeon nucleus rotundus neurons. *Nature Neuroscience, 1,* 296-303.

Tinbergen, N. (1959). Comparative studies of the behaviour of gulls (*Laridae*): a progress report. *Behaviour, 15,* 1-70.

Todd, I. A., & Mackintosh, N. J. (1990). Evidence for perceptual learning in pigeons' recognition memory for pictures. *Quarterly Journal of Experimental Psychology, 42B,* 385-400.

Trillmich, F. (1976). Learning experiments on individual recognition in budgerigars (*Melopsittacus undulatus*). *Zeitschrift für Tierpsychologie, 41,* 372-395.

Turner, R. A. (1965). Social feeding in birds. *Behaviour, 24,* 1-46.

Varela, F. J., Palacios, A. G., & Goldsmith, T. H. (1993). Color vision of birds. In H. P. Zeigler & H. J. Bischoff (Eds.), *Vision, brain, and behavior in birds* (pp. 77-98). Cambridge, MA: MIT Press.

Verhave, T. (1966). The pigeon as a quality-control inspector. In R. Ulrich, T. Stachnik, & J. Mabry (Eds.), *Control of human behavior* (pp. 242-246). Glenview: Scott Foresman.

Watanabe, S. (1993). Object-picture equivalence in the pigeon: An analysis with natural concept and pseudoconcept discriminations. *Behavioural Processes, 30,* 225-232.

Watanabe, S. (1997). Visual discrimination of real objects and pictures in pigeons. *Animal Learning and Behavior, 25,* 185-192.

Watanabe, S., & Furuya, I. (1997). Video display for study of avian visual cognition: From psychophysics to sign language. *International Journal of Comparative Psychology, 10,* 111-127.

Watanabe, S., Lea, S. E. G., & Dittrich, W. H. (1993). What can we learn from experiments on pigeon concept discrimination? In H. P. Zeigler & H. J. Bischof (Eds.), *Vision, brain, and behavior in birds* (pp. 47-61). Cambridge, MA: MIT Press.

Watanabe, S., Sakamoto, J., & Wakita, M. (1995). Pigeons' discrimination of paintings by Monet and Picasso. *Journal of the Experimental Analysis of Behavior, 63,* 165-174.

Watanabe, S., Yamashita, M., & Wakita, M. (1993). Discrimination of video-images of conspecific individuals in Bengalese finches. *Journal of Ethology, 11,* 67-72.

Wilkie, D. M., Willson, R. J., & Kardal, S. (1989). Pigeons discriminate pictures of a geographic location. *Animal Learning and Behavior, 17,* 163-171.

Wilkie, D. M., Willson, R. J., & MacDonald, S. E. (1992). Animal's perception and memory for places. In W. K. Honig & G. Fetterman (Eds.), *Cognitive aspects of stimulus control* (pp. 89-112). Hillsdale, NJ: Erlbaum.

Wohlschläger, A., Jäger, R., & Delius, J. D. (1993). Head and eye movements in unrestrained pigeons (*Columba livia*). *Journal of Comparative Psychology, 107,* 313-319.

Wright, A. A. (1989). Memory processing by pigeons, monkeys and people. *Psychology of Learning and Memory, 2,* 25-70.

Wright, A. A., Cook, R. G., Rivera, J. J., Sands, S. F., & Delius, J. D. (1988). Concept learning by pigeons: matching-to-sample with trial-unique video picture stimuli. *Animal Learning and Behavior, 16,* 436-444.

The pigeon's perception of
depth-rotated shapes

Jessie J. Peissig,[1] Michael E. Young,[1]
Edward Wasserman,[1] and Irving Biederman[2]

1. University of Iowa, USA
2. University of Southern California, USA

Abstract

Past investigations into the pigeon's recognition of three-dimensional objects that are pictured at several different views have yielded mixed evidence of viewpoint-invariant performance. In our study, we used single, computer-rendered geons (arch, brick, cone, cylinder, pyramid, and wedge) that involved food reinforcement at only one view (Experiment 1) or at five different views (Experiment 2). One-view training produced reliable stimulus generalization to a majority of nonreinforced views of the geon; five-view training produced reliable stimulus generalization to all nonreinforced views of the geon. These results are discussed in regard to both viewer-centered and object-centered theories of object recognition.

Key words: Object perception, visual recognition, shape discrimination.

Correspondence should be sent to Jessie J. Peissig or Edward A. Wasserman, Department of Psychology, University of Iowa, Iowa City, IA 52242-1407, USA (e-mail: jessie-peissig@uiowa.edu or ed-wasserman@uiowa.edu).

INTRODUCTION

All organisms must discriminate stimuli that satisfy biological needs from those that are life-threatening. As well, those organisms that maneuver effectively throughout their highly heterogeneous environment will have an evolutionary advantage over those that do not. These and other challenges of survival require object recognition.

For most organisms, vision is the primary sensory system that is used for object recognition. The visual system has the seemingly impossible task of quickly and efficiently identifying the hundreds of thousands of objects that enter the field of vision each day. Nevertheless, organisms are evidently quite able to do so despite dramatic changes in viewing angle and distance that a single object may reflect on repeated encounters. Although vision is the most extensively studied sensory system, we are still far from having a complete understanding of its ability to perform complex tasks such as object recognition.

One of the most sophisticated chores performed by the visual system is the recognition of objects from novel views. Even though the organism often sees an object at a variety of views within a single encounter, future encounters may occur in which the object is seen from an entirely different viewpoint. Recognizing novel views is especially difficult because an object's two-dimensional image can change radically as our viewpoint changes, rendering a strict template-matching scheme highly inefficient. For example, as an object rotates in depth, some of its parts may be revealed and other parts may be concealed. A comprehensive theory of object recognition must account for our ability to identify objects despite widely varying two-dimensional retinal images.

Because of the particular complexity inherent in recognizing objects when they are rotated in depth, a large amount of research has investigated the effects of depth rotation on human object recognition. This work has shown that, under some conditions, rotation in depth has little or no effect on either the speed or the accuracy of object recognition (Biederman, 1987; Biederman & Gerhardstein, 1993); under other conditions, however, rotation in depth produces marked impairments in the speed and the accuracy of object recognition (Edelman & Bülthoff, 1992; Rock & DiVita, 1987; Tarr, 1995; Tarr & Pinker, 1989). Exactly why these contrasting findings emerge is not yet fully understood, but it is being actively researched.

One theory of object recognition, recognition-by-components (RBC), suggests a set of circumstances under which rotating an object in depth will have little or no effect on object recognition (Biederman & Gerhardstein, 1993, 1995); these circumstances are defined by three jointly sufficient criteria. The first criterion is that the object must be composed of distinct parts. A crumpled towel lying on the floor, for example, does not contain readily discriminable components or "geons" (geometric ions). The second criterion is that a distinctive geon structural description (GSD) for each object can be formed. A GSD includes all of the geons of an object plus their spatial relations to one another. It would be practically impossible, therefore, to create objects with distinctive GSDs from the same number of common parts, like bricks. The GSDs might not be identical, but they would be similar enough that they would not be considered distinctive. The third criterion requires that the GSD remains the same as the object is rotated in depth. If some parts of the object are no longer visible and others come into view as the object is rotated in depth, then recognition will not be viewpoint-invariant.

If these three criteria are not met, then the organism might have to use viewpoint-dependent processes to identify an object. Because viewpoint-dependent processes require some type of normalization process to match the retinal image to the stored representation, the organism will require more time to identify an object – if indeed it can be recognized at all.

Animal research

Although most visual object recognition research has studied human participants, for a variety of reasons an animal model is especially useful for investigative purposes. With humans, there is always the possibility that they have seen similar stimuli prior to the experiment, which may affect performance. Using animals as experimental subjects allows us to control the organism's prior history with the stimuli. In addition, humans may use verbal labels in recognition tasks, making it difficult to know if the data reflect visual processing alone or visual processing combined with higher-level processes, such as language. With non-human subjects, we eliminate the possibility that the subjects are using verbal labels; thus, we can be more certain that the recorded behavioral effects are principally due to processing in the visual system. A final advantage of an animal model is the broader range of investigative methods that are possible; single-unit recording and lesion studies are two such examples of research that is effectively limited to nonhuman organisms.

A large portion of the animal work involving visual object recognition has looked for areas of the brain that are associated with object recognition. Gross, Bender, and Rocha-Miranda (1969) reported single-unit recording data in monkeys that implicated a specific part of the brain – the inferotemporal cortex (IT) – as important in object recognition. Gross et al. (1969) found IT cells with unusually large receptive fields that seemed to respond selectively to complex visual stimuli (Gross et al., 1969, 1972). In addition, other researchers have found that ablation of area TE (the anterior region of IT) in monkeys produces severe impairments in visual object recognition (Ungerleider & Mishkin, 1982). This converging evidence has implicated IT as a locus of visual object recognition in monkeys.

In more recent research, Tanaka (1996) used single-unit recordings to examine the precise organizational properties of TE. He found that cells in TEd (the dorsal area of TE) are maximally responsive to moderately complex stimuli, as Gross et al. (1969) had proposed. Tanaka (1996) found that these cells exhibit a columnar organization based on stimulus characteristics. Within this columnar organization, individual cells may code information about small changes in object position, orientation, or size, while still maintaining an overall pattern across cells associated with a specific object. This mechanism for representing object features may be the basis for the types of calculations that are required for visual object recognition.

Logothetis, Pauls, Bülthoff, and Poggio (1994) used monkeys in behavioral studies of visual object recognition. Their monkeys viewed a novel object once at a single rotation. The monkeys were then required to respond in an old-new recognition task; they pressed one lever to indicate they had seen the object before ("old") and another lever to indicate they had not seen the object before ("new"). The previously viewed objects (those requiring an "old" response) were shown at different rotations from the one that was seen during the initial viewing. The distractor objects (those requiring a "new" response) were either from the same class of objects (and shared many features with the target object) or from a different class of objects (and shared few features with the target object). The stimuli included one group of wire objects that resembled bent paper clips, one group of amoeboid-like objects that were roughly spherical with protrusions and concavities, and one group of unrelated, common objects. The group of common objects included items such as a teapot. Logethetis et al. (1994) found that on "old" trials with the wire-frame and amoeboid objects, the farther the object was rotated from the initial viewing rotation, the more difficult it was for the monkeys to recognize it as an "old" object; however, on "old" trials with the common objects, the monkeys exhibited viewpoint-invariant performance. These results indicate that monkeys are capable of both viewpoint-dependent and viewpoint-invariant performance.

Although the stimuli in the Logethetis et al. (1994) study did include shading and texture cues, they did not meet all three criteria for invariant object recognition proposed by Biederman and Gerhardstein (1993). For example, the wire-frame objects were not composed of distinctive GSDs. The amoeboid-like objects were not decomposable into distinctive parts and were not composed of distinctive GSDs. Thus, based on these three structural criteria, rotation costs were expected and found. Depending on the rotation, the common objects may have revealed and concealed parts as they rotated, thus violating Biederman and Gerhardstein's third criterion. The common objects were able to form GSDs distinct from one another, however, unlike the other two classes of stimuli. Thus we would expect that the common objects would yield results that were more viewpoint-invariant in nature than the other two classes of objects; at some rotations, however, viewpoint-dependent behavior might be expected. Logethetis et al. (1994) report results that generally accord with this analysis.

Pigeon research

Although much animal research in object recognition has used primates, the use of pigeons to study visual object recognition is increasing. In early studies, researchers found that pigeons trained to discriminate among real, three-dimensional objects show significant transfer in discrimination tasks involving two-dimensional photographs and line drawing/silhouettes of those objects (Delius, 1992; Lumsden, 1977). Delius (1992) reported that pigeons' accuracy with different kinds of pictorial stimuli was generally lower than with novel examples of the real objects (84.3%): the pigeons generalized most to black-and-white photographs (79.1%), slightly less to drawings (70.8%), and least to color photographs (68.7%). The pigeons' discriminative performance was, however, reliably above chance to all three types of two-dimensional portrayals.

These studies demonstrate a correspondence between the pigeon's perceptual processing of three-dimensional objects and the corresponding two-dimensional representations of those objects. Despite these persuasive data, it is still unclear if pigeons have the cognitive capabilities to derive three-dimensional structure from two-dimensional line drawings. Cerella's (1977) study suggests that pigeons cannot do so. In Experiment 1, Cerella (1977) taught pigeons to respond discriminatively to a line drawing of a square, which served as the S+ (reinforced stimulus), and to line drawings of random quadrilaterals, which served as the S-s (nonreinforced stimuli). The random quadrilaterals consisted of four lines in which the angles of intersection were not all equal to 90°. Although it took several months to do so, the pigeons eventually learned this discrimination. Once they had learned to discriminate squares from nonsquares, Cerella replaced the square S+ with random polar projections of a precise cube. The S-s were replaced with stimuli that were created by making small, random shifts in the vertices of the cube; these S-s had the same number of lines and vertices as the cube, but they had no three-dimensional structure. The pigeons' performance dropped to chance for discrimination of the cube from the noncubes; despite prodigious training (150 sessions), the pigeons were never able to master the discrimination.

In Experiment 2, Cerella (1977) attempted to train pigeons to discriminate the true cube from the noncube forms; he did so by first training pigeons with a single rotation of the cube and then gradually adding novel rotations to the training set once the pigeons had evidenced discriminative performance. The pigeons were unable to learn the full set of rotations along the X, Y, and Z axes (9,261 views); they performed only slightly worse when they discriminated two classes of abstract objects with no three-dimensional structure. Cerella (1977) concluded that the pigeons were not deriving the three-dimensional structure from the two-dimensional stimuli.

We would argue that, in Cerella's Experiment 1, the pigeons were expected to transfer discrimination from a two-dimensional stimulus (square) to three-dimensional stimuli (rotations of a cube). The square could be perceived as a forward facing cube with no other sides visible, but this would be an accidental view (an accidental view is one in which the property of the image is not correlated with the actual three-dimensional property of the object; Biederman, 1987). Because an accidental view obscures important information about three-dimensional structure, it is hardly surprising that the pigeons did not generalize the discrimination. As to Cerella's Experiment 2, the pigeons would have had to learn about a phenomenal number of stimuli (9,261 views), some of which may have included accidental views, in order to have exhibited complete stimulus invariance; their failure to do so is, again, not surprising.

Although in Cerella's 1977 study pigeons were unable to learn all rotations of a three-dimensional object, the two-dimensional stimuli that he used contained minimal depth information. In order to derive three-dimensionality, the pigeon may need a much richer two-dimensional representation. Wasserman, Gagliardi, Cook, Kirpatrick-Steger, Astley, and Biederman (1996) found that pigeons were capable of generalizing their visual recognition performance to novel depth rotations of an object when they were trained with line drawings of complex objects; the stimuli included a chair, a flashlight, a desk lamp, and an airplane, each of which comprised several different kinds of geons. The pigeons were trained using a four-alternative forced-choice procedure. In Experiment 1b, the pigeons learned to associate one view of each of the four objects with a different choice key. Once they had acquired the discrimination, the pigeons were tested with novel views of the four objects that were rotated in depth as much as 133° from the trained view. Across all four objects, the birds exhibited significant stimulus generalization to the novel views.

Although significant rotation generalization was found, the pigeons did not exhibit invariant generalization to all novel views in testing; their performance showed a systematic decrease in accuracy as the novel testing views were rotated farther away from the training view. This result could be attributed to many factors. For example, the multi-geon stimuli used by Wasserman et al. (1996) revealed and concealed parts as they were rotated in depth; hence, the GSDs of the four training stimuli were not consistent at all testing rotations, thus violating one of Biederman and Gerhardstein's (1993) structural criteria. Once a part was no longer visible or a new part was revealed, the pigeons should have greater difficulty matching it to the stored representation of that object. This difficulty is especially likely when the pigeon is trained with only one view of an object, which limits the amount of structural information that is available. In the natural environment, organisms usually see an object from many different viewpoints as they move around the object or it moves around them; this experience makes it less likely that a previously unseen part will appear when the object is seen from a novel viewpoint. The disappearance of parts should also be less detrimental to recognition after experience with many different views, because the organism may have already seen the object from viewpoints in which previously seen parts are hidden from direct view.

Wasserman et al. (1996) were indeed able to reduce or to virtually eliminate the decrement in recognition accuracy to novel testing views by training pigeons with three different views of the objects. Training with more views should broaden the pigeon's experiential base and provide it with a more complete and robust three-dimensional representation of the object. In Experiment 2a, Wasserman et al. (1996) again trained pigeons in the four-alternative forced-choice task. Four groups served. One was trained with a single view, just as in Experiment 1b. In the remaining three, the pigeons were trained with three views involving different degrees of rotation: one group was trained with views that varied over a 67° span, a second group with views that varied over a 133° span, and a third group with views that varied over a 267° span. In general, training with three views resulted in smaller decreases in accuracy for untrained views of the objects than did training with only a single view; as well, the rotation costs were smallest for the group that was trained with the broadest range of rotation views (267°).

The current study

The goal of the current study was to investigate object recognition in pigeons by using stimuli that satisfy all three of the structural criteria for viewpoint-invariant performance proposed by Biederman and Gerhardstein (1993). Prior research has suggested that these criteria may apply to object recognition in pigeons as well as humans (Wasserman et al., 1996; Biederman & Gerhardstein, 1993). Specifically, if pigeons are trained with stimuli that meet all three structural criteria, then they should show broad rotation generalization. If the birds nevertheless exhibit decrements in generalization performance, then we can be confident that this result is not due to a violation of one or more of the criteria. This study cannot make definitive distinctions regarding the internal processes involved in object recognition. Although performance can be classified as viewpoint-invariant or viewpoint-specific, it is a much more difficult task to identify the underlying processes producing these behaviors, as evidenced by the ongoing debates in the human literature (Biederman & Gerhardstein, 1995; Tarr & Bülthoff, 1995). The current study can, however, determine whether the three criteria proposed by Biederman and Gerhardstein (1993) are sufficient for guaranteeing viewpoint-invariant behavior. If pigeons exhibit viewpoint-dependent performance even when the criteria are met, then some other factor(s) must be producing the behavior.

In Experiment 1, the discriminative stimuli were simple geometric shapes (single geons) with realistic shading and lighting cues to suggest their three-dimensional shape. Only one view of an object was associated with reinforcement in order to determine the amount of rotation generalization that the pigeons exhibit to other, nonreinforced views under training conditions involving the minimal amount of rotation information. In Experiment 2, we further explored the pigeon's ability to derive three-dimensional structure from two-dimensional representations by training birds with five reinforced views of an object rather than with only one. We expected this increased rotational information to have a positive influence on rotation generalization if prior results (Wasserman et al., 1996) were not merely the result of the use of multi-geon objects.

EXPERIMENT 1

In Experiment 1, we used single-geon objects to test the pigeon's ability to generalize conditioned responding from one view of an object to other views of the same object. We used a go/no-go discrimination task to measure the pigeon's perceived similarity among several different views of an object. The pigeon was required to peck at the S+ to obtain food reinforcement ("go" trials), and did not receive food for responding at an S- ("no-go" trial). Only one view of a geon (the "target" geon) served as the S+; the S-s included all other views of the target geon. By analyzing the errors of commission that the pigeon makes when it learns to discriminate the S-s from the S+, we can determine which S- views appear more similar to the S+ and which appear more different from the S+; the more similar an S- appears to the S+, the more errors it should commit. In addition to the target geon (which involved reinforcement at only one view), we also included a "foil" geon that was not associated with reinforcement at any view. The foil geon was used as a basis for assessing the magnitude of conditioned responding to the nonreinforced views of the target geon; geon-appropriate responding would be indicated by more responding to the nonreinforced views of the target geon than to the nonreinforced views of the foil geon.

Method

Subjects. The subjects were eight feral pigeons. They were maintained at 85% of their free-feed weights by controlled daily feeding. Prior to the onset of the present experiment, the pigeons had participated in unrelated studies.

Apparatus. The pigeons were trained in four specially-constructed plywood chambers. One side of each chamber consisted of a large opening with an aluminum frame attached to the outside of the box. Inside the frame was a clear touch screen (Elmwood Sensors DuraTouch Model #70056-001, Pawtucket, RI) that was coated with mylar for durability. The subjects' pecks to the touch screen were processed by a serial controller board (Elographics Model #E271-2200, Oak Ridge, TN). A brushed aluminum panel was placed directly in front of the screen to allow subjects access to limited portions of the video monitor. Although there were five openings in the aluminum panel, this experiment utilized only the central 7 cm × 7 cm display in which the stimuli appeared. In the rear of the chamber, a clear Plexiglas food container was placed level with a wire mesh floor to prevent subjects from perching on the food cup. Noyes 45-mg pigeon pellets were delivered through a vinyl tube into the food cup using a rotary pellet dispenser (Model #ENV-203M; MED Associates, Lafayette, IN). During experimental sessions, constant illumination was provided by a houselight mounted on the upper rear wall of the chamber. A digital I/O interface board (National Instruments Model #NB-DIO-24, Austin, TX) controlled the pellet dispenser and the houselight.

Control of peripheral stimuli (via the I/O interface) and recording of the pigeons' responses (via the serial controller board) were accomplished by two Apple Macintosh IIci and two Apple Macintosh Quadra 650 computers. The pigeon's monitor and an identical monitor located in an adjacent room were connected by a video splitter (VOPEX-2M, Network Technologies Inc., Aurora, OH) for the Apple Macintosh IIci computers, and a distribution amplifier (MAC/2 DA 2, Extron Electronics, Santa Fe Springs, CA) for the Quadra 650's. The programs were developed in Hypercard 2.3.

Stimuli. Stimuli were gray-scale drawings that were rendered in Raydream Designer 4 at 150 dpi (dots per inch) resolution. The stimuli were approximately 2 to 3 centimeters wide and 3 centimeters high and consisted of a brick, a cone, a cylinder, and a pyramid, varying from one another by at least one nonaccidental property (Biederman, 1987). For example, a cone and a pyramid differ only by the edge of the cross-section, which is curved for the cone and straight for the pyramid. The stimuli only varied by at most two nonaccidental properties (the cone has a curved, contracted cross-section and the brick has a straight, constant cross-section). We rendered the geons with one long axis to allow alignment at specific views; the 0° views for all of the geons have identical long axis orientations. Each geon was rotated in depth by 36° steps to provide us with 10 different views spanning a full 360° of rotation.

Procedure. Two pigeons were assigned to each of four training conditions ($N = 8$): brick target with cone foil, cone target with brick foil, cylinder target with pyramid foil, and pyramid target with cylinder foil (hereafter designated brick+/cone-, cone+/brick-, cylinder+/pyramid-, and pyramid+/cylinder-, respectively). The stimuli were paired so that the two geons in each condition always differed by two nonaccidental properties. The reinforced view (S+) of the target geon was arbitrarily chosen and was designated as the 0° view.

At the beginning of a trial, the center display area was illuminated with a white field. A single peck anywhere within the display area turned on the stimulus. On a nonreinforced ("no-go") trial, the stimulus remained on for 15 s, after which the display area darkened and the intertrial interval began; all pecks during the 15 s were recorded. On a reinforced ("go") trial, the stimulus remained on for 15 s and the first peck after 15 s was followed by food reinforcement; the number of pecks during the first 15 s was recorded. The intertrial interval ranged from 6 to 10 s (mean of 8 s). Responses were reinforced with 1 to 3 pellets of food, determined for each pigeon by its weight. On any given trial, the bird saw a single geon at a particular view on the monitor.

The experiment comprised two phases: Baseline training and Discrimination training. During Baseline training, responses to all stimuli were reinforced. Once the pigeons responded consistently to the stimuli during Baseline, they were moved to the Discrimination phase, during which only responses to the 0° view of the target geon were reinforced; responses to any other stimuli were not reinforced.

For both the Baseline and Discrimination phases, we used a randomized block design. In Baseline, a 30-trial block consisted of one presentation of each of the 10 views of the target geon and one presentation of each of the 10 views of the foil geon; the view of the target geon that was chosen to be the S+ for the Discrimination phase was also presented an additional 10 times. Thus, the view of the target geon that would later serve as the S+ was presented a total of 11 times in each block. Each session of Baseline training consisted of five 30-trial blocks for a total of 150 trials.

In the Discrimination phase, each block included a single, nonreinforced presentation of each of the 10 views of the target geon and a single, nonreinforced presentation of each of the 10 views of the foil geon; the S+ was also given 10 more times followed by food reinforcement. Thus, the S+ was presented 10 times with reinforcement and 1 time without reinforcement. This method of reinforcing the S+ on 91% of its presentations was used to ensure that the birds would continue responding vigorously to the S+ while giving the birds an equal number of nonreinforced trials with the 1 S+ picture and each of the 19 different S- pictures. The data used for statistical analysis came only from the nonreinforced trials, allowing each of the 20 pictorial stimuli to contribute equally. This design produced a total of 30 trials in each block: 11 trials with the S+ (10 reinforced and 1 nonreinforced) and 19 trials with the S-s (all nonreinforced). Each session of Discrimination training included five 30-trial blocks for a total of 150 trials.

To assess responding to each of the 20 pictorial stimuli, we used the pecking data of each pigeon after it began to discriminate the reinforced from the nonreinforced displays, but before its discrimination was complete. We began collecting data for each bird when the number of pecks to any of the S-s fell to 67% or less of that to the S+ in a single session. Data collection ended when the number of pecks to any 18 of the 19 S-s fell to 33% or less of that to the S+ in a single session (this was the best level of discrimination learning that was achieved by all eight pigeons).

Results and discussion

Baseline training took between 5 and 7 days for each of the birds to complete. The number of scored days in Discrimination training ranged from 3 to 29. The birds in the pyramid+/cylinder- condition took the fewest days to reach criterion ($M = 4.5$) and the birds in the cylinder+/pyramid- condition took the most days to reach criterion ($M = 18.5$). Birds in the remaining conditions took an intermediate number of days to reach criterion (brick+/cone-, $M = 5.5$; cone+/brick-, $M = 7.5$).

Figure 1 shows responding to the target and foil geons, averaged across the eight pigeons and the four conditions. The spokes of the graph indicate the percentage of pecks to the S+ view of the target geon, calculated by dividing the number of pecks to each stimulus by the number of pecks to the S+ and multiplying by 100;[1] necessarily, the score was 100% to the S+ view of the target geon. These percentages were calculated for each session and then an overall mean was used for Figure 1. Places where the gray area intersects the spokes represent the percentage of S+ pecks to the target geon; for example, the percentage of S+ pecks at the -36° view is 50%. Places where the spokes are intersected by the filled circles (connected by the black lines) represent the percentage of S+ pecks to the foil geon.

Responding to the target geon was highest at the reinforced view and showed a large generalization decrement as the object was rotated away from the S+ view. The pigeons exhibited a mild asymmetry in responding to rotations of the target geon, largely because the -108° view involved a higher percentage of S+ responses than did the less extreme rotation of -72°. Responding to the foil geon was highest at the view that matched the rotation of the reinforced view of the target. Still, the percentage of S+ responses to the foil geon was quite low across all views. With one exception (at -144°) where the scores were tied, the pigeons responded more to the nonreinforced views of the target geon than to the corresponding views of the foil geon.

---

1. These percentages were calculated for each pigeon individually and then averaged across birds.

We analyzed these data using a repeated measures, full factorial analysis of variance (ANOVA) of Geon (target vs. foil), View (-144°, -108°, -72°, -36°, 0°, 36°, 72°, 108°, 144°, 180°), and Condition (brick+/cone-, cone+/brick-, cylinder+/pyramid-, pyramid+/cylinder-). The dependent measure was the rate of response to each stimulus. The pigeons responded more to the target geon than to the foil geon, as evidenced by a statistically significant main effect of Geon, $F(1, 4) = 38.02$, $p < .01$. There was also a statistically significant interaction of Geon by View, $F(9, 50) = 18.73$, $p < .0001$; this interaction indicated that the difference in the peck rates between the target and foil geons varied across views. As illustrated in Figure 1, the target-foil disparity was greatest at the 0° reinforced view and it was lower at the other

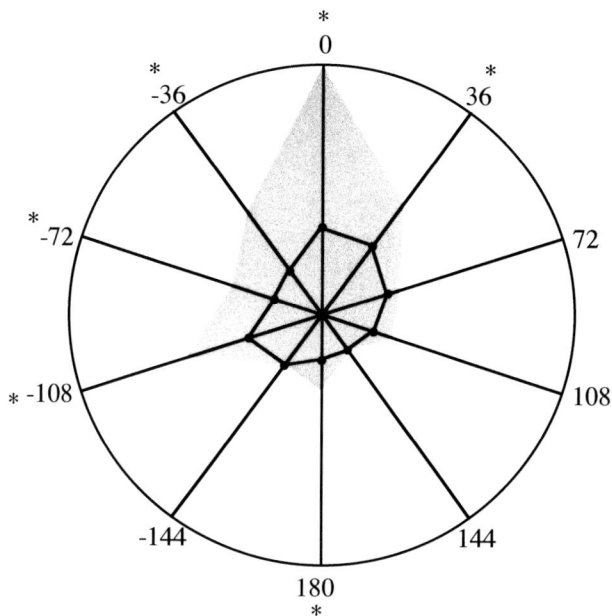

Figure 1. The results of Experiment 1 averaged across all four geon conditions.
Plotted on the spokes are the rates of pecking to each view of the target geon divided by the rate of pecking to the 0° view of the target geon multiplied by 100 to yield a percentage score. The gray area represents responding to views of the target geon and the filled circles connected by the black lines represent responding to views of the foil geon. Asterisks denote views at which responding to the target geons was reliably greater than responding to the foil geon.
* = $p < .05$.

depth rotations. Planned orthogonal comparisons ($\alpha = 0.05$) between the target versus foil geons at each rotation indicated that at the -108°, -72°, -36°, 0°, 36°, and 180° rotations, there was significantly more responding to the target geon than to the foil geon; there were no significant differences in responding to the target and foil geons at the -144°, 72°, 108°, and 144° rotations.

The pigeons exhibited geon-specific responding in the individual training conditions, as shown in Figure 2.[2] The pigeons in the brick+/ cone- condition (Figure 2a) showed high responding at the 0° S+ view and at the nonreinforced -108°, 180°, and 72° views of the target geon. Responding was actually a bit higher to the foil geon than to the target geon at the 36° and 108° views. The pigeons in the cone+/brick- condition (Figure 2b) showed a very regular generalization gradient, with greater target than foil responding at the 72°, 36°, 0°, -36°, -72°, and -108° views. The pigeons in the cylinder+/pyramid- condition (Figure 2c) showed substantial rotational asymmetry, with greater target than foil responding at the -108°, -72°, -36°, 0°, and 36° views; responding to the foil geon was greater than to the target geon at the 72°, 108°, and 144° views. The pigeons in the pyramid+/cylinder- condition (Figure 2d) also exhibited a rotational asymmetry, with greater target than foil responding to the -36°, 0°, 36°, 72°, 108°, 144°, and 180° views; responding to the foil geon was greater than to the target geon at the -108° and -144° views.

Over the course of Discrimination training, the pigeons exhibited a marked decline in responding to the S- views of the target geon; this result is not surprising because the birds only received reinforcement for responding to the S+ view. It is more important to appreciate that, for the majority of the nonreinforced views, responding across all birds and all conditions was significantly higher to the target geon than to the corresponding views of the foil geon. Any increased responding to the S- views of the target geon is actually counterproductive, as it involves wasted energy and possibly frustrative nonreward. This high responding to other views of the target geon suggests that the pigeons did recognize the rotated target geon as the same object as S+, even for S- views rotated as far away from S+ as 180°.

---

2. These percentages were calculated for each pigeon individually and then averaged across birds.

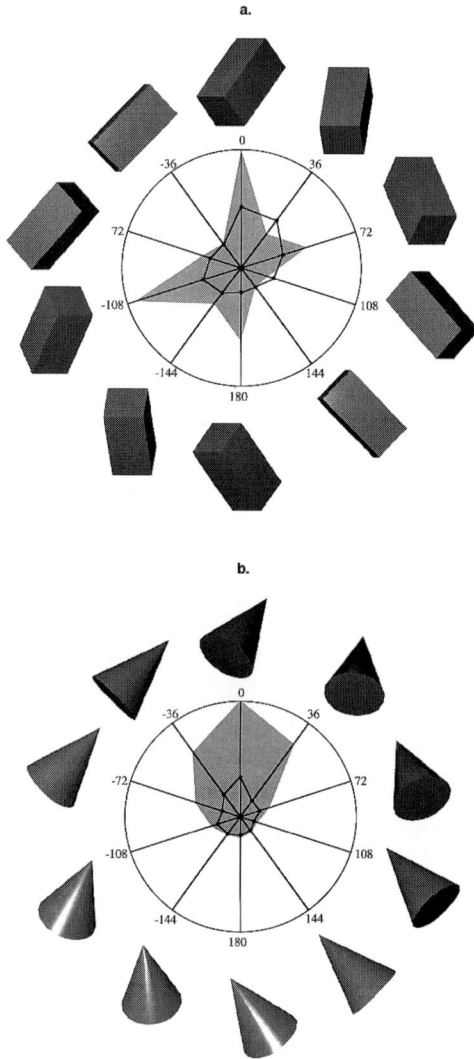

Figure 2. The results for each condition of Experiment 1: (a) brick+/cone-,
(b) cone+/brick-, (c) cylinder+/pyramid-, and (d) pyramid+/cylinder-.
Plotted on the spokes are the rates of pecking to each view of the target geon
divided by the rate of pecking to the 0° view of the target geon multiplied by

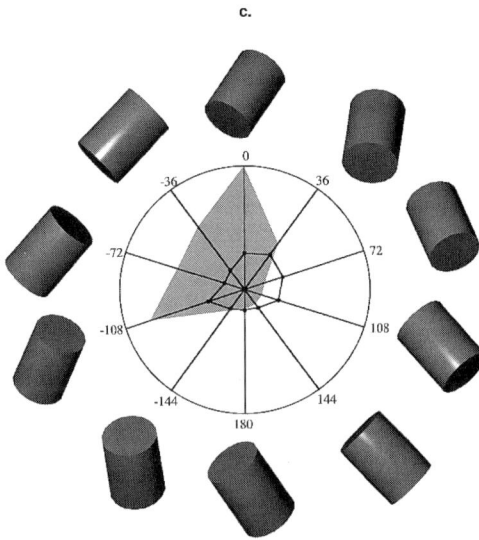

c.

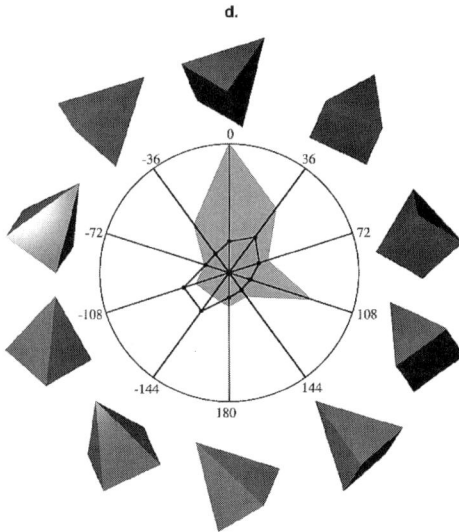

d.

100 to yield a percentage score. The gray area represents responding to views of the target geon and the filled circles connected by the black lines represent responding to views of the foil geon.

These results therefore indicate that the pigeon is capable of generalizing conditioned responding from a single reinforced view of an object to other nonreinforced views of the same object.[3] The fact that responding to the majority of nonreinforced views of the target geon was significantly above responding to the corresponding views of the foil geon is especially noteworthy because the target geon and the foil geon in each condition differed from one another by only two nonaccidental properties.

The pigeons did nevertheless exhibit a systematic decrease in conditioned responding as the target geon was rotated away from the reinforced view, thus failing to show viewpoint-invariant performance to the nonreinforced views of the target geon.

EXPERIMENT 2

Experiment 1 clearly demonstrated that pigeons can generalize their conditioned responses to other depth-rotated views of a geon when the birds' responses were reinforced at only one view, although the generalization was not viewpoint-invariant. In Experiment 2, we wanted to explore further the pigeon's ability to exhibit viewpoint-invariant responding. The pigeons in Experiment 2 were trained with five views of the target geon, rather than with only one as in Experiment 1. This change should better encourage the pigeons to form a viewpoint-independent representation of the target geon. Multiple-views training is arguably more ecologically valid, because organisms are rarely restricted to one view of an object when they encounter it in the natural environment.

The basic design of this experiment was similar to that used in Experiment 1. Now, however, five reinforced views of the target geon were interleaved with five nonreinforced views. We expected strong conditioned responding to the reinforced views; we also expected strong conditioned responding to the interpolated, nonreinforced views. Indeed, we wondered whether or not the pigeons could effectively learn to

---

3. It is possible, of course, that the pigeon's behavior could have been produced by generalized inhibition among S-s, but the generalization decrement observed would still be indicative of viewpoint-dependent behavior.

withhold responding to the nonreinforced views. As in Experiment 1, we again expected responding to both reinforced and nonreinforced views of the target geon to exceed responding to all of the views of the foil geon.

Method

Subjects. The subjects were four different feral pigeons. By controlled daily feeding, the pigeons were maintained at 85% of their free-feeding weights. Prior to the onset of the present experiment, the pigeons had participated in unrelated studies.

Apparatus. The pigeons were trained in four specially-constructed plywood chambers that were slightly different from those used in Experiment 1. These chambers used a different touch screen (Accutouch Model #002744-FTM-K1; Elographics, Oak Ridge, TN) and serial controller board (Model #E271-2210, Elographics). In addition, control of peripheral stimuli (via the I/O interface) and recording of the pigeons' responses (via the serial controller board) were accomplished by four Apple Macintosh 7100/66 Power PC computers. The pigeon's monitor and an identical monitor located in an adjacent room were connected by a different distribution amplifier (Model #MAC/2 DA2; Extron Electronic, Sante Fe Springs, CA) than that used in Experiment 1.

Stimuli. The stimuli used in this experiment were slightly different from those used in Experiment 1. The stimuli ranged in size from 2 to 4 centimeters in width and from 2 to 4 centimeters in height; they were rendered in Raydream Designer 4 at 300 dpi resolution. The stimuli consisted of an arch and a wedge that varied from one another by three nonaccidental properties (curved vs. straight edge of axis, constant vs. contracted axis, and symmetry; Biederman, 1987). Varying the objects by more than two nonaccidental properties (as in Experiment 1) should make the foil geon easier to discriminate from the target geon; if the pigeons learn more quickly to discriminate between the target and foil geon, then the task may be more sensitive to differences between the nonreinforced views of the target geon and all views of the foil geon. The geons were rotated in depth by 36° intervals to yield 10 different views of each geon.

Procedure. Two pigeons were assigned to each of two conditions: arch+ and wedge+. In the arch+ condition, the arch served as the target geon and the wedge served as the foil; in the wedge+ condition, the wedge served as the target geon and the arch served as the foil. The experiment consisted of two different phases: Preliminary Discrimination and Final Discrimination.

At the beginning of a trial, the center display area was illuminated with a white field. A single peck anywhere within that display area turned on the discriminative stimulus in the center display area. On a nonreinforced ("no-go") trial, the stimulus remained on for 15 s, after which the display area darkened and the intertrial interval began; all pecks during the 15 s were recorded. On a reinforced ("go") trial, the stimulus remained on for 15 s, and the first peck after the 15 s was followed by reinforcement; the number of pecks during the first 15 s was recorded. The intertrial interval ranged from 6 to 10 s (mean of 8 s). The pigeons' responses were reinforced with 1 to 3 pellets of food, determined for each bird by its weight.

During Preliminary Discrimination training, the pigeons' responses were reinforced to five views of the target geon that were equally spaced at $72°$ intervals: $-144°$, $-72°$, $0°$, $72°$, and $144°$. The pigeons' responses were not reinforced to a black-and-white "brick wall" pattern (S-). We trained the pigeons to respond differentially to the five reinforced views in order to record any spontaneous generalization that might occur to the five nonreinforced views of the target geon when they were introduced in Final Discrimination training. Before moving from Preliminary to Final Discrimination training, the pigeons were required to meet a criterion of five consecutive sessions in which the peck rate to the S- was less than 33% of the mean peck rate to the S+s.

In Preliminary Discrimination training, we used a randomized block design. Within each block, there were four trials each with the five S+ views of the target geon (20 trials) and 20 trials with the brick wall S-, for a total of 40 trials. Each daily session consisted of five blocks for a total of 200 trials per day (5 blocks of 40 trials).

During Final Discrimination training, the birds continued training with the five S+ views of the target geon. We added five novel nonreinforced views of the target geon, that were rotated at equal distances from the reinforced views ($-108°$, $-36°$, $36°$, $108°$, and $180°$); we also introduced 10 nonreinforced views of a foil geon shown at $36°$ intervals. We used a randomized block design. Each block consisted of one nonreinforced trial with each of the 10 views of the target geon and each of the 10 views of the foil geon, for a total of 20 nonreinforced trials. In addition, the five S+ views of the target geon were each presented four times, for a total of 20 reinforced trials. This procedure resulted in reinforcement on 80% of the S+ presentations. This method was used to assure that the pigeons would continue to respond to the S+s while keeping the number of nonreinforced trials with the S+s and the S-s equal. Thus, each block comprised a total of 40 trials (20 nonreinforced and 20 reinforced trials). There were five blocks in each session for a total of 200 trials (5 blocks of 40 trials). Analyses only used data from the nonreinforced trials.

In Experiment 1, data collection did not begin until the pigeons had reached a specific initial criterion; in Experiment 2, Preliminary Discrimination training taught the subjects to discriminate between the S+ views of the target geon and a single negative stimulus (the "brick wall" pattern). Therefore, data collection began on Day 1 of Final Discrimination training to determine if any spontaneous generalization would occur to other views of the target geon or to any views of the foil geon. Initial data collection continued until a pigeon's responding to each of the foils had fallen to 33% or less of responding to the reinforced target views; these scores were calculated by dividing the peck rate to each individual view of the foil geon by the mean of the peck rates for the five S+ views of the target geon (for each session). After the birds met criterion, data were collected for an additional 20 days session to determine if the pigeons would soon learn to discriminate between the reinforced and nonreinforced views of the target geon.

Results and discussion

The number of days to reach criterion in Final Discrimination training ranged from 5 to 30. The birds in the arch+ condition took longer to reach criterion ($M = 17.5$ days) than the birds in the wedge+ condition ($M = 10.5$ days).

Figure 3 shows mean responding to the target geon, averaged across the reinforced and nonreinforced views separately; it also shows responding to the foil geon, averaged across all 10 views. The data are separately shown both before and after criterion, with the sessions prior to and including the day of attaining criterion included in the pre-criterion measure and the 20 sessions after the pigeons met criterion included in the post-criterion measure. Responding is represented as the percentage of pecks to the five S+s, calculated by dividing the number of pecks to each stimulus by the mean number of pecks to the five S+s and multiplying by 100.[4]

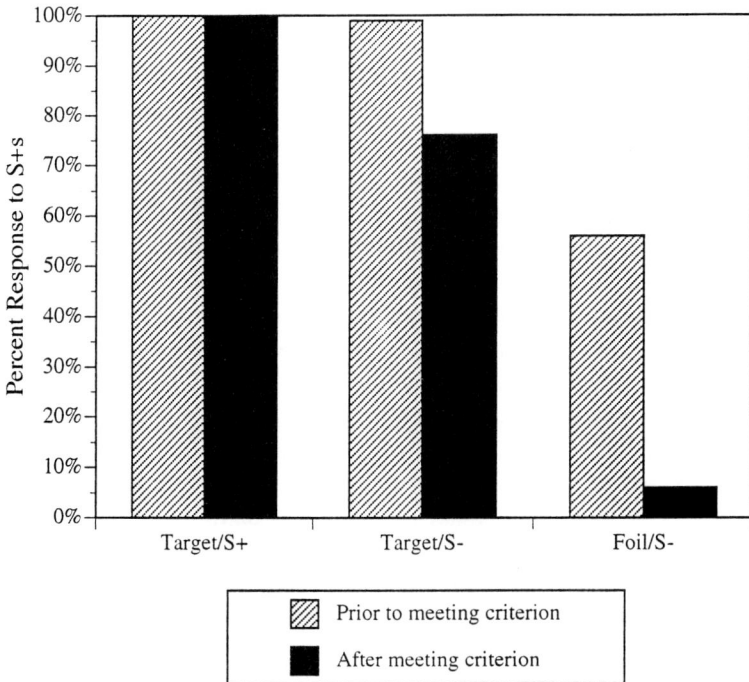

Figure 3. The results of Experiment 2 averaged across training conditions and depth-rotated object views.
The bars indicate the mean peck rate to each type of stimulus divided by the mean peck rate to the S+s multiplied by 100 to yield a percentage score. The striped bars represent responding prior to and including the session on which each pigeon met the foil discrimination criterion. The solid bars represent responding during the 20 days following the session on which each bird met the foil discrimination criterion.

---

4. These percentages were calculated for each pigeon individually and then averaged across birds.

Both before and after meeting the criterion, the pigeons responded most to the reinforced views of the target geon and least to views of the foil geon. Before meeting criterion, the pigeons' percentage of S+ responses to the nonreinforced views of the target geon was virtually the same as for the reinforced views, indicating no discrimination between the S- and S+ views of the target geon. After meeting criterion, the pigeons exhibited a slightly lower percentage of S+ responses to the nonreinforced views of the target geon than to the reinforced views, but this percentage was still well above responding to the foil geon which was almost zero.

Figure 4 shows responding to each view of the target geon in the two training conditions before the pigeons had met criterion (responding to foils falling to less than or equal to 33% of that to the S+s). Places where the gray area intersects the spokes represent the percentage of S+ pecks to the target geon. The inner circle represents the overall mean percentage of S+ responding to the foil geon; because the two geons used in this experiment had no clear longitudinal axis and could not be aligned with one another, we averaged the scores for all views of the foil geon. The outer circle represents a score of 100%; because the mean of the five S+s combined must equal 100%, some individual S+ scores will be slightly above and others slightly below 100%.

The arch+ and wedge+ conditions were very similar to one another prior to the pigeons' meeting criterion; in both conditions, the pigeons responded more to all views of the target geon than to any views of the foil geon. In addition, there were no clear differences in the percentage of S+ responding for reinforced and nonreinforced views of the target geon in either condition; the percentage of S+ responding to all views of the target geon was well above average responding to the foil geon, regardless of whether the picture was an S+ or an S- view of the target geon.

Figure 5 shows responding to each view of the target geon in the two training conditions collected for 20 days after the pigeons had met criterion (peck rates to the foils had fallen to 33% or less than peck rates to the S+s). Even after 20 additional days of discrimination training, pigeons in the arch+ condition exhibited very little evidence of having learned to discriminate between the S+ and S- views of the arch; although responding is slightly lower at the -108°, -36°, and 36° views, the decrease is small (Figure 5a). In the wedge+ condition, the pigeons did show more pronounced decreases in responding to some S- views of

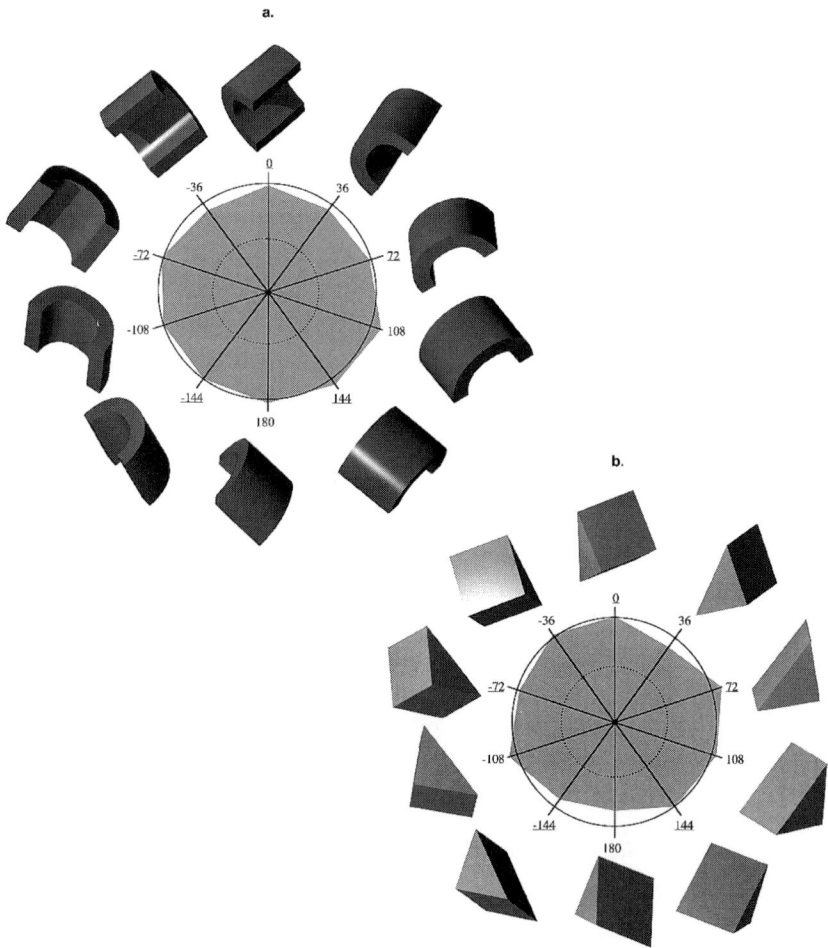

*Figure 4. The results for the arch+ and wedge+ conditions of Experiment 2
for the sessions up to and including the session on which each pigeon met the
foil discrimination criterion.*
Plotted on the spokes are the rates of pecking to each view of the target geon
divided by the mean rate of pecking across the five reinforced views of target
geon (underlined) multiplied by 100 to yield a percentage score. The inner
circle is the mean rate of pecking to all views of the foil geon divided by the
mean rate of pecking across the five reinforced views of target geon multiplied
by 100.

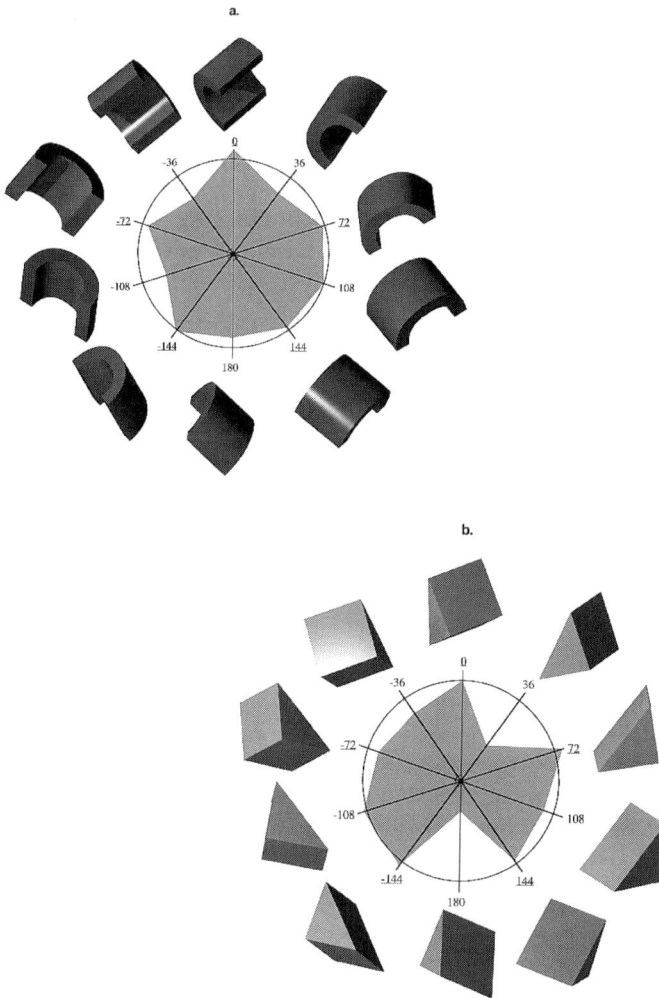

Figure 5. The results for the arch+ and wedge+ conditions of Experiment 2 for the 20 sessions following the session on which each subject met the foil discrimination criterion.
Plotted on the spokes are the rates of pecking to each view of the target geon divided by the rates of pecking across the five reinforced views of target geon (underlined) multiplied by 100 to yield a percentage score. The inner circle is the mean rate of pecking to all views of the foil geon divided by the mean rate of pecking across the five reinforced views of target geon multiplied by 100.

the target geon; responding at the 36° and 180° views is well below that of the adjacent S+ views (Figure 5b). These signs of discriminating the S+ from the S- views of the target geon notwithstanding, responding to all views of the target geon still exceeded average responding to the foil geon.

For all statistical analyses of the data in Experiment 2, a nested design was necessary because the pigeons received reinforced and nonreinforced views of the target geon, but only nonreinforced views of the foil geon. As noted earlier, because the two geons could not be aligned, comparing specific views of the target and foil geons was not possible; thus, the different views of the foil geon were collapsed into a single mean score. Further, preliminary analyses found no statistically significant differences between the training conditions, so we collapsed the data across the two conditions in order to provide greater statistical power.

The first day of Final Discrimination training was analyzed to see if Preliminary Discrimination training had produced any discrimination between the target and foil geons. We analyzed the data for Day 1 of Final Discrimination training using a full factorial, repeated measures ANOVA of Reinforcement (S+ vs. S-) nested under Geon (target vs. foil). The dependent measure was the rate of pecking to each of the stimuli. Neither of the two main effects was statistically significant, indicating that Preliminary Discrimination training had no measurable effect on responding on Day 1 of Final Discrimination training.

We next analyzed the pre-criterion and post-criterion data separately.[5] We analyzed the pre-criterion data using a full factorial, repeated measures ANOVA of Reinforcement (S+ vs. S-) nested under Geon (target vs. foil). The dependent measure was the daily peck rate to each stimulus. Even though five views of the target geon were not reinforced, pigeons responded more to the target geon than to the foil geon, as evidenced by a statistically significant main effect of Geon, $F(1, 3) = 17.91, p < 0.05$. The main effect of Reinforcement nested under Geon class was not significant, $F(1, 9) = 1.76, p > .05$, indicating that there was no significant difference in responding to the S+ and S- views of the target geon.

---

5. We could not analyze the data separately for each condition because there were only two subjects per condition, which led to a lack of statistical power.

The post-criterion data were analyzed using the same model as the pre-criterion data. The dependent measure was the peck rate to each stimulus during the 20 post-criterion training sessions. The pigeons again responded more to the target geon than to the foil geon; the main effect of Geon was statistically significant, $F(1, 3) = 18.17, p < 0.05$. The main effect of Reinforcement nested under Geon class was not quite statistically significant, $F(1, 3) = 6.63, p = 0.08$. Thus, despite an additional 20 days of post-criterion training, there was only slim evidence of discrimination between the reinforced and nonreinforced views of the target geon.

In summary, after training with five equally spaced views of an object, pigeons exhibited strong rotation generalization to interpolated views of the same object. The birds exhibited great difficulty in learning to stop responding to the S- views of the target geon. This difficulty was not due to a general inability to discriminate among the experimental stimuli, because the pigeons very quickly and completely learned to cease responding to multiple views of the foil geon. Therefore, it appears that in Experiment 2, stimulus generalization from the reinforced views was sufficiently strong to ensure very high rates of responding to the nonreinforced views of the target geon.

This strong stimulus generalization produced largely viewpoint-invariant responding, in contrast to the viewpoint-specific responding in Experiment 1. We can be relatively certain that the increased generalization exhibited by the pigeons in Experiment 2 was due almost exclusively to training with five views, and not to stimulus differences (i.e., the number of accidental properties); we have found similar increases in generalization when comparing pigeons trained with one view to those with trained five views using the same stimuli in a four-alternative forced-choice task (Peissig, Young, Wasserman, & Biederman, 1999a).

GENERAL DISCUSSION

The results of our study indicate that pigeons generalize conditioned responding from reinforced to nonreinforced depth rotations of a target geon. In Experiment 1, the pigeons received food reinforcement at only one view of the target geon; nonetheless, at a majority of depth rotations of the target geon, they exhibited significantly more responding to the target geon than they did to the foil geon. Thus, we observed rotation generalization even when the pigeons had only one reinforced view of an object from which to extrapolate the structure of the object. In Experiment 2, we reinforced responding at five equally spaced views of the target geon to improve the likelihood that the pigeons would form a robust three-dimensional representation of the object. This type of training is more similar to naturalistic conditions in which an object is seen from a variety of different viewpoints. Here, the pigeons exhibited even stronger generalization to the interpolated, nonreinforced views of the target geon; in fact, the pigeons were unable to significantly decrease their responding to the nonreinforced views of the target geon, despite 20 days of overtraining.

It is possible that the results we obtained, especially the viewpoint-dependent performance in Experiment 1, may be due to two-dimensional stimulus properties. We cannot be certain that the pigeons were indeed perceiving the stimuli as three-dimensional and using the derived three-dimensional structure to perform the tasks. Previous research has shown, however, that pigeons are capable of perceiving the three-dimensionality of two-dimensional representations. For example, Delius (1992) demonstrated that pigeons were capable of generalizing from real objects to photographs of stimuli. Pigeons also have the ability to form a single class of objects containing both real objects and photographs of those objects (Watanabe, 1997). Despite evidence that pigeons are capable of perceiving the three-dimensionality of two-dimensional representations, it is possible that in our experiments they used simple, two-dimensional features, such as dark and light patches due to shading or the shape of the silhouette, to learn the discriminations. A pixel-matching analysis of stimuli identical to those used in Experiment 2 indicated that these types of simple features were inadequate at predicting the generalization exhibited by different pigeons in similar experiments (Peissig, Young, Wasserman, & Biederman, 1999b).

It is also possible that the pigeons used two-dimensional geometric features (e.g., edge location, edge length, or vertex types and their locations) to perform the tasks. Unfortunately, we are not aware of any widely accepted models that are capable of a geometric analysis of complex, shaded images such as ours. This limitation makes it difficult to quantify the role of two-dimensional features in our tasks. Ruling out two-dimensional features may be irrelevant, however, because human research has demonstrated that qualitative variations in geometric features can influence object recognition (Tarr, Bülthoff, Zabinski, &

Blanz, 1997). Some alternative theories of object recognition propose that a three-dimensional representation is unnecessary for recognition, and that two-dimensional feature extraction may be sufficient under some circumstances (Poggio & Edelman, 1990). Therefore, even if pigeons are using two-dimensional features to perform the discrimination, this may not be a distinctly different process from that used by humans.

There is also experimental evidence that three-dimensional information can be used by pigeons to enhance performance in a task similar to ours. In a more naturalistic study, pigeons were exposed to real objects in their home cages (Watanabe, this issue). When these pigeons were later required to perform a discrimination task with photographs of the same objects, they showed more generalization to novel views than did pigeons that had not been exposed to the real objects. The results of Watanabe's experiment could be a result of exposure to multiple views of an object, as in Experiment 2 of our study. Watanabe's experiment is notable not only for corroborating our results, but also for demonstrating that pigeons can use knowledge about real objects to enhance their performance with two-dimensional representations of those objects.

Theoretical interpretations

The differences between our pigeons' responding in Experiments 1 and 2 can be explained by current theories of object recognition in humans.

In object-centered theories, such as Biederman's (1987) RBC, the frame of reference is the object. Initially, the organism decomposes the object into simple, three-dimensional geometric forms or geons. The organism then recreates the three-dimensional structure of the object based on the spatial relationship among the geons. Finally, the organism compares the structure derived from the retinal image to the many three-dimensional representations of objects that are stored in its memory to determine if there is a match. Because the stored representations are three-dimensional and have a reference point separate from the viewer, objects should be recognized independent of viewpoint.

In Experiment 1, the absence of a difference in conditioned responding between some views of the target geon and the foil geon could be due to a lack of sensitivity in our task. If the pigeons had learned to cease responding to nonreinforced views of the geons too quickly, then floor effects might prevent the detection of target-foil differences. In addition, RBC does not predict that organisms are utterly oblivious to object viewpoint; rather, it predicts that recognition is independent of viewpoint. The results of Experiment 1 may reflect the pigeon's sensitivity to rotations in depth that are independent of the recognition process. It is also possible that the generalization decrement that we observed in Experiment 1 was due to the specific emphasis that the training procedure places on object viewpoint as a discriminative stimulus.

In Experiment 2, the pigeons received reinforcement for responding to five views of the target geon rather than to one view, as in Experiment 1; training with multiple views should increase the likelihood that the pigeons will exhibit viewpoint-invariant behavior. In Experiment 2, our results accorded with RBC theory. The pigeons responded significantly more to all nonreinforced views of the target geon than to any views of the foil geon. Even after overtraining, the pigeons were unable to reliably discriminate between the reinforced and the nonreinforced views of the target geon. These results provided clear evidence of viewpoint-invariant responding.

Our results, however, can also be explained in terms of theories other than RBC. One widely-accepted alternative theory is the multiple-views theory proposed by Tarr and Pinker (1989). Multiple-views theory is an example of a viewer-centered account of object recognition. In viewer-centered theories, the representations that are stored in memory reflect the specific viewpoint(s) from which the organism has previously encountered an object (Edelman & Bülthoff, 1992; Tarr & Bülthoff, 1995; Ullman, 1989). The organism mentally transforms the retinal image when there are differences in size and/or viewpoint between the current image and prior stored representation(s). These transformations have cognitive costs that are reflected in performance. Because performance may vary systematically depending on viewpoint, recognition will be viewpoint-dependent. Viewpoint-dependent theories thus anticipate that rotating an object may have significant effects on object recognition.

In Experiment 1, the pigeons did not respond to the target significantly more than the foils at all views – primarily those rotations that were farthest from the training view. The multiple-views theory would propose that the costs of transformation at the distant rotations were greater than for nearer rotations where target responding was significantly above the foils. These types of rotation costs would be most notable in Experiment 1, because the rotational distance between the reinforced target view and nonreinforced views spanned 36° to 180°. When pigeons received reinforcement at multiple views of an object in Experiment 2, they did exhibit viewpoint-invariant performance. The multiple-views theory anticipates this result; if the pigeons stored all of the reinforced views in memory, then the rotation costs for the nonreinforced views would be minimal because the greatest amount of transformation that would ever be required would be only 36°. Thus, the multiple-views and RBC theories of object recognition each provide plausible theoretical explanations of the data in our two experiments.

That our study was not able to decisively support RBC or multiple-views theory is not surprising. Studies using human participants have encountered similar problems. The difficulty stems from our inability to determine the underlying recognition process by looking at behavior performance. RBC predicts viewpoint invariance, but only under certain conditions. If the objects reveal and conceal parts, for example, then RBC predicts that performance will be viewpoint-dependent, even though the underlying mechanism would still essentially be object-centered. Likewise, multiple-views theory predicts viewpoint dependence, unless the organism has many views of an object stored in memory. With a vast number of representations for a single object, performance would be viewpoint invariant, although the underlying mechanisms would still be viewer-centered. Thus, even though the two existing classes of theories initially appear diametrically opposed, on closer analysis they yield nearly identical predictions making it almost impossible to clearly support one over the other.

Conclusions

The goal of our study was to investigate visual object recognition in pigeons by using stimuli that meet all of the structural criteria for viewpoint-invariant performance proposed by Biederman and Gerhardstein (1993). Previous animal studies, including those conducted in our own laboratory (e.g., Wasserman et al., 1996), did not meet all three criteria, thus making it difficult to interpret failures to observe viewpoint-invariant performance. In the present study involving stimuli that met all three criteria, our pigeons did not exhibit viewpoint-invariant performance in Experiment 1, when training involved only a single object view; but, when we increased the number of object views to five in Experiment 2, our pigeons did show viewpoint-invariant performance. Based on these results, we can conclude that the three criteria proposed by Biederman and Gerhardstein (1993) are not the only factors that determine whether performance will be viewpoint-invariant or viewpoint-dependent; the number of training views also plays a critical role. Future research using the present experimental stimuli and training procedures clearly holds the promise of shedding further light on when and why viewpoint-invariant discriminative responding will be observed.

In addition to analyzing the structural criteria and learning experiences that may be vital for viewpoint-invariant recognition performance, our laboratory is keenly interested in discovering whether pigeons and humans enlist similar discrimination processes to recognize objects. Other research studying visual object recognition has shown that many stimulus features that are important for human object recognition are also important for pigeons (Kirkpatrick-Steger & Wasserman, 1996; Van Hamme, Wasserman, & Biederman, 1992; Wasserman, Kirkpatrick-Steger, Van Hamme, & Biederman, 1993). The present experiments have provided us with further evidence that can help to assess the species generality of visual recognition processes.

ACKNOWLEDGEMENTS

This research was supported by National Institute of Mental Health Grant, MH 47313. We would like to thank B. J. Terrones and H. Kingery for their assistance collecting data.

REFERENCES

Biederman, I. (1987). Recognition-by-components: A theory of human image understanding. *Psychological Review, 94,* 115-147.

Biederman, I., & Gerhardstein, P. C. (1993). Recognizing depth-rotated objects: Evidence and conditions for three-dimensional viewpoint invariance. *Journal of Experimental Psychology: Human Perception and Performance, 19,* 1162-1182.

Biederman, I., & Gerhardstein, P. C. (1995). Viewpoint-dependent mechanisms in visual object recognition: Reply to Tarr and Bülthoff (1995).

Journal of Experimental Psychology: Human Perception and Performance, 21, 1506-1514.

Cerella, J. (1977). Absence of perspective processing in the pigeon. *Pattern Recognition, 9,* 65-68.

Delius, J. D. (1992). Categorical discrimination of objects and pictures by pigeons. *Animal Learning and Behavior, 20,* 301-311.

Edelman, S., & Bülthoff, H. H. (1992). Orientation dependence in the recognition of familiar and novel views of three-dimensional objects. *Vision Research, 32,* 2385-2400.

Gross, C. G., Bender, D. G., & Rocha-Miranda, C. E. (1969). Visual receptive fields of neurons in inferotemporal cortex of the monkey. *Science, 166,* 1303-1306.

Gross, C. G., Rocha-Miranda, C. E., & Bender, D. G. (1972). Visual properties of neurons in inferotemporal cortex. *Journal of Neurophysiology, 35,* 96-111.

Kirkpatrick-Steger, K., & Wasserman, E. A. (1996). The what and the where of the pigeon's processing of complex visual stimuli. *Journal of Experimental Psychology: Animal Behavior Processes, 22,* 60-67.

Logothetis, N. K., Pauls, J., Bülthoff, H. H., & Poggio, T. (1994). View-dependent object recognition by monkeys. *Current Biology, 4,* 401-413.

Lumsden, E. A. (1977). Generalizations of an operant response to photographs and drawings/silhouettes of a three-dimensional object at various viewpoints. *Bulletin of the Psychonomic Society, 10,* 405-407.

Peissig, J. J., Young, M. E., Wasserman, E. A., & Biederman, I. (1999a). The pigeon's ability to form a generalized representation. Unpublished manuscript.

Peissig, J. J., Young, M. E., Wasserman, E. A., & Biederman, I. (1999b). Seeing things from a different angle: The pigeon's recognition of single geons rotated in depth. Unpublished manuscript.

Poggio, T., & Edelman, S. (1990). A network that learns to recognize three-dimensional objects. *Nature, 343,* 263-266.

Rock, I., & DiVita, J. (1987). A case of viewer-centered perception. *Cognitive Psychology, 19,* 280-293.

Tanaka, K. (1996). Inferotemporal cortex and object vision. *Annual Review of Neuroscience, 19,* 109-139.

Tarr, M. J. (1995). Rotating objects to recognize them: A case study on the role of viewpoint dependency in the recognition of three-dimensional objects. *Psychonomic Bulletin and Review, 2,* 55-82.

Tarr, M. J., & Bülthoff, H. H. (1995). Is human object recognition better described by geon structural descriptions or multiple views? Comment on Biederman and Gerhardstein (1993). *Journal of Experimental Psychology: Human Perception and Performance, 21,* 1494-1505.

Tarr, M. J., Bülthoff, H. H, Zabinski, M., & Blanz, V. (1997). To what extent do unique parts influence recognition across changes in viewpoint? *Psychological Science, 8,* 282-289.

Tarr, M. J., & Pinker, S. (1989). Mental rotation and orientation-dependence in shape recognition. *Cognitive Psychology, 21,* 233-282.

Ullman, S. (1989). Aligning pictorial descriptions: An approach to object recognition. *Cognition, 32,* 193-253.

Ungerleider, L. G., & Mishkin, M. (1982). Two cortical visual systems. In D. J. Ingle, M. A Goodale, & R. J. W. Mansfield (Eds.), *Analysis of visual behavior* (pp. 549-586). Cambridge, MA: MIT Press.

Van Hamme, L. J., Wasserman, E. A., & Biederman, I. (1992). Discrimination of contour-deleted images by pigeons. *Journal of Experimental Psychology: Animal Behavior Processes, 18,* 387-399.

Wasserman, E. A., Gagliardi, J. L., Cook, B. R., Kirkpatrick-Steger, K., Astley, S. L., & Biederman, I. (1996). The pigeon's recognition of drawings of depth-rotated objects. *Journal of Experimental Psychology: Animal Behavior Processes, 22,* 205-221.

Wasserman, E. A., Kirkpatrick-Steger, K., Van Hamme, L. J., & Biederman, I. (1993). Pigeons are sensitive to the spatial organization of complex visual stimuli. *Psychological Science, 4,* 336-341.

Watanabe, S. (1997). Visual discrimination of real objects and pictures in pigeons. *Animal Learning and Behavior, 25,* 185-192.

How do pigeons see pictures?
Recognition of the real world from
its 2-D representation

Shigeru Watanabe

Keio University, Tokyo, Japan

Abstract

Picture perception in birds was examined from four points of view: correlation, interaction, distortion, and transfer. The main question raised was whether they have the cognitive ability to relate pictures to the real world. Pigeons were found to see photographs but not line drawings as representations of real objects. Also, they did not see partly occluded figures as hidden objects, or occluding figures as hiding objects. These findings suggest that pigeons' cognition of line drawings and partly occluded objects differs from ours.

Key words: Visual discrimination, bird, object recognition.

Correspondence should be sent to Shigeru Watanabe, Department of Psychology, Keio University, Mita 2-15-45, Minato-Ku, Tokyo, Japan (e-mail: swat@flet.keio.ac.jp).

INTRODUCTION

Do animals see a picture of a real object as a representation of that object? Since Herrnstein and Loveland (1964), there have been many studies on avian visual concept discrimination using slides of complex natural stimuli such as a tree, a fish, or a man-made object (Herrnstein & De Villiers, 1980; Herrnstein, Loveland, & Cabe, 1976; Lubow, 1974). A picture does not simply mean a reduction from 3-D (three dimensions) to 2-D (two dimensions). Considerable information is lost depending on whether the picture is a photograph, a painting, a line drawing cartoon, a video image, etc. In this chapter, I will try to answer this question based on four different kinds of experimental studies. The first was a correlational study; if an animal's behavior with a picture is similar to that to its behavior with a real object, the animal can be regarded as seeing the picture as a representation of the real object. The second was an interaction study; if experience with real objects affects the animal's behavior towards pictures, or if experience with pictures affects its behavior towards the real world, the animal's behavior is controlled by the relationship between the picture and the real world. The third was a distortion study; if artificial distortion of pictures to obtain a naturally impossible image, such as a randomly scrambled picture of the body parts of a bird, disturbs the animal's behavior, it will be inferred that the animal sees the real world in the pictures. The last was a direct transfer study; if the animal shows transfer of discrimination with real objects to that with pictures, or vice versa, the animal notices equivalence between the real world and the pictures.

CORRELATIONAL STUDY

Many model experiments in the field of ethology on behavior-releasing stimuli suggest that a single feature of a natural stimulus can control innate animal behavior. In some cases, even a simple 2-D model of a natural stimulus can elicit the innate behavior. In other words, an abstracted feature can function similarly to a real-world stimulus, as when a red spot on a stick releases the same behavior in an infant gull as the real beak of its parents. If an animal behaves to pictures the same way as it does to one of its conspecifics, then it may simply mean confusion between real objects and pictures. Confusion is just the lack of ability to perceptually discriminate between pictures and real objects. In this sense, confusion is totally different from our perception of pictures as representations of the real world. For example, the amount of consumption of different foods by a person gives a measure of his/her food preferences. Food preferences can also be measured by asking the subject to sort pictures of different foods according to preference. The two measurements should agree, because the subject knows the pictures to be representations of the real foods. If someone tries to eat the pictures, then that person does not see the pictures as representations of food but confuses them with real food. Thus, in order to test whether an animal has the ability to see pictures as representations of real-world objects, it is necessary to compare discriminative behavior to real objects in a particular setting, with behavior towards pictures in another setting requiring a different response.

Using an operant chamber, I trained pigeons to peck at a screen on which a color slide of corn was projected, with food reinforcement, and then tested them with slides of differently colored corn (unpublished experiment). The subjects produced pecking responses most frequently to slides of natural corn (original stimulus), next to red corn, and the least frequently, to green corn. After the test, real corn colored with food dye was offered to the subjects. The colored corn kernels were scattered on a floor and eating behaviors were observed. They ate uncolored corn first, red corn next, and green corn last, in the same order of frequency as they pecked at the slides. Thus, the discriminative behavior measured in the operant chamber agreed with the discriminative behavior observed in the feeding situation. Because the pecking response as an operant was functionally different from the eating behavior, the correlation suggests that the pigeons saw the slides as representations of the corn. However, another possible explanation of the correlation is a generalization gradient along the color dimension. The natural color of corn (yellow) is closer to red than green. Pigeons might show a stimulus generalization in operant and eating situations alike. We examined this possibility in the interaction study.

INTERACTION STUDY

In a similar training and generalization experiment using color slides, the subjects also responded less frequently to pictures of red corn. Then,

I offered corn colored red with food dye to the subjects (Watanabe, Lea, & Dittrich, 1993) to make them get accustomed to eating red corn. The subjects easily learned to eat the red corn. After this, when discriminative behavior was tested again in the operant chamber using the same slides, the frequency of the operant response to the slides showing red corn increased. Next, I offered red corn coated with methyl anthranilate, a bitter chemical. The subjects quickly learned to avoid the red corn. The test in the operant chamber after this aversive experience showed a decrease in response to the slides of red corn. In this experiment, experience with real objects was found to modify the discriminative operant behavior, both in positive and negative ways. What the subjects learned in the operant chamber was a "concept of edible corn", because eating experience affected the discriminative behavior. In other words, the pigeons saw representations of real corn in the pictures.

The next example of an interaction study is an experiment on so-called viewpoint invariance. Identifying the same object when viewed from different positions is an important visual ability of animals. Viewpoint invariance, especially for 2-D images of an unusual 3-D object, requires sophisticated visual processing because it is practically impossible to memorize the huge number of individual 2-D images of a 3-D object. Experience with real objects is known to affect viewpoint invariance for human observers (e.g., Edelman & Bulthoff, 1992; Tarr, 1995). Rock and DiVita (1987) reported a lack of viewpoint invariance in human subjects who did not have experience with the test stimuli. Monkeys could learn to identify novel wire-shaped objects, but the monkeys were not able to recognize the objects when they were rotated more than 40 degrees (Logothetis, Pauls, Bulthoff, & Poggio, 1994). Cerella (1990) trained pigeons to respond to a 2-D image of a wire shape, then tested them with the same shape rotated about the x-, y-, or z-axis. The pigeons showed a consistent decrease in responses as a function of the degree of rotation. Recently, Wasserman, Gagliardi, Astley, Cook, and Kirkpatrick-Steger (1996) obtained a generalization gradient as a function of the degree of rotation using line drawings. These results are indicative of poor viewpoint invariance in pigeons for 2-D projections of 3-D objects. I reexamined viewpoint invariance using color video images of a stainless steel feeder and a coffee mug (Watanabe, 1997a). Pigeons were trained in visual discrimination using a TV monitor. One group of pigeons was trained to peck the screen when the feeder appeared on it, while the other group was trained to peck the screen when the mug appeared. After training, the pigeons were tested with several different pictures, such as a bottom view or side view of the object lying horizontally. The subjects showed generalization from the original view of the feeder to images of these unfamiliar views, but not from the original coffee mug to its unfamiliar views. Thus, viewpoint invariance depends on the kind of stimulus. The feeder was a familiar object and the mug, an unfamiliar one, because the birds ate mixed grain from the feeder every day in their living cages. Apparently, experience with the real 3-D objects facilitated recognition of the unusual 2-D views.

Watanabe (1999) placed real objects (a pair of wood blocks) in pigeons' living cages to familiarize the subjects with them. The position of the blocks was deliberately changed at least twice a day in addition to any changes caused by movements of the birds. Then the birds were trained in the discrimination of video images of the objects. The video images were displayed on a TV monitor in an operant chamber. The birds learned to discriminate the familiar stimuli more quickly than unfamiliar stimuli. This effect may be considered as a type of latent learning, with the exception that real objects were used in the exposure phase, and their 2-D images in the learning phase. This facilitative effect on the learning of 2-D images of exposure to 3-D objects suggests perceptual equivalence between real objects and their images projected on a TV monitor.

After acquiring the discrimination, the subjects were given a viewpoint invariance test in which unusual views, such as an upside down or bottom view, of the discriminative stimuli appeared on the monitor. The subjects responded more frequently to the unusual stimuli when the original stimulus was familiar than when it was unfamiliar. Thus, familiarization with the real objects enhanced viewpoint invariance of the 2-D images.

A similar facilitative effect by exposure to real objects has been reported for the discrimination of social stimuli. Bradshaw and Dawkins (1993) trained hens to discriminate slides of familiar and unfamiliar conspecifics. The hens discriminated novel views of conspecifics better when the conspecifics were familiar. Landscape discrimination is also within the scope of the interaction study. Wilkie, Wilson, and Kardel (1989) trained pigeons that had experience in homing to a specific location and pigeons that did not, to discriminate photographs of the vicinity of that location from photographs of novel locations. Acquisition of the discrimination was slightly better in the subjects that had homing experience.

These interaction studies suggest that 2-D image discrimination is facilitated by experience with 3-D stimuli. On the other hand, the effects of experience with 2-D images on the discrimination of 3-D objects are still unclear in animal studies, although it is indisputable that humans are able to master the bidirectional 2-D/3-D interaction.

DISTORTION STUDY

The basic principles of the distortion study are as follows. If a given type of distortion is naturally impossible in the real world, the distortion of a picture should disturb animal behavior. Such a disruption of behavior suggests that the animal sees the picture as a representation of the real world. There are several different ways of distorting an object. Here I describe rotation, incompleteness, partial occlusion, and scrambling.

Rotation of pictures

Two-dimensional rotation is a simple distortion. There is a one-to-one correspondence between each element in the rotated and original figures. Particularly, the left-right mirror image is easy to identify. In other words, it is hard to discriminate between the left-right mirror images. For pigeons, left-right mirror images were shown to be less discriminable than upside-down mirror images (Lohmann, Delius, Holland, & Friesel, 1988). Pigeons had trouble forming the concept of left-right orientation in the discrimination of photographs of birds (Watanabe & Sato, 1984), while they could discriminate the vertical orientation of photographs of humans, monkeys, or pigeons (Jitsumori & Ohkubo, 1996).

A photograph is a relatively precise projection of a 3-D object onto a 2-D medium. A painting, however, is not a simple 2-D image of the 3-D world; instead, it is the product of the artist's mental activities, especially for paintings from after the impressionist period. Thus, paintings are distorted 2-D images. Pigeons were found to discriminate Monet's paintings from Picasso's (Watanabe, Wakita, & Sakamoto, 1995). They were able to generalize, not only to novel paintings by these artists, but also from Monet to Renoir or Cezanne, and from Picasso to Braque or Matisse. Did the pigeons see the paintings as representations of the real world? They continued to respond to the left-right mirror image of these paintings. However, when Monet's paintings were presented upside down, the pigeons no longer responsed, although they still discriminated reversed Monet from reversed Picasso. Thus, upside-down presentation lowered the responding rate but not discrimination itself. Other studies on the effects of natural photograph rotation (Wasserman, Kiedinger, & Bhatt, 1988) or pigeon face rotation (Phelps & Roberts, 1994) also showed maintenance of discrimination and less effectiveness in triger-ring schedule-induced attack in pigeons than normal pictures (Looney & Cohen, 1974).

On the other hand, upside-down Picasso paintings did not suppress responses. If we look at impressionist art, it is generally easy to recognize the object; it is much harder to do so in abstract paintings. If the paintings are meaningless for the viewer, upside-down images are acceptable. This case is similar to mental rotation of geometric figures in pigeons (Delius & Holland, 1995). Delius and Holland measured the reaction time of birds in a matching-to-sample task and found that pigeons easily identified rotated geometric figures. These studies suggest that pigeons see representations of the real world in paintings by impressionists, but not in abstract pictures.

Incompleteness and abstraction of prototype

Incomplete figures are another example of distortion. Can birds compensate for an incomplete picture? Van Hamme, Wasserman, and Biederman (1992) used two complementary sets of incomplete line drawings. Two complementary pictures shared the same geon but no features. The pigeons showed transfer from one set to the complementary set, suggesting "geon" recognition. Similarly, pigeons trained on incomplete drawings of a triangle or a rectangle showed generalization to complete figures (White, Alsop, & Williams, 1993). Kirkpatrick-Steger, Biederman, and Wasserman (1998) compared depletion of one or three geons in line drawing discrimination and found that depletion of one geon did not disturb accuracy of discrimination but that of three geons significantly reduced it. Fragmentation was investigated by

Brodbeck (1997) using priming effects. After pigeons were trained to discriminate slides of cats and cars, presentation of a warning stimulus improved the recognition of fragmented pictures that were 50 percent obscured. Even when the warning stimulus did not specifically cue the car or cat, the subjects still discriminated the pictures above chance level.

These experiments suggest that pigeons have the ability to complete figures. However, it is not clear whether the subjects see the figures as representations of real objects. The stimuli used in these experiments were rough drawings or meaningless figures and pigeons are considered to be poor at identifying line drawings (Looney & Cohen, 1974).

The ability to complete incomplete figures can be considered as a kind of "prototype learning" where the subject abstracts an ideal pattern from distorted exemplars. In pigeons, however, no decisive evidence of prototype learning has been reported. I trained pigeons to discriminate between triangles made of six dots that were slight distortions of the prototype, and six random dots (Watanabe, 1988). The position of each dot in the original prototype triangle was moved one pixel up or down and one pixel left or right at distortion level 1, and 2 pixels up or down and 2 pixels left or right at distortion level 2, and so on. Because these distorted triangles and random dot patterns were generated by a computer on each trial using a random generator function, the probability of seeing the exactly same pattern during the training was negligibly small. After the birds learned discrimination between level 2 distorted triangles and random dots, generalization by degree of distortion was tested. During the test, triangles of level 1, 2, 3, 4, or 5 and the original triangle were presented. The pigeons had never seen the original triangle during the discriminative training. They showed a response peak on the trained triangles (level 2 distortion) and responded less to less distorted or more distorted triangles. There was no peak on the prototype. In other words, the pigeons did not abstract the prototype triangle from its distorted exemplars. However, in the case of polymorphous concept discrimination in which a complex of discrete features of artificial butterfly patterns were the stimulus categories, pigeons abstracted a prototype (Jitsumori, 1996). The subjects had seen each feature during the discriminative training in this experiment, whereas no dots in the prototype triangle had ever been presented in my experiments. This procedural difference, in addition to a difference in the stimulus patterns, may be responsible for the discrepancy in the results.

Partial occlusion

Partial occlusion is another way of generating incomplete images. Cerella (1980), who trained pigeons with complete triangles and then tested them with incomplete triangles and partly occluded triangles, found that the pigeons responded less to partly occluded figures. Pigeons trained to classify figures into complete and incomplete by a two-key-choice procedure showed that they did not include partly occluded figures in the category of completed figures (Sekuler, Lee, & Shettleworth, 1996). To test the recognition of ecologically significant stimuli, Watanabe and Furuya (1997) trained pigeons on discrimination between still video images of a pigeon's head poking above a board and the board without the head, and then tested them with the pigeon's head without the board, the entire body of the pigeon, and the original image of the head above the board. The subjects responded indifferentially to all of these images, suggesting that a local cue or a limited feature (the head) was enough to control their discriminative behavior. In other words, the pigeons did not see a hidden pigeon in the image of the pigeon's head poking above the board. This observation is consistent with Cellera's results. Pigeons ignore the occluded part of an object when they see an overlapping 2-D image.

Contrary to these pigeon studies, Regolin and Vallortigara (1995) found amodal completion in newly hatched chicks. The chickens were imprinted with a triangle, then tested with a partially occluded triangle and fragments of the triangle for 3 days after hatching. They chose the occluded triangle. Even though a triangle is a geometric figure, it became a "social" stimulus through the imprinting process. In some sense, the imprinted triangle is a more natural stimulus than an image of pigeon on a TV monitor. Rearing with the triangle gave the subjects much experience of seeing it from many different angles. Total exposure to the stimulus in the imprinting experiment may have been longer than usual operant training. These factors, in addition to a species difference, may be the cause of the contradictory results. Thus, perception of partially occluded object in birds is still open for further research.

Scrambling

Cartoons are another example of distorted 2-D images. In cartoons, a well-known figure such as a politician is easily identified even though the drawing is considerably deformed with respect to the real image. A cartoon is a mixture of omission and exaggeration of specific features. There must be some rule of distortion, however. The spatial arrangement of the body parts is believed to be one of the rules. The head, arms, body, and legs must be arranged in some specific spatial order for the cartoon to be identified as a representation of an "intact" human being. This rule can be considered as a type of "naive theory". Images of human beings should follow the rules for arranging body parts. Cerella (1980) successfully trained pigeons to discriminate the cartoon character "Charlie Brown". The subjects showed generalization to novel images of Charlie Brown, and thus seemed to have acquired the Charlie Brown concept. After the discrimination, Cerella found that scrambled images of Charlie Brown were perceived by the pigeons the same way as the intact cartoons, although the scrambled figures were easily distinguished from the originals by human observers. These results suggest that constituent elements are crucial for pigeons' visual cognition, and that the spatial arrangement of the elements is not important.

Van Hamme et al. (1992) trained pigeons using incomplete line drawings of an elephant, a mushroom, a chair, etc., and tested them with spatially scrambled pictures. Although response accuracy decreased considerably, the subjects still responded above chance level. These results are consistent with Cerella's observation; that is, pigeons paid less attention to the spatial arrangement of the stimulus. Wasserman, Kirkpatrick-Steger, Van Hamme, and Biederman (1993) reexamined the role of spatial arrangement in bird cognition. They trained pigeons with a four-choice procedure to peck a different key in the presence of each of four line drawings of artificial objects (a desk lamp, an iron, a water can, and a sailboat). Correct response rate on original stimuli was 81% but for scrambled ones, it was 52% on average. Scrambling remarkably reduced accuracy, even though the pigeons discriminated the scrambled stimuli well above the chance level (25%). This result is not compatible with Cerella's. Scrambling was reexamined again by Kirkpatrick-Steger and Wasserman (1996). They found that the position of an individual component relative to the picture's other components was important, and thus concluded that pigeons use both components and spatial arrangements as cues in visual cognition. Their results support the idea of joint processing of "what" and "where" information in the visual cognition of pigeons. Kirkpatrick-Steger et al. (1998) replicated their previous experiment with a systematically designed way of scrambling, and showed that the spatial organization of geons is a major contributor to picture recognition. However, accuracy on scrambled stimuli was around 60%, which, again, is well above the chance level (25%), although accuracy on the original stimuli was 88%. One crucial point in these experiments for our purposes here in this chapter is the use of line drawings as stimuli. As described earlier, pigeons may lack the ability to integrate lines to reconstruct the perspectives of the original 3-D object. They may see line drawings in much the same way as we do, but it does not mean they see line drawings as representations of real objects.

In fact, scrambling caused a severe reduction in responses in pigeons when slides of conspecifics were used as stimuli. Watanabe and Ito (1991) trained pigeons to discriminate color slides of heads of two pigeons, and found that scrambling the elements, such as the eyes and beak, severely reduced the subjects' responses. Budgerigars also showed longer reaction times in an experiment using scrambled stimuli after discrimination of conspecific faces (Brown & Dooling, 1993). These experiments suggest that scrambling disturbs visual discrimination of conspecifics. The reported difference in the effects of scrambling between the experiment using Charlie Brown (Cerella, 1980) and that using pigeon slides (Watanabe & Ito, 1991) may be attributed to the difference in the type of stimuli (line drawings vs. slides, or human images vs. conspecific images).

To clarify the determining factor of response suppression in a scrambled discriminative stimulus, I trained pigeons on four discrimination tasks (Watanabe, submitted). One was discrimination of color slides of one particular person and other people, the second was discrimination of color slides of pigeons and other birds, the third was discrimination of cartoons of one character and other characters, and the fourth was discrimination of cartoons of pigeons and other birds. For human cartoons, a Japanese cartoon character named "Sazae San" and other characters taken from the same cartoon book were used. For pigeon cartoon discrimination, a cartoon of a pigeon called "Arashi" and those of other birds taken from the same cartoon book were used. After the subjects learned the discrimination, two tests were carried out. One was a test of generalization to new stimuli that belonged to the same category as the training stimuli but that had never been shown during training, and the second test was with scrambled training stimuli. Generalization to new stimuli was observed in the pigeon photographs, human photographs, and pigeon cartoons, but not in the human cartoons. The pigeons seemed to employ a categorical classification strategy for photograph discrimination, but a one-by-one memorization strategy for human cartoon discrimination. Scrambling reduced responses to the photographic stimuli, especially the conspecific photographs, but not to the cartoon stimuli, especially the human cartoons. Pictures of scrambled human or pigeon bodies do not match what pigeons see in a natural environment. Therefore, if the subjects see these scrambled images as representations of real humans or real pigeons, such abnormality should cause response suppression, according to the naive theory about the spatial arrangement of the body. Conversely, if the birds see the cartoons as meaningless patterns, responses to the scrambled human cartoon should be disturbed.

The results of the experiments were consistent with the finding that pigeons show decreased responses to inverted paintings by Monet but not to those by Picasso (Watanabe et al., 1995). The lack of a response disturbance on inverted Picasso paintings shows that the pigeons ignored the spatial orientation in the pictures. The disturbance on scrambled photographs is consistent with the suppression of responses on disoriented paintings.

DIRECT TRANSFER

The experiments described above are indicative of animal perception of pictures. However, the most straightforward way to know how animals relate real-world objects to pictures is to investigate the transfer of real-object discrimination to discrimination of their pictures.

Photographs

Cross-modality matching between real objects and pictures is one of the most powerful tools in the demonstration of direct transfer. Apes exhibited picture-object equivalence in cross-modality matching (Davenport & Rogers, 1971). Although there have been no such cross-matching experiments with birds, transfer after discrimination training with real objects or pictures has been examined in several studies. For example, Lumsden (1977) trained pigeons in orientation discrimination with real objects and found that the generalization gradient with photographs was similar to that with real objects. Delius (1992) trained pigeons in the categorical discrimination of real objects. The subjects learned to discriminate spherical objects from nonspherical ones. They transferred the spherical concept to color or black and white photographs of the objects. Real-to-photograph transfer has been observed with ecologically more important stimuli. Budgerigars showed that transfer of live conspecific discrimination to that of their slides was possible in a T-maze experiment (Trillmich, 1976). These experiments are proof of transfer from real objects to pictures. There is one contradictory report, however. Cole and Honig (1994) trained pigeons to discriminate pictures of the two ends of a room, then trained them to find food in the actual room. The subjects showed transfer from the pictures of the room to the room itself, but training with the real room did not improve discrimination of the pictures.

If birds show transfer from the real world to photographs, it does not necessarily mean that they have perceptual equivalence between real objects and photographs. In fact, budgerigars did not transfer discrimination of slides of conspecifics to real conspecifics, although they showed transfer in the opposite direction (Trillmich, 1976). Watanabe (1993) trained one group of pigeons with real objects, and then tested them with printed photographs, and trained and tested another group in the reverse order. Four kinds of grains and seeds (corn, peas, buckwheat, and wheat) and four non-edible objects (stone, twig, yellow paper clip, and nut) were used as stimuli. The stimuli were pasted on small pieces of cardboard. Color photographs of the grains and other objects printed in actual size and cut out along the edges, were also pasted on cardboard and used as 2-D stimuli.

The pigeons exhibited bidirectional transfer between the real objects and their photographs. Transfer from the objects to the pictures was better than the opposite transfer, although the difference was not statistically significant. The results thus demonstrated object-to-picture and picture-to-object transfer. However, when the subjects were trained in pseudoconcept discrimination in which one arbitrary group of stimuli consisted of two kinds of grains and two kinds of non-edible objects and the other group, of the remaining two kinds of grains and two kinds of objects, they could learn this discrimination but did not show transfer in either direction. During the discrimination training, the subjects had to learn the stimuli one-by-one based on local cues, because categorization based on food versus non-food could not be employed to accomplish the task. Local cues, such as a minor change in color or shape, might become irrelevant when the stimuli were changed from real to photographs or vice versa.

Bidirectional transfer may simply indicate confusion between real objects and their pictures. Humans can see photographs as representations of real objects but do not confuse them. To eliminate the possibility that pigeons cannot discriminate pictures from real objects, I trained two groups of pigeons (Watanabe, 1997b). Four different kinds of foods and four different kinds of objects such as those used in the previous transfer experiment were used. This time, however, the real stimuli and photographic stimuli were mixed and presented in random order. The task for one group was discrimination between food and non-food. In this task, the difference between real objects and photographs was irrelevant for discrimination. The other group was trained to discriminate objects from photographs. The subjects in this group had to ignore the fact that the stimuli were food or non-food. Both groups successfully learned the discrimination. There was no statistically significant difference in acquisition between the two groups. Therefore, the pigeons were able to discriminate real objects and their photographs or classify real objects and their pictures into one category, depending on the task requirement. When new stimuli were introduced, both groups showed generalization to the new stimuli. However, when the stimuli (both real objects and pictures) were painted black, the real vs. picture discrimination group maintained the discrimination ability, whereas the food vs. non-food discrimination group failed. That is, the pigeons were able to discriminate real 3-D objects from their 2-D pictures without a color cue.

Baboons showed some difficulty in learning to discriminate photographs of food versus non-food after they had learned discrimination on the same task with real objects (Bovet & Vauclair, 1998). According to the authors, the baboons seemed to classify pictures as non-food stimuli. This was not the case in pigeons.

Line drawings

A line drawing has a contour and an enclosed area, but no closed surface. Therefore, when a line drawing is used as a stimulus, the subject is required to identify the enclosed area as a surface. Although Blough and Blough (1997) demonstrated similarity of line form perception between humans and pigeons, birds may not see line drawings as representations of real objects. Cabe (1976) trained pigeons to discriminate two real solid objects painted white, and tested transfer with reversal training. The birds showed transfer from objects to photographs and from objects to silhouettes, but not from objects to line drawings. So, pigeons do not seem to perceive a line-enclosed area as the surface of a 3-D object. Pigeons seem to lack not only 3-D object to line drawing transfer but also line drawing to 3-D object transfer, because pigeons that had been trained to discriminate between drawings of a three-dimensional cube and a distorted cube did not transfer of the discrimination when a rotated cube was presented (Cerella, 1977). On the other hand, pigeons do seem to transfer from 2-D figures to line drawings, because Lombardi and Delius (1988) demonstrated transfer from silhouette shapes to outline figures in pigeons using a matching-to-sample procedure. These results suggest that pigeons do not have the ability to reconstruct 3-D objects from line drawings.

Video images

How about video images? Recently, computer-controlled image projection systems with a video monitor and a laser disk have been used widely for experiments. Such systems have advantages over the conventional slide projector, due to ease of control and freedom in modifying images via graphic software. However, the video system has some setbacks when used as a stimulus-presenting device for animals. In general, a still video image is not as crisp as a printed photograph. The color-producing system of TV monitors is designed for the trichromatic eye of humans. Therefore, color images on a TV monitor may look different from natural ones for animals whose color perception is different from ours, e.g., pigeons, which have a component that is sensitive to ultraviolet. There is another problem related to the CFF (critical frequency of fusion) in video displays. The refresh rate of a TV screen is 60 Hz, even in the most advanced high-definition system. A higher CFF in pigeons than in humans has been obtained (Powell, 1967; Emmerton, 1983). The measured CFF was 145 Hz when the brightness of the stimuli was 100000 cd/m2, and approximately 100 Hz when the brightness was reduced to 100 cd/m2. Considering that the average brightness of commercial TV sets is about 60 to 70 cd/m2, and that the CFF of pigeons at 70 cd/m2 is 58 cps as extrapolated on Powell's curve, pigeons' high CFF may not be a crucial disturbing factor if the brightness of the screen is low enough.

I trained pigeons with real objects (a cone or a ball) and then retrained them with videotaped images of the same objects (Watanabe, in preparation). The birds showed a temporary decrease in the correct response rate on the first transfer session, but performed well on the second session. Thus, transfer from real objects to video images was confirmed, at least in terms of training retention. On the other hand, when I trained pigeons with videotaped images first, and then retrained them with the real objects, they showed only slight transfer of discrimination. These results indicate that the transfer is not symmetrical.

Patterson-Kane, Nicole, Foster, and Temple (1997) trained hens to discriminate between red and green cards, between a white hen and no hen, and between a white hen and a brown hen, using a Y-maze. When tested with video images instead of real objects, the hens performed better than chance level for the red vs. green cards, and the hen vs. no hen, but not for the white vs. brown hen. These results suggest that for hens, a video image is identical to a real stimulus when a simple stimulus is used, but not when a complex 3-D stimulus is used.

However, there are discrepancies among the results of exposure to videotaped images in pigeons. Ryan and Lea (1994) reported that pigeons did not show any social behavior to life-size moving video images of conspecifics, while Shimizu (1998) showed that courtship behavior was elicited in male pigeons by videotaped images of female pigeons but not by those of non-pigeon birds. Similarly, Zebra finches that were exposed to the display of silent videotaped images of conspecifics responded with song (Adret, 1997). These discrepancies may result from differences in stimulus conditions such as brightness.

CONCLUSION

Humans and most avian species have sophisticated visual functions. Ancestors of primates and those of birds may have lived in a common ecological niche requiring them to jump from tree to tree to find food and to avoid predators. In such an environment, visual information processing plays an important role in knowing the precise distance and three-dimensional arrangement of leaves and hidden objects. Examination of picture cognition in birds suggests that they see photographs and still video images as representations of real objects, but not line drawings. Another important difference between our visual cognition and avian cognition is in the discrimination of partly occluded pictures. Pigeons cannot identify occluded and occluding objects in a 2-D image. These findings characterize the limitations of the avian ability to reconstruct a 3-D image from a 2-D image.

ACKNOWLEDGEMENTS

This research was supported by a Grant-in-Aid for the Promotion of the Sciences (#09207150).

REFERENCES

Adret, P. (1997). Discrimination of video images by zebra finches (*Taeniopygia guttata*): Direct evidence from song performance. *Journal of Comparative Psychology, 111,* 115-125.

Blough, D. S., & Blough, P. M. (1997). Form perception and attention in pigeons. *Animal Learning and Behavior, 25,* 1-20.

Bovet, D., & Vauclair, J. (1998). Functional categorization of objects and of their pictures in baboons (*Papio anubis*). *Learning and Motivation, 29,* 309-392.

Bradshaw, R. H., & Dawkins, M. S. (1993). Slides of conspecifics as representatives of real animals in laying hens (*Gallus domestics*). *Behavioural Processes, 28,* 165-172.

Brodbeck, D. R. (1997). Picture fragment completion: priming in the pigeon. *Journal of Experimental Psychology: Animal Behavior Processes, 23,* 461-468.

Brown, S. D., & Dooling, R. J (1993). Perception of conspecific faces by budgerigars (*Melopsittacus undulatus*): II. Synthetic models. *Journal of Comparative Psychology, 107,* 48-60.

Cabe, P. A. (1976). Transfer of discrimination from solid objects to pictures by pigeons: A test of theoretical models of pictorial perception. *Perception and Psychophysics, 19,* 545-550.

Cerella, J. (1977). Absence of perspective processing in the pigeon. *Pattern Recognition, 9,* 65-68.

Cerella, J. (1980). The pigeon's analysis of pictures. *Pattern Recognition, 12,* 1-6.

Cerella, J. (1990). Shape constancy in the pigeon: The perspective transformations decomposed. In M. L. Commons, R. J. Herrnstein, S. M. Kosslyn,

& D. B. Mumford (Eds.), *Quantitative analysis of behavior: Behavioral approaches to pattern recognition and concept formation* (pp. 37-57). Hillsdale, NJ: Lawrence Erlbaum.

Cole, P. D., & Honig, W. K. (1994). Transfer of a discrimination by pigeons (*Columba livia*) between pictured locations and the represented environments. *Journal of Comparative Psychology, 108,* 189-198.

Davenport, R. K., & Rogers, G. M. (1971). Perception of photographs by apes. *Behaviour, 31,* 318-320.

Delius, J. D. (1992). Categorical discrimination of objects and pictures by pigeons. *Animal Learning and Behavior, 20,* 301-311.

Delius, J. D., & Holland, V. D. (1995). Orientation invariant pattern recognition by pigeons (*Columba livia*) and humans (*Homo sapiens*). *Journal of Comparative Psychology, 109,* 278-290.

Edelman, S., & Bulthoff, H. H. (1992). Orientation dependence in the recognition of familiar and novel views of three-dimensional objects. *Vision Research, 32,* 2385-2400.

Emmerton, J. (1983). Vision. In M. Abs (Ed.), *Physiology and behavior of the pigeon* (pp. 245-266). New York: Academic Press.

Herrnstein, R. J., & De Villiers, P. A. (1980). Fish as a natural category for people and pigeons. In G. H. Bower (Ed.), *The psychology of learning and memory*. New York: Academic Press.

Herrnstein, R. J., & Loveland, D. H. (1964). Complex visual concept in the pigeon. *Science, 146,* 549-551.

Herrnstein, R. J., Loveland, D. H., & Cabe, C. (1976). Natural concepts in pigeons. *Journal of Experimental Psychology: Animal Behavior Processes, 2,* 285-302.

Jitsumori, M. (1996). A prototype effect and categorization of artificial polymorphous stimuli in pigeons. *Journal of Experimental Psychology: Animal Behavior Processes, 22,* 405-419.

Jitsumori, M., & Ohkubo, O. (1996). Orientation discrimination and categorization of photographs of natural objects by pigeons. *Behavioural Processes, 33,* 205-226.

Kirkpatrick-Steger, K., Biederman, I., & Wasserman, E. A. (1998). Effects of geon deletion, scrambling, and movement on picture recognition in pigeons. *Journal of Experimental Psychology: Animal Behavior Processes, 24,* 34-46.

Kirkpatrick-Steger, K., & Wasserman, E. A. (1996). The what and the where of the pigeon's processing of complex visual stimuli. *Journal of Experimental Psychology: Animal Behavior Processes, 22,* 60-67.

Logothetis, N. K., Pauls, J., Bulthoff, H. N., & Poggio, T. (1994). View-dependent object recognition by monkeys. *Current Biology, 4,* 401-414.

Lohmann, A., Delius, J. D., Holland, V. D., & Friesel, M. F. (1988). Discrimination of shape reflections and shape orientations by *Columba livia*. *Journal of Comparative Psychology, 102,* 3-13.

Lombardi, C. M., & Delius, J. D. (1988). Pattern recognition invariance in pigeons (*Columba livia*): outline, color and contrast. *International Journal of Comparative Psychology, 2,* 83-101.

Looney, T. A., & Cohen, P. S. (1974). Pictorial target control of schedule-induced attack in white Carneaux pigeons. *Journal of Experimental Analysis of Behavior, 21,* 571-584.

Lubow, R. E. (1974). Higher order concept formation in the pigeon. *Journal of Experimental Analysis of Behavior, 21,* 475-483.

Lumsden, E. A. (1977). Generalization of an operant response to photographs and drawings/silhouettes of a three-dimensional object at various orientations. *Bulletin of the Psychonomic Society, 10,* 405-407.

Patterson-Kane, E., Nicole, C. J., Foster, T. M., & Temple, W. (1997). Limited perception of video images by domestic hens. *Animal Behavior, 53,* 951-963.

Phelps, M. T., & Roberts, W. A. (1994). Memory for pictures of upright and inverted primate faces in humans (*Homo sapiens*), squirrel monkeys (*Saimiri sciureus*), and pigeons (*Columba livia*). *Journal of Comparative Psychology, 108,* 114-125.

Powell, R.W. (1967). The pulse-to-cycle fraction as a determinant of critical flicker fusion in the pigeon. *The Psychological Record, 17,* 151-160.

Regolin, L., & Vallortigara, G. (1995). Perception of partly occluded objects by young chicks. *Perception and Psychophysics, 57,* 971-976.

Rock, I., & DiVita, J. (1987). A case of viewer-centered object perception. *Cognitive Psychology, 19,* 280-293.

Ryan, C. M. E., & Lea, S. E. G. (1994). Images of conspecifics as categories to be discriminated by pigeons and chickens: slides, video tapes, stuffed birds and real birds. *Behavioural Processes, 33,* 155-176.

Sekuler, A. B., Lee, J. A. J., & Shettleworth, S. J. (1996). Pigeons do not complete partly occluded figures. *Perception, 25,* 1109-1120.

Shimizu, T. (1998). Conspecific recognition in pigeons (*Columba livia*) using dynamic video images. *Behaviour, 135,* 43-53.

Tarr, M. J. (1995). Rotating objects to recognize them: A case study on the role of view point dependency in the recognition of three-dimensional objects. *Psychonomic Bulletin and Review, 2,* 55-82.

Trillmich, F. (1976). Learning experiments on individual recognition in budgerigars. *Zeitschrift für Tierpsychologie, 41,* 372-395.

Van Hamme, L. J., Wasserman, E. A., & Biederman, I. (1992). Discrimination of contour-delated images by pigeons. *Journal of Experimental Psychology: Animal Behavior Processes, 18,* 387-399.

Wasserman, E. A., Gagliardi, J. L., Astley, S. L., Cook, B. R., & Kirkpatrick-Steger, K. (1996). The pigeon's recognition of drawings of depth-rotated stimuli. *Journal of Experimental Psychology: Animal Behavior Processes, 22,* 205-221.

Wasserman, E. A., Kiedinger, R. R., & Bhatt, R. S. (1988). Conceptual behavior in pigeons: Categories, subcategories and pseudocategories. *Journal of Experimental Psychology: Animal Behavior Processes, 14,* 235-246.

Wasserman, E. A., Kirkpatrick-Steger, K., Van Hamme, L. J., & Biederman, I. (1993). Pigeons are sensitive to the spatial organization of complex visual stimuli. *Psychological Science, 4,* 336-341.

Watanabe, S. (1988). Failure of visual prototype learning in the pigeon. *Animal Learning and Behavior, 16,* 147-152.

Watanabe, S. (1993). Object-picture equivalence in the pigeon: An analysis with natural concept and pseudoconcept discriminations. *Behavioural Processes, 30,* 225-232.

Watanabe, S. (1997a). An instance of viewpoint consistency in pigeon object recognition. *Behavioural Processes, 39,* 247-261.

Watanabe, S. (1997b). Discrimination and integration of real objects and their pictures in the pigeon. *Animal Learning and Behavior, 25,* 247-267.

Watanabe, S. (1999). Enhancement of view point invariance by experience in pigeons. *Cahiers de Psychologie Cognitive/Current Psychology of Cognition, 18,* 321-335.

Watanabe, S. (in press). Discrimination of cartoons and photographs in pigeons: Effects of scrambling of elements. *Behavioural Processes.*

Watanabe, S. (in preparation). Transfer of discrimination from real objects to video images.

Watanabe, S., & Furuya, I. (1997). Usage of video display for study of visual cognition in pigeons. *International Journal of Comparative Psychology, 10,* 111-127.

Watanabe, S., & Ito, Y. (1991). Individual recognition in pigeon. *Bird Behaviour, 36,* 20-29.

Watanabe, S., Lea, S. E. G., & Dittrich, W. H. (1993). What can we learn from experiments on pigeon concept discrimination. In P. H. Zeigler & H.-J. Bischof (Eds.), *Vision, brain and behavior in birds* (pp. 352-376). Cambridge, MA: MIT Press.

Watanabe, S., & Sato,Y. (1984). Pigeon's discrimination of the orientation of other birds (in Japanese). *Sociology, Psychology and Education, 24,* 45-54.

Watanabe, S., Wakita, M., & Sakamoto, J. (1995). Discrimination of Monet and Picasso in pigeons. *Journal of the Experimental Analysis of Behavior, 63,* 165-174.

White, K. G., Alsop, B., & Williams, L. (1993). Prototype identification and categorization of incomplete figures by pigeons. *Behavioural Processes, 30,* 253-258.

Wilkie, D. M.,Wilson, R. J., & Kardel, S. (1989). Pigeons discriminate pictures of a geographic location. *Animal Learning and Behavior, 17,* 163-171.

Use of pictures to investigate aspects
of pigeons' spatial cognition

Donald M. Wilkie

The University of British Columbia, Vancouver, BC, Canada

Abstract

In the literature on animals' spatial cognition several investigators have started to use photographs and digitized computer images as stimulus materials. In the current paper a representative overview of this research is described. Research on the following topics is reviewed: 1) habitat preference in migrating birds, 2) conceptual categorization of naturalistic spatial locations, 3) pigeons' use of landmarks in pictures of naturalistic spatial locations, 4) pigeons' attention to certain features in naturalistic spatial locations, and 5) pigeons' attention to the natural horizon. The paper concludes by describing the broad generalizations that emerge from this research.

Key words: Discrimination of outdoor geographic locations, places, landmarks, feature-positive discrimination, color slides, digitized images, touchscreen, pigeons.

Correspondence should be sent to Donald M. Wilkie, Department of Psychology, The University of British Columbia, Vancouver, BC, Canada V6T 1Z4 (e-mail: dwilkie@cortex.psych.ubc.ca).

INTRODUCTION

A vast amount of research has been conducted investigating animal's processing of spatial information. In laboratory investigation of processes such as spatial memory, "place" is typically narrowly defined (e.g., an arm of a radial maze, a hidden platform in a water maze) in an environment (e.g., a small laboratory room) that is typically impoverished in terms of the variety of stimuli present and does not contain naturalistic spatial cues such as the sky, sun and shadows, an horizon, and vegetation and other features that are integral parts of natural, geographic places. In this article a representative sampling of research on spatial cognition that uses pictures of natural geographic places is described. Some of the findings from this research go well beyond the conclusions possible using conventional laboratory paradigms and arbitrary stimuli.

HABITAT PREFERENCE IN MIGRATING BIRDS

Migration is a remarkable spatial ability in which many animals, and birds especially, travel huge distances from one spatial location to another. The summer and winter locations often are very distinctive in terms of visual appearance. Roberts and Weigl (1984) studied dark-eyed junco's preferences for summer and winter habitats, using photographs of the two habitats. Because juncos migrate over considerable distances and with significant energy expenditures, these researchers expected that the juncos would show a preference for the appropriate (summer or winter) pictures of habitat, which is what was found.

Roberts and Weigl tested wild-caught dark-eyed juncos' preferences for slides of natural habitat in a two-compartment chamber. Each compartment of the test chamber contained a perch mounted in front of a window. A projection screen could be viewed through each window and baffles in the middle of the chamber ensured that only the adjacent projected image was visible. The images were color slides of the juncos' summer and winter habitats. Summer slides were of a grassland-conifer forest and winter slides were of open southern mixed pine and hardwood forest. Roberts and Weigl wanted to determine if juncos would show preferences (defined as time spent in front of a slide) for slides of winter and summer habitats that were a function of their season of capture. Would birds captured in the winter prefer winter habitat slides and would birds captured later in the year prefer summer slides?

Ten juncos were captured in their winter habitat (Winston-Salem, North Carolina) between November 28 and January 22; 15 birds were caught in the same location between January 31 and March 7. The birds of the former group were designated the winter group and were put on a winter photoperiod (9L:15D) in the colony. The other birds, the summer group, were placed on a summer photoperiod (15L:9D). Each subject was given two 90-min tests in which slide preference was recorded in terms of the amount of time a subject perched in front of a summer or winter slide. The results were clear. The winter group preferred the winter slide, spending 71% of the time perched in front of this slide. The summer group preferred the summer slide, spending 73 % of the time in front of it.

Roberts and Weigl collected some other data that are also of interest. Field studies had shown that larger dominant adult males generally migrate relatively short distances from the summer breeding grounds. Smaller females generally migrate the furthest. These field observations allowed Roberts and Weigl to predict that habitat (i.e., slide) preference should be correlated with size/dominance: Preference for the winter slide should be inversely related to size, with smaller birds showing the strongest preference. This prediction was confirmed. The correlation between wing cord length and time spent viewing the winter slide was -0.896 and correlation between winter preference and body weight was -0.757.

DISCRIMINATION OF LARGE-SCALE
GEOGRAPHIC LOCATIONS

Roberts and Weigl's subjects discriminated pictures of outdoor geographic locations that were differentiated by the type of vegetation. Two studies (Honig & Stewart, 1988; Wilkie, Willson, & Kardal, 1989; see also Kendrick, 1992, for somewhat related research) have also demonstrated picture discriminations between outdoor locations, using operant discrimination procedures. In these studies the rewarded (S+) pictures were taken from several perspectives in a particular geographic location.

Our study (Wilkie, Willson, & Kardal, 1989) originated from an interest in the long-standing and unresolved issue of whether homing pigeons use visual recognition of place during navigation. Although most reviews of the homing pigeon literature (e.g., Bingman, 1998) state that homing pigeons rely on visual landmarks in the immediate vicinity of their loft, the extent of the evidence for this is not great. A demonstration that homing pigeons can discriminate between pictures of their actual geographic home and other similar geographic areas would provide additional, albeit indirect, evidence that homing pigeons may use visual recognition of landmarks and topography, at least when they are close to home. We asked if our pigeons could discriminate between pictures taken in the vicinity of the loft to which they had been trained to home and pictures of other areas they had not visited. To determine if homing experience was necessary in order to discriminate pictures of this place, non-homing control pigeons were also tested.

During the experiment all pigeons lived in a colony in which the light/dark cycle was adjusted every few days so that light onset and offset matched actual sunrise and sunset times. The homing group received training to fly to a cage on the roof of UBC's Psychology Building. The birds were first released from the roof several times before being released four times from each of four more distant sites, each of which was more distant than the preceding site. These sites, large grassy areas, were 1.5, 4.1, 7.8, and 17.8 km from home. After these releases the subjects were released several more times from the roof. Near the end of this outdoor training, picture discrimination training was started.

Picture discrimination training was implemented in a Skinner box containing a grain dispenser and a 16×15 cm pecking key made from rear-projection Plexiglas. All subjects received training to discriminate between two sets of slides, one set (S+) consisting of slides taken in the general vicinity of UBC's Psychology Building and the other set (S-) taken at locations known to not have been visited by our homing subjects. Figures 1 and 2 show representative examples of the S+ and S-slides.

The pigeons learned the initial slide discrimination extremely rapidly. After only 12 sessions of training (48 S+ trials, 48 S- trials; approximately 30 min of training) discrimination ratios (the ratio of responding on S+ trials to total responses on both S+ and S- trials) were about .80. The homing pigeons tended to discriminate the S+ and S- slides slightly better than the non-homers but this difference was not statistically significant. After training both groups of subjects received transfer tests in

Figure 1. Representative S+ slide used in the Wilkie, Willson, and Kardal (1989) study. This picture was taken from the roof of the Psychology Building at UBC where the homing pigeons' loft was located.

Figure 2. Representative S- slide used in the Wilkie, Willson, and Kardal (1989) study. This slide was taken from a rooftop location on the campus of Dalhousie University in Halifax, Nova Scotia.

which novel pictures of the S+ and S- locations were introduced. The slightly superior discrimination ability of the homers shown in acquisition was again evident during the first three transfer tests. This difference was statistically significant. It is interesting to note that at this point in the experiment the homing pigeons were still being given outdoor flight training. After the third transfer test outdoor flights ceased due to inclement weather. Thereafter performance in the two groups converged. Both groups were about 80% correct in classifying novel slides for the very first time.

Our results show that pigeons are capable of discriminating a broadly-defined outdoor geographic location depicted in a series of color slides. The only defining feature of the S+ slides was that the slides were of a particular location centered on the spot to which the homing pigeons flew. Some slides were oriented towards the Psychology Building but others were oriented away from this building. Some contained views of this building but others did not. Some were taken at ground level; others from rooftops of multi-story buildings. The S- slides contained a similar variety of content. The fact that our subjects learned the discrimination between S+ and S- locations quickly and displayed good transfer to slides viewed for the very first time suggests that the discrimination was a categorical one. Although it has been well established by prior research that pigeons are capable of making categorical discriminations of such natural stimuli as fish, people, and trees, our results and those of Honig and Stewart (1988) are apparently the first showing that pigeons are capable of making categorical discriminations of outdoor geographic locations. In our experiment the locations were broadly defined. Although most S+ slides were taken within 0.5 km of the Psychology Building, the geographic features visible in the slides define an area consisting of many kilometers.

Honig and Stewart (1988) demonstrated categorical discrimination of a more restricted outdoor location. In their study pigeons (who did not have outdoor experience) discriminated photographs taken at several ground-level spots ("standpoints") in each of two separate locations on the Dalhousie University campus. The features visible in their slides probably defined a geographic area of approximately 50 meters at most. Discrimination training consisted of 23 to 33 sessions (for different birds) in which 32 S+ and 32 S- slides were presented on a 5 cm square key. Their birds learned to discriminate the two pictorially-presented locations and showed good transfer to novel slides of the two locations.

Honig and Stewart included a rote memorization control group. For these subjects, slides of the two locations were randomly assigned to the S+ and S- sets. As in similar experiments (e.g., Edwards & Honig, 1987) the rote memorization group learned the discrimination between S+ and S-, but much more slowly and to a lesser extent (see Cole & Honig, 1994, for related research).

Honig and Stewart's (1988) results and the results for our control subjects show that pigeons can learn to recognize an outdoor geographic location in the absence of experience in the locations depicted in the slides. In one way this finding is analogous to the findings that laboratory pigeons can discriminate pictures representing natural categories, such as fish, with which they probably have had no or only limited experience. Since pigeons can come to recognize a place without directly experiencing the location, by somehow integrating a series of overlapping snapshot views, this may indicate that our procedure of presenting a succession of images in some way mimics the natural way in which places are recognized. This idea is well developed in the insect spatial cognition literature (see Judd & Collett, 1998).

LANDMARK USE IN NATURAL OUTDOOR SCENES

Many animals use visual cues ("landmarks") in the process of piloting to particular spatial locations. Cheng (e.g., Cheng, 1988, 1989) has developed both a paradigm to study animals' use of landmarks and a criterion for identifying whether a particular visual cue is a landmark. The procedures are simple; food is buried in a discrete, fixed location under the uniform substrate of an open field. Various objects, placed in fixed locations in the open field, serve as potential landmarks to enable subjects (hungry pigeons) to find the hidden food. Objects are identified as effective landmarks if the bird's searching behavior is shifted in the same direction, and to approximately the same extent, as a shifted object. The bird's searching behavior during both training and shift tests is measured using video tape from an overhead video camera. Use of this paradigm has led to the discovery of certain regularities in landmark use (e.g., landmarks closer to the goal are weighted more heavily than are distant landmarks; Cheng, 1989).

In the original version of the landmark paradigm the "open field" was a wooden-chip covered floor of a laboratory room (Cheng, 1988).

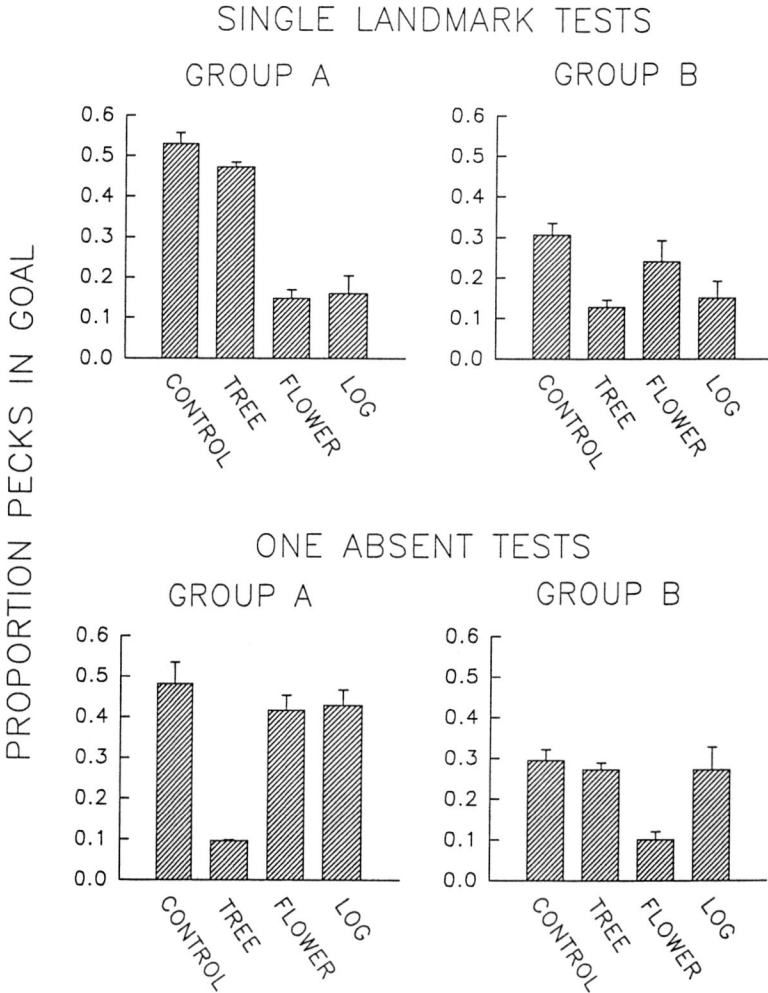

Figure 3. Data from Spetch and Wilkie's (1994) study.
The digitized image that the birds viewed is shown in Figure 6 (A). For group
A birds, the goal was located closest to the tree whereas for group B birds, the
goal was located closest to the flower. For both groups the proportion of pecks
made in the goal area is shown. In Control sessions, all three landmarks were
present. In Single landmark tests, only one landmark was presented. In One
absent tests, one of the three landmarks was removed. Group A birds' pecking
was controlled by the tree; group B birds' pecking was controlled by the
flower.

Spetch, Cheng, and Mondloch (1992; see also Spetch & Mondloch, 1993) extended the paradigm to a computer-controlled VGA monitor/touchscreen apparatus. Hungry pigeons received food rewards for pecking at an unmarked location on the monitor. Landmarks were computer-generated graphics (e.g., blue rectangle). Spetch et al. found that pigeons' use of landmarks in this apparatus was similar in many respects to that observed in the original open field version of the task.

The computerized landmark task has several advantages over the open field version, one of which is automated data collection by the touchscreen system which records the XY coordinates of each peck. Another advantage is that computers are capable of presenting large, high quality, colored images. In recent research, Spetch and Wilkie (1994) have extended the Spetch et al. (1992) touchscreen procedure to one in which pigeons view a digitized image of an actual outdoor location (a grassy field) such as might be encountered by a feral pigeon. Again, the pigeons are trained to peck at an unmarked spot on the monitor. In that research, it was found that pigeons use certain parts of the scene (e.g., a tree) as landmarks to locate the hidden goal (see Figure 3).

Peck location was shifted when the landmark was shifted, demonstrating control of search behavior by the landmark. Landmarks nearest to the goal controlled peck location the most, suggesting that landmarks most proximate to a goal are weighed most heavily by foragers.

WHAT FEATURES IN LANDSCAPE SCENES ARE ATTENDED TO?

Wilkie, Mak, and Saksida (1994) provided another, complementary, type of evidence of landmark use by animals. A second, and more important, goal was the development of a paradigm in which an animal's responding to the image of a digitized outdoor scene can indicate what components, parts, or features of real-world scenes are attended to. As in Spetch and Wilkie (1994), we used computer generated images of outdoor scenes on a touchscreen-equipped monitor. One of the constraints inherent in the search paradigm is that pigeons tend to rely on visual cues closest to the target location as landmarks. Thus, which cues act as landmarks to guide search behavior may be determined more by spatial proximity rather than natural saliency. In the Wilkie, Mak, and

Saksida experiment we attempted to remove this constraint and permit subjects to show us which part(s) of an outdoor scene are most salient.

We attempted to do this by using a procedure similar to the "feature-positive" discrimination procedure first reported by Jenkins and Sainsbury (1969) and later elaborated upon by Edwards and Honig (1987). Jenkins and Sainsbury (1969) trained pigeons to discriminate between a S+ and a S- differentiated only by a single feature (e.g., three circles vs. two circles and a star). Two groups of pigeons were tested, one for which the feature was on the S+, and a second for which the feature was on the S-. The feature-positive group learned the discrimination much more rapidly than the feature-negative group. The explanation for this "feature positive effect" was discovered when the location of the pigeons' pecks to the displays was recorded. Feature-positive subjects were found to localize their pecks on the distinctive feature before eliminating responses to the S-. Feature-negative subjects, on the other hand, only gradually eliminated responding to the feature and localized responding on the common features of the two displays. The same general pattern of results was reported by Edwards and Honig (1987) who trained pigeons to discriminate complex visual images. Their stimuli were photographic slides of a scene with a person present, and the same scene with the person absent. Groups of pigeons were trained to discriminate this "present/absent" category with the feature (person) either serving as S+ or S-. Again feature-positive subjects learned more rapidly.

For the purposes of our research, the important finding of Jenkins and Sainsbury (1969) was that pigeons physically peck at the distinguishing feature of the S+. In the present research, we used this phenomenon to see what aspects of an outdoor scene are treated as features (i.e., are pecked at) by pigeons. Pigeons were trained on a two image

Figure 4. Data from the Wilkie, Mak, and Saksida (1994) study.
Panel A shows the S+; the S- was the same image in which grass was "pasted" over the three objects in the S+. The data are from a single subject. Panel B shows acquisition scores. Panel C shows the frequency distribution of pecks at the S+ image. Panel D shows modal X and Y peck locations. The three stars show the location of the three objects (tree, flower pot, and log). Panels E and F show the same data for sessions in which the three objects were shifted to new locations. For this subject most pecks were located in the vicinity of the flower pot.

A

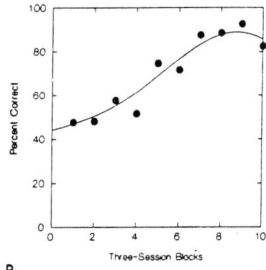

B

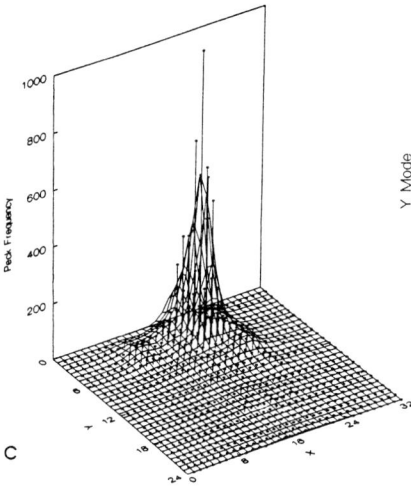

C

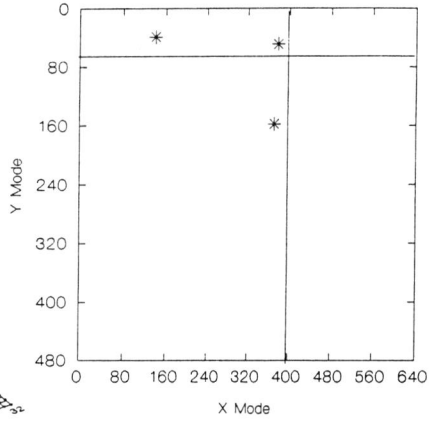

D

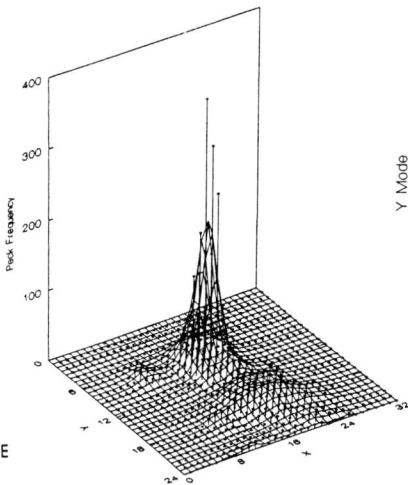

E

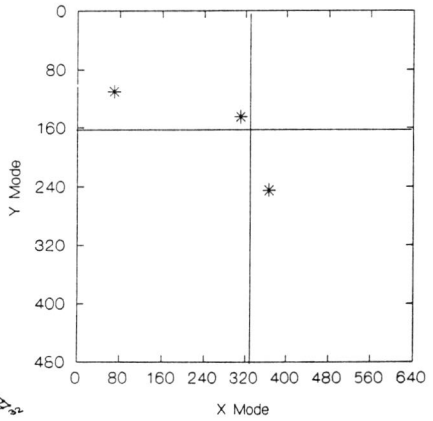

F

discrimination of an outdoor location. The S+ image was a grassy field containing a small tree, a planter containing flowers, and a log. The S- was the field with the tree, flowers, and log removed. A touchscreen was used to record the location of pecks to the two images.

Subjects readily discriminated the S+ and S- images. After several sessions of discrimination training, subjects pecked infrequently at the S- image. The location of pecks to the S- image was quite variable. Pecks to the S+ images, on the other hand, were very spatially concentrated. One subject pecked in the vicinity of the flowers while another subject pecked in the vicinity of the tree. Both subjects pecked the S+ images most frequently in a very small area (1 bin, 20 by 20 pixels, less than 1 square cm) near the center of the landmark (see Figure 4). Peck distributions shifted as landmark location in the S+ image was shifted, satisfying the criteria for landmark identification.

FEATURE ANALYSIS IN UNSTAGED
OUTDOOR LOCATIONS

Ongoing, unpublished research also demonstrates the feasibility of using touchscreen technology in conjunction with a procedure similar to "feature positive" discrimination as a way of assessing which feature(s) of complex, naturalistic, unstaged, outdoor environments subjects attended to. This procedure capitalized on the tendency of pigeons to peck at the distinguishing feature of the S+.

We have used this feature positive task to test hypotheses about homing pigeons' navigation to their home loft. Homing pigeons have a remarkable ability to quickly find their way home from distant, novel release sites. There is some evidence that they use visual information, at least closer to home (see review by Bingman, 1998). As a source of hypotheses about how they might do this, I have checked into how human aviators navigate using Visual Flight Rules (VFR). They often seem to use the shape of the horizon for map information. Honey bees also appear to use horizon landmarks (Southwick & Buchmann, 1995).

In the first experiment, we trained three pigeons to discriminate between a S+ (a landscape consisting of the ocean in the foreground, an horizon of land features, and the sky) and a S- (ocean only) displayed on a touchscreen-equipped computer monitor. Subjects received 40 trials each day. The S+ and S- images were presented for 12 s, in a randomized order. The X,Y location of each peck was recorded. The birds learned the discrimination to a high level (about 90% correct after 30 sessions of training). The pigeons concentrated their S+ pecks at the horizon, suggesting that horizon information is salient feature (see Figure 5). When a different sized image of the scene was presented, peck location followed the horizon feature across or up and down on the touch screen. In another experiment, discrimination was better when the S+ contained an horizon than when it did not contain an horizon, again suggesting that features on the horizon are salient. Each of the four pigeons in that study discriminated a S+ with an horizon about 4-5% better than a S+ without an horizon.

CONCLUSIONS

Recent research shows that it is possible to investigate animals' spatial cognition through the use of colored photographs and digitized computer images. The present paper provides a representative overview of five such investigations. The broad generalizations that emerge from these studies are: 1) migrating birds show preferences for photographs of seasonally-appropriate landscapes, strongly suggesting that they recognize a correspondence between pictures and the depicted outdoor scenes; 2) pigeons can form conceptual, categorical discriminations of medium and large scale outdoor locations, even without direct experience with these locations, suggesting that place recognition may occur through the integration of a series of individual images of the location; 3) pigeons foraging behavior directed at a hidden food goal located on a touchscreen, displaying a picture of an outdoor location, is controlled by landmarks in the picture nearest the goal, suggesting that proximate landmarks to goals are weighted the most heavily; 4) pigeons' discrimination between a S+ (an outdoor image consisting of several objects) and a S- (a featureless outdoor image) consistently peck at one feature, a finding that provides a way of assessing which aspects of landscapes are most salient; 5) the latter procedure was used to show that the horizon is a salient feature in outdoor landscape discriminations. Most of the questions posed in these investigations could not have been investigated to the same extent without the use of pictorial technologies.

Figure 5. Peck location data from the unpublished Wilkie study.
The image shown is the S+; the ocean is shown in the foreground, behind it is a tree-covered peninsula, and behind that is an island and snow-covered mountains. The S- was an image of the ocean. The white lines show the mean peck locations in the X and Y dimensions. All three pigeons pecked at the peninsula. They continued to peck at this feature when a novel image was presented. The different panels show data from three pigeons.

ACKNOWLEDGEMENTS

This research was supported by the Natural Sciences and Engineering Research Council of Canada (NSERC). The research described in the last section was done with the able assistance of Jennifer Galloway, Kerry Jo Parker, Aiko Yamamoto, and Tracy Tanchuk.

REFERENCES

Bingham, V. P. (1998). Spatial representations and homing pigeon navigation. In S. Healy (Ed.), *Spatial representation in animals* (pp. 68-85). Oxford: Oxford University Press.

Cole, P. D., & Honig, W. K. (1994). Transfer of a discrimination by pigeons (*Columba livia*) between pictured locations and the represented environment. *Journal of Comparative Psychology, 108,* 189-198.

Cheng, K. (1988). Some psychophysics of pigeons' use of landmarks. *Journal of Comparative Physiology A, 162,* 815-826.

Cheng, K. (1989). The vector sum model of pigeon landmark use. *Journal of Experimental Psychology: Animal Behavior Processes, 15,* 366-375.

Edwards, C. A., & Honig, W. K. (1987). Memorization and "feature selection" in the acquisition of natural concepts in pigeons. *Learning and Motivation, 18,* 235-260.

Honig, W. K., & Stewart, K. (1988). Pigeons can discriminate locations presented in pictures. *Journal of Experimental Analysis of Behavior, 50,* 541-551.

Jenkins, H. M., & Sainsbury, R. S. (1969). The development of stimulus control through differential reinforcement. In N. J. Mackintosh & W. K. Honig (Eds.), *Fundamental issues in associative learning* (pp. 123-161). Halifax: Dalhousie University Press.

Judd, S. P. D., & Collett, T. S. (1998). Multiple stored views and landmark guidance in ants. *Nature, 392,* 710-714.

Kendrick, D. F. (1992). Pigeon's concept of experienced and non-experienced real-world locations: Discrimination and generalization across seasonal variation. In W. K. Honig and J. G. Fetterman (Eds.), *Cognitive aspects of stimulus control* (pp. 113-134). Hillsdale, NJ: Erlbaum.

Roberts, E. P., Jr., & Weigl, P. D. (1984). Habitat preference in the dark-eyed junco (*Junco hyemalis*): The role of photoperiod and dominance. *Animal Behaviour, 32,* 709-714.

Southwick, E. E., & Buchmann, S. L. (1995). Effects of horizon landmarks on homing success in honey bees. *American Naturalist, 146,* 748-764.

Spetch, M. L., Cheng, K., & Mondloch, M. V. (1992). Landmark use by pigeons in a touch-screen spatial search task. *Animal Learning and Behavior, 20,* 281-292.

Spetch. M. L., & Mondloch, M. V. (1993). Control of pigeons' spatial search by graphic landmarks in a touch-screen task. *Journal of Experimental Psychology: Animal Behavior Processes, 19,* 353-372.

Spetch, M. L., & Wilkie, D. M. (1994). Pigeon's use of natural landmarks presented in digitized images. *Learning and Motivation, 25,* 245-275.

Wilkie, D. M., Mak, T., & Saksida, L. M. (1994). Pigeons' landmark use as revealed in a "feature-positive", digitized landscape, touchscreen paradigm. *Behavioural Processes, 32,* 87-100.

Wilkie, D. M., Willson, R. J., & Kardal, S. (1989). Pigeons discriminate pictures of a geographic location. *Animal Learning and Behavior, 17,* 163-171.

Recognition of objects and spatial relations in pictures across changes in viewpoint

Marcia L. Spetch, Debbie M. Kelly, and Sheri Reid

University of Alberta, Edmonton, Canada

Abstract. The ability to recognize objects or places despite variation in viewpoint seems fundamental to many adaptive behaviors. But do animals recognize objects or places in static pictures across changes in view? In Experiment 1, pigeons with prior outdoor experience were trained to locate an unmarked goal in 6 views of a scene presented on a touch-screen monitor. The goal location was fixed relative to landmarks in the scene, but 2-D vectors from landmarks to the goal varied across views. Pigeons learned the task, but showed poor transfer to novel views. Their performance resembled that previously seen in laboratory-raised pigeons with the same images, but differed from that previously seen in outdoor-experienced pigeons trained with more views of a different scene. Thus, stimulus and/or training factors, rather than outdoor experience, may determine degree of transfer to novel views. Experiment 2 explored pigeons' object recognition across changes in viewpoint. One group discriminated objects composed of identical parts and another group discriminated objects composed of different parts. Baseline accuracy was higher for the different-parts group, but transfer to novel views was comparable across groups. Both groups generalized across views, but accuracy decreased with rotation from the nearest training view. Implications for the use of pictorial stimuli to study cognitive processes in animals are discussed.

Key words: Landmark-based search, object recognition, picture processing, pigeons, scene recognition, viewpoint dependence.

Correspondence should be sent to Marcia L. Spetch, Department of Psychology, University of Alberta, Edmonton, AB T6G 2E9, Canada (e-mail: mspetch@ualberta.ca).

INTRODUCTION

For the past three decades, many cognitive and perceptual processes have been investigated in animals through presentation of pictorial stimuli. Studies investigating processes such as object recognition, categorization, and spatial learning using colored slides or digitized images have clearly shown that pigeons process and remember rich visual details in pictorial stimuli. Although this work has provided sufficient evidence to justify the use of such stimuli for investigation of many cognitive processes, much remains to be known about exactly how pictorial stimuli are perceived by pigeons, and to what extent pigeons' perception of pictorial stimuli is similar to their perception of real-world objects and scenes. For example, questions such as whether pigeons detect three-dimensionality of objects and scenes, and whether they can recognize pictures as representations of real world objects or scenes have been addressed in recent work but remain in need of further investigation (see D'Eath, 1998, for an excellent recent review). Understanding how pigeons perceive pictorial information is important, both because it will advance our understanding of basic avian visual cognition and because it will facilitate interpretation of results of studies using pictorial stimuli to investigate other cognitive processes.

There have been two main approaches to the question of whether pigeons and other avian species recognize pictures as representations of the real world. One has been to test for transfer of a learned response from pictures to real objects or scenes and vice versa. Evidence from studies taking this approach has been mixed, with several studies finding some degree of transfer (Cabe, 1976; Cole & Honig, 1994; Looney & Cohen, 1974; Watanabe, 1993; Wilkie, Willson, & Kardal, 1989), but others not (Bradshaw & Dawkins, 1993; Dawkins, Guilford, Braithwaite, & Krebs, 1996; Lechelt & Spetch, 1997). Another approach has been to look for appropriate behavioral responses, such as courtship, preferences, or aggressive behaviors to pictures of biologically significant stimuli, such as a picture of a conspecific. Again, the results have been mixed. For example, Looney and Cohen (1974) found that pigeons attacked and pecked at the head area of pigeons presented in color photographs when induced to display aggression by interruptions in feeding. However, Dawkins (1996) failed to find evidence of socially appropriate behaviors by hens toward photographs of conspecifics; although the hens chose flock-mates over unfamiliar birds as feeding companions, they did not show a significant preference for photographs of flock mates. Very recently, Shimizu (1998) found that courtship behavior by male pigeons to video images of female pigeons was equivalent to that shown to live female pigeons, and substantially greater than that shown to video images of a cockatoo. Courtship displays were more vigorous when the video was in motion and when the head region was available. By contrast, Ryan and Lea (1994) failed to observe socially-appropriate responses from pigeons to life-size moving images of pigeons. Differences between studies in stimuli, task requirements, and species investigated could underlie some of the discrepancies in results. Moreover caution must be taken in interpreting failures to treat pictorial stimuli as real objects or scenes. As discussed extensively in a recent review by D'Eath (1998), pictorial stimuli are clearly impoverished representations of the real world and may not portray some visual features, such as color, accurately to non-human visual systems. Further distortions may occur when video stimuli are used, because screen refreshing may result in the perception of flicker for animals with high critical flicker-fusion thresholds.

Evidence has also been mixed on the issue of whether pigeons perceive three-dimensional depth information in pictures. One approach to this question has been to seek evidence of known perceptual illusions that may result from the perception of depth. One such illusion is the Ponzo illusion in which two parallel bars are located between two converging lines. To humans, the bar near the apex of the lines looks longer than the bar further away, possibly because linear perspective cues provide the illusion of depth. Pigeons as well as other animals have been found to show perception of such an illusion (horses, Timney & Keil, 1996; monkeys, Bayne & Davis, 1983; and pigeons, Fujita, Blough, & Blough, 1991, 1993), although the specific characteristics of the illusion are not completely identical with that found in humans (Fujita et al., 1991, 1993). Another known perceptual phenomenon that presumably indicates depth perception is completion of partially occluded objects. Although chicks (Lea, Slater, & Ryan, 1996; Regolin & Vallortigara, 1995), mice (Kanizsa, Renzi, Conte, Compostela, & Guerani, 1993), and monkeys (Osada & Schiller, 1994) have been found to show completion of occluded objects, pigeons have thus far failed to show this effect (Cerella, 1980; Sekuler, Lee, & Shettleworth, 1996).

Another approach has been to assess the ability to discriminate between two-dimensional and three-dimensional objects presented in pictures. Hershberger (1970) trained chicks to discriminate convex and concave dents in an aluminum panel and found that their discrimination transferred to photographs of the training dents, suggesting that they could detect depth from the shading information present in photographic stimuli. More recently, Reid and Spetch (1999) trained pigeons on a "3-dimensionality concept" using a large set of object pairs that were displayed side by side in digitized images. The target object was 3-dimensional, and provided both shading and perspective cues for depth. The shading and/or perspective cues were absent or distorted for the distractor object. The pigeons learned to select the 3-dimensional object, and their accuracy remained above chance on transfer tests with completely novel target and distractor objects. At the very least, these results suggest that pigeons can form a concept based on pictorial cues that distinguish 2-dimensional and 3-dimensional objects; whether they actually see the pictures as representations of 3-dimensional objects is more difficult to determine.

The present research addresses a slightly different aspect of pigeons' picture perception, namely, the extent to which their recognition of spatial relationships and objects presented in pictures generalizes across changes in perspective. In natural settings, animals are frequently faced with the problem of recognizing places and objects from different viewpoints, due to their own movement or to the movement of an external object. Quick and accurate object and place recognition despite changes in position of the object or viewer would appear to benefit many adaptive behaviors, such as returning to a nest or feeding site, recognizing a conspecific, or avoiding predators. Thus, an interesting question from the perspective of picture processing is whether animals can readily and accurately recognize spatial relationships and objects in pictures across changes in viewpoint. The two experiments reported here follow from studies on pigeons recently conducted in our laboratory. The first uses a landmark-based search task and investigates pigeons' ability to generalize spatial localization across different views of a complex naturalistic scene. The second concerns pigeons' generalization of object recognition across changes in orientation. In both studies, the basic procedure involved training with a set of views and then testing for transfer to novel views.

EXPERIMENT 1

In several studies we have shown that pigeons can use visual land-marks in images of a scene to accurately locate a small unmarked area in the scene (Lechelt & Spetch, 1997; Spetch & Wilkie, 1994; Spetch, Kelly, & Lechelt, 1998). This demonstrates the processing of visual details in the scene and of spatial relationships, but by itself does not tell us whether the scene is processed as a representation of three-dimensional space. In a recent study (Spetch et al., 1998), we attempted to address this question by training pigeons with images that showed a scene from different viewpoints. The pigeons' task was to find a small unmarked location in the scene. When shown from different viewpoints, the 2-dimensional spatial relationships between visual landmarks and the unmarked spot changed across images, even though the depicted three dimensional relationships in the scene were invariant. Thus, if the images were processed only in terms of two-dimensional relationships, this would be equivalent to training the birds to find a goal that moved about with respect to the landmarks. Not only should such learning be difficult because it would require memorization of different two-dimensional relationships for each trained image, but we would also expect little transfer to novel viewpoints because these would provide new two-dimensional relationships. On the other hand, if the images were processed in terms of the underlying three-dimensional relationships in the depicted scene, then only one set of landmark-goal relationships need be learned, and transfer to novel viewpoints should be possible because the same three-dimensional relationships exist. In Experiment 1 of Spetch et al. (1998), pigeons were trained with six different views of an outdoor scene and then tested for transfer to six novel views. The pigeons used were laboratory Silver King pigeons with no outdoor experience. The pigeons learned the task but showed poor transfer to the novel views. In a second experiment, racing pigeons with prior outdoor experience were trained with 28 different views of a different outdoor scene and then were tested with 18 novel views. The birds again learned the task, albeit slowly, and in this case, good transfer to the novel views was found. This study showed that transfer of landmark-based search can occur under a restricted set of conditions. However, it did not isolate which condition(s) are critical for transfer because several factors changed between the first and second experiments, including the past experience and strain of the pigeons, the nature of the scene and visual landmarks, and the number of training and test views. Any or all of these factors could account for the difference in transfer results.

The present study represents a first attempt to determine whether subject factors (past experience or strain of pigeon) or stimulus factors (type of scene or number of training and test orientations) are more important for the occurrence of good transfer across changes in viewpoint. Accordingly, we trained and tested outdoor-experienced racing pigeons with the stimulus materials and training conditions that had generated poor transfer in laboratory pigeons. If prior outdoor experience and/or strain of pigeon are critical in the emergence of transfer across orientations, then these birds might show superior transfer to novel orientations than had been observed for the laboratory pigeons. On the other hand, if the nature of the stimulus and/or the number of training and test orientations are critical, then racing pigeons might also show poor transfer performance under these conditions.

Method

Subjects. The subjects were 4 adult pigeons obtained from the same local pigeon racer who supplied the pigeons used in Spetch et al. (1998). The pigeons in this and the previous studies were a local strain bred specifically for racing performance. They had previous outdoor experience through their participation in races, but they were naive with respect to experimental procedures and the scene depicted in the images. For at least four weeks prior to, and throughout the experiment, the birds were housed indoors in large individual cages under a 12 hour light/dark cycle (lights on at 6:00 a.m.). All birds were maintained at approximately 85 % of their free-feeding weights by Kay Tee pigeon pellets obtained after experimental sessions and mixed grain during experimental sessions. Water and grit were available ad libitum in the home cages.

Apparatus, stimuli, and search space. The apparatus and search space were identical to those used in Experiment 1 of Spetch et al. (1998). The custom-built experimental chamber was 44 cm high, 32 cm deep, and 74 cm wide (inside dimensions), with a large opening in the back wall which provided access to the surface of a Zenith 1492 color monitor with attached infrared touch frame (Carroll Touch, 1492 Smart Frame). Spacers separated the touch frame by approximately 3 cm from the opening, and by approximately 1.6 cm from the monitor. Two Gerbrands grain feeders were mounted on the back wall, one on each side of the monitor, with the feeder openings 8.5 cm from the sides of the monitor opening, and 17 cm from the floor. Lamps located within each feeder illuminated feeder presentations and photocells in each hopper measured head entries to limit eating times. Experimental contingencies and response detection were controlled by a microcomputer located in an adjacent room. The touch frame was programmed to detect individual responses (i.e., detection of a beam break, and subsequent return to an unbroken state before another response would be recorded). The search space was a rectangular area, approximately 26 × 20 cm, on the surface of the color monitor.

The images used for training and for testing were the same as those used in Experiment 1 of Spetch et al. (1998). The procedures for producing and editing the images, and for matching the goal location to touch-screen coordinates, are described in Spetch et al. (1998). The training images displayed six different views of an outdoor scene which contained three landmarks (a chair, potted flowers, and a pile of logs) near the goal, as well as several visually distinct background cues (house, flowers, trees, etc.). These views had been selected to be noticeably different from one another and to differ from one another in the absolute location of the goal on the computer screen. A blue plastic box marked the goal area in images used during preliminary training only. The goal marker was absent in the images used during the later stages of training and during all testing. The test images used during the first test series consisted of six novel views of the same scene. These novel views differed from the training views both in visual appearance and in the location of the goal on the computer screen. During a second test series, the images used for testing were derived from the six training images but had some of the visual information (the nearby landmarks, the background cues, or both) edited out of the scene.

Procedure

– *Preliminary training*. Each bird first received one or two sessions of training to eat from the raised illuminated hopper. All birds then received several sessions of training with a modified autoshaping procedure to establish reliable pecking at the monitor. Initially, a 2-cm blue square was intermittently presented in various screen locations against a green background, with 60-s intertrial intervals (ITI). The blue square remained on until the bird pecked at it, or until 8 s elapsed, and then food was presented. Once reliable pecking was established to the blue square, the six images shown in the top of Figure 1 were introduced (with a rectangular goal marker present as illustrated in the first image). Pecks in a 2-cm area centered at the goal marker were reinforced immediately; otherwise the display terminated with food after 8 s. For the final session of preliminary training, the ITI was decreased to 5 s and the image stayed on until a peck in the goal area was recorded.

– *Search training.* The procedure used for search training was identical to that used in Experiment 1 of Spetch et al. (1998). During initial search training sessions, the goal marker was gradually eliminated so that the pigeons needed to rely on visual cues in the scene to find the goal. This was accomplished by presenting images that were edited so that the marker was covered with patches of grass. Images were created in which the grass covered about 50%, 75%, and finally 100% of the marker (all, except the top left, images in Figure 1 show examples of images with the marker 100% covered). This phase of search training continued until the bird completed (by pecking in the goal area) at least 80 trials in a 60 m session with the goal marker absent. During the next few sessions, the number of pecks in the goal required to terminate the trial and obtain food was increased to 2, and then to 3. Next, a consecutive peck requirement was added such that the last two pecks recorded had to be consecutive pecks in the goal area. Thus, the response requirement during the final stage of training and for all subsequent baseline sessions was a minimum of three pecks in the goal with the last two

Figure 1. Images used for training and testing in Experiment 1.
The top set of images shows the 6 training views. The rectangular target marker is shown for illustrative purposes in the top left image; except during the preliminary training sessions, this marker was edited out of all images used for training and test sessions. The middle set of images shows the novel views presented during the transfer tests, and the bottom set of images shows the test images that were edited to remove the landmarks (NoLm), the background cues (NoBk), or both (None), respectively.

Training Images

1   2   3

4   5   6

Novel Images

1   2   3

4   5   6

Testing Images

1   2   3

pecks being consecutive goal pecks. Each increment in the response requirement was implemented only if the bird completed 80 trials in a session. During the last set of search training sessions, the percentage of trials on which reinforcement was available decreased from 100% to 50%. On unreinforced trials, completion of the response requirement terminated the display but no food was presented. Each bird remained on 50% reinforcement for at least 5 sessions and advanced to the test phase only after completing at least 80 trials on each of the last two sessions. Rate of learning varied considerably, with 2 birds requiring less than 100 sessions (76 and 99), and 2 birds requiring over 200 sessions (217 and 224).

– *Testing*. All birds received two test series, separated by a return to baseline training for two or more sessions, depending upon performance. A single baseline training session also followed every third test session within each test series. Each test session consisted of 50% reinforced baseline trials. The remaining trials consisted of unreinforced baseline trials, control trials that were visually identical to baseline trials but were procedurally the same as test trials, and test trials with novel or altered images. On control and test trials, the image terminated without reinforcement 8 s following the second peck recorded anywhere on the screen.

The first series was a transfer test in which six novel views of the scene were presented on test trials (middle images in panel of Figure 1). For the second test series, the images presented on test trials had been edited to remove all three local landmarks ("No Lms"), to remove all of the background information ("No Bk"), or to remove both the landmarks and the background ("None"). Examples of these images are shown in the bottom panel of Figure 1. Tests were conducted with edited images of each of the six training views.

Data recording and analysis. All data presented are from unreinforced control and test trials. Data were recorded and analyzed in the same manner as in Spetch et al. (1998). Each response was recorded as touch-screen coordinates that ranged from 0 to 640 in the horizontal dimension and from 0 to 480 in the vertical dimension. The first three pecks made on every trial, and all pecks that fell within 20 pixels from the far edges of the search space, were excluded from the analysis (see Spetch et al., 1998).

Responses were considered correct if they were within 25 pixels of the center of the goal in both the horizontal and vertical dimensions. Accuracy was calculated as correct responses divided by the total responses. All accuracy scores presented are averaged across all test trials of that type.

The accuracy level expected on the basis of chance is very low. For example, random responding on the screen would generate accuracy levels of less than .01. If pigeons learned to respond only within the range of screen locations in which the goal is sometimes found (a range that spanned 230 by 178 pixels), then the probability of a response falling in the 50 by 50 pixel goal area as a result of random responding in this restricted range is .06.

For all statistical tests, our criterion for significance was $p < .05$.

Results

The top graph in Figure 2 shows accuracy scores on the control trials, averaged across the six training views, and on transfer test trials, averaged across the six novel views. For comparison we also show the results obtained by Spetch et al. (1998), with the middle graph showing the results they obtained with lab pigeons that were trained and tested on the same stimuli used here, and the bottom graph showing the results they obtained with racing pigeons that were trained and tested on a different scene and a larger set of viewpoints. The racing pigeons in the present study showed a significant decrement in accuracy when tested with novel views, $t(3) = 15.77$, and thus appear more similar to the lab pigeons of the previous study than to the racing pigeons of the previous study.

The top panel of Figure 3 shows mean accuracy for each of the individual trained and novel images for the racing pigeons in the present study. For comparison, the middle and bottom graphs, respectively, show mean accuracy for the same individual images for the lab pigeons and for humans tests in Spetch et al. (1998). As can be seen, there was a strong positive correlation between the scores obtained by the two sets of pigeons ($r = 0.907$). By contrast, the scores obtained by humans were not positively correlated with the scores obtained by either the racing pigeons ($r = -0.130$) or the lab pigeons ($r = -0.109$).

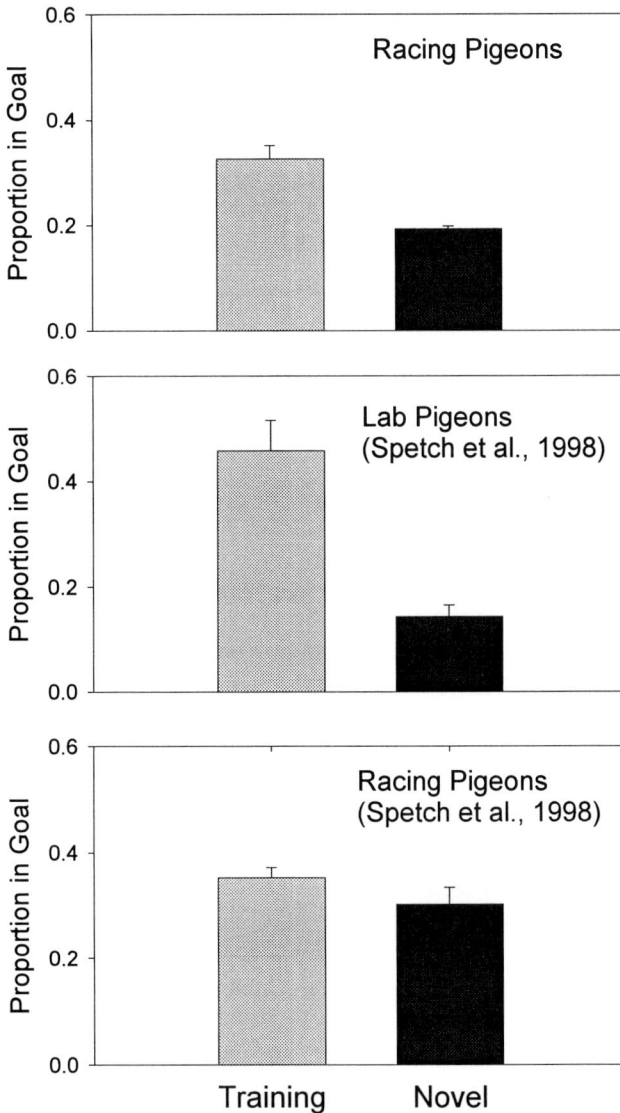

Figure 2. Mean accuracy during transfer tests, averaged across the six train-ing images and the six novel images, for the racing pigeons of the present experiment, the laboratory pigeons tested by Spetch et al. (1998) with these same images, and the racing pigeons in Spetch et al. (1998) that were tested with a different set of images.
Error bars represent standard error of the mean.

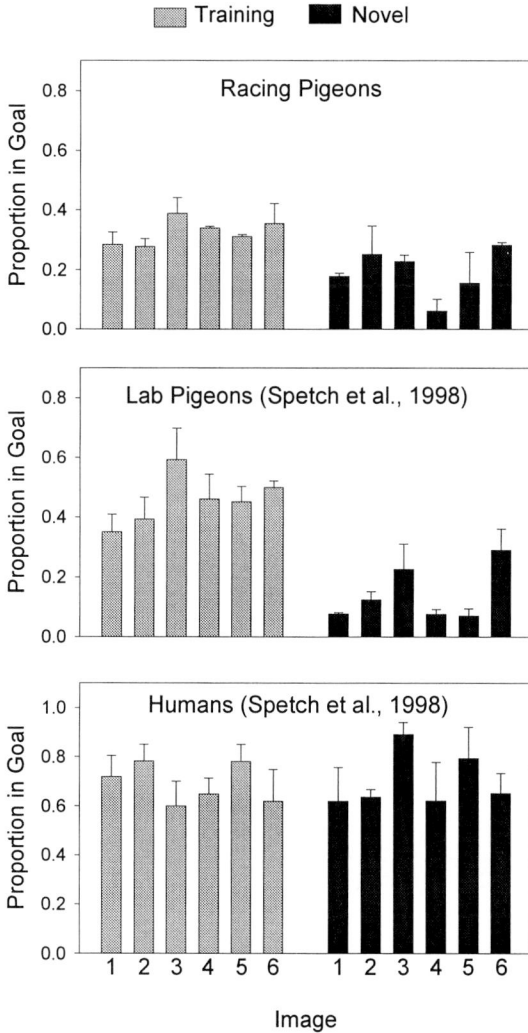

Figure 3. Mean accuracy for each of the individual training and novel images presented during transfer tests for a) the racing pigeons of the present experiment (top), b) the laboratory pigeons tested by Spetch et al. (1998), and c) the humans tested by Spetch et al. (1988).

The same set of images was used in each case, and the images correspond to the order shown in Figure 1. Error bars represent standard error of the mean.

The top graph in Figure 4 shows mean accuracy scores on control and test trials during the landmark and background removal tests. Accuracy is averaged across the six views used for each image type. A repeated measures ANOVA revealed a significant effect of Image type, $F(3, 9) = 10.53$. For comparison, results for the lab pigeons and the humans tested in Spetch et al. (1998) on the identical tests are shown in the middle and bottom graphs, respectively. It appears that both sets of

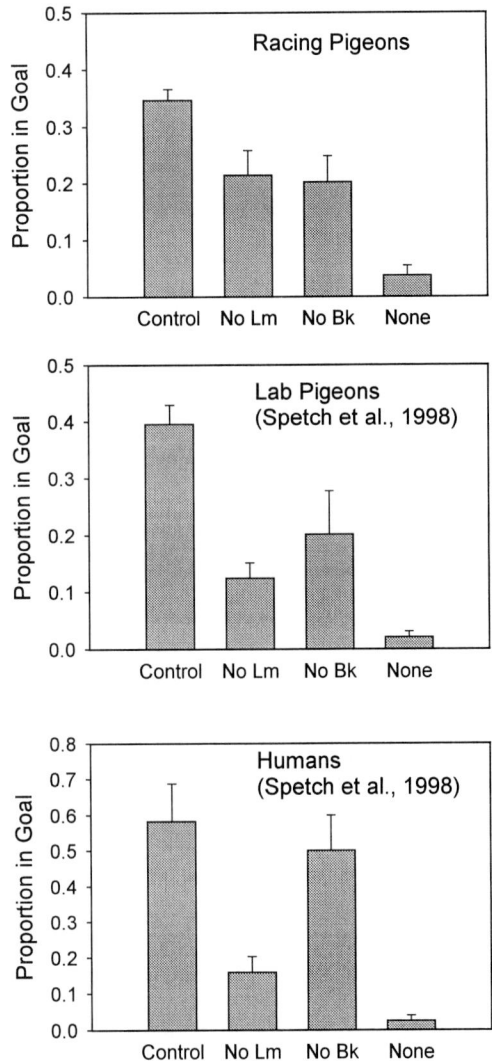

Figure 4. Mean accuracy on control trials with the training images, and on test trials with images that were edited to remove the landmarks (NoLm), the background cues (NoBk), or both (None).
Error bars represent standard error of the mean.

pigeons depended to some extent on both the landmarks and the background to respond accurately, whereas humans showed almost exclusive reliance on the landmarks.

Discussion

The results of this experiment failed to support the hypothesis that subject factors (either outdoor experience or strain of pigeons) is a major determinant of whether pigeons process spatial information in pictures in a way that allows transfer to novel viewpoints. Instead, the results of this experiment, which used racing pigeons with prior outdoor experience, are remarkably similar to the previously reported results with lab pigeons. In fact, the very strong positive correlation between the two sets of pigeons in their accuracy on individual images suggests that they processed the information in the pictures in a similar fashion, thus showing good agreement in which viewpoints were easy and which were hard. The decrement in accuracy shown by both sets of pigeons to removal of landmarks or removal of background cues is also consistent with similar spatial information processing, especially given that humans showed disruption only by removal of the landmarks. It appears, then, that the superior transfer to novel images shown by racing pigeons in the Spetch et al. (1998) study was probably due to the use of a different scene that may have provided more salient pictorial cues to depth, and/or the considerably larger set of viewpoints used in training (28) and testing (18).

The finding that transfer of spatial search to novel viewpoints occurs only under certain training or stimulus conditions is perhaps not surprising given the complexity of the task. The novel views not only change the 2-dimensional spatial relationships between the various landmarks in the image, they also alter the appearance of the landmark objects due to the novel orientation from which they are seen. Thus, in order for birds to transfer to novel views they not only would need to recognize and respond appropriately to the spatial relationships at the new orientation, but they would also need to recognize the objects that serve as landmarks despite changes in their appearance from the novel perspective. Difficulties with either of these steps would reduce accuracy on transfer tests. Experiment 2 explores factors that may influence pigeons' ability to recognize objects across changes in their orientation.

EXPERIMENT 2

In Experiment 2, we investigated pigeons' object recognition across changes in viewpoint. Both the task and the stimuli used were less complex than those used in Experiment 1. The task was a simple two-choice discrimination and the stimuli were digitized images of individual objects filmed against a featureless background. These stimuli provided some of the components of a natural scene (e.g., shading cues), but removed much of the complexity thereby allowing us to easily and precisely manipulate characteristics and orientation of the objects presented during training and testing.

The ability to recognize objects seen from different angles is perhaps one of the most fundamental tasks of perception, and it is likely equally critical in the lives of animals as in the lives of humans. Results of studies investigating this ability in pigeons using pictorial stimuli have produced a mixed set of results. Several studies have investigated pigeons' recognition of two-dimensional shapes across rotations in the frontal plane. In some studies, the pigeons were trained with stimuli presented in a particular orientation and then tested for transfer to novel orientations. Although good transfer sometimes occurred to particular orientations (e.g., 180° rotations), transfer was surprisingly poor to some of the novel orientations (e.g., Morgan, Fitch, Holman, & Lea, 1976; Towe, 1954; Vetter & Hearst, 1968). By contrast, Hollard and Delius (1982) and Delius and Hollard (1995) trained pigeons to select an object that matched a sample object and then tested the pigeons with rotations of the comparison objects to produce orientation disparity. With this procedure, the pigeons showed rotational invariance in terms of accuracy and reaction time, both when the incorrect comparisons were mirror images of the objects and when the incorrect comparisons were arbitrary different shapes. It seems likely that rotational invariance as measured by disparity in orientation of simultaneously presented objects is not the same as rotational invariance as measured by tests with novel orientations.

Studies of pigeons' recognition of 3-dimensional objects rotated in depth have also produced variable results. Some studies have found little or no transfer to novel orientations (Cerella, 1977, 1990), some have found rotational invariance for a familiar but not for an unfamiliar object (Watanabe, 1997), and some have found generalization functions in which discriminative performance decreases systematically as an object is rotated further away from the training orientation (Lumsden, 1970, 1977; Lumsden & Pullen, 1970; Reynolds, 1961; Wasserman, Gagliardi, Cook, Kirkpatrick-Steger, Astley, & Biederman, 1996). For example, Lumsden (1970) trained pigeons to discriminate between real 3-dimensional objects that differed in shape. Each object was presented in a single orientation. During subsequent tests, responding to the positive (S+) object decreased systematically as it was rotated further away from the training orientation, with a secondary peak at the mirror-image orientation of the S+.

Wasserman et al. (1996) studied pigeons' generalization to novel depth rotations of line drawings of 3-dimensional objects. In one experiment, pigeons were trained to discriminate line drawings of four distinct objects (i.e., an aeroplane, a chair, a lamp, and a flashlight) presented at a single training orientation. Choice accuracy on tests with novel orientations was well above chance, but decreased as a function of rotation away from the training view. Increasing the training views from one to three increased the degree of generalization to novel rotations.

Taken together, results to date suggest that pigeons can, but do not always, recognize objects in novel orientations. Although rotational invariance can occur, more typically, accuracy decreases as the object is rotated away from the training view.

A great deal of research in humans has been directed toward the question of whether object recognition is object-centered, and hence viewpoint invariant, or viewer centered, and hence viewpoint dependent (e.g., see Biederman & Gerhardstein, 1993; Edelman & Bülthoff, 1992; Jolicoeur & Humphrey, in press; Tarr & Pinker, 1989). Contemporary examples of the viewpoint-independent approach are the recognition-by-components (RBC) theory (Biederman, 1987) and its more recent version, the geon-structural-description (GSD) theory (Biederman & Gerhardstein, 1993, 1995). Both versions hold that objects are represented in memory as structural descriptions of the spatial relations among simple, volumetric, 3-dimensional parts, called geons. Recognition depends equally on the particular geons comprising an object and their spatial arrangements. Thus, viewpoint-depended recognition can be attained provided that (1) an object's image can be decomposed into geons, (2) the arrangement of geons provides a structural description that is distinct from other arrangements, and (3) the structural description of the object is the same across different views. If these conditions are met, recognition should be constant regardless of distance from the training view.

By contrast, multiple-view theories (Bülthoff & Edelman, 1992; Humphrey & Kahn, 1992; Tarr, 1995; Tarr & Bülthoff, 1995; Tarr & Pinker, 1989) assume that objects are encoded within a viewpoint-dependent frame of reference, and are represented as a collection of familiar views that reflect the precise metric (appearance) properties of each experienced viewpoint. Unless the object contains diagnostic features that are not shared by other objects, recognition should vary systematically with distance to the nearest represented viewpoint, because novel percepts must be transformed to match the frame of reference for the nearest stored view. Consequently, recognition speed and/or accuracy should decrease as a function of rotation away from the encoded view(s). More recently, Tarr and Bülthoff (1995; see also Hayward & Tarr, 1997) stated that viewpoint-dependent normalization mechanisms should be expected to dominate recognition when discriminating between visually similar objects, whereas viewpoint–independent mechanisms should predominate when discriminating between visually-dissimilar objects.

Although the issue of whether basic object-recognition processes in humans are object or viewer centered remains controversial, some consistent findings have emerged from studies of humans' recognition of rotated objects. In particular, the composition of the object is critical, with viewpoint invariance most likely to be found if the target object contains a "diagnostic feature" that is not shared by the distractor objects. In fact, both of the aforementioned approaches assume that recognition will be viewpoint invariant if an object can be recognized on the basis of diagnostic features. An interesting question is whether presence of diagnostic features is equally important for pigeons' recognition of depth-rotated objects.

Several of the studies previously described have used objects that contain diagnostic features and have failed to find viewpoint-invariant object recognition in pigeons. Nevertheless, such features may improve generalization of object recognition to novel rotations. The present study is the second of two series of studies designed to directly address the role of stimulus characteristics, and in particular diagnostic features, on pigeons' recognition of rotated 3-dimensional objects. Our first studies (Spetch, Friedman, & Reid, submitted) suggested that pigeons' ability to recognize objects in novel orientations may not benefit from the presence of a single diagnostic feature to the same extent as humans. In those studies, pigeons and humans were trained to discriminate between two artificially-created objects shown in two different orientations, and then were tested with four novel orientations. The stimuli and experimental conditions were designed to replicate those used in a recent study with humans by Tarr, Bülthoff, Zabinski, and Blanz (1997). The objects were wire frames with different global shapes and in different conditions, either 0, 1, 3, or 5 distinctive parts were added to the objects. In the condition with one added part, the distinctive part differed across objects and could serve as a diagnostic feature. In this case, discrimination between the objects would be possible without attention to the global object shape. Tarr et al. found a large difference between conditions, with the 1-geon condition yielding much less viewpoint dependence than the other three conditions. The humans in Spetch et al. (submitted) also appeared able to use the distinctive part as a diagnostic feature and showed viewpoint invariance in their recognition accuracy in the 1-part condition. Pigeons, however, showed viewpoint dependence in all conditions.

The present study was a systematic variation of the Spetch et al. (submitted) study and was designed to further assess whether pigeons' ability to recognize objects in novel orientations benefits from the presence of a distinctively shaped part that could serve as a diagnostic feature. In the present study, rather than using computer-drawn grey-scale objects, we used digitized images of real objects that were videotaped in various rotations. Although these objects were unfamiliar arbitrary shapes, they provided natural shading cues and thus might appear more realistic than computer drawn objects. The design of this study also differed from the one conducted by Spetch et al. (submitted) in several ways. First, the previous study used a within-subjects design in which all subjects were trained and tested within each object-part condition, whereas we used a between-group design in which some pigeons were trained with objects containing distinctive parts, and others were trained with objects containing identical parts. It seemed possible that sensitivity to the presence of diagnostic features might be greater in a between-subjects design in which only one object discrimination is learned. Second, whereas pigeons in the Spetch et al. study were trained to discriminate one target (S+) object from one distractor (S-) object in each condition, pigeons in the present study were trained to discriminate between one S+ and three S- objects; this might enhance attention to the distinctive features present in the S+ object. And finally, we trained the pigeons with a larger set of orientations (6 rather than 2). Any of these changes might enhance the pigeons' ability to use diagnostic features to recognize objects in novel orientations.

In the present study, one group of pigeons was trained to discriminate objects composed of identical parts and the other was trained to discriminate objects composed of distinctly different parts. Both groups were then tested for transfer to six novel orientations, five of which differed from the nearest training view by only 22°, and one of which differed from the nearest training view by 67°. Based on the literature on object recognition in humans, pigeons in the different-parts group should show less viewpoint-dependence than pigeons in the same-parts group.

Method

Subjects. The subjects were nine Silver King pigeons. Four birds served in the same-parts group and five birds served in the different-parts group. All birds had previous experience with operant chambers equipped with touch-frames but none had previously served in an object discrimination task. All birds were maintained as in Experiment 1.

Apparatus. The apparatus was the same as that described in Experiment 1.

Stimuli. The stimulus set consisted of five different objects created from red Lego™ pieces attached together to form a geometric pattern. Four of the objects were created from the same set of pieces, arranged to form four different global shapes. One of these objects was used as the S+ for the same-parts group and the other three served as the S- objects for both groups. The fifth object was composed of a different set of four pieces and served at the S+ for the different-parts group. The objects and orientations used during training and testing are shown in Figures 5 and 6, respectively. Column 1 shows the S+ for the same-parts group at each rotation, column 2 shows the S+ for the different-parts group at each rotation, and column 3 shows samples of the three objects used as the S- objects for both groups, with each object shown at two of the six rotations used. Images of the objects were created by videotaping each object at each orientation, and then capturing still frames as gif images using a frame grabber system (Creative Labs Video Blaster). These images were then edited using Photofinish software (Zsoft) to create stimulus displays in which a positive and a negative objects were presented side by side. Each object was centered in a rectangular area of approximately 11 cm wide by 16 cm high. The objects were approximately 5.5 cm along the long axis and 4.2 cm along the short axis. Each object was presented equally often on the left and the right during all training and testing conditions.

Procedure. Sessions were conducted at approximately the same time each day, 5, or 6 days per week. Sessions lasted until all scheduled trials were completed or for a maximum of 1 hour. The monitor screen was cleaned at the end of each day and between sessions as needed.

Pretraining. All birds had previous experience in spatial search tasks conducted on the touch screen and hence were trained at pecking the monitor screen, but none had previously participated in a two-choice discrimination task. Each bird was initially given one or two sessions with an autoshaping procedure in order to establish pecking to the stimulus display used in this study. Each autoshaping trial began with the presentation of a stimulus pair, consisting of an S+ and an S- object. The stimulus pair remained illuminated for 8 s or until a peck was recorded within the rectangular area containing the S+ object; the completion of either event resulted in access to a food hopper. Each of the training stimulus pairs (described in the following section) was presented equally often in a randomly-determined order within each autoshaping session. Trials were separated by a 40-s ITI.

Discrimination training. The stimulus pairs used in training were composed of the S+ object and one of the three S- objects, presented in one of six orientations: 0°, 45°, 90°, 135°, 180°, and 225°. For each picture pair, the two objects were presented in the same orientation. For each combination of S- object and orientation, the S+ was shown once on the right and once on the left, making 36 picture pairs for each group. Each of these picture pairs was presented equally often in each session but the order of presentation was randomly determined. Each trial began with the presentation of a stimulus pair that remained on until the pigeon pecked at one of the two objects. Pecks to the S+ object

Training Orientations

S+
Same

S+
Diff

S-
Both

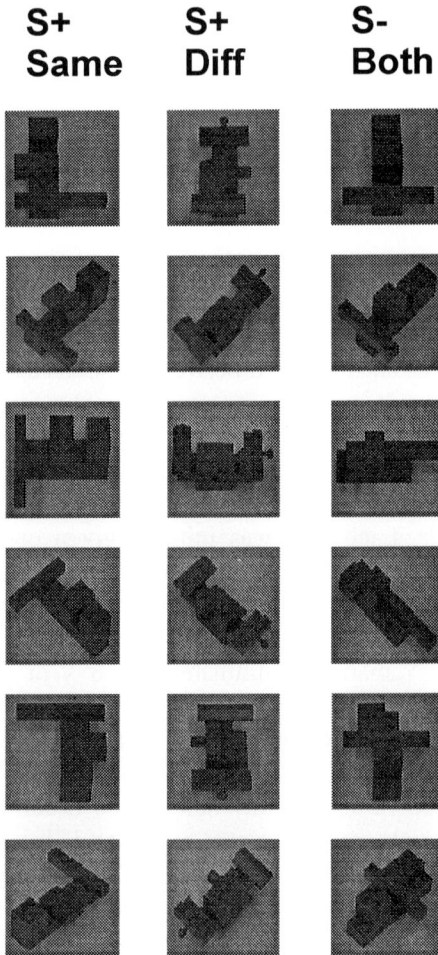

Figure 5. Illustration of the stimuli used during training in Experiment 2.
Column 1 represents the S+ of the same-parts group in each of the 6 training orientations. Column 2 represents the S+ of the different-parts group presented in each of the 6 training orientations. Column 3 represents the 3 S-s presented in two training orientations each. The resolution of the images presented to the pigeons was superior to that reproduced here.

Test Orientations

| S+ | S+ | S- |
| Same | Diff | Both |

Figure 6. Illustration of the novel orientations used during testing in Experiment 2.
Column 1 represents the S+ of the same-parts group in each of the 6 testing orientations. Column 2 represents the S+ of the different-parts group presented in each of the 6 testing orientations. Column 3 represents the 3 S-objects presented in two testing orientations each. The resolution of the images presented to the pigeons was superior to that reproduced here.

were rewarded with a 2-s access to a randomly selected food hopper. Pecks to the S- object terminated the trial without reward and initiated a correction procedure in which the same stimulus pair was represented until the pigeon made a correct choice. Correction trials were not used in the determination of accuracy. The intertrial interval (ITI) was 2 s during which the monitor was blank. Each pigeon was trained until it reached an average of 80% correct responding over four sessions. The birds in the same-parts group took an average of 37 sessions to reach criterion and the birds in the different-parts group took an average of 16 sessions to reach criterion. The birds then received 5 sessions of training with a 50% reinforcement schedule prior to transfer testing. During these sessions, correct pecks ended with food with a probability of 0.5 and otherwise ended with no food.

Transfer tests. Each transfer test session included a mixture of rein-forced baseline trials with training picture pairs, as well as unreinforced probe trials. On probe trials, the trial ended without reinforcement as soon as the pigeon pecked at either object, but the correction procedure was not instituted following incorrect choices. Half of the probe trials served as controls and presented the training picture pairs. The other half of the probe trials presented novel picture pairs. Two transfer test series were conducted, each consisting of three sessions.

Test series one: Transfer to novel depth rotations. Recognition of the objects was tested at six novel orientations: 22°, 67°, 112°, 157°, 202°, or 292°. The first five of these were only 22° from one of the training values, whereas the last one was 67° from the nearest training value. As in training, the two objects were shown in matching orientation.

Test series two: Disparity in orientation of the two objects. This test series examined the effect of presenting the two objects in disparate orientations. Hollard and Delius (1982) and Delius and Hollard (1995) found no effect of disparity in orientation between two simultaneously-presented objects in a matching-to-sample procedure with pigeons. Our test investigates whether disparity between the orientation of simultane-ously presented objects influences pigeons' ability to discriminate the target object from the distractor within a simple discrimination proce-dure. In this test, a selected set of training orientations (0°, 45°, and 90°) were presented on probe trials. On control trials, both objects were shown in the same orientation. On test trials, the objects were shown with a 45° disparity in the orientation of the two objects (i.e., one at 0° and one at 45°, or one at 45° and one at 90°), or with a 90° disparity in the orientation of the two objects (one at 0° and one at 90°).

Results

The top graph in Figure 7 shows pigeons' performance on the probe tests with the training orientations and the novel orientations for each group. The different-parts group was clearly more accurate than the same-parts group, but both groups showed a reduction in accuracy with novel orientations compared to training orientations. A mixed-model ANOVA, with Groups as a between-subject factor and Orientation type (trained vs. novel) as a within-subjects factor confirmed that there was a significant main effect of Group, $F(1, 7) = 26.04$, and Orientation type, $F(1, 7) = 20.72$, but no interaction between Group and Orientation type, $F(1, 7) = 0.18$. Although both groups showed a reduction in accuracy with novel orientations, average accuracy with novel orientations was nevertheless well above chance level (50%) for both groups, $t(3) = 8.35$ and $t(4) = 31.11$ for the same-parts and different-parts groups, respectively.

To determine whether accuracy varied depending on the degree of rotation from the nearest training orientation, we further analyzed the accuracy data in terms of whether the image presented on probe trials was rotated by 0°, 22°, or 67° from the nearest training value. The 0° rotation was the average of the six control orientations, and the 22° rotation score was the average of the first five novel orientations (i.e., 22°, 67°, 112°, 157°, and 202°). The 67° rotation score was the 292° orientation. The middle graph in Figure 7 shows accuracy as a function of rotation. A two-way mixed-model ANOVA revealed a highly significant effect of Group, $F(1, 7) = 50.94$, and of rotation, $F(2, 14) = 26.06$, but the Group × Rotation interaction did not approach significance, $F(2, 15) = 0.26$. Polynomial contrasts revealed a significant linear trend for the Rotation factor, $F(1, 7) = 31.61$. Thus, both groups showed a decrement in accuracy that varied linearly with the degree of rotation from the nearest training value. Although the different-parts group was more accurate than the same-parts group, they showed an equivalent disruption in accuracy as a function of rotation.

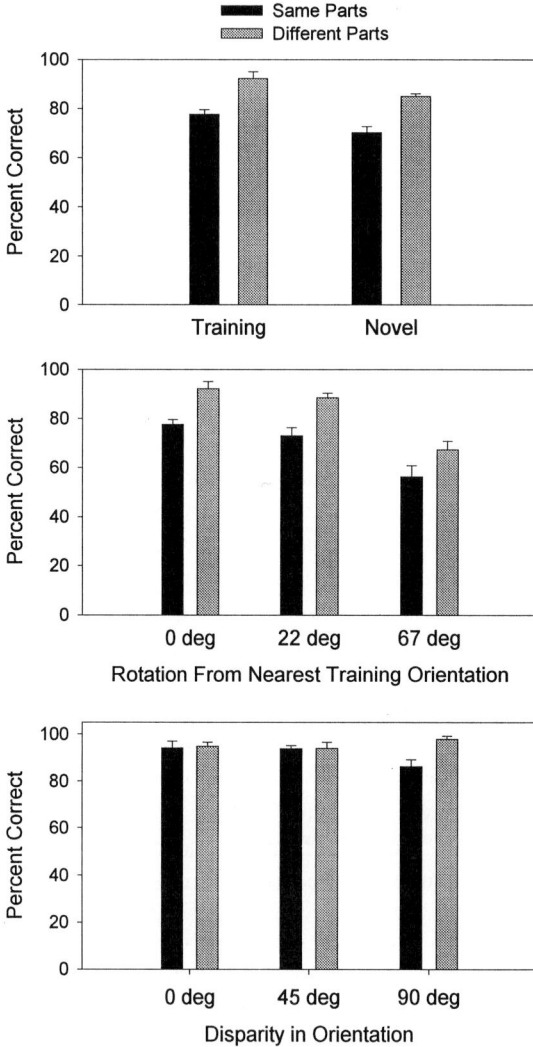

Figure 7. Top: Percentage of correct responses on test trials with training and novel orientations for the different-parts and the same-parts groups in test series 1 of Experiment 2. Middle: Percentage of correct responses on test trials as a function of degree of rotation from the nearest training view for the different-parts and the same-parts groups in test series 1 of Experiment 2. Bottom: Percentage of correct responses as a function of degree of disparity in orientation between the two simultaneously presented objects for the different-parts and the same-parts groups in test series 2 of Experiment 2.

The bottom graph in Figure 7 shows accuracy as a function of disparity in orientation between the two comparison objects (0°, 45°, or 90°). As can be seen, the effect of disparity appeared to vary slightly across groups, with the same-parts group showing a slight decrease in accuracy as a function of disparity and the different-parts group showing no effect of disparity. An ANOVA revealed no significant effect of Group, $F(1, 7) = 3.36$ or of disparity, $F(2, 14) = 0.94$, but the Group × Disparity interaction was significant, $F(2, 14) = 5.94$. However, subsequent one-way ANOVAs within each group failed to reveal a significant effect of disparity within either the same-parts group, $F(2, 6) = 3.54$, or the different-parts group, $F(2, 8) = 1.98$. Thus, the significant interaction term appeared due to the opposite direction of the functions, with the same-parts group showing slightly reduced accuracy as orientation disparity increased and the different-parts group showing slightly increased accuracy at greater orientation disparity.

Discussion

Pigeons in both the same-parts and different-parts groups transferred the discrimination to novel depth-rotations. That is, both groups performed significantly above chance on unreinforced tests with the objects presented in novel orientations. Pigeons in the different-parts group showed higher overall levels of discrimination accuracy than pigeons in the same-parts group, but they displayed equivalent disruption in response to the novel orientations. Specifically, accuracy decreased systematically as a function of rotation from the nearest training value, whether the objects were composed of the same or of different parts.

The higher accuracy for birds in the different-parts group than for birds in the same-parts group indicates that the distinctive parts facilitated the discrimination between the objects. In this context, it is particularly interesting that the presence of distinctive parts did not produce viewpoint invariance. Apparently, the birds could use the distinctive features to more accurately discriminate the positive from the negative object, but these distinctive parts failed to enhance their recognition of these objects when shown in novel depth rotations.

The finding that generalization to novel views was not enhanced by distinctive features is consistent with other recent results obtained in our laboratory (Spetch et al., submitted). The present study differed from the previous one in the nature of the stimulus (digitized images of objects rather than computer drawn objects) and in the number of training orientations. Thus, the lack of an effect of distinctive parts on generalization to novel rotations appears to have considerable generality.

The finding that accuracy decreased when objects were presented in novel orientations is consistent with multiple-view models of object recognition (Bülthoff & Edelman, 1992; Humphrey & Kahn, 1992; Tarr, 1995; Tarr & Bülthoff, 1995; Tarr & Pinker, 1989). According to such models, viewpoint-dependent recognition is the result of the visual system having to transform the unfamiliar orientation of an object to a familiar one represented in memory. This transformation process results in a cost either in accuracy or reaction time. The finding that accuracy decreased as a function of degree of rotation from the nearest stored view is consistent with the assumption that some sort of normalization process is needed to transform novel percepts to the nearest stored orientation. This result is also consistent with findings by Wasserman et al. (1996) in which pigeons that were trained on only one view and then tested with multiple novel views showed decrements in performance as a function of distance from the familiar view.

Accuracy was not affected by the disparity in orientation between the target and distractor object, a finding that is consistent with results obtained by Hollard and Delius (1982) and Delius and Hollard (1995) using a matching-to-sample task. Thus, rotational invariance as assessed by disparity between simultaneously presented objects appears to be a general phenomenon in pigeons. However, invariance with respect to disparity is clearly different than invariance in recognition of novel object rotations.

GENERAL DISCUSSION

Our tentative conclusions based on the present set of results and those of previous studies are that pigeons can: 1) extract detailed information from pictures, 2) discriminate between objects on the basis of complex information such as spatial relationships, pictorial depth cues, and global shapes, and 3) generalize well to novel viewpoints under at least some circumstances. Nevertheless, the processes pigeons use for these accomplishments might not be the same as those used by humans.

Several aspects of the present results suggest that, at least under some circumstances, pigeons may process pictorial information in a fundamental different way than humans do. First, the results of Experiment 1 showed a striking correspondence between the pattern of transfer and test results for the outdoor-experienced racing pigeons in the present study and the laboratory-reared Silver King pigeons of the previous study (Spetch et al., 1998). Not only did both sets of pigeons show poor transfer to novel views, they also showed a very high positive correlation between their accuracy on individual training and transfer images, suggesting good agreement between the two sets of pigeons on the difficulty level of each image. This is particularly interesting given the lack of correlation between pigeons and humans (in fact the correlation was slightly negative). Thus it appears that the pigeons and humans may have attended to different information in the pictures, and/or encoded the information in a different way. Additional evidence for a difference in attention or encoding by pigeons and humans comes from the landmark and background removal tests. Whereas pigeons in both the present and previous studies were disrupted by removal of either the nearby landmarks or the background, humans showed a substantial disruption for landmark removal but not for background removal.

So why were the racing pigeons in Spetch et al. (1998) able to transfer well to novel views? We suspect that the most likely reason is the large number of training views (28) used in that study. Given that recognition of objects at novel orientations is enhanced if more views are provided in training (e.g., Wasserman et al., 1996), recognition of the landmark objects in the novel views was likely facilitated by having seen the landmarks from a larger set of orientations during training. In addition, the large set of views presumably provided a much stronger basis for extraction of the spatial relationships. Finally, training with a large set would discourage any attempt to solve the task by treating each image as an independent scene and memorizing the spatial relationship between the landmarks and goal separately for each scene. Training with a large set of exemplars also enhances concept learning and transfer to novel exemplars (e.g., Cook, Wright, & Kendrick, 1990). Perhaps because adult humans have extensive experience in viewing pictures as representations of the real world, a large set of training views is not necessary to produce accurate transfer to novel views. Thus, the difference between humans and pigeons could reflect experiential factors rather than a fundamental difference between avian and human visual cognition.

In Experiment 2, pigeons showed good generalization to novel rotations of a 3-dimensional object after training with several views of the object. Nevertheless, their generalization was not perfect in that they showed a systematic decrease in accuracy for novel rotations, and particularly for the rotation that was farthest from the nearest training view. Surprisingly, in this study and in a previous one (Spetch et al., submitted), the presence of diagnostic features that distinguished the positive object from the negative objects, did not enhance the degree of transfer to novel views. Although baseline accuracy was higher when the objects contained diagnostic features (indicating that such features were noticed), the degree of viewpoint dependence (i.e., the decrement with novel views) was equivalent whether or not the objects contained diagnostic features. This result contrasts with that typically found for humans (Spetch et al., submitted; Tarr et al., 1997).

Given our argument that animals must be able to quickly and accurately recognize objects and places despite changes in their orientation, one has to wonder why orientation invariance in pigeons rarely occurs and may require specialized training procedures, such as the very large set of views used in Experiment 2 of Spetch et al. (1998). We suspect that the reason is that static pictorial stimuli are impoverished in numerous ways relative to the visual information available to pigeons in the real world. For example, in the real world, movement of the external stimuli or the viewer may play a critical role in both depth perception and object or scene recognition (see Cook & Katz, 1999). Interestingly, one of the strongest demonstrations that pigeons reacted to a pictorial display as a representation of the real world was with the use of video images, and movement was shown to be a critical determinant (Shimizu, 1998). Self movement through an environment produces motion parallax, which may provide the most salient cues to depth for defining and segregating objects. In addition, natural experiences likely provide a very large and continuous set of views of a scene or object. In fact, animals often approach and systematically explore novel objects, places or spatial relationships (e.g., Heinrich, 1995; Poucet, Chapuis, Durup, & Thinus-Blanc, 1986), and this investigatory behavior presumably provides an extensive record of what the object or place looks like from different distances or angles. Even in cases for which it would be adaptive to show accurate recognition after only a single brief exposure (e.g., recognition of a predator), movement of the object (e.g., predator) or observer may nevertheless provide quite a range of views, and other cues in addition to visual ones may contribute to the recognition. Thus, recognition of scenes or objects presented in pictures may typically be viewpoint-dependent except when several views have been experienced. Natural experience with a real world object may often provide the necessary multiple view training. Consistent with this possibility, Watanabe (1997) found rotational invariance for images of a familiar object but not for images of an unfamiliar one. Additional studies varying familiarity and viewing experiences would be beneficial.

If one accepts that static pictures provide very impoverished stimuli relative to those that may operate in the real world, then one may question the appropriateness of their use for studying cognitive processes in animals. We suggest that in most cases, the use of pictorial stimuli is nevertheless appropriate and can yield valuable information about general processes. For example, in studies of landmark use for spatial search, we have found that results obtained with pictorial stimuli on the touch screen generalize well to real environments and vice versa (e.g., see Spetch, Cheng, & Mondloch, 1992; Spetch & Wilkie, 1994; Spetch, 1995; Spetch, Cheng & MacDonald, 1996; Spetch, Cheng, MacDonald, Linkenhoker, Kelly, & Doerkson, 1997). Cognitive processes such as concept learning (e.g., Wasserman, Kiedinger, & Bhatt, 1988) are likely well tapped through the use of pictorial stimuli. Pictorial stimuli should even be useful for assessing perceptual processes in animals, provided that one does not conclude that they are tapping the limits of such perceptual abilities. Thus, static pictorial stimuli are extremely valuable tools for the study of cognitive processes in animals, but interpretations of the results should not assume that they serve as complete representations of the real world. However, recent advances in technology, such as the creation of virtual reality programs, offer promising means to enrich pictorial stimuli to provide both self-induced and object-induced motion cues. Thus, the future holds exciting possibilities for the investigation of visual perception and cognition in animals.

ACKNOWLEDGEMENTS

This research was supported by a Natural Sciences and Engineering Research Council of Canada research grant held by the first author. We thank K. Steinbring for assistance with the research, and D. Treit for comments on the manuscript.

REFERENCES

Bayne, K. A. L., & Davis, R. T. (1983). Susceptibility of rhesus monkeys (*Macaca mulatta*) to the Ponzo illusion. *Bulletin of the Psychonomic Society, 21,* 476-478.

Biederman, I. (1987). Recognition-by-components: A theory of human image understanding. *Psychological Review, 94,* 115-147.

Biederman, I., & Gerhardstein, P. C. (1993). Recognizing depth-rotated objects: Evidence and conditions for three-dimensional viewpoint invariance. *Journal of Experimental Psychology: Human Perception and Performance, 19,* 1162-1182.

Biederman, I., & Gerhardstein, P. C. (1995). Viewpoint-dependent mechanisms in visual object recognition: Reply to Tarr and Bülthoff (1995). *Journal of Experimental Psychology: Human Perception and Performance, 21,* 1506-1514.

Bradshaw, R. H., & Dawkins, M. H. (1993). Slides of conspecifics as representatives of real animals in laying hens (*Gallus domesticus*). *Behavioural Processes, 28,* 165-172.

Bülthoff, H. H., & Edelman, S. (1992). Psychophysical support for a two-dimensional view interpolation theory of object recognition. *Proceedings of the National Academy of Sciences, 89,* 60-64.

Cabe, P. A. (1976). Transfer of discrimination from solid objects to pictures by pigeons: A test of theoretical models of pictorial perception. *Perception and Psychophysics, 19,* 545-550.

Cerella, J. (1977). Absence of perspective processing in the pigeon. *Pattern Recognition, 9,* 65-68.

Cerella, J. (1980). The pigeons' analysis of pictures. *Pattern Recognition, 12,* 1-6.

Cerella, J. (1990). Pigeon pattern perception: Limits on perspective invariance. *Perception, 19,* 141-159.

Cole, P. D., & Honig, W. K. (1994). Transfer of a discrimination by pigeons (*Columbia livia*) between pictured locations and the represented environments. *Journal of Comparative Psychology, 108,* 189-198.

Cook, R. G., & Katz, J. S. (1999). Dynamic object perception by pigeons. *Journal of Experimental Psychology: Animal Behavior Processes, 25,* 194-210.

Cook, R. G., Wright, A. A., & Kendrick, D. F. (1990). Visual categorization in pigeons. In M. L. Commons, R. Herrnstein, S. M. Kosslyn, & D. B. Mumford (Eds.), *Quantitative analysis of behavior: Behavioral approaches to pattern recognition and concept formation* (pp. 187-241). Hillsdale, NJ: Lawrence Erlbaum.

Dawkins, M. S. (1996). Distance and the social recognition in hens: Implications for the use of photographs as social stimuli. *Behaviour, 133,* 663-680.

Dawkins, M. S., Guilford, T., Braithwaite, V. A., & Krebs, J. R. (1996). Discrimination and recognition of photographs of places by homing pigeons. *Behavioural Processes, 36,* 27-38.

D'Eath, R. B. (1998). Can video images imitate real stimuli in animal behaviour experiments? *Biological Review, 73,* 267-292.

Delius, J. D., & Hollard, V. D. (1995). Orientation invariant pattern recognition by pigeons (*Columba livia*) and humans (*Homo sapiens*). *Journal of Comparative Psychology, 109,* 278-290.

Edelman, S., & Bülthoff, H. H. (1992). Orientation dependence in the recognition of familiar and novel views of 3D objects. *Vision Research, 32,* 2385-2400.

Fujita, K., Blough, D. S., & Blough, P. M. (1991). Pigeons see the Ponzo illusion. *Animal Learning and Behavior, 19,* 283-293.

Fujita, K., Blough, D. S., & Blough, P. M. (1993). Effects of the inclination of context lines on perception of the Ponzo illusion by pigeons. *Animal Learning and Behavior, 21,* 29-34.

Hayward, W. G., & Tarr, M. J. (1997). Testing conditions for viewpoint invariance in object recognition. *Journal of Experimental Psychology: Human Perception and Performance, 23,* 1511-1521.

Heinrich, B. (1995). Neophilia and exploration in juvenile common ravens, *Corvus corax. Animal Behaviour, 50,* 695-704.

Hershberger, W. (1970). Attached-shadow orientation perceived as depth by chickens reared in an environment illuminated from below. *Journal of Comparative and Physiological Psychology, 73,* 407-411.

Hollard, V. D., & Delius, J. D. (1982). Rotational invariance in visual pattern recognition by pigeons and humans. *Science, 218,* 804-806.

Humphrey, G. K., & Khan, S. C. (1992). Recognizing novel views of three-dimensional objects. *Canadian Journal of Psychology, 46,* 170-190.

Jolicoeur, P., & Humphrey, G. K. (In press). Perception of rotated two-dimensional and three-dimensional objects and visual shapes. In V. Walsh & J. Kulikowski (Eds.), *Visual constancies: Why things look as they do.* Cambridge, UK: Cambridge University Press.

Kanizsa, G., Renzi, P., Conte, S., Compostela, C., & Guerani, L. (1993). Amodal completion in mouse vision. *Perception, 22,* 713-721.

Lea, S. E. G., Slater, A. M., & Ryan, C. M. E. (1996). Perception of object unity in chicks: A comparison with the human infant. *Infant Behavior and Development, 19,* 501-504.

Lechelt, D. P., & Spetch, M. L. (1997). Pigeons' use of landmarks for spatial search in a laboratory arena and in digitized images of the arena. *Learning and Motivation, 28,* 424-445.

Looney, T. A., & Cohen, P. S. (1974). Pictorial target control of schedule-induced attack in White Carneaux pigeons. *Journal of Experimental Analysis of Behavior, 21,* 571-584.

Lumsden, E. A. (1970). Implication of the equivalence of mirror-image stimuli for object constancy. *Psychonomic Science, 19,* 55-56.

Lumsden, E. A. (1977). Generalization of an operant response to photographs and drawings/silhouettes of a three-dimensional object at various orientations. *Bulletin of the Psychonomic Society, 10,* 405-407.

Lumsden, E. A., & Pullen, M. R. (1970). Object orientation as a dimension of stimulus generalization. *Psychonomic Science, 18,* 149-150.

Morgan, M. J., Fitch, M. D., Holman, J. G., & Lea, S. E. G. (1976). Pigeons learn the concept of 'A'. *Perception, 5,* 57-66.

Osada, Y., & Schiller, P. H. (1994). Can monkeys see objects under conditions of transparency and occlusion? *Investigative Ophthalmology and Visual Science*, Supplement, 35, 1664.

Poucet, B., Chapuis, N., Durup, M., & Thinus-Blanc, C. (1986). A study of exploratory behavior as an index of spatial knowledge in hamsters. *Animal Learning and Behavior, 14,* 93-100.

Regolin, L., & Vallortigara, G. (1995). Perception of partly occluded objects by young chicks. *Perception and Psychophysics, 57,* 971-976.

Reid, S., & Spetch, M. L. (1999). Perception of pictorial depth cues by pigeons. *Psychonomic Bulletin and Review, 5,* 698-704.

Ryan, C. M. E., & Lea, S. E. G. (1994). Images of conspecifics as categories to be discriminated by pigeons and chickens: Slides, video tapes, stuffed birds and live birds. *Behavioural Processes, 33,* 155-176.

Reynolds, G. S. (1961). Contrast, generalization, and the process of discrimination. *Journal of the Experimental Analysis of Behavior, 4,* 289-294.

Sekuler, A. B., Lee, J. A. J., & Shettleworth, S. J. (1996). Pigeons do not complete partly occluded figures. *Perception, 25,* 1109-1120.

Spetch, M. L. (1995). Overshadowing in landmark learning: Touch-screen studies with pigeons and humans. *Journal of Experimental Psychology: Animal Behavior Processes, 21,* 166-181.

Spetch, M. L., Cheng, K., & MacDonald, S. E. (1996). Learning the configuration of a landmark array: I. Touch-screen studies with pigeons and humans. *Journal of Comparative Psychology, 110,* 55-68.

Spetch, M. L., Cheng, K., MacDonald, S. E., Linkenhoker, B., Kelly, D., & Doerkson, S. (1997). Use of landmark configuration by pigeons and human: II. Generality across search tasks. *Journal of Comparative Psychology, 111,* 14-24.

Spetch, M. L., Cheng, K., & Mondloch, M. V. (1992). Landmark use by pigeons in a touch-screen spatial search task. *Animal Learning and Behavior, 20,* 281-292.

Spetch, M. L., Kelly, D. M., & Lechelt, D. P. (1998). Encoding of spatial information in images of an outdoor scene by pigeons and humans. *Animal Learning and Behavior, 26,* 85-102.

Spetch, M. L., Friedman, A., & Reid, S. L. (Submitted). The effect of distinctive parts on recognition of depth-rotated objects by pigeons and humans.

Spetch, M. L., & Wilkie, D. M. (1994). Pigeons' use of landmarks presented in digitized images. *Learning and Motivation, 25,* 245-275.

Shimizu, T. (1998). Conspecific recognition in pigeons (*Columba livia*) using dynamic video images. *Behaviour, 135,* 43-53.

Tarr, M. J. (1995). Rotating objects to recognize them: A case study on the role of viewpoint dependency in the recognition of three-dimensional objects. *Psychonomic Bulletin and Review, 2,* 55-82.

Tarr, M. J., & Bülthoff, H. H. (1995). Is human object recognition better described by geon structural descriptions or by multiple views? Comment on Biederman and Gerhardstein (1993). *Journal of Experimental Psychology: Human Perception and Performance, 21,* 1494-1505.

Tarr, M. J., Bülthoff, H. H., Zabinski, M., & Blanz, V. (1997). To what extent do unique parts influence recognition across changes in viewpoint? *Psychological Science, 8,* 282-289.

Tarr, M. J., & Pinker, S. (1989). Mental rotation and orientation-dependence in shape recognition. *Cognitive Science, 21,* 233-282.

Timney, B., & Keil, K. (1996). Horses are sensitive to pictorial depth cues. *Perception, 25,* 1121-1128.

Towe, A. L. (1954). A study of figural equivalence in the pigeon. *Journal of Comparative and Physiological Psychology, 47,* 283-287.

Vetter, G. H., & Hearst, E. (1968). Generalization and discrimination of shape orientation in the pigeon. *Journal of the Experimental Analysis of Behavior, 11,* 753-765.

Wasserman, E. A., Gagliardi, J. L., Cook, B. R., Kirkpatrick-Steger, K., Astley, S. L., & Biederman, I. (1996). The pigeon's recognition of drawings of depth-rotated stimuli. *Journal of Experimental Psychology: Animal Behavior Processes, 22,* 205-221.

Wasserman, E. A., Kiedinger, R. E., & Bhatt, R. S. (1988). Conceptual behavior in pigeons: Categories, subcategories and pseudocategories. *Journal of Experimental Psychology: Animal Behavior Processes, 14,* 235-246.

Watanabe, S. (1993). Object-picture equivalence in the pigeon: An analysis with natural concepts and pseudoconcept discriminations. *Behavioural Processes, 30,* 225-232.

Watanabe, S. (1997). An instance of viewpoint consistency in pigeon object recognition. *Behavioural Processes, 39,* 215-312.

Wilkie, D. M., Willson, R. J., & Kardal, S. (1989). Pigeons discriminate pictures of a geographic location. *Animal Learning and Behavior, 17,* 163-171.

Picture perception in animals
J. Fagot (Ed.)

What do birds see in moving video images?

Stephen E. G. Lea[1] and Winand H. Dittrich[1,2]

1. University of Exeter, UK
2. University of Hertfordshire, UK

Abstract

Ecological and physiological evidence suggests that motion should be very important in the vision of birds, as it is in human vision. However, because of technical difficulties, and uncertainty about the suitability of current video and computer technology for presenting moving stimuli to birds, there has been relatively little research on avian perceptual and cognitive processing of motion. The present article first reviews what we know about birds' processing of moving video images. Although the bird's eye view differs from the human view, static video images are effective stimuli for birds, and pigeons can respond to apparent motion as though it was real motion. Using video images, birds have been shown to discriminate still from moving images, between moving shapes, and between categories of movement. There is some but not complete evidence of transfer between moving video images and the real objects they represent. Movement may aid the process of feature integration, and it gives rise to some but not all of the cognitive effects that it leads to in humans – for example birds do seem to track a temporarily invisible moving object correctly, but they do not respond distinctively to causal movements. Secondly, the paper reviews some questions that are now open for research, but have not yet been properly addressed, for

Order of authorship was determined by tossing a two-pence coin.
Correspondence may be sent either to W. H. Dittrich, Psychology Department, University of Hertfordshire, Hatfield, AL10 9AB, UK (w.h.dittrich@herts.ac.uk) or S. E. G. Lea, Psychology Department, University of Exeter, Exeter, EX4 4QG, UK (s.e.g.lea@exeter.ac.uk).

example the psychophysics of video images, the relative salience of movement cues in pattern discrimination, movement after effects and the role of movement in depth perception and individual recognition. There remain some things we can never know about how birds see video stimuli, because of problems that include the impossibility of sharing the subjective experience of any other individual, or of entering into the perceptions of animals whose perceptual and cognitive processes and experience are different from our own.

Key words: Vision, motion, perception, animal cognition, video, pigeon, bird.

INTRODUCTION

For birds almost everything that is visually important moves. There are two senses in which this is true. First, it is true from an ecological or evolutionary point of view: the stimuli that any animal needs to see are mostly in motion – either because they move themselves, or because the animal itself is in motion when it perceives them: it follows that visual systems will be adapted to see moving stimuli (cf. Gibson, 1969). Predators and prey are both likely to be seen in motion, as are social partners, whether the social contact is concerned with aggression, mating, parenting, or affiliation. Movement information seems to be crucial for behavioural decisions about inter- or intraspecific companions or competitors which share the same environment. Even inanimate objects such as nest sites usually need to be perceived when the animal is moving in relation to them. Furthermore, in some cases, the functional meaning of a stimulus is determined by its movement characteristics. Most obviously, a potential predator or aggressor approaching carries a different meaning than the same stimulus backing away, but even the identification of an object can be affected by the way it moves: the classic demonstration is Lorenz and Tinbergen's hawk/duck model (Tinbergen, 1951), which was claimed to elicit avoidance responses if moved in one direction but was ignored if it moved in the other. Unsurprisingly, this case is not as simple as it seemed at first, and the effective stimulus for eliciting antipredator behaviour has since been shown in both turkeys (Schleidt, 1961) and chickens (Evans, Macedonia, &

Marler, 1993) to be characterised by a specific relation between size, shape, and speed of movement, and in addition by the social context. But the importance of these other factors does not detract from the crucial role of movement. Many other aspects of birds' behavioural adaptations also depend crucially on precise and sometimes quite subtle visual discriminations of the speed and direction of movement: obvious examples include landing from flight, pecking, catching insects, and courtship. Thus movement is critical to the biological uses of sight, in maintaining orientation while moving around, avoiding predators, catching prey, or finding a potential mate.

The second sense in which everything that is visually important moves may well be a consequence of these fundamental ecological facts. At least as far as humans are concerned (and humans are the species whose visual system we know most about), the way our visual systems actually work means that only stimuli whose retinal images move or change can be seen at all: this is a consequence of properties of fundamental structural components of the eye. At the earliest levels of visual processing, static and unchanging information is discarded, so that only information about moving or changing retinal images reaches levels of the nervous system where it is capable of triggering any response other than an adjustment of the visual system itself. Since this discarding is a result of such fundamental properties, it is likely to apply also to birds. But in mammals, at least, later stages of visual processing partly undo this most basic privileging of motion information. Through nystagmus and other mechanisms, the eyes are in constant motion, ensuring that unchanging external objects can still be seen. It remains true, however, that the photochemical and neural bases of vision give a bias towards the perception of moving stimuli, with nystagmus seemingly a complementary principle to mitigate the effects of this fundamental bias. It cannot be taken for granted that the nystagmic reflex functions in the same way for birds as for mammals, or even that it occurs at all in every species, though most birds do seem to show something like nystagmus (McKenna & Wallman, 1985). In primates, nystagmic reflexes to moving stimuli are part of a complete and relatively encapsulated visual module that serves the needs of the duplex retina. In comparison, we assume, in birds much more processing capacity seems to be dedicated to moving and changing stimuli. It follows that for birds, much more than for primates, even information about the shape and condition of the environment is unlikely to be obtained from perception of static objects; rather such "where questions" will be answered by information processes tuned to changing or moving stimuli. Therefore, the role of motion information and the question of how birds process moving images have to take into account that these processes have been shaped on one side by ecological demands and on the other side by structural (e.g., biochemical, anatomical) requirements of the bird's eye and its neural substrate.

If it is true that everything that is important in a bird's visual world moves, it follows that any response that a bird makes to its world must be based on incomplete information. Even in a static world, an organism can only form a limited impression of its environment: it only sees a limited number of the many possible views of the objects in its world. But once those objects, or the subject, start to move, the problems become many times worse: the number of trajectories they could follow, and hence the number of ways of seeing them, become infinite in a nontrivial sense. We have argued elsewhere (Dittrich & Lea, 1993) that this property of moving stimuli means that the perception of moving objects is inevitably categorical, and that if a bird is to react adaptively to moving stimuli, the limited views that the bird receives of a moving object must be integrated into "concepts". Such concepts are, of course, strictly based on the information that the organism receives from its sensory system, and their properties are open to empirical investigation. In recent years, researchers have not only asked how stimuli are perceived ("perception") and then associated with each other ("learning"), but have also increasingly asked about the properties by which these stimuli are encoded, stored, and transformed. These questions lead naturally to the realisation that we are investigating "animal cognition" (cf. Vauclair, 1996). But the investigation needs to be firmly biologically based. There is plentiful evidence that an organism's senses are adaptive structures, formed by its particular environment and evolutionary constraints. It is increasingly accepted that the same must be true of what the organism does with the sensory information it receives. It follows that we can expect to find a variety both of sensory structures and of information processing strategies in different bird groups. We therefore need to take an evolutionary-cognitive approach to birds' response to visual movement. This modern approach extends both the classical ethologists' approach, which mainly focussed on behaviour, and the earlier work on animal cognition (e.g., Köhler, 1925; Tolman, 1932), which largely ignored any fitness considerations beyond a simple belief that cognitive ability would be fitness-enhancing.

Although it is obvious that moving stimuli are important, their study in non-human subjects has lagged behind that of static stimuli, simply because they are more complicated to specify, generate, and control, especially if they are going to be presented in an ecologically valid way. Ever since good quality video recording and playback systems became cheaply available, it has been clear that they offer a potentially valuable tool for overcoming these problems, and allowing moving stimuli to take their proper place in the study of animal perception. Furthermore their potential has been radically increased by the increasing availability, and decreasing cost, of computer image-editing techniques, together with systems for random access to different video scenes. Yet there has been considerable hesitation among the research community in making use of these technical advances.

We believe that this hesitation arises because comparative psychologists, collectively, have not been sure of the answer to the question that forms our title. It is one thing to show a snatch of a videotape to an animal; it is another to know what perceptual and cognitive effects that image has. The further distant the taxa we are working with are from the primates, the more acute the possible problems are, because the further from the primates we go, the fewer assumptions we can make about the similarity between our subjects' visual systems and visual experiences and our own. Since it is likely that at least 150 million years of independent evolution separate the modern mammal and bird visual systems, there is clearly much that we should not take for granted when presenting a bird with any video display system designed for the human eye (see Meyer, 1977).

The specific technical problems arising in the use of modern video technology in animal behaviour experiments are discussed in detail by D'Eath (1998). D'Eath's important paper primarily addresses the methodological question of the extent to which video stimuli can be used as substitutes for real objects in experiments. Obviously our concerns overlap with his, but we are seeking to go beyond the question of object-image equivalence, and to see what can (and cannot) be said about birds' visual experience in the presence of video stimuli. Despite the technical difficulties, there are three distinct reasons why it would be interesting to know more about the visual effects of video displays on birds. The first is the practical question D'Eath addresses, which is perhaps of interest only to the research community: if we could establish to what extent video displays can substitute for real stimuli, we would know just when they would be a useful tool in experimental work and when they would lead to misleading results. The second is more theoretical: similarities and differences in the effects of video images on human and bird visual systems would help us understand the similarities and differences between those systems. In so doing, they would help in the grand comparative project of exploiting the natural experiment that evolution has performed for us, in producing two apparently independently evolved groups of homoio-therms, both with advanced visual systems, but with significant dif-ferences in brain anatomy. That natural experiment offers us a way of discovering whether a particular anatomy is necessary or sufficient for particular kinds of visual brain function. Third, the use of video stimuli offers one path into the more intractable question about what particular stimuli actually "look like" to animals of other species, in the present case birds. That is a question that can only be posed within the framework of a systematic study of animal cognition, and even within that framework it requires careful justification and interpretation if our discussion is not to descend into mere anthropomorphism. But brute demonstrations of ani-mals' capabilities have a way of moving the argument past apparent logi-cal stumbling blocks, and as we shall discuss below, moving stimuli are an area where some striking demonstrations have already been achieved, and others might be possible.

The rest of this paper is divided into three main sections, addressing three questions. What is there that we know already about the effects of moving video displays on birds? What is there that we do not yet know, but could find out? And what is there that we can, in principle, never know? Although the present article concentrates on birds, many of the points we discuss here are generally relevant to animal studies using video images. Certainly these same three questions need to be asked about any species when it is proposed to use video techniques in experiments.

WHAT DO WE KNOW ALREADY?

This section provides the empirical heart of our paper; here we attempt to categorise the existing literature relevant to moving image discrimina-tion by birds, and to make a preliminary assessment of it.

The bird's eye view differs from the human view

The first thing we know is that, as noted above, the anatomy and phy-siology of birds' visual systems are different from ours. What does it really mean to get a bird's eye view? Not, certainly, just seeing something from above.

For example, humans have a 180° visual field, of which 120° is binocular, so that for most of our visual field objects are viewed by both eyes at once. A pigeon, however, has a visual field of 340°, i.e., almost all the way around its head, but the fields of view of the two eyes overlap by only 20°. Not surprisingly, therefore, most studies of bird vision have concentrated on two-dimensional aspects of perception, even though stereo vision can be demonstrated in the frontal region (e.g., McFadden & Wild, 1986). Also, the anatomy of the bird's eye is very different from that of a typical mammal (Martin, 1993). Birds generally have flatter eyeballs than mammals and have severe limitations on swivelling their eyeballs as mammals can, relying on head movements instead. When a bird looks at an object outside the area of binocularity, it may compensate by turning and tilting the head, to look first from one angle, then from another. These head movements may also be used to achieve motion parallax, and also bring the important parts of the scene onto areas of its retina with high photoreceptor density. Most birds have some kind of fovea, and about half of those studied have more than one. These dense cell areas are distributed in very different places in different bird species, leading to very different orienting head movements. The potential influence of a third major difference between bird and human vision, namely, the number of different photosensitive receptors, has often been underestimated (but see Thompson, Palacios, & Varela, 1992; Bennett, Cuthill, & Norris, 1994). For example, the pigeon's spectral sensitivity covers a range from ultraviolet to the near infrared (Blough, 1957; Wortel, Wubbels, & Nuboer, 1984; Remy & Emmerton, 1989), and probably involves at least five different receptor types, as discussed in more detail below.

The second important preliminary point is that there is much variation between species of birds. There are particular variations in visual fields (Martin, 1999). Variations in visual acuity, and its dependence on light level are also wide (Martin, 1993), though arguably no wider than would be found in the mammals, even if it is unlikely that any mammal approaches the theoretical maximum of spatial acuity as closely as the falcons (e.g., Reymond, 1987). These variations have important practical implications for the questions under discussion in this paper: the same quality of video presentation will not be appropriate for all species.

These structural differences and variations do not make the study of birds' vision uninteresting to those whose primary interest is in human vision. On the contrary, a comparative approach offers an essential perspective. So long as it is based on biological principles, and not on mere botanising, it is the one approach that can enable us to understand the ecological demands on visual perception and cognition (e.g., Kamil, 1988; Delius, 1992; Dittrich, Gilbert, Green, McGregor, & Grewcock, 1993; Shettleworth, 1993). In the remainder of this section, therefore, we look at what a comparative approach has brought to the study of moving images.

Static video images are effective stimuli for birds

An important starting point is that, despite the differences between human and avian visual apparatus, static video images are relatively unproblematic. Numerous studies (e.g., Wright, Cook, Rivera, Sands, & Delius, 1988; Blough, 1992, 1993; Wasserman, Hugart, & Kirkpatrick-Steger, 1995; Spetch, 1995; Cook, Cavoto, Katz, & Cavoto, 1997; Young, Wasserman, & Dalrymple, 1997) have exploited the fact that still images presented on conventional visual display units can be effective discriminative stimuli for birds. Furthermore, in experiments such as those of Kirkpatrick-Steger, Wasserman, and Biederman (1996) and Jitsumori and Yoshihara (1997), analysis of generalisation to partial and deformed versions of still video stimuli has shown that details of the displays affect responding in lawful ways that make sense in terms of known perceptual principles.

The fact that static video images seem to function perfectly well as stimuli for pigeons is important, because it overcomes a number of possible objections to the use of videos for presenting moving images. Conventional video display units are, as has already been pointed out, designed for the human visual system. Two ways in which the avian and human visual systems are known to differ are in their mechanisms of handling colour information and in their sensitivity to flicker. The implications of these differences for perception of video displays have been discussed in detail by D'Eath (1998), and virtually all the concerns he raises are as significant for static video stimuli as for moving ones – some of them more so. So the general success of experiments using static video stimuli enables us to sidestep some of his arguments.

Consider first colour. As we have already discussed, birds' eyes contain receptor cells of more distinct kinds (in the sense of having different sensitivity spectra) than are found in humans. It does not necessarily follow that birds' colour vision is more elaborate than humans': as Brindley (1970, p. 234) explains, Stiles found it necessary to postulate five or more distinct colour mechanisms in human eyes, but this is not reflected in any detectable pentachromacy. So far we lack the basic colour psychophysics on avian colour mixture that would enable us to say how many primaries are needed to match an arbitrary colour for any bird. But we do know that the variations in spectral sensitivity are achieved by different mechanisms in birds and humans, with filters of different absorption sensitivities located in front of a single pigment in birds rather than the variation between pigments found in humans and other primates (e.g., Martin, 1993; Varela, Palacios, & Goldsmith, 1993). Typical avian colour vision seems to involve at least five different receptor types (rods, plus a minimum of four distinct classes of single cones) with a variety of oil droplets enhancing spectral tuning of the photopigments (Bowmaker, Heath, Wilkie, & Hunt 1997; Das, Wilkie, Hunt, & Bowmaker 1999). It is therefore clear that even if avian colour vision is only trichromatic, its colour mixture properties will be different from those of human colour vision, and there is indeed empirical evidence to support this conclusion (e.g., Wright & Cumming, 1971). Since video displays use trichromatic mixing tuned to human colour psychophysics, it is almost inevitable that the relation between the colours of real objects and their video images is not as accurate for birds as it is for humans. The problems of colour are exacerbated by the fact that video images make no attempt to reproduce the ultra-violet content of the light reflected from real objects. It is known that many species of birds can detect ultra-violet light, and its presence can affect colour matches (Wright, 1972). Indeed, merely filtering out ultra-violet light can distort or prevent birds' natural responses to real objects (Hunt, Cuthill, Swaddle, & Bennett, 1997), and this is likely to be a general problem since most ordinary glass and plastic windows used in experimental apparatus are likely to block some ultra-violet transmission – though it has been shown that using such a window does not necessarily prevent discrimination of live conspecifics (D'Eath & Dawkins, 1996). Given all these potential problems with colour in video displays, it is reassuring that pigeons do successfully discriminate still video stimuli. Whatever distortions of colour video presentation produces, they are not such as to render stimuli so disordered or disturbing that birds cannot extract any information at all from them.

A second issue that the success of experiments with static video images enables us to sidestep is that of flicker. Any conventional video display is subject to a refresh rate of 50-60 Hz. This is too fast to interfere with human vision: under dim viewing conditions, human critical flicker fusion frequency (CFFF) is approximately 18 Hz (e.g., Cornsweet, 1970), and even in typical photopic viewing conditions, CFFF is unlikely to be above 30 Hz. However, Hendricks (1966) claimed much higher critical frequency in experiments with pigeons, up to 77 Hz, which means that birds may well be able to perceive the periodic redrawing of a normal video display. However, as in humans thresholds were at lower frequencies for lower light intensities, and were as low as 6 Hz at the lowest intensities tested. Ginsburg and Nilsson (1971) found a similar trend in budgerigars, though the critical frequency was above 20 Hz at all the intensities they tested. These figures put potential question marks over birds' perception of conventional video tape stimuli, though when images are presented on computer monitors, which may have refresh rates of 80-140 Hz, problems are less likely. In any case, the question marks are to a great extent removed by the success of experiments on the discrimination of static video images. Some issues do remain, however. Presumably, if screen persistence is high enough, the periodic redrawing of the video image will not produce any actual flickering effect with a static stimulus, so it is not surprising if discrimination of static stimuli is not disturbed by flicker. With moving stimuli, however, excessive persistence might produce a smeared image to a bird's eye, while a low refresh rate might produce a stroboscopic effect. Experiments in which smearing or stroboscopic images were produced deliberately might help show whether normal moving video images have these effects.

Pigeons can respond to apparent motion as though it was real motion

A second important preliminary point, again not involving moving video displays as such, is the demonstration in birds of another basic phenomenon of human vision, apparent movement. If an object disappears from one position and reappears in another, humans usually see it as moving smoothly between the two. Apparent movement is frequently related to the existence of a critical clicker fusion frequency, but in humans, apparent movement can be seen when the interval between the disappearance and reappearance of the object (50-200 ms) is substantially greater than would be predicted from the critical flicker fusion frequency alone (50-60 ms). (Obviously the critical interval also depends on the distance moved, but this is irrelevant to the present argument.) All moving video displays rely on apparent movement, since the display is only renewed a limited number of times per second. Thus, if video displays are to be used with birds, it is vital to show they too respond appropriately to apparent movement. Siegel (1970) showed that pigeons could discriminate simple static shapes from the same shapes in apparent movement at speeds of between 4 and 64 Hz; the distances moved are not fully specified in Siegel's paper, but they seem to have been on the order of 2° to 30° of visual angle. Subsequently, Siegel (1971) trained pigeons to discriminate horizontal from vertical movements of a simple stimulus, and claimed perfect transfer between real and apparent movements in test trials.

Pigeons can discriminate between shapes moving on a video screen

Thus video screens as such pose no problems, and nor does the apparent motion on which all video presentations depend. We therefore turn to a consideration of moving video images as such. The first point that can be made is that birds can discriminate simple shapes when they are moved on a conventional video or computer screen. For example, Pisacreta (1982) trained birds to track shapes moving, in a staccato fashion, at various rates across a screen; although colour and form contributed most to the discrimination, movement rate affected levels of generalisation. In a rather more sophisticated investigation, Emmerton (1986) showed that when monochromatic stimuli were displayed on a fast oscilloscope screen, so that there should have been no uncontrolled problems with flicker, and colour was irrelevant, pigeons could be trained successfully to discriminate movement patterns. The patterns in themselves were complex: they were Lissajous figures, which are produced by moving a dot on an oscilloscope screen with independent sinusoidal motions in the vertical and horizontal dimensions. But the particular figures used as positive and negative stimuli were consistent from trial to trial, so Emmerton's experiment was not a category discrimination in the way that so many movement discrimination tasks necessarily are. However, category discrimination is also possible. In an unpublished experiment, Watanabe, Lea, Ryan, and Ghosh have shown very strong transfer of a discrimination between static and moving video stimuli. In a conventional successive discrimination operant task, pigeons were trained to discriminate between pictures of birds and pictures of trees presented on a computer screen. Generalisation tests at the end of the experiment showed that this was true category discrimination, since response to new kinds of trees and new kinds of birds was appropriate. Critical for our present argument, however, were tests where the original training stimuli were presented in either smooth or staccato motion: the birds showed clear generalisation of the discrimination to these new versions of the stimuli, showing that information present in the static stimuli was preserved when they were moving.

Pigeons can discriminate still from moving video images

The second point that is well established is that birds can discriminate moving from still images on video screens. This was formally demonstrated by Dittrich and Lea (1993), using a discriminated autoshaping design with pigeons. Birds readily learned to peck in the presence of moving images of conspecifics and to withhold pecks in the presence of still versions of the same images; the opposite discrimination, however, could only be demonstrated in extinction. This asymmetry of discrimination is an example of the feature-positive effect described by Jenkins and Sainsbury (1970), and it implies that movement is a "marked" feature of the visual world for pigeons. Furthermore, Dittrich and Lea reported a generalisation gradient for moving images and showed that discrimination was independent of size, perspective or viewing angle, brightness, and colour.

Birds can perform concept discriminations of moving images

Third, it is established that moving images, like still images, fall into well-defined categories for birds. Dittrich, Lea, Barrett, and Gurr (1998, Experiments 1 and 2) demonstrated that pigeons could be trained to distinguish moving images of conspecifics from one another on the basis of the movement's category membership such as pecking or walking. The different scenes in each category were not identical, and as in any "concept discrimination", it is likely that several different cues would be needed to make a reliable discrimination between the two sets (cf. Lea, 1984). A standard control procedure in concept discriminations is to use a "pseudoconcept" group, for whom the positive and negative sets cut across what, for the human experimenter, is the natural classification of the stimuli. The sets can either both lie within a single natural conceptual class, or can both include members of two different classes; Lea and Ryan (1990), called these "random" and "perverse" pseudoconcepts, respectively. Pigeons can generally learn discriminations based on random pseudoconcepts, sometimes remarkably well (e.g., Vaughan & Greene, 1984), presumably relying on rote learning. Perverse pseudoconcepts are another matter, however: if the arbitrary stimulus sets cut across a categorisation that is meaningful for the subjects as well as the experimenter, we can predict that discriminating the sets will be very difficult. Dittrich et al. (1998, Experiment 1) found that, in a discrimination between categories of movements, control birds trained in a perverse pseudoconcept task uniformly failed to discriminate. This result shows not only that the discrimination between categories in the experimental birds did not depend merely on rote learning of instances, but also that movements that belong to the same category to human eyes are also similar to one another from the pigeon's point of view.

In unpublished experiments, Lea, Domken, Ryan, and Dittrich have extended the results of Dittrich et al. (1998). Using the same discriminated autoshaping procedure as Dittrich et al., and the same stimuli as Dittrich et al. used in their Experiment 2, we successfully trained bantam hens to discriminate video images of pigeons pecking from corresponding images of pigeons walking. This result shows not just that the capacity to make discriminations between categories of movements is not confined to pigeons, but also that it is not confined to images of conspecifics, which might be supposed to have some special status. In fact, as in experiments using colour slide stimuli (Ryan & Lea, 1994), the chickens learned to discriminate pigeon stimuli rather faster than pigeons did.

Discrimination can be achieved using movement cues alone

Fourth, we know that birds can achieve discrimination between movement categories using cues that are derived from the movements themselves, and not from, say, particular static views of the object that are uniquely revealed by certain movements. Dittrich et al. (1998, Experiment 3) showed that pigeons could be trained in movement category discriminations using scenes of pecking and walking movements that were represented only by a handful of points of light, the arrangement Johansson (1973) described as a "biological motion" display; the unpublished experiment of Lea, Domken, Ryan, and Dittrich, referred to above, extended this result also to chickens. Further evidence on the same point comes from an experiment of Lea, Dittrich, Ryan, and Siemann (1998). In this experiment, we studied pigeons' response to the Michotte (1963) "launch event", in which one abstract form moves across a screen and makes contact with another which then moves off; we found that at least some birds could discriminate the absolute movement direction of the second object. In addition, we can show that such pure motion cues must play a part in discrimination even of fully-lit displays. This is shown in Dittrich et al.'s (1998) Experiment 2, where birds that had been trained to discriminate pecking and walking with fully-detailed video scenes were then tested with point-light scenes of the same movement categories. There was some transfer of the discrimination. In our unpublished experiment with chickens, we used a more sensitive test of transfer, and we were able to demonstrate generalisation both from the full-detail to the point-light stimuli, and in the reverse direction.

To what extent is there transfer between moving video images and the objects they represent?

The question everyone would like to answer, of course, is whether birds recognise the object that a moving video image is trying to represent. In some ways, this question belongs among those that can never be answered, as we shall discuss in the final section of this paper. But there are versions of it that are open to empirical test: most obviously, birds can be trained on a discrimination between video images, and tested for transfer to the corresponding real objects, or vice versa. There are as yet no experiments successfully testing transfer of learned discriminations between moving video images and real objects, and there are some well documented failures. Nonetheless, there is enough evidence for us to be sure that, for at least some stimuli and at least some birds, moving video images must contain some of the same perceptual information as the real objects they portray. A study by D'Eath and Dawkins (1996) illustrates both the negative and the positive evidence. This paper showed that when hens were exposed to either familiar and unfamiliar conspecifics behind Perspex screens, they began to feed more quickly near a familiar bird; but when the experiment was repeated with life-size colour video images, they showed no discrimination. Since Ryan (1982) and Ryan and Lea (1994) had shown that chickens were quite easily trained to discriminate between images of different unfamiliar individuals when static colour slides were used as stimuli, D'Eath and Dawkins' results suggest that there may be some particular problem with video stimuli in general, or with the display conditions used. One possible explanation is the rapid habituation to the video displays, which D'Eath and Dawkins report. It may well be that the test birds habituated to the video images so rapidly that they did not look at them for long enough for images of different individuals to acquire differential control over behaviour. This would also be consistent with the positive side of D'Eath and Dawkins' results: the hens did show discrimination between movement categories, taking longer to approach video images of hens in threat-like postures than those in normal postures. Habituation to threats is normally relatively slow. Interestingly, the authors emphasise that the hens initially showed typical response patterns which were synchronised with the content of the video images, e.g., pecking to the head region of the chickens in the images.

An alternative account of the results of D'Eath and Dawkins (1996) is that video presentation degrades some particular kind of information that hens rely on for discrimination between individuals, while information required for cruder discriminations, e.g., between movement categories, is preserved. Given the results of Ryan (1982) and Ryan and Lea (1994), we would have to assume that the information required for individual discrimination is preserved in colour slides, but this is at least plausible: the two image formation technologies are, after all, very different. Several experiments have directly tested whether instinctual responses could be elicited by video depictions of the moving stimuli that normally trigger them off. Some failures have been reported; for example, Ryan and Lea (1994) found that pigeons gave no evidence of social response to a life-size video image of a pigeon that had just been exposed to a novel conspecific. But there have been several successful demonstrations in other birds. Evans and Marler (1991) showed that a video image of a hen would have the same effect as a live hen in increasing a cockerel's production of alarm calls (though in this experiment the video image was accompanied by its sound track, which may have been critical). Similarly, Evans, Macedonia, and Marler (1993) showed that a video image of a potential aerial predator would elicit alarm calls, and that variation in the video stimuli produced sensible, correlated variations in the response. McQuoid and Galef (1993) showed that video tapes of Burmese jungle fowl (the wild form of the domestic chicken) feeding successfully elicited increased feeding in conspecifics. Adret (1997) used the same video technique to demonstrate that zebra finches responded with song to video images of birds compared to non-bird images. He confirmed that the movement characteristics of the bird images had a stimulating effect on singing. Video images of females can trigger courtship behaviour in male pigeons. In contrast, no or much shorter instinctual responses were recorded when control images (empty chamber, other bird) were presented (Shimizu, 1998). Shimizu also found that the head region compared to the body region elicited stronger responses, and that moving birds were more effective stimuli than static images of the females. An account of video problems that focusses on individual recognition can also explain another failure that has been reported: Pepperberg, Naughton, and Banta (1998), and Pepperberg, Gardiner, and Luttrell (in press) showed that two African Grey parrots failed to learn new vocalisations from a videotape of a conspecific model, though they learned successfully from live sessions with the same conspecific. Since Pepperberg has repeatedly stressed the importance of social factors in the learning of vocalisations by parrots, this result would be consistent with failure on the part of the subjects to recognise their tutor in the video display.

It is tempting to conclude, therefore, that moving video images contain enough information for discrimination of movement categories, but not enough (or the wrong information) for discrimination of individuals. Evidence against this conclusion, however, comes from a result of Watanabe, Yamashita, and Wakita (1993). They found that Bengalese finches could discriminate conspecific individuals based on visual cues from still and moving video images, but they could find no evidence for any elicitation of species-specific response patterns.

Does movement affect the processing of feature information?

More speculatively, we propose that motion information may have a feature-binding role, and that video presentation of motion is adequate for this purpose (see Dittrich & Lea, 1993). A key issue in pattern recognition is the extent to which a collection of features is analysed as if they constituted a single object. Biederman (1987) proposes a theory of pattern recognition that depends on what he calls "geons", higher in level than a simple feature like an edge or a corner, but below the level of a whole object. Kirkpatrick-Steger, Wasserman, and Biederman (1996, 1998) have successfully applied a geon-based analysis to pigeons' discrimination of static outline drawings. But there are some well known cases in which pigeons do not show any apparent integration of features; for example, Cerella (1980) reported that pigeons showed no generalisation decrement when a cartoon of the "Peanuts" character Charlie Brown was replaced with a drawing in which the features were scrambled at random. We suggest that in some situations movement may facilitate the integration of a collection of features into a geon; this would be a longer-term version of the well known rule of "common fate" in human visual perception, first discussed by the Gestalt psychologists (e.g., Wertheimer, 1923). We have already described our experiments showing that pigeons and chickens can be trained to discriminate movement categories using "biological motion" point light displays (Dittrich et al., 1998; Lea et al., unpublished data). In addition to simple discrimination, however, in both species we were able to demonstrate transfer from fully-detailed images to the point-light displays, and in the chickens at least there was evidence for transfer in the reverse direction. This implies that the birds successfully integrated the movement of the points of light so that their resemblance to the moving solid object could be perceived.

A standard experimental test of visual integration involves a stimulus in which a vertical object is shown occluded by a horizontal bar, and subsequent tests, with no occluder present, allow response either to the entire, unoccluded object, or to the separated parts that were visible to either side of the occluder. Two experiments have used this paradigm with birds, and they obtained opposite results. Sekuler, Lee, and Shettleworth (1996) reported generalisation from an occluded bar to its two elements, whereas Lea, Slater, and Ryan (1996) reported generalisation to the whole object. There were many differences between the two experiments (Sekuler et al. used a discrimination learning situation with adult pigeons, whereas Lea et al. used imprinting with recently hatched chickens), but for our present argument what matters is that in Sekuler et al.'s (1996) experiment, the occluded object was stationary, while in Lea et al.'s it was continually moving. Obviously the hypothesis that movement plays a critical role in feature integration requires more direct experimental test, but it is interesting that such different lines of evidence support it.

The cognitive consequences of moving video images

In humans, an important property of moving stimuli is that they give rise to particular cognitions. Several attempts have been made to detect corresponding cognitions in birds, using stimuli presented on video or computer screens.

A standard test of cognition in both developmental and comparative psychology involves a visual barrier: an object disappears behind some kind of screen and reappears soon afterwards. An organism that can extrapolate the object's motion trajectory behind a barrier can then recognise the emerging object as the same one that disappeared earlier, and indeed can anticipate its reappearance. Domestic chicks seem to perform this task well (Etienne, 1973) using real objects, and Pepperberg, Willner, and Gravitz (1997) have studied how the capacity emerges in a Grey parrot. Although the cognitive processes underlying this kind of recognition have not been studied extensively in birds, it can be assumed that some kind of cognitive representation of the moving image is crucial (Vauclair, 1996, chapter 3; Pepperberg et al., 1997). A series of experiments testing this hypothesis (Neiworth & Rilling, 1987; Rilling & Neiworth, 1991) provide a further demonstration of the information pigeons can extract from moving video displays. Rilling and Neiworth claimed that their results were evidence that pigeons have mental imagery: they held that pigeons transform the seen movement into a mental representation which moves continuously and thus accurately represents the location of the occluded stimulus. For our purposes, the plausibility of this claim is less important than the technique of the experiments they used to support it. Using a video screen, they presented bars that moved like a clock-hand, rotating either with constant velocity through some fixed angle, or in a way that violated constant velocity. In one task, pigeons had to discriminate between constant and changing velocity, under conditions where the bar disappeared during a delay and reappeared at a final stop location. In principle, of course, it is possible to calculate the location where the bar should reappear if it is moving at constant velocity. After successful discrimination of the bar motion with a final stop position at 3 o'clock and 6 o'clock, the birds were tested at the novel locations of 4 o'clock and 7 o'clock. Successful discrimination in the novel situation was interpreted as evidence for mental imagery. Rilling and Neiworth in fact go further and postulate that pigeons can store complex visual information in a picture-like form which is used for further transformations, forming an analogue image of the physical environment. From our present point of view, however, the issue of imagery does not matter. However the pigeons achieved their successful generalisation, they can only have done it by extracting considerable information about the bar's trajectory from the video display. In other words, the moving video image was an effective stimulus for them, and it was able to trigger behaviour appropriate to its probable time and place of reappearance.

A second characteristic cognitive consequence of movement in human vision is the perception of causality. In the light of Rilling and Neiworth's results, it can be expected that the birds would be able to use the information inherent in displays that demonstrate Michotte's launch event. In the Michotte display, an incoming square A moves towards a stationary square B; after collision square A stops moving and B moves off. To the human eye, this gives a strong impression that square A causes square B to move, but minor variations in the trajectories of the two squares (e.g., a delay between A stopping and B starting to move) can degrade this sharply. Lea et al. (1998) trained pigeons to discriminate between versions of the Michotte display that do, and do not, look causal to humans. It was found that pigeons could discriminate all the visual features that, for humans, distinguish apparently causal from apparently non-causal versions of the stimuli. But the causal versions did not constitute a category in any sense: there was no spontaneous generalisation from one causal stimulus to another, or from one non-causal stimulus to another. Here, then, we find a property that moving video stimuli have for humans that they do not, on the evidence available so far, have for birds: the capacity to give an impression of causality. Interestingly, Cheng, Spetch, and Miceli (1996) reported that pigeons seem to average duration and spatial information when they have to predict the location, at a specified time, of a stimulus moving steadily on a screen. This confirms Lea et al.'s claim that the basic operations required for causal processing are available to pigeons, and is also consistent with the results obtained by Neiworth and Rilling.

This brief survey of what we now know about birds' response to moving video images has not, perhaps, revealed many surprises. While the literature is not extensive, it is sufficient to establish that moving video images have most of the simple visual properties for birds (or at least for pigeons and chickens) that they do for humans. With that encouragement, it is worth considering what subtler visual properties of moving stimuli deserve investigation.

WHAT WE COULD KNOW (BUT DON'T YET)

Strictly speaking, "what we could know" is an infinite set. In this section of the paper, however, our aim is to identify some lines of enquiry that look, on the basis of the literature just reviewed, as though they would be profitable, and achievable given present or reasonably feasible technology. It is an attempt to forecast what we might be reviewing if we revisit the present topic in five or ten years' time. The point of this attempt is not just speculative, of course; it gives us a further opportunity to comment on the strengths and weaknesses of the literature we have just summarised. More important, it allows us to distinguish questions that can be answered from a further set of questions, discussed in the section after this one, that though fascinating turn out on inspection to be unanswerable.

How reliable are the phenomena reported so far?

The first thing we could know is whether or not the phenomena that have so far been discovered are reliable. The current literature is, in general, relatively weak. Most of the effects outlined above rest on one or two experiments, and in some cases those experiments were done with fewer subjects than is really desirable, or for other reasons are not yet conclusive. So a first desideratum would be confirming evidence for the phenomena we have already reviewed. The need is not for simple replications, but for what Sidman (1960) calls "systematic replication": testing the basic phenomena with different subjects, responses, or versions of the stimuli, to make sure that they are robust. An important aspect of systematic replication is replication by different teams of researchers, working in different laboratories, to ensure that details of laboratory practice are not leading to artefact. Of course, systematic replication is needed in all research areas, but it is a particular concern in discrimination of moving video images, for two reasons. The first reason is that, until recently, the experiments were technically very difficult, so experimenters used as few subjects as they could, and made other compromises in experimental design; for example, when presenting stimuli from video tape, it is not realistic to use a different random stimulus sequence in every session, so there is a possibility that birds solve a supposedly perceptual problem by learning the sequence of positive and negative trials. The second reason why systematic replication is particularly needed is the large number and wide range of the parameters of the stimulus displays. It is inevitable that not all relevant details will be reported in research reports, both because the researchers are psychologists not television engineers, and because we do not know in advance what aspects of a video display are important to avian observers.

The psychophysics of the video image

A second very basic thing that we need to know, and could find out, is what is the nature and quality of the video image as perceived by a bird's eye. We need answers to a whole series of questions about the accuracy with which the bird's eye separates out the different channels of information inherent in video images – form, as well as colour and motion. For example, we can ask what the range of effective wavelengths is, or what the spatial resolution the receptors can achieve. Since the pioneering work of Blough (1956, 1957), many psychophysical studies have been undertaken with different bird species, to characterise various sensory thresholds. However, these experiments have been done under, as nearly as possible, optically ideal conditions. As we have seen (and as D'Eath, 1998, explains in greater detail), video images are far from ideal; furthermore in many situations we want to study the effect of video images on relatively freely moving birds. We need to know how much information is available to a bird viewing a video image in a fairly natural way. On the specific issue of motion perception, velocity-detection thresholds of pigeons have been found to range from 4.1 to 6.1°/sec (Hodos, Smith, & Bonbright, 1975; Mulvanny, 1978). However, these values are for frontal-viewing conditions and it can be expected that under lateral viewing conditions (e.g., optic flow) threshold levels may vary, as the lateral field seems to be adapted to faster moving stimuli. A full psychophysics of the video image also undoubtedly needs to address the possible differences in the processing of images in birds' frontal and lateral visual fields. Clear threshold differences between different groups of birds depending on their ecology can also be expected. So psychophysical studies are certainly needed; but a full answer about the information that video displays deliver will only emerge if future studies address the question at different levels – physiological, behavioural, and cognitive.

The importance of motion in vision

The third question, or set of questions, that could and should be investigated relates directly to our opening arguments for the importance of
movement in vision. Just how important is movement for birds' visual
perception? As we discussed above, for humans, objects that are totally
static on the retina quickly cease to generate any visual effect. Electrophysiological experiments suggest that the cessation of visual effect of
static objects is found in amphibians (Lettvin, Maturana, McCulloch, &
Pitts, 1959; Ewert, 1987). Would it be possible to devise a behavioural
test of this phenomenon, and apply it to birds? It is not obvious how, but
the challenge is an important one. At present, we do not really know
whether movement is as vital in avian as in mammalian vision. Nor is it a
foregone conclusion that it must be. At a physiological level, visual
motion information may not be handled by the same neural structures as
static information. In primates, for example, motion is processed via the
magnocellular pathway (e.g., Mishkin, Ungerleider, & Macko, 1983;
Livingstone & Hubel, 1988), indicating that large neural resources are
made available to process information about object motion or the movements of other animals. The organisation of the pigeon's retina and visual
pathways is different from that in mammals (e.g., Shimizu & Karten,
1993; Engelage & Bischof, 1993), and there may or may not be separate
neural systems for handling moving stimuli. An answer to that question
depends on physiological research, of course, but as Skinner (1938) puts
it, the analysis of behavioural mechanisms controlling the responses to
moving stimuli offers neurophysiology "a rigorous and quantitative statement of the program before it" (p. 438). Thus, comparisons of birds'
behaviour towards static and moving video images should give an idea of
whether a separation of the same sort as is seen in mammals is plausible.
In other words, is it plausible to assume that the bird's brain is modu-
larised (e.g., form, colour, and motion) in the same way as the mammal's
brain seems to be? Can the notion of neural modularisation be successfully extended to other taxa, and if it can, are the modules the same?
There has been considerable refinement and revision of the original concept of two separate visual pathways in mammals, one dealing with form
and colour and the other with motion information, in the light of new
physiological, anatomical, and behavioural evidence (e.g., Goodale &
Milner, 1992; Shipp & Zeki 1995). But the general idea of modularity
stands firm, whereas there are still no physiological data available either

confirming or rejecting a specialised pathway or module for handling motion information in the bird's brain. Without more behavioural and cognitive information, we do not know what we should be looking for, physiologically. For example, far too little is known about either the neural and cognitive mechanisms by which a flying bird catches flying insects – quite in contrast to our thorough understanding of the corresponding mechanisms in bats.

One simple case of the importance of motion in vision should be relatively easy to test. Physiological evidence and ecological argument unite to suggest that an object moving against a static background should have greater salience than otherwise similar, static objects, and in humans it is a fact of common experience that this is true. Discrimination learning techniques are easily adapted to test which of multiple available features are the most salient (e.g., Reynolds, 1961), so it should be very easy to test whether this salience differential applies to birds.

Optic flow

Stimulation involving "optic flow" has not been considered in detail here, but this is an area where video displays could prove extremely useful to test behavioural and neural responses to the motions of the whole visual field that are normally closely linked with self-motion. There is good evidence that birds possess the neurological apparatus to respond to optic flow variations (see, e.g., Wang, Jiang, & Frost, 1993; Wylie, Linkenhoker, & Lau, 1997; Wylie, Bischof, & Frost, 1998), and some birds at least have a clear ecological need to do so (see, e.g., Lee & Reddish, 1981). Behavioural experiments to link these two lines of research are obviously called for.

After-effects of movement

The study of after-effects has been one of the ways in which simple psychophysical experiments have been able to shed light on physiological processes within the visual system. Very little has been done to study after-effects in non-human animals. However, in humans, movement generates a number of powerful after-effects, and with video displays it should in principle be easy enough to test for their existence in birds. We could, for example, train pigeons to make different responses to gratings drifting to the right or the left, and then expose them to static gratings after a prolonged period of right or left drift. From the point of view of exploring visual processing, an even more interesting possibility is the investigation of contingent after-effects, of the kind first reported by McCollough (1965). Roberts (1984) found that the simple McCollough colour-orientation contingent after-effect can be detected in pigeons, and Lea, Earle, and Ryan (in press) have replicated her result using entirely different procedures. So the general principle of contingent after-effects seems to hold in bird vision. In humans, there are some striking McCollough effects involving moving stimuli, including rotation of spirals; it should be possible to extend the techniques of Lea et al. to test whether these also exist in birds.

Movement and depth

Another ecologically important role of movement in human vision is to facilitate the perception of depth. Binocular disparity is of surprisingly limited use in giving a stereo effect in human vision, since at distances greater than six metres, interoptic disparity falls well below the threshold for detection. But movements of the subject's head or body will produce motion parallax in objects at much greater distances. Since birds are capable of much more rapid travel than humans who are unaided by machines, they need to take notice of visual depth at great distances, and are likely to be much better adapted to do so than we are. Furthermore, most birds have in any case only rather limited binocular fields of view, which are adapted for vision at close quarters. It is a reasonable guess, therefore, that at medium and long distances, motion parallax is very important in birds' visual depth discrimination, though testing this hypothesis behaviourally is likely to be a severe test of experimental ingenuity. The hypothesis is, however, supported by the long established fact that there are cells in the pigeon visual system that respond to relative motion between objects and background (e.g., Frost & Nakayama, 1983). Motion parallax is not the only possible cue to depth, of course: Lee and Reddish (1981) showed how optic flow could account for the depth discrimination required in plunge-diving birds such as the gannet.

Individual recognition

One area where it is possible but quite unproven that movement may be of importance in the vision of at least some bird species is individual recognition. Ryan and Lea (1994, Experiment 1) reported surprisingly poor results in an experiment where pigeons were trained in a concept discrimination where the categories to be discriminated were colour slides of other individual pigeons (or chickens). Chickens, on the other hand, learned the identical discriminations much more quickly. Dawkins (1995) reported that chickens could only discriminate conspecifics when they were very close to each other (less than 10 cm), and therefore assumed that chickens can only use their lower frontal visual field for social recognition. She interpreted this constraint as an adaptive characteristic, because jungle fowl tend to live in small groups. Her assumptions about individual recognition mechanisms and group living are rather arbitrary, but they do have the advantage of generating specific predictions which seem testable; furthermore, it certainly is important to bear in mind the different use of frontal and lateral visual fields in birds. However, Dawkins' assumptions would not explain the differences in performance Ryan and Lea found between pigeons and chickens. One possible explanation, which seems plausible to anyone who has kept both chickens and pigeons socially, is that pigeons are more inclined than chickens to discriminate social partners by the way they move rather than by static features. Even for humans, gait seems a powerful cue for individual recognition, and it has been claimed that familiar individuals can be recognised with no more than the gait cues given by Johansson point-light stimuli (Cutting & Kozlowski, 1977). In our laboratory, where pigeons live in aviaries, we are aware of using gait as a way of recognising individual birds. Experiments like Ryan and Lea's Experiment 1, but using video images, seem to offer an obvious way of testing this hypothesis. However, as we noted above, there is some evidence that birds do not readily discriminate images of different conspecifics on a video screen, so the experiments may not be as easy as they appear. Individual recognition is by no means the only issue of interest in the fast developing area of social cognition, of course. Other questions would be how important movement cues or parameters are in receiving specific social displays accurately. Dittrich and Lea (1994) showed that humans could infer intentionality from movement patterns: it would be interesting to see whether this relatively abstract discrimination is also possible for birds. Video images are the ideal tool to address such questions in the future.

Comparative issues

The topics we have highlighted above have been chosen out of a large pool of open questions about the way birds in general perceive moving video images. In addition, there are important questions about how such perception differs between different groups of birds, as a function of both phylogeny and ecology. Almost all current research has been carried out with pigeons or chickens. These two species differ in some useful ways: pigeons have extraordinary abilities at long-distance flight and homing, whereas chickens make relatively little use of flight. But neither is truly flightless, and neither catches prey on the wing, two adaptations that seem likely to have massive implications for visual motion perception. There are many other such adaptations. For example, there is an obvious need of more study of psittacids' behavioural responses to video movies. As already discussed, Pepperberg et al. (1998, in press) found that parrots did not learn new vocalisations from a videotape of a conspecific model; on the other hand, Pepperberg et al. (1998) report unpublished data showing interaction with video taped representations of objects. If parrots' vocal mimicry abilities rest on a general cognitive capacity, rather than being domain-specific, we could predict some interesting learning phenomena in relation to body movements based on the video-image model. Water birds, which have to see through two mediums of very different optical properties, also need to be studied: would it be possible for a video display to elicit the kinds of judgement about movement that a kingfisher or a heron must make in order to catch its prey? And if so, what would be the required viewing conditions? More generally, given the enormous variety of specific visual adaptations in birds (see, for example, Martin, 1993, 1999), it seems likely that some aspects of birds' response to video images will come to light only when additional species are exposed to such images. Furthermore, a truly comparative approach may throw additional light on some of the general questions we have posed in this section.

Summary

To sum up, therefore, what more can we hope to know about what birds see in moving video images? Two kinds of difficulties are involved in trying to answer this question, and in the past they have been confused because neither could really be overcome. The first difficulty is fundamental, and cannot be overcome: we cannot ask the birds what a video image looks like to them; we can only use their behavioural responses to guide our inferences. We return to this problem in the next and final section of the paper. In this present section, however, we have put our question into a relatively simple form, and considered what use birds, here mainly pigeons, can make of the information available from video images. We have shown that sophisticated and difficult experimental work is needed to answer even this kind of question. Whatever the experimental problems, however, this second kind of difficulty is not fundamental; it is related to the availability and costs of video/computer technology in a modern laboratory. More, better and cheaper technology is rapidly becoming available. It is therefore possible to conceive of a powerful research programme to answer questions about birds' behaviour in relation to their perception of visual movement. It is instructive to draw a parallel with the work of one of the founders of ethology, Karl von Frisch. Through careful experimentation he showed that bees had colour vision, that they used landmarks for orientation, and that their ability to discriminate shapes was well developed. Most astonishingly, bees seemed to be able to communicate some of their percepts to other hive members although the details of the bees' abilities are still a matter of debate (e.g., von Frisch, 1967; Gould, 1976; Gould, Dyer, & Towne, 1985). Thus much can be known about what another animal does with its visual input. The continuing debate associated with the topic of vision in bees is also highly instructive for our current discussion on the bird's view of video images, for example in relation to the use of ultra-violet regions of the spectrum, and the possible importance of mental images. The comparison with bees also makes the point that some technical difficulties will not go away, at least for the time being: it is reputed that the bee's critical flicker fusion frequency is around 300 Hz, so that any ideas of using virtual reality flowers to investigate bees' vision, for example, are mere fiction at present.

WHAT WE CAN NEVER KNOW

The brief list given above only scratches the surface of the research that might be done using moving video images: there is, no doubt, an infinite list of further experiments that could be attempted. But there are limits of principle on our possible knowledge. Some of the most obvious questions are, arguably, impossible to answer.

What we would all, in one sense, like to know is what a video image looks like to a bird, taking into account all the evidence we have about birds' visual physiology and psychology. If we construe the words "looks like" in a narrow sense, this question can indeed be answered: if we carry out discrimination training followed by transfer tests, we are establishing what other stimuli are functionally similar to the original image. But in a more fundamental sense we can never know whether the robin, presented with a video image of a conspecific, "sees it as" another robin. Only in fiction can we pretend to know how far a bird's visual "Umwelt" is accessible to conscious scrutiny in the same way as our own – not least because of our ignorance of the cognitive bases of our own mental images.

While this conclusion is obvious enough, it is worth briefly analysing the reasons that drive us to draw it. There are at least three problems. The first is the fundamental problem of other minds; the second is the problem of interspecific differences in sensory and cognitive apparatus; and the third is the problem of the relationship between sense organs and experience.

The first issue is the problem of private events. Nagel (1974) posed the question appositely in the title of his paper: "What is it like to be a bat?". There is a sense in which no individual human knows or can know what the world looks like even to another human, and we *a fortiori* cannot expect to leap this gulf of principle with an animal of another species. Thus the issue is not merely the indirectness of evidence about animals' percepts, but the inaccessibility in principle of such evidence. Suppose that a robin exposed to a video tape of a conspecific does indeed emit fixed action patterns that are normally elicited by another robin. Does that mean that it has seen the image as a conspecific? Surely not, unless we are also going to say that the herring gull chick, from which Tinbergen and Perdeck (1950) elicited begging responses using a red knitting needle, saw the knitting needle as its parent's bill. We know that these two stimuli elicit the same response, but if it makes any sense at all to talk about the gull chick's subjective visual experiences, it is hard to believe that such different stimuli do not elicit different experiences. But how can we know? In the case of a human, we could ask, but with other animals, is there any alternative to the sterile proscriptions of behaviourism, which would not even allow us to pose the question? As a matter of fact, however, we do not have to rely on suppositions about whether the knitting needle and the bill give rise to the same visual experiences, since in principle at least this could be tested by seeing whether different responses could be attached to them by conditioning. But how far can such a behaviouristic approach to the mind be taken? Heyes and Dickinson (1990) have sought to apply behaviouristic criteria to study the subjective components of behaviour, such as intentionality, but they fail to solve the problem of reconciling the contradictory approaches of studying animals' behaviour and asking questions about their subjective minds. Furthermore a thoroughgoing behaviourism regards people's utterances about their minds as no more than another form of behaviour, and no more privileged than the gull chick's begging responses as an indication of subjective experience.

If the problem of other minds was all we had to contend with, things would not be too bad. Most of us would be content to have as sure a knowledge of what the world looks like to a robin as we have of what it looks like a fellow-human, even if a philosopher tells us that such knowledge is not as good as we often think. Unfortunately, in the case of other species we are faced with a second set of barriers, specifically different sensory apparatus and different cognitive concepts. This poses particularly acute problems where birds' sensory resources are richer than our own, for example in the case of colour vision, discussed above: how can we even imagine what the world would look like if we had five independent colour channels? But even where birds' visual apparatus seems inferior to ours, it is not obvious that we can adopt their point of view. Can a trichromatic human really say what the world looks like to his/her dichromatic brother? This point tends to undermine some well-intentioned attempts to do more justice to the birds' view of the world. For example, Bennett et al. (1994) argue that, "... it is apparent that a research program in color cognition is necessary, for if we wish to understand evolutionary hypotheses involving color we need to understand how animals perceive colors. Color ... is a product of the brain of the animal perceiving the object." In pursuing such a programme, it is easy to forget that when we attempt to construct what an image for a bird would look like, we are simply constructing the way the world would appear to us as if our optical apparatus and visual system suddenly changed to be the same as those of the birds in question, but our visual cognitions remained those that had been formed by a lifetime of experience with the human optical apparatus and visual system.

Finally, however, even if we knew what the world looks like to a robin we would have no idea what the robin's experience of this world would be. Experiences are private events which cannot directly be shared with others. Obviously, we cannot ask a robin to describe its visual experience, we can only make inferences from its behaviour; and there is good reason from human psychology to believe that behaviour is at best an unreliable guide to a person's visual experience. Even with the most sophisticated form of behaviour we know, language, we can do only the most imperfect justice to the richness of our visual experiences, and sometimes it gets things plain wrong, for example in astronomical observation (Sheehan, 1988), in visual illusions, or in some neuropsychological conditions: for example, when the right parietal cortex is damaged in humans, a profound contralateral behavioural neglect is reported, which cannot easily be attributed to perceptual errors or biases (Parkin, 1996). If perceptual input can lead to behavioural error, we have to acknowledge that behaviour can mislead us about the accompanying perceptual experience. Our first problem, the issue of the subjectivity of experience, makes this third issue of the possible unreliability of the links between behaviour and visual experience even more delicate. To truly adopt a bird's eye view would require us to change our perspective, but we cannot know what the bird's perspective really is. How do birds see the world? At one level, the question is unanswerable, and in consequence, there are some things we can never know about what birds see in moving video images.

All these are fairly obvious and well-worn arguments. It is important to note, however, that though they are important and fundamental, they are surprisingly limited in scope so far as the empirical study of cognitive processes in birds is concerned. As we noted at the beginning of this paper, recent years have seen an explosion of interest in "animal cognition" (see Pearce, 1997; Roberts, 1998; Vauclair, 1996). A cognitive approach to animal behaviour poses several questions that behaviourism would have regarded as unanswerable. Do pigeons have concepts? If they do, what is the intention and extension of their concept of a "pecking movement"? Is a video depiction of another pigeon pecking an instance of this concept, or not? Nothing in this section has ruled that these questions are unanswerable. And from an opposite perspective, confident proscriptions like Geach's (1971, p. 17), "The life of brutes lacks so much that is integral to human life that it can only be misleading to say that they have concepts like us" now look a little quaint. On the contrary, it now seems artificial not to use the word "concept" when describing the perceptual and cognitive processes by which birds respond to complex and variable stimuli; and the previous two sections have shown that answers to questions about motion concepts are now within our reach. As D'Eath (1998) points out, a video image differs from the real object it depicts in many ways. There are the psychophysical differences we have focussed on above, and there are also "behavioural" differences – for example, the video image is often silent, and a video image of a conspecific does not respond to the subject bird's own behaviour as a real conspecific would. We may not be able to enter into a bird's experience of the video image. But we can know whether these differences between image and reality are important, and which of them are more important than others. To admit that birds have the cognitive capacity to form concepts is to acknowledge that the content of their concepts might well be different from ours, but those differences are open to empirical investigation; it is not impossible to decide to what extent the bird's concept of the object depicted corresponds to ours, or differs.

CONCLUSIONS

So there are some things that we can know. In these latter two sections, we have allowed ourselves to stray away from a narrow discussion of moving video stimuli, to a consideration of moving stimuli more generally. The reason is simple: the results cited in the first section give us considerable confidence that the conventional video display is indeed, if not a perfect tool, a highly acceptable tool for investigating birds' perception and cognition of visual movement. The first answer to the question our title poses, therefore, is a confident, "Something not exactly like, but not altogether unlike, the objects the images depict". Some of the ways in which the image is a good and bad match to the real object are discussed in the first section. Because we are interested in investigating birds' visual cognitive capacities, not just their natural responses, we reach a somewhat more optimistic conclusion about the usefulness of video images than D'Eath (1998). In the second section, therefore, we were able to assume that we could use video images as a tool to investigate many interesting questions about how birds see motion in general. Progress on these questions, however, depends crucially on avoiding getting ensnared in the unanswerable questions listed in our third section. Unfortunately, these unanswerable questions include, precisely, those that many people most spontaneously ask. But if real progress is to be made, researchers must move on from fruitless attempts to reconstruct the real colours of the real video image of conspecifics for birds. Instead, we need a research programme on birds' vision that raises empirically tractable and ecologically valid questions about sensory physiology and cognitive processing. Such investigation of the bird's view of the world may sound more modest than an attempt to see the world through a bird's eyes; but it stands a better chance of contributing to a unified understanding of vision in all animal groups.

REFERENCES

Adret, P. (1997). Discrimination of video images by zebra finches (*Taeniopygia guttata*): Direct evidence from song performance. *Journal of Comparative Psychology, 111,* 115-125.

Bennett, A. T. D., Cuthill, I., & Norris, K. J. (1994). Sexual selection and the mismeasure of color. *American Naturalist, 144,* 848-860.

Biederman, I. (1987). Recognition-by-components: A theory of human image understanding. *Psychological Review, 94,* 115-147.

Blough, D. S. (1956). Dark adaptation in the pigeon. *Journal of Comparative and Physiological Psychology, 49,* 425-430.

Blough, D. S. (1957). Spectral sensitivity in the pigeon. *Journal of the Optical Society of America, 47,* 827-833.

Blough, D. S. (1992). Effects of stimulus frequency and reinforcement variables on reaction-time. *Journal of the Experimental Analysis of Behavior, 57,* 47-50.

Blough, D. S. (1993). Reaction-time drifts identify objects of attention in pigeon visual-search. *Journal of Experimental Psychology: Animal Behavior Processes, 19,* 107-120.

Bowmaker, J. K., Heath, L. A., Wilkie, S. E., & Hunt, D. M. (1997). Visual pigments and oil droplets from six classes of photoreceptor in the retina of birds. *Vision Research, 37,* 2183-2194.

Brindley, G. S. (1970). *Physiology of the retina and the visual pathway* (2nd edn). London: Arnold.

Cerella, J. (1980). The pigeon's analysis of pictures. *Pattern Recognition, 12,* 1-6.

Cheng, K., Spetch, M. L., & Miceli, P. (1996). Averaging temporal duration and spatial position. *Journal of Experimental Psychology: Animal Behavior Processes, 22,* 175-182.

Cook, R. G., Cavoto, B. R., Katz, J. S., & Cavoto, K. K. (1997). Pigeon perception and discrimination of rapidly changing texture stimuli. *Journal of Experimental Psychology: Animal Behavior Processes, 23,* 390-400.

Cornsweet, T. N. (1970). *Visual perception.* New York: Academic Press.

Cutting, J. E., & Kozlowski, L. (1977). Recognition of friends by their walk. *Bulletin of the Psychonomic Society, 9,* 353-356.

D'Eath, R. B. (1998). Can video images imitate real stimuli in animal behaviour experiments? *Biological Reviews, 73,* 267-292.

D'Eath, R., & Dawkins, M. S. (1996). Laying hens do not discriminate between video images of conspecifics. *Animal Behaviour, 52,* 903-912.

Das, D., Wilkie, S. E., Hunt, D. M., & Bowmaker, J. K (1999). Visual pigments and oil droplets in the retina of a passerine bird, the canary *Serinus canaria*: microspectrophotometry and opsin sequences. *Vision Research* (in press).

Dawkins, M. S. (1995). How do hens view other hens? The use of lateral and binocular visual fields in social recognition. *Behaviour, 132,* 591-606.

Delius, J. D. (1992). Categorical discrimination of objects and pictures by pigeons. *Animal Learning and Behavior, 20,* 301-311.

Dittrich, W. H., Gilbert, F., Green, P., McGregor, P., & Grewcock, D. (1993). Imperfect mimicry: a pigeon's perspective. *Proceedings of the Royal Society of London, Series B,* 251, 195-200.

Dittrich, W. H., & Lea, S. E. G. (1993). Motion as a natural category for pigeons: Generalisation and a feature-positive effect. *Journal of the Experimental Analysis of Behavior, 59,* 115-129.

Dittrich, W. H., & Lea, S. E. G. (1994). Visual perception of intentional motion. *Perception, 23,* 253-268.

Dittrich, W. H., Lea, S. E. G., Barrett, J., & Gurr, P. R. (1998). Categorisation of natural movements by pigeons: Visual concept discrimination and biological motion. *Journal of the Experimental Analysis of Behaviour, 70,* 281-299.

Emmerton, J. (1986). The pigeon's discrimination of movement patterns (Lissajous figures) and contour-dependent rotational invariance. *Perception, 15,* 573-588.

Engelage, J., & Bischof, H.-J. (1993). The organization of the tectofugal pathway in birds: A comparative review. In H. P. Zeigler & H.-J. Bischof (Eds.), *Vision, brain, and behavior in birds* (pp. 137-158). Cambridge, MA: MIT Press.

Etienne, A. (1973). Searching behaviour towards a disappearing prey in the domestic chick as affected by preliminary experience. *Animal Behaviour, 21,* 749-761.

Evans, C. S., Macedonia, J. M., & Marler, P. (1993). Effects of apparent size and speed on the response of chickens (*Gallus gallus*) to computer-generated stimulations of aerial predators. *Animal Behaviour, 41,* 1-11.

Evans, C. S., & Marler, P. (1991). On the video images as social stimuli in birds: audience effects on alarm calling. *Animal Behaviour, 41,* 17-26.

Ewert, J. P. (1987). Neuroethology of releasing mechanisms: Prey-catching in toads. *Behavioral and Brain Sciences, 10,* 337-368.

Frisch, K. von (1967). *The dance language and orientation of bees.* Cambridge, MA: Belknap.

Frost, B. J., & Nakayama, K. (1983). Single visual neurons code opposing motion independent of direction. *Science, 220,* 744-745.

Geach, P. (1971). *Mental acts.* London: Routledge & Kegan Paul.

Gibson, E. J. (1969). *Principles of perceptual learning and development.* New York: Appleton-Century-Crofts.

Ginsburg, N., & Nilsson, V. (1971). Measuring flicker thresholds in the budgerigar. *Journal of the Experimental Analysis of Behavior, 15,* 189-192.

Goodale, M. A., & Milner, A. D. (1992). Separate visual pathways for perception and action. *Trends in Neurosciences, 15,* 20-25.

Gould, J. L. (1976). The dance-language controversy. *Quarterly Review of Biology, 51,* 211-244.

Gould, J. L., Dyer, F. C., & Towne, W. F. (1985). Recent progress in understanding the honey bee dance language. *Fortschritte der Zoologie, 31,* 141-161.

Hendricks, J. (1966). Flicker thresholds as determined by a modified conditioned suppression procedure. *Journal of the Experimental Analysis of Behavior, 9,* 501-506.

Heyes, C., & Dickinson, A. (1990). The intentionality of animal action. *Mind and Language, 5,* 87-104.

Hodos, W., Smith, L., & Bonbright, J. C. (1975). Detection of the velocity of movement of visual stimuli by pigeons. *Journal of the Experimental Analysis of Behavior, 25,* 143-156.

Hunt, S., Cuthill, I. C., Swaddle, J. P., & Bennett, A. T. D. (1997). Ultraviolet vision and band-colour preferences in female zebra finches. *Animal Behaviour, 54,* 1383-1392.

Jenkins, H. M., & Sainsbury, R. S. (1970). Discrimination learning with the distinctive feature on positive or negative trials. In D. I. Mostofsky (Ed.), *Attention: Contemporary theory and analysis* (pp. 239-273). New York: Appleton-Century-Crofts.

Jitsumori, M., & Yoshihara, M. (1997). Categorical discrimination of human facial expressions by pigeons: A test of the linear feature model. *Quarterly Journal of Experimental Psychology, 50B,* 253-268.

Johansson, G. (1973). Visual perception of biological motion and a model for its analysis. *Perception and Psychophysics, 14,* 201-211.

Kamil, A. C. (1988). A synthetic approach to the study of animal intelligence. In D. W. Leger (Ed.), *Nebraska Symposium on Motivation, Volume 35: Comparative perspectives in modern psychology* (pp. 257-308). Lincoln, NB: University of Nebraska Press.

Kirkpatrick-Steger, K., Wasserman, E. A., & Biederman, I. (1996). Effects of spatial rearrangement of object components on picture-recognition in pigeons. *Journal of the Experimental Analysis of Behavior, 65,* 465-475.

Kirkpatrick-Steger, K., Wasserman, E. A., & Biederman, I. (1998). Effects of geon deletion, scrambling, and movement on picture recognition in pigeons. *Journal of Experimental Psychology: Animal Behavior Processes, 24,* 34-46.

Köhler, W. (1925). *The mentality of apes.* London: Routledge & Kegan Paul.

Lea, S. E. G. (1984). In what sense do pigeons learn concepts? In H. L. Roitblat, T. G. Bever, & H. S. Terrace (Eds.), *Animal cognition* (pp. 263-276). Hillsdale, NJ: Erlbaum.

Lea, S. E. G., Dittrich, W. H., Ryan, C. M. E., & Siemann, M. (1998). Pigeons and the Michotte launch event: Discrimination, but not of causality. Paper read at the July conference of the Experimental Psychology Society, York.

Lea, S. E. G., Earle, D. C., & Ryan, C. M. E. (in press). The McCollough effect in pigeons: Tests of persistence and spatial-frequency specificity. *Behavioural Processes.*

Lea, S. E. G., & Ryan, C. M. E. (1990). Unnatural concepts and the theory of concept discrimination in birds. In M. L. Commons, R. J. Herrnstein, S. Kosslyn, & D. Mumford (Eds.), *Quantitative analyses of behavior, Vol. 8: Behavioral approaches to pattern recognition and concept formation* (pp. 165-185). Hillsdale, NJ: Erlbaum.

Lea, S. E. G., Slater, A. M., & Ryan, C. M. E. (1996). Perception of object unity in chicks: a comparison with the human infant. *Infant Behavior and Development, 19,* 501-504.

Lee, D. N., & Reddish, P. E. (1981). Plummeting gannets: a paradigm of ecological optics. *Nature, 293,* 293-294.

Lettvin, J. W., Maturana, H. R., McCulloch, W. S., & Pitts, W. H. (1959). What the frog's eye tells the frog's brain. *Proceedings of the Institute of Radio Engineers, 47,* 1940-1951.

Livingstone, M., & Hubel, D. (1988). Segregation of form, color, movement, and depth: Anatomy, physiology and perception. *Science, 240,* 740-749.

Martin, G. (1999). Optical structure and visual field in birds: their relationship with foraging behaviour and ecology. In S. N. Archer et al. (Eds.), *Adaptive mechanisms in the ecology of vision* (pp. 485-508). Kluwer: Dordrecht.

Martin, G. R. (1993). Producing the image. In H. P. Zeigler & H.-J. Bischof (Eds.), *Vision, brain, and behavior in birds* (pp. 5-24). Cambridge, MA: The MIT Press.

McCollough, C. (1965). Color adaptation of edge detectors in the human visual system. *Science, 149,* 1115-1116.

McFadden, S. A., & Wild, J. M. (1986). Binocular depth perception in the pigeon (*Columba livia*). *Journal of the Experimental Analysis of Behavior, 45,* 149-160.

McKenna, O. C., & Wallman, J. (1985). Accessory optic-system and pretectum of birds - comparisons with those of other vertebrates. *Brain Behavior and Evolution, 26,* 91-116.

McQuoid, L. M., & Galef, B. G. (1993). Social stimuli influencing feeding behaviour of Burmese fowl: a video analysis. *Animal Behaviour, 46,* 13-22.

Meyer, D. B. (1977). The avian eye and its adaptation. In F. Crescitelli (Ed.), *Handbook of sensory physiology* (vol. III, pp. 549-611). Berlin: Springer.

Michotte, A. (1963). *The perception of causality* (2nd ed.). London: Methuen.

Mishkin, M., Ungerleider, L. G., & Macko, K. A. (1983). Object vision and spatial vision: Two cortical pathways. *Trends in Neurosciences, 6,* 414-417.

Mulvanny, P. (1978). Velocity discrimination by pigeons. *Vision Research, 18,* 531-536.

Nagel, T. (1974). What is it like to be a bat? *Philosophical Review, 83,* 435-450.

Neiworth, J. J., & Rilling, M. E. (1987). A method for studying imagery in animals. *Journal of Experimental Psychology: Animal Behavior Processes, 13,* 203-214.

Parkin, A. J. (1996). *Explorations in cognitive neuropsychology.* Oxford: Blackwell.

Pearce, J. M. (1997). *Animal learning and cognition* (2nd edition). Hove: Psychology Press.

Pepperberg, I. M., Gardiner, L. I., & Luttrell, L. J. (in press). Limited contextual vocal learning in the grey parrot (*Psittacus erithacus*): The effect of interactive co-viewers on videotaped instruction. *Journal of Comparative Psychology.*

Pepperberg, I. M., Naughton, J. R., & Banta, P. A. (1998). Allospecific vocal learning by grey parrots (*Psittacus erithacus*): a failure of videotaped instruction under certain conditions. *Behavioural Processes, 42,* 139-158.

Pepperberg, I. M., Willner, M. R., & Gravitz, L. B. (1997). Development of Piagetian object permanence in a grey parrot (*Psittacus erithacus*). *Journal of Comparative Psychology, 111,* 63- 75.

Pisacreta, R. (1982). Stimulus control of the pigeon's ability to peck a moving target. *Journal of the Experimental Analysis of Behavior, 37,* 301-309.

Remy, M., & Emmerton, J. (1989). Behavioral spectral sensitivities of different retinal areas in pigeons. *Behavioural Neuroscience, 103,* 170-177.

Reymond, L. (1987). Spatial visual acuity of the falcon, *Falco berigora*: A behavioural, optical and anatomical investigation. *Vision Research, 27,* 1859-1874.

Reynolds, G. S. (1961). Attention in the pigeon. *Journal of the Experimental Analysis of Behavior, 4,* 203-208.

Rilling, M. E., & Neiworth, J. J. (1991). How animals use images. *Science Progress, 75,* 439-452.

Roberts, J. E. (1984). Pigeons experience orientation-contingent chromatic aftereffects. *Perception and Psychophysics, 36,* 309-314.

Roberts, W. (1998). *Principles of animal cognition.* Boston, MA: McGraw-Hill.

Ryan, C. M. E. (1982). Concept formation and individual recognition in the domestic chicken (*Gallus gallus*). *Behaviour Analysis Letters, 2,* 213-220.

Ryan, C. M. E., & Lea, S. E. G. (1994). Images of conspecifics as categories to be discriminated by pigeons and chickens: slides, video tapes, stuffed birds and live birds. *Behavioural Processes, 33,* 155-175.

Schleidt, W. M. (1961). Reaktionen von Truthühnern auf fliegende Raubvögel und Versuche zur Analyse ihrer AAM's. *Zeitschrift für Tierpsychologie, 18,* 534-560.

Sekuler, A. B., Lee, J. A. J., & Shettleworth, S. J. (1996). Pigeons do not complete partly occluded figures. *Perception, 25,* 1109-1120.

Sheehan, W (1988). *Planets and perception: Telescopic views and interpretations, 1609-1909.* Tempe, AZ: University of Arizona Press.

Shettleworth, S. J. (1993). Where is the comparison in comparative cognition? *Psychological Science, 4,* 179-184.

Shimizu, T. (1998). Conspecific recognition in pigeons (*Columba livia*) using dynamic video images. *Behaviour, 135,* 43-53.

Shimizu, T., & Karten, H. J. (1993). The avian visual system and the evolution of the neocortex. In H. P. Zeigler & H.-J. Bischof (Eds.), *Vision, brain, and behavior in birds* (pp. 103-114). Cambridge, MA: The MIT Press.

Shipp, S., & Zeki, S. (1995). Segregation and convergence of specialised pathways in macaque visual cortex. *Journal of Anatomy, 187,* 547-562.

Sidman, M. (1960). *Tactics of scientific research.* New York: Basic Books.

Siegel, R. K. (1970). Apparent movement detection in the pigeon. *Journal of the Experimental Analysis of Behavior, 14,* 93-97.

Siegel, R. K. (1971). Apparent movement and real movement detection in the pigeon: Stimulus generalisation. *Journal of the Experimental Analysis of Behavior, 16,* 189-192.

Skinner, B. F. (1938). *The behavior of organisms.* New York: Appleton-Century-Crofts.

Spetch, M. L. (1995). Overshadowing in landmark learning - touch-screen studies with pigeons and humans. *Journal of Experimental Psychology: Animal Behavior Processes, 21,* 166-181.

Thompson, E., Palacios, A., & Varela, F. J. (1992). Ways of coloring: Comparative color vision as a case study for cognitive science. *Behavioral and Brain Sciences, 15,* 1-74.

Tinbergen, M. (1951). *The study of instinct.* London: Oxford University Press.

Tinbergen, N., & Perdeck, A. C. (1950). On the stimulus situation releasing the begging response in the newly-hatched herring gull chick (*Larus a. argentatus Pont*). *Behaviour, 3,* 1-38.

Tolman, E. C. (1932). *Purposive behavior in animals and men.* New York: Century.

Varela, F. J., Palacios, A. G., & Goldsmith, T. H. (1993). Color vision of birds. In P. H. Zeigler & H.-J. Bischof (Eds.), *Vision, brain, and behavior in birds* (pp. 77-98). Cambridge, MA: MIT Press.

Vauclair, J. (1996). *Animal cognition.* Cambridge, MA: Harvard University Press.

Vaughan, W., & Greene, S. L. (1984). Pigeon visual memory capacity. *Journal of Experimental Psychology: Animal Behavior Processes, 10,* 256-271.

Wang, Y.-C., Jiang, S., & Frost, B. J. (1993) Visual processing in pigeon *nucleus rotundus*: Luminance, color, motion, and looming subdivisions. *Visual Neuroscience, 10,* 21-30.

Wasserman, E. A., Hugart, J. A., & Kirkpatrick-Steger, K. (1995). Pigeons show same-different conceptualization after training with complex visual stimuli. *Journal of Experimental Psychology: Animal Behavior Processes, 21,* 248-252.

Watanabe, S., Yamashita, M., & Wakita, M. (1993). Discrimination of video images of conspecific individuals in Bengalese finches. *Journal of Ethology, 11,* 67-72.

Wertheimer, M. (1923). Untersuchungen zur Lehre von der Gestalt, II. *Psychologische Forschung, 4,* 301-50.

Wortel, J. F., Wubbels, R. J., & Nuboer, J. F. (1984). Photopic spectral sensitivity of the red and the yellow field of the pigeon retina. *Vision Research, 24,* 1107-1113.

Wright, A. A. (1972). The influence of ultraviolet radiation on the pigeon's color discrimination. *Journal of the Experimental Analysis of Behavior, 17,* 325-337.

Wright, A. A., Cook, R. G., Rivera, J. J., Sands, S. F., & Delius, J. D. (1988). Concept learning by pigeons: Matching-to-sample with trial-unique video picture stimuli. *Animal Learning and Behavior, 16,* 436-444.

Wright, A. A., & Cumming, W. W. (1971). Color-naming functions for the pigeon. *Journal of the Experimental Analysis of Behavior, 15,* 7-17.

Wylie, D. R. W., Bischof, W. F., & Frost, B. J. (1998). Common reference frame for neural coding of translational and rotational optic flow. *Nature, 392,* 278-282.

Wylie, D. R. W., Linkenhoker, B., & Lau, K. L. (1997). Projections of the nucleus of the basal optic root in pigeons (*Columba livia*) revealed with biotinylated dextram amine. *Journal of Comparative Neurology, 384,* 517-536.

Young, M. E., Wasserman, E. A., & Dalrymple, R. M. (1997). Memory-based same-different conceptualization by pigeons. *Psychonomic Bulletin and Review, 4,* 552-558.

Pictorial same-different categorical learning and discrimination in pigeons

Robert G. Cook, Jeffrey S. Katz,
and Debbie M. Kelly

Tufts University, Medford, MA, USA

Abstract. Two experiments examined the range of conditions over which five pigeons previously demonstrated to have a generalized same-different concept would transfer this behavior. Using two-alternative choice task that required discrimination of odd-item Different displays, in which contrasting elements were present, from Same displays, in which all of the elements were identical, these birds were transfer tested to novel display types that were outside the stimulus range of their established discriminative behavior. Experiment 1 found evidence of positive transfer for a majority of the birds to semi-realistic gray scale pictures of objects from four categories (birds, flowers, fish, and humans). Experiment 2 found evidence of positive transfer for a majority of the pigeons to realistic gray scale and color photographs of objects from six categories (birds, flowers, cars, cats, dogs, and buildings). The results suggest these pigeons possessed a generalized rule that could be applied to novel stimuli from outside their direct experience, and add to the growing evidence that pigeons can form broadly-defined relational same-different concepts.

Key words: Pigeon discrimination learning, concept formation, picture perception.

Correspondence should be sent to Dr. Robert G. Cook, Department of Psychology, Tufts University, Medford, MA 02155, USA (e-mail: rcook1@ emerald.tufts.edu).

The twin issues of concept formation and picture perception in animals have been intimately intertwined almost from their modern inception (Herrnstein & Loveland, 1964). The most common method for studying categorization by animals, for instance, has typically employed photographs of realistic objects and scenes in various go/no-go and choice discrimination procedures. Using such tasks, it has been found that object concepts, such as those formed by pictures of trees, cars, cats, flowers, birds, mammals, fish, oak leaves, and humans, can be easily acquired by pigeons (Bhatt, Wasserman, Reynolds, & Knauss, 1988; Cerella, 1979; Cook, Wright, & Kendrick, 1990; Herrnstein, Loveland, & Cable, 1976; Herrnstein & De Villiers, 1980). This article keeps with this tradition by simultaneously investigating concept formation and picture perception in animals. Our focus is slightly different, however, in that we will be examining how pigeons transfer and respond to picture stimuli as presented and tested in a relational same-different task.

Identity and non-identity relations are among the most fundamental of psychological discriminations and at the core of many types of advanced intellectual functions and behaviors. One popular means of studying these relations has been the same-different task. In this task, the subject is required to respond *same* when all of the stimuli on a display are identical and respond *different* if one, or more, of the stimuli is different from the others. Although the same-different task has been commonly used with nonhuman primates (King, 1973; Oden, Thompson, & Premack, 1990; Premack, 1983; Robinson, 1955, 1960; Sands, Lincoln, & Wright 1982; Shyan, Wright, Cook, & Jitsumori, 1987; Thompson & Oden, 1996; Thompson, Oden, & Boysen, 1997; Wright, Cook, & Kendrick, 1989; Wright, Santiago, & Sands, 1984), its use in the study of perception and categorization in other animals has been relatively limited. In the case of pigeons, for instance, early attempts to use same-different choice procedures met with only limited success in teaching them the generalized categories of Same and Different (Edwards, Jagielo, & Zentall, 1983; Fetterman, 1991; Santiago & Wright, 1984). Such results have lead some to suggest that this type of relational concept may be beyond the intellectual faculties of this particular creature (Pearce, 1991; Premack, 1978, 1983; Wright, Santiago, Urcuioli, & Sands, 1983).

Research from our lab has recently suggested, however, that pigeons may have an unappreciated capacity for learning and using abstract

Same and Different concepts (Cook, Cavoto, & Cavoto, 1995; Cook, Katz, & Cavoto, 1997, 1998; Cook & Wixted, 1997). This raises the possibility that this integral component of intelligent behavior is more widespread in the animal kingdom than previously supposed. To better understand the processes underlying this abstract behavior in pigeons and its relation to primate conceptual behavior, two new experiments using pictorial stimuli of real objects were conducted.

The experiments grew directly out of Cook et al.'s (1997) experiments on same-different concept learning using multiple types or classes of stimulus displays. Because these experiments form the foundation for the questions explored in the current work, it is important to describe their procedures and results in some detail. Cook et al. trained pigeons to choose a *same* choice hopper when all of the stimuli on a computerized display were identical and to choose a *different* choice hopper when the component stimuli were different from one another. They used four classes of computer-generated stimuli designed to prevent simple or irrelevant perceptual features from differentiating the Same and Different displays. Examples of Same and Different displays from each of these four classes or display types are shown in Figure 1. The *texture display type* was the same as originally tested by Cook et al. (1995). The Same displays consisted of the repetition of a single element in a larger array on the computer display, while the Different displays had a contrasting odd region of elements, differing in either color or shape, randomly located within this larger array. The *feature display type* was similar to the texture displays in organization, but required the pigeons to detect a contrasting odd region based on global differences among the elements. This global discrimination was required by the addition of irrelevant local variation among either the shape or color properties of the individual elements. The *geometric display type* consisted of a 3×2 array of large colored shapes in which the contrasting difference was defined by a single element rather than a block of smaller elements as in the above two display types. The *object display type* consisted of an array of colored digitized images of natural objects (flowers and birds). Collectively, these four dissimilar display types and their component elements were used to create a very large and highly variable set of polymorphic, global contrasts in which no single direct perceptual feature, other than the categorical relation of their elements, consistently separated the Same and Different displays.

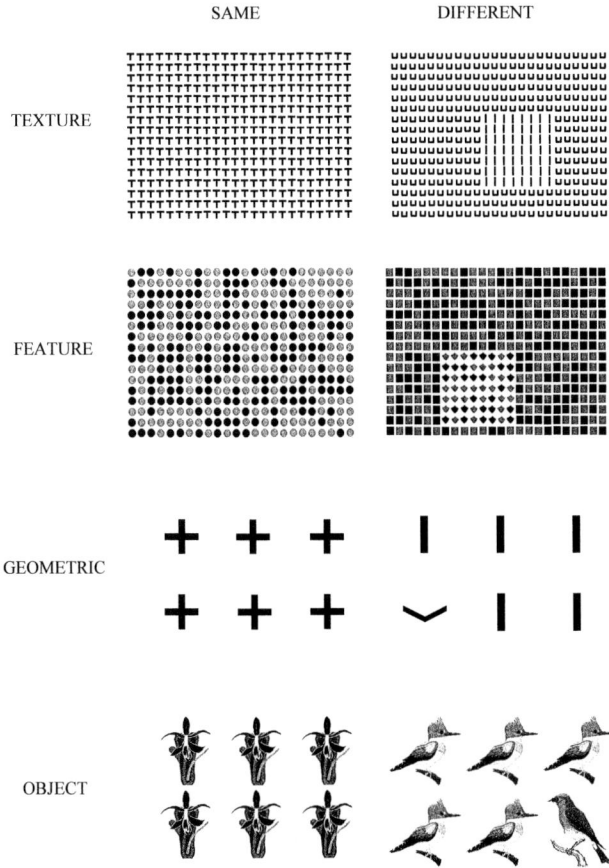

Figure 1. Representative examples of the original four display types used by Cook, Katz, and Cavoto (1997) in training the pigeons tested in these experiments.

The different gray levels in this black and white reproduction represent different colors. The left column shows examples of Same displays for each display type (the example for the feature display type depicts a shape-Same display). The right column shows examples of Different displays for each display type (the examples for the texture, feature, and geometric display types depict shape-Different displays). Note that all figures actually appeared on a black background (see examples in Figure 2). (Adapted from the *Journal of Experimental Psychology: Animal Behavior Processes, 23,* 417-433. Copyright 1997 by American Psychological Association.)

Cook et al. (1997) found that pigeons easily learned to classify the Same and Different displays created from these multidimensional stimuli. Two findings were of particular interest. First, they found that learning proceeded at the same rate for all four display types, suggesting that only a single common discrimination rule was being used with each of them. Second, they found that this Same-Different discrimination transferred to novel examples from within each stimulus class (further details and the entire set of training and test stimuli used by Cook et al. (1997) can be seen at http://www.pigeon.psy.tufts.edu/jep/). Together, these results provide some of the strongest evidence yet that pigeons can classify stimuli according to their generalized same-different relations.

One potential advantage of such conceptual representations is that they allow behavioral flexibility, permitting an animal to use old behaviors in new stimulus situations. As such, a key test of any animal's putative conceptual behavior is to establish the range or domain of conditions over which a particular concept extends. The more abstract the conceptual representation, the greater the range of the novel conditions over which it should be applicable. Like in object categorization experiments, Cook et al.'s (1997) relational categorization experiments tested novel exemplars only from within the same stimulus classes as experienced in training. If these pigeons truly possessed an abstract same-different concept, however, they should be able to transfer to novel exemplars drawn from visual stimuli that lie outside of these training classes as well.

The goal of the present experiments was to explore further the boundary conditions of the same-different conceptual behavior attained by Cook et al.'s (1997) pigeons. This was done in two different ways. The first way involved testing these same pigeons with gray scale versions of the object display type. The original study had only used colored pictures of the objects during training and testing. Subsequent cluster analyses had suggested that this color information played the major role in differentiating the identity and non-identity relations of these displays – and raised questions about exactly what was being perceived and extracted from these picture stimuli. Given this apparent reliance on color, we wondered whether these pigeons would be able to transfer to object displays in which this color information had been eliminated. The second way of examining the scope of their discrimination involved testing the animals with a completely new display type. This fifth stimulus class was created from realistic color and gray scale photographs of objects drawn from six different natural categories. These photographic displays created a visual pattern that was quite different from those created by the four stimulus classes previously experienced by the birds. Would the pigeons be able to transfer their learned discrimination to these complex and realistic pictures? If so, it would suggest that their conceptual behavior had sufficient breadth to generalize to dissimilar visual elements that were outside those used in training. As discussed later, these new experiments involving pictorial stimuli not only extend our knowledge about the conceptual behavior of animals, but in keeping with the mutualism pointed to earlier, also contribute to our understanding of what animals perceive in pictures.

EXPERIMENT 1

The first experiment examined how well the pigeons would transfer to object displays in which color information had been eliminated. Despite the semi-realistic appearance of the objects, a cluster analysis in the earlier study (Cook et al., 1997) had determined it was the dominant colors of these multidimensional displays that appeared to be the basis for their discrimination. For example, it was more difficult for the pigeons to respond *different* when a display was composed of red cardinals and a red poinsettia than when made from red cardinals and a bluebird. We were interested in knowing how exclusive this dimensional bias was and to what extent shape-related information could mediate discrimination of this class of picture stimuli. With these goals in mind, we transfer tested the birds with Same and Different displays that were gray scale renderings of the colored object stimuli (see Figure 2). This test also gave us an opportunity to examine transfer to a novel image medium not previously experienced by the pigeons.

The birds and testing procedures were the same as used by Cook et al. (1997), although the number of training elements used to create each of the display types had increased since the original report. The number of colors and shapes used to create the texture, feature, and geometric displays for each daily session had increased from eight to twelve. For the color object displays, the number of object stimuli had increased from 16 pictures representing two categories to 32 pictures representing four categories (12 birds, 12 flowers, 4 fish, and 4 humans). These new object stimuli had been included in their daily testing for at least fifty sessions prior to this experiment. Each bird was accurately making same-different judgments with all four display types at the beginning of the experiment, except in one case. One bird, Magic, although doing well with all other displays, was performing at near chance levels with geometric displays requiring a shape discrimination. This was of some concern to us because the novel gray scale object test displays used the same basic organization and similarly contained no relevant color information.

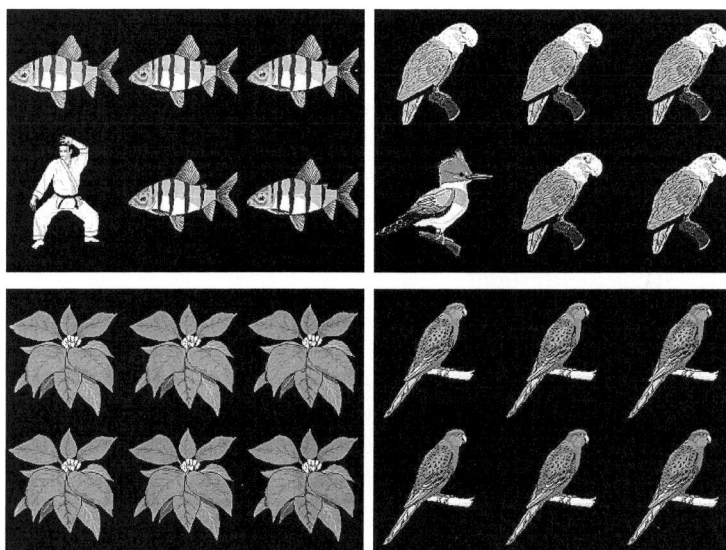

Figure 2. Two representative examples of Different and Same gray scale object displays used in testing the pigeons in Experiment 1.

Method

Animals. The same five male White Carneaux pigeons (Palmetto Pigeon Plant, Sumter, SC) were tested in the experiment as in Cook et al. (1997). They were maintained between 80% and 85% of their free-feeding weights during testing. During this period, they had free access to water and grit in their home cages, which were housed in a colony room with a 12:12 LD cycle.

Apparatus. Testing was conducted in a flat-black Plexiglas chamber (38 cm wide × 36 cm deep × 39.3 cm high). All stimuli were presented by computer on a color monitor (COMPAQ 151FS; Houston, TX) visible through a 27.5 × 21 cm viewing window in the middle of the front panel. The viewing window's bottom edge was 18 cm above the chamber floor. Mounted in this window, 2 cm in front of the color monitor, was a touchscreen (Elographics AccuTouch Model E274-SFC; Oak Ridge, TN) which was used to detect pecks to the monitor screen. A clear thin acetate sheet was placed in front of the touchscreen to protect it. A 28v houselight was located in the ceiling of the box and illuminated at all times, except when an incorrect choice was made. Identical food hoppers (Coulbourn #E14-10, Allentown, PA) were located in the center of the front panel and the right and left walls of the chamber. The side hoppers were located 3.5 cm from the front panel with their openings flush to the floor. The center hopper was not used in these experiments and was inactive. Infrared LEDs mounted 1.5 cm within each hopper were used to detect a bird's head within the opening.

Experimental events were controlled and recorded with a 486-class computer. A video card (VGA Wonder; ATI Technologies, Scarborough, Ontario) controlled the monitor in the SVGA graphics mode (800 × 600 pixels). Computer-controlled relays (Metrabyte, Taunton, MA) operated the hoppers and houselight. Stimulus and event programming were done with QuickBasic (Microsoft; Redmond, WA) with an attached graphics library (GX Graphics; Houston, TX).

Procedure

Basic display organizations. All of the baseline displays tested in the present study were based on the procedures described in Cook et al.

(1997). As such, each is only briefly outlined below and differences from that study noted. All displays were 18 × 12 cm in size, and arranged in either a *texture* or a *visual search* organization. The texture and feature displays were configured using the texture organization (see Figure 1). These consisted of 384 small elements (3 to 6 mm in size) arranged in a 24 × 16 matrix at .75 cm intervals. The Different displays for this organization contained a randomly located 8 × 7 target region within a surrounding region of distractor elements. The geometric and object displays were configured using the visual search organization. They consisted of 6 large elements (3 to 5.5 cm in size) arranged in a 3 × 2 matrix at 6 cm intervals. The Different displays in this organization contained a single target element randomly located within the surrounding set of distractor elements.

Texture displays. One hundred and forty four elements, derived from the pairwise combination of 12 different shapes and 12 different colors, were used to make the texture displays. The Same displays were made by repeating one of these 144 elements at all 384 locations in the texture array. The Different displays were made by the pairwise combination of target and distractor elements contrasting in either color or shape. All together 1584 color-Different, 1584 shape-Different, and 144 Same texture displays could be generated and tested.

Feature displays. The same 144 elements were used to create the feature displays. The Different displays of this type were made by a mixture of four elements. The selection and arrangement of these four elements were such that the global difference between the two elements forming the target and the two elements forming the distractor regions differed consistently in either their color or shape (see Cook, 1992b, & Cook et al., 1997, for more details). The local mixture of the two elements within these contrast regions was spatially randomized along the globally irrelevant dimension (color in shape relevant displays; shape in color relevant displays). The number of feature displays depends on how they are counted. Given the randomization of the component elements on each trial, the exact repetition of a feature display rarely occurred. Discounting this factor, there were 8712 color-Different, 8712 shape-Different, and 792 color-Same and 792 shape-Same feature displays of this type.

Geometric displays. The same 144 elements were used to create these displays, except that the 12 shapes were about ten times larger than in the above two display types. The Different displays were made by combining these elements so that the target element differed from the five distractors in terms of either its color or shape. The Same displays were made by repeating the identical element six times within each display. All together 1584 color-Different, 1584 shape-Different, and 144 Same geometric displays could be generated and tested.

Object displays. The baseline displays of this display type were made from semi-realistic color pictures of 32 color objects drawn from four categories: birds (12 exemplars), flowers (12), human figures (4), and fish (4). These objects were created from Corel graphics clip art and were 4.5 to 5.5 cm in size. They were presented as 256-color PCX images. Based on these 32 objects, there were 992 Different displays and 32 Same displays that could be generated and tested. The gray scale images used in the transfer test were made by modifying the above set of color objects using the gray scale operator in our graphics software (Paint Shop Pro versions 3 & 4). Some minor adjustments in the brightness and contrast of the resulting gray scale pictures were done as needed. Due to screen limitations, the gray scale pictures were restricted to 24 levels of gray.

Discrimination testing. Each trial began with a peck to the ready signal, followed by presentation of a randomly selected Same or Different display from any of the four stimulus classes. A target-directed FR (TD-FR) procedure was employed for presenting the stimulus displays. In this procedure, the pigeons were required to peck five times at the target of the Different displays in order to enter a trial's choice phase. Pecks to the distractor area of the Different displays were recorded, but not counted toward the completion of the TD-FR requirement. Because Same displays have no target area, the number of pecks required to enter the choice phase of these trials was individually yoked to prior Different trials of that display type. This ensured that an equivalent number of pecks were made to each type. The number of pecks made on individual Different trials of each display type was kept in a pushdown stack and used on the Same trials of that type as they were randomly scheduled to appear. If this stack was temporarily empty due to the chance randomization of trials, the mean number of responses from previous Different trials of that display type from earlier in the session was used. When a Same trial was the first one of a session, five pecks were required to enter the choice phase.

After completing the TD-FR requirement, the left and right choice hoppers were illuminated allowing a choice to be made. The stimulus display remained visible until a choice was made. If the correct hopper was entered, it was raised for 2 s. If the incorrect hopper was entered, the hopper lights were turned off and the overhead houselight extinguished for 15 s. An 8-s intertrial interval (ITI) followed either outcome. Daily baseline sessions prior to transfer testing consisted of 160 trials. Each of the four display types was tested 40 times (20 randomly selected Same and 20 randomly selected Different trials [10 color and 10 shape, except for object displays]). The testing order of these 160 randomly selected displays was also randomized every session.

Gray scale transfer test. This transfer test consisted of four 160-trial sessions. For each of these sessions, eight gray scale object transfer trials (4 Same/4 Different) replaced eight randomly selected baseline trials. The only constraint was that these gray scale transfer trials not appear in the first twenty trials of a session. Each session tested four separate gray scale objects (2 birds and 2 flowers), with each picture appearing once in either the role of the target or distractor on Different trials and once as a Same trial. Across sessions eight separate gray scale objects (4 birds and 4 flowers) were tested in trial-unique combinations, except for repeating each of the Same trials twice. These gray scale probe trials were conducted just like the baseline trials except that they simply ended after the bird's choice, with no reinforcement or time-out being delivered.

Integration of gray scale objects into daily testing. Twenty-six sessions after the completion of the above transfer test, 32 gray scale objects (8 familiar and 24 novel) were integrated into the birds' daily testing. These sessions still consisted of 160 trials. The 40 object trials, however, were now equally divided between 20 color (10 Same/Different) and 20 gray scale (10 Same/Different) trials. These gray scale displays were made from the same set of 32 objects as the colored displays, except for their transformation into the gray scale format. All choice responses on these gray scale trials were now reinforced in accord with the same contingencies as the other display types.

Results and discussion

During transfer testing, performance on all four baseline display types remained good (mean choice accuracy = 83.2%). On trials testing the color dimension or colored objects, mean performance was 88.3% (texture = 94.6%; feature = 88.2%; geometric = 87.5%; object = 82.7%). On trials testing the shape dimension, mean performance was 80.6% (texture = 87.2%; feature = 86.4%; geometric = 68.3%). The individual birds discriminated well overall (Astro = 81.7%; Barkley = 84.7%; Rosie = 85.7%; Judy = 80.4%; Magic = 78.7%), except for Magic's continued chance discrimination of shape geometric displays (51.5%).

The pigeons showed significant above chance transfer to the novel gray scale object displays. Mean choice accuracy across the four non-reinforced test sessions for the gray scale transfer displays was 63.8%.

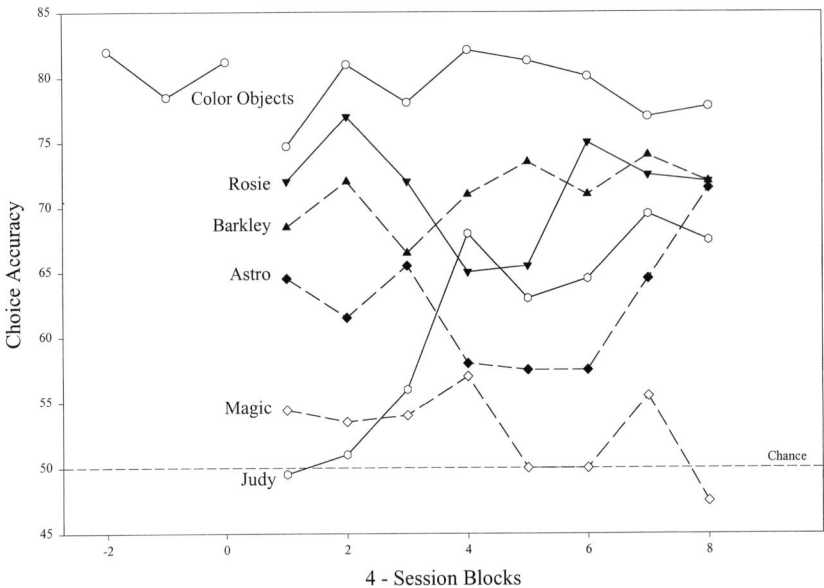

Figure 3. Mean choice accuracy for each bird with gray scale object displays upon integration into the birds' daily testing regime. Also included is mean choice accuracy for the color object displays over this testing period and the twelve prior sessions.

This latter value was significantly greater than expected by chance, $t(4)$ = 4.1, but significantly below that recorded for the baseline color object displays (82.7%), $t(4)$ = 11.4 (all statistical tests in this paper were evaluated using an alpha level of $p < .05$).

Figure 3 shows mean choice accuracy with the expanded set of gray scale object displays upon integration into daily testing. For comparison, accuracy with color objects over these sessions and the 12 sessions prior to this introduction is included. Upon the introduction of the gray scale displays there was a brief reduction in accuracy with the color object displays, but otherwise the new displays had little effect on color performance. In general, the gray scale displays were easily integrated into each bird's working repertoire, except for Magic. Three birds (Rosie, Barkley, and Astro) responded accurately with this larger set of gray scale displays upon their introduction. The fourth bird's (Judy) accuracy was low at the beginning, but improved rapidly with this type of display after 10 sessions. The fifth bird's (Magic) accuracy with this type of display was low from the beginning and never improved with testing.

This experiment revealed evidence of significant transfer to object displays constructed from shape-related information only. This was manifested in the significant above chance performance in the first transfer test and by the good transfer shown by three of the birds when the expanded set of mostly novel gray scale object displays were integrated into their daily testing. In this latter test, some individual differences among the birds emerged. Besides the three successful birds (Astro, Barkley, Rosie), the fourth bird (Judy) transferred poorly to the expanded set, but quickly improved. The fifth bird (Magic) failed to discriminate this larger set of gray scale displays despite extended testing.

The first implication of these results is that four of the five birds were capable of extracting and using shape-related information in discriminating the objects in these picture displays. Whereas the earlier study had found color information dominated when present (Cook et al., 1997), this was obviously not the entire story. Given their capacity to transfer and discriminate these gray scale object displays, some form of shape-related information was available to the birds as well. This shape information was not as salient as the color information, however, as performance with the gray scale displays was consistently and significantly lower than with the color version of the same image. This is not too surprising, color information often dominates shape information in dimensionally redundant displays across a wide variety of species. What is more important here is that this shape information was available in these object displays.

Given that color was not mediating this performance, what was it in the gray scale object displays that permitted their discrimination? Whatever the source it must have something in common with the color displays, as indicated by the transient interference in the color performance upon the introduction of the matched gray scale displays. One possibility is that the same "object" figure was recognized across the differing color and gray scale formats. These gray scale displays also potentially differed along a number of simpler dimensions, such as their brightness, total area, and perimeter. Were any of these features important in mediating the discrimination? Using a larger data set collected after these experiments (and described in the General discussion section), we examined the correlation between accuracy and the corresponding difference in physical area, brightness, perimeter, and major orientation for all possible pairwise combinations of the object pictures. These four measures were derived for the individual objects using a public domain image measurement software package (UTHSCSA Image Tool V2.0) and an in-house Visual Basic program. These measures were selected because they seemed the most salient simple features of the object displays. The correlations between these features and gray scale and color object performance for the 2256 different combinations of object pictures are listed in Table 1 (Same trials were excluded; 48 object pictures were included in the larger data set). These analyses found that total area and perimeter had significant, but very small, correlations with

Table 1
Product-moment correlations between Simple image properties and accuracy on object displays

	Area	Perimeter	Orientation	Brightness
Shape	.13**	.06**	-.03	.02
Color	.09**	.07**	-.01	.04*

Note: ** probability of < .001; * probability of < .05; $N = 2256$.

gray scale performance, and that total area, perimeter, and gray scale brightness had similar-sized and significant correlations with color performance. Nevertheless even the largest significant correlation, between gray scale accuracy and total area ($r = .13$), accounted for less than 2% of the variance in choice behavior. These weak feature-oriented correlations suggest that the image properties of the gray scale displays controlling the birds' same-different accuracy are not simple in nature.

The second implication of these transfer results is their consistency with the hypothesis that these birds used a generalized same-different concept to perform the current task. There are two caveats to this conclusion. The first is that two birds did not robustly transfer their discrimination. We reserve for the moment comments on Judy's performance until the discussion of Experiment 2, but the explanation of Magic's transfer failure is straightforward. This bird appeared only to encode color information from the visual search displays. This was true whether they were composed of objects or geometric shapes. In both cases, its performance was poor or near chance. Even after additional training not described here, this bird never improved on geometric shape or gray scale object displays. This can not be simply attributed to an inability to process shape information, as this bird did perform shape discriminations with the smaller elements of the texture displays. Further, this bird had once performed reasonably well with geometric shape displays earlier in its training (Cook et al., 1997). Why this bird could now not extract shape information from these types of displays is not clear, except to note that a larger set of stimuli was being tested. Nevertheless, this bird's persistent attention to color information or its inability to process shape information from large separated elements are likely the reasons this bird failed to transfer to the gray scale displays. Given repeated attempts to enhance this bird's performance with such displays, we eventually discontinued its testing.

The second caveat to keep in mind is that the birds already had extensive experience with shape discriminations as presented in the geometric displays. Although these shapes were abstract and looked very different from the gray scale pictures tested here, to the extent that these two forms of shape discriminations were seen as similar, the current experiment may not have been a particularly stiff test of the breadth of the birds' conceptual boundary.

EXPERIMENT 2

Experiment 2 provided a much stronger test of the potential abstractness of the pigeons' same-different rule. It involved testing for transfer
to a new class of stimuli with which the birds had no experience –
photographic pictures of real objects. For the experiment, realistic color
and gray scale photographs of objects from six different natural categories were transfer tested. This new photographic display used the same

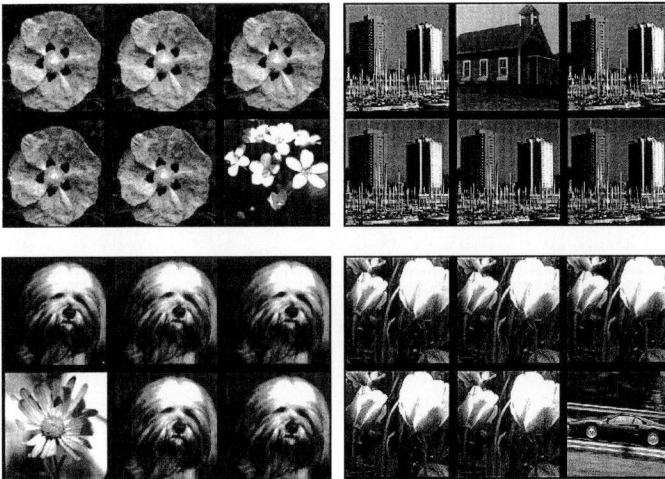

*Figure 4. Representative examples of Different photographic displays used in
testing the pigeons in Experiment 2.*
Same displays were also tested, but are not shown. These examples are further
divided by whether the displays represent a within-category or between-
category pairing of the objects portrayed in the photographs (see General
discussion).

visual search organization as the geometric and object displays (see examples in Figure 4). Two of the categories tested may have been familiar (birds and flowers) to the pigeons given their experience with object displays, but the other four were completely novel (dogs, buildings, cars, and cats).

These new photographic displays looked very different from the other four types of displays. Nevertheless, they had several interesting similarities and differences worth noting from the four classes of familiar displays. For instance, their spatially extended area caused them not to resemble the more widely separated and isolated elements of the other visual search displays. In this way, they were more like the texture displays in their fuller coverage of the computer screen. They differed from the texture displays, however, in being comprised of large multidimensional patterns with color and shape differences both within each image (and irrelevant to the Same-different choice required of the pigeons) and between adjacent images. They were similar to the object displays in that they exemplified objects from natural categories, but in a more realistic way. Unlike the object displays, however, it was necessary to parse the object figure from the surrounding background in order to identify this category membership.

Would the birds transfer their same-different discrimination to these novel and distinctive displays? If they did, it would be important because it would indicate that the generality of their same-different concept extended to visual stimuli drawn from outside the range of their training experience, and not just to those created from established display classes.

Method

Animals, apparatus, and baseline procedures. The same pigeons, except for Magic, and apparatus were used as in Experiment 1. One month prior to this experiment the number of pictures used in the daily testing of object displays was expanded to 48 color and 48 gray scale pictures (18 birds, 18 flowers, 6 fish, 6 humans) and the number of elements for the texture, feature, and geometric displays was increased to 16 colors and 18 shapes. These were added without problem. No other changes in the daily testing procedures were made.

Procedure

Photographic tests – familiar categories. This test examined transfer to novel photographic images from categories previously used with the object displays. This new photograph display type used the same 3 × 2 configuration of elements as used with the geometric and object display types. The photographs were selected from a variety of commercial image packages. Each color picture was modified to fit a 200 × 200 pixel area and presented as a 256-color PCX image. A corresponding set of gray scale pictures was also created (24 gray levels). Each picture consisted of a foreground object on a background. This foreground object occupied, on average, about 50% of the total area of the photograph as determined by the image analysis software (UTHSCSA Image Tool V2.0) mentioned previously.

The first transfer test consisted of sixteen 160-trial test sessions. Each session started with equal numbers of randomly ordered texture, feature, object, and geometric displays. Eight photograph test trials (4 Same/4 Different) were then randomly inserted into a session, with each one replacing one of the baseline trials. The only restriction was that these test trials not occur in the first twenty trials of a session.

The first four transfer sessions (1-4) tested color photographs of four birds and four flowers. Four photographs (2 birds/2 flowers) were tested in a session, with each session testing a different trial-unique combination of images. For each session, the four Same trials were created using each of the four pictures. The four Different trials consisted of novel pairwise combinations of the four photographs, with each tested once as the odd item and once as the surrounding element in a session. As such, over the first four sessions of the experiment, each Different trial was either made from novel photographs and/or novel combinations and arrangement of the photographs. Each Same trial was repeated once in either the third and fourth sessions. All test trial choices ended without consequence, and were followed immediately by an 8-s inter-trial interval. The next four transfer sessions (5-8) tested the same set of color photographs using the same procedure, but this time correct choices were reinforced to prevent the birds from extinguishing responding to this distinctive display type.

The next set of eight test sessions tested the gray scale versions of these images using the same procedure. The first four sessions (9-12) tested non-reinforced trial unique combinations (except for the need to repeat the Same displays once) of gray scale photographs and the last four sessions (13-16) tested reinforced presentations of the pictures.

A second set of transfer tests using eight novel pictures (4 birds and 4 flowers) from these familiar categories was also conducted. The first eight sessions of this second test examined only gray scale pictures using the same trial and session procedures (four sessions non-reinforced, then four sessions reinforced). This gray scale transfer test was conducted after the first novel category test described below. Later, a second set of eight sessions (first four sessions non-reinforced/second four sessions reinforced) testing the color photographs of these same birds and flowers was conducted. This color transfer test was done after the last novel category test described below.

Photographic tests – novel categories. These tests examined transfer to novel photographic images from categories not previously tested. Two sets of tests were conducted. The first tested for transfer to novel pictures of dogs and buildings and the second tested novel pictures of cars and cats.

The first of these tests simultaneously used novel color and gray scale pictures of four dogs and four buildings, and were again arranged to make as many trial-unique combinations as possible. It lasted eight sessions. Eight photograph test trials (4 Different [2 color and 2 gray scale]/4 Same [2 color and 2 gray scale]) randomly replaced baseline trials within a standard 160-trial session. Choices on test trials were not reinforced in any of these sessions.

The second test used novel gray scale and colored photographs of four cars and four cats. It consisted of sixteen 160-trial sessions. Each session again tested eight photograph test trials (4 Same/4 Different) using the same procedures as described above. The first four sessions (1-4) tested non-reinforced presentations of the gray scale Same and Different trials of these photographic stimuli and the next four sessions (5-8) tested reinforced presentations of these pictures. The next set of eight sessions tested the color photographs of these same four cats and four cars. The first four sessions (9-12) involved non-reinforced presentations of the color test trials, while the last four sessions (13-16) tested reinforced presentations of the photographs.

Integration of the photographic display type. Following the completion of these novel transfer tests, the photographic display type was integrated into the birds' daily testing. Each of these sessions still consisted of 160 trials, but the numbers of texture, feature, object, and geometric trials were reduced from 40 to 32 per session. The remaining 32 trials (16 color [8 Same/8 Different] and 16 gray scale [8 Same/8 Different]) were randomly generated from color and gray scale photographs of four birds, four flowers, four cars, and four cats selected from the above transfer tests.

For Astro, Rosie, and Barkley this period of testing lasted 32 sessions. After these 32 sessions, Judy was still not accurately performing with the photographic display type. This bird was then moved to another identical chamber and daily testing continued except for one change. This consisted of using a correction procedure used exclusively for trials testing photographs (each such trial being repeated until correct). Every third session was conducted without this correction procedure. Judy was tested for 72 additional sessions using this photographic-only correction procedure. Twenty sessions later, a transfer test using 8 novel photographic stimuli (4 birds and 4 flowers) was conducted using the same design as employed for the first familiar category test described above.

Results

Baseline performance. The addition of the photographic displays had no influence on the established same-different discriminations. Mean performance with non-photographic baseline displays across all transfer sessions was 83.7%. For trials testing the color dimension or colored objects, mean performance was 88% (texture = 93.1%; feature = 87%; geometric = 86.8%; object = 85.2%). For trials testing the shape dimension or gray scale objects, mean performance was 79.4% (texture = 86.5%; feature = 82.3%; geometric = 75.3; object = 73.3%).

Photographic transfer test performance. The overall results from the photograph transfer tests are rather easily summarized. Three of the birds (Barkley, Rosie, and Astro) showed consistently and significantly above chance transfer to the photographic stimuli (mean all tests = 69.1%), while the fourth bird (Judy) did not (53.1%). The top panel of Figure 5 shows the mean choice accuracy for the three successful birds on color (black bars) and gray scale (gray bars) trials for each of the four separate category transfer tests. For these birds, discrimination transfer to color photographs (73.8%) was significantly better than to gray scale photographs (64.5%). The bottom four panels show transfer performance for each individual bird. The first three panels show the three successful birds, while the panel in the lower right shows the data for the unsuccessful fourth bird (Judy). As can be seen, this latter bird performed poorly with the photographic images in all four tests.

Familiar categories. Because there was little difference between the two transfer tests using bird and flower photographs, these results were combined for the purposes of analysis. Barkley and Rosie overall showed excellent transfer to the photographic displays, Astro's transfer was slightly more modest, and Judy's was poor. When compared to the critical binomial value, each individual bird's accuracy for each transfer test was significantly greater than the chance expectation (50%), except for Judy's performance on both colored photographs tests and the first gray scale transfer test. Mean accuracy for the successful three birds was 74.8% for color and 68.3% for gray scale photographs in both tests (Judy's data were excluded from the following analyses). A three-way repeated measures ANOVA (dimension × reinforcement × test) comparing choice accuracy between gray scale and color photographs across the reinforced and non-reinforced phases of the two transfer tests revealed a significant difference between color and gray scale accuracy, $F(1, 2) = 558.7$, but no effect of reinforcement (non-reinforced = 71.7%, reinforced = 71.4%), or other higher order interactions. Further evidence that the absence and then presence of reinforcement had no effect on transfer performance comes from looking at transfer accuracy during just the first session with any new set of photographs. It was not remarkably different from that seen across all of the transfer sessions (Astro = 71.8%; Barkley = 68.7%; Rosie = 71.8%).

Novel categories. For the two transfer tests using novel pictures of buildings, dogs, cars, and cats, Barkley and Rosie continued to show very good transfer, Astro's transfer was again more modest, and Judy continued to do poorly. When compared to the critical binomial value, each individual bird's accuracy for each transfer test was significantly greater than the chance expectation, except for Judy's performance in every test, and Astro's and Rosie's performance with the gray scale pictures of dogs and buildings.

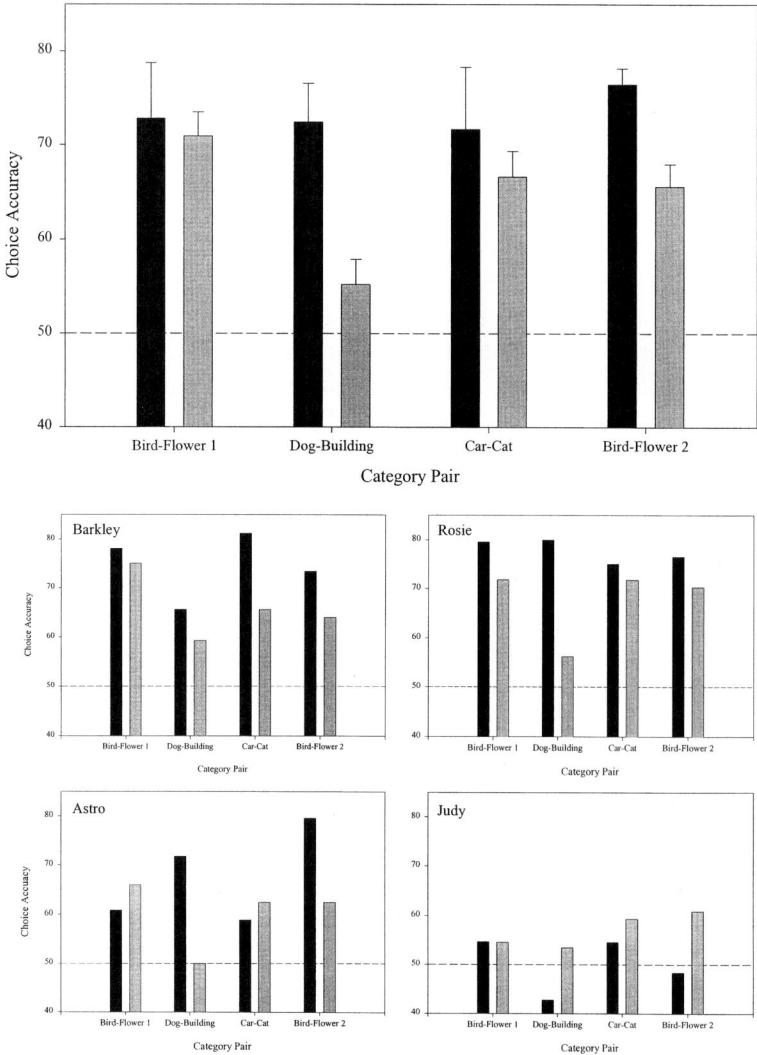

Figure 5. Mean choice accuracy with novel color (black bars) and gray scale (gray bars) photographic displays during the four category transfer tests of Experiment 2.
The top panel shows mean accuracy for all birds, except for Judy. The bottom four panels show accuracy for the same test conditions for the individual birds. The dotted reference line in each panel depicts chance performance in this task.

Mean accuracy for the successful three birds over these novel category tests was 72.4% for the color and 61% for the gray scale transfer tests (again Judy's data were not included in the analyses below). A three-way repeated measures ANOVA (dimension × reinforcement × test) comparing choice accuracy between gray scale and colored pictures in the reinforced and non-reinforced phases of the two tests again revealed a significant difference between color and gray scale accuracy, $F(1, 2) = 33.7$, but no significant effect of reinforcement (non-reinforced = 66.9%, reinforced = 66.1%), or other higher order interactions. Mean transfer accuracy during just the first session with each new set of images was not markedly different from that recorded over all of the transfer sessions (Astro = 66.2%; Barkley = 75.5%; Rosie = 75%).

Integration of the photographic display type. Figure 6 shows mean accuracy with the photographic displays (color and gray scale trials combined) after their integration into daily testing for the four individual birds. For the three birds that transferred in the above tests, integration of the photographic display type was swift. Each began at a level of accuracy highly characteristic of their earlier transfer data and then improved over the next 10 to 20 sessions. Figure 6 also shows that the bird showing the poorest transfer, Judy, eventually learned to perform accurately with the photographic displays. But unlike the other birds, its acquisition was slow and only really began upon the introduction of the correction procedure (block 9; Figure 6 shows only the data from sessions in which the photographic-only correction procedure was not used). The results of the subsequent transfer test conducted with Judy after learning to discriminate photographs showed significant transfer to both novel color (67.5%) and gray scale (67.5%) photographs of birds and flowers.

Discussion

This experiment revealed a pattern of excellent to good same-different transfer to a novel stimulus class in three of the four pigeons. Novel color photographs overall supported better transfer and performance than did matching gray scale photographs, as this additional dimensional information again helped the discrimination. This positive transfer to a novel and perceptually distinct display type strengthens the hypothesis that at least a majority of these birds were employing an abstract same-different concept. It documents for the first time transfer to novel exemplars from outside the stimulus range of their established discriminative behavior. As such, these results continue to build the scientific case that these non-primates may be truly capable of abstract conceptual behavior.

One should not ignore the exception to this important conclusion represented by the results of the fourth bird, Judy. This bird showed little capacity to deal with the novel photographic displays. It performed poorly on all of the initial transfer tests and upon the introduction of the photographs into daily testing. Judy's approach to this complex visual discrimination was clearly different in some fundamental way from the apparently conceptual approach of the other birds. Interestingly, Judy did eventually learn to discriminate and transfer to novel photographic stimuli, but only with extended training. These difficulties, combined with the similar pattern of behavior with gray scale object displays in

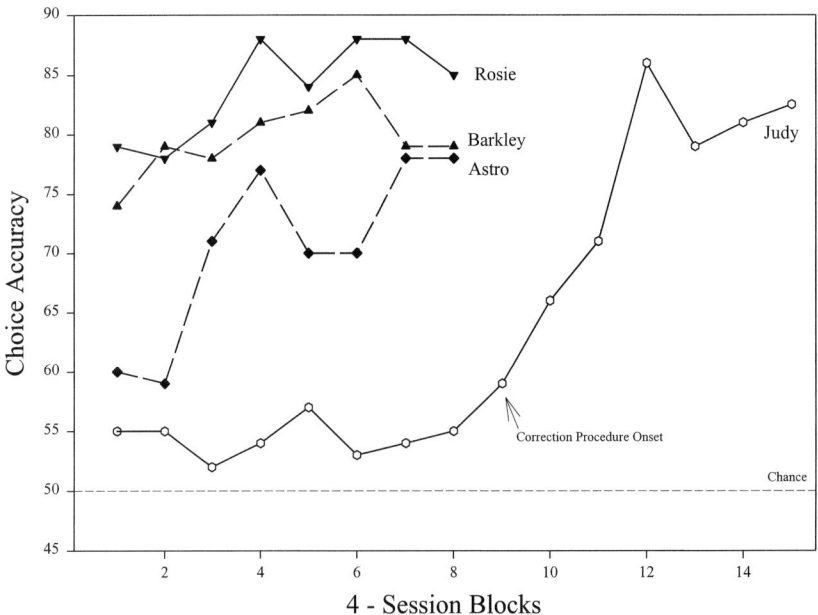

Figure 6. Mean choice accuracy for each bird with photographic stimuli upon their integration into the birds' daily testing regime.

Experiment 1, indicate that this bird's discriminative rule did not flexibly accommodate novel display types. While the bird's rule was applicable to novel stimuli created from within the familiar stimulus classes (the last transfer test, Cook et al., 1997), and hence abstract in one sense, this behavior seems restricted to only previously experienced classes. Nevertheless, with experience, this bird did eventually learn to discriminate large numbers of these new photographic stimuli. This combination of stimulus specificity and discriminative elasticity forms an interesting paradox. How can this bird perform so well with such a large quantity of displays, with very different stimuli, and contrasting organizations, yet still not be able to readily transfer to stimuli from outside the range of training? Past research has generally found that increasing the number of training exemplars is a key factor in determining the degree of transfer shown by pigeons (Kendrick, Wright, & Cook, 1990; Wright, Cook, Rivera, Sands, & Delius, 1988; Wasserman & Bhatt, 1992).

This transfer failure is likely not due to any form of sensory deficit, since this bird did eventually learn to perform the photographic discriminations. Given how long it took this bird to acquire the photographic discrimination, it is also difficult to attribute its transfer failure to simple neophobia. In fact, it looks as if the acquisition of the photographic discrimination was essentially an entirely new habit, showing no savings whatsoever in comparison to the time taken to learn the original discrimination with four display types ($\approx$ 50 sessions; Cook et al., 1997). One possibility is that this bird had learned a number of highly stimulus-specific rules. This is the most common explanation for failures of transfer found in less complex conditional discriminations (e.g., Carter & Werner, 1978; Holmes, 1979; Wright et al., 1988). We think this is unlikely, however, because it would require memorizing responses to an extraordinarily large number of very infrequently presented displays.

Another possibility is that this bird tried to take advantage of the asymmetrical number of possible Same and Different displays by learning some form of default rule (cf. Grant 1991; Sherburne & Zentall, 1993; Wixted, 1993). Given the relative proportion of Same and Different displays, the most efficient and logical default rule would be "go to one choice hopper for highly familiar displays (i.e., Same displays), else go to the other choice hopper". Given such a rule, it fails to explain why this bird, and indeed most birds, showed a strong empirical tendency to respond *same* to novel displays (cf. Cook et al., 1995, and Cook & Wixted, 1997, for other evidence against such a default account).

Finally, it is possible that this bird learned a variant of a same-different decision rule, but one strictly applied to display types with a familiar look and feel. This account has the appeal of providing for the trial-to-trial flexibility needed to respond to the large number of displays, while accounting for the within-class, but not between-class, transfer observed with this particular animal. If display type familiarity were the only limiting factor, however, it does seem to us that the photographic displays should have been accommodated more quickly and without needing to resort to a correction procedure.

One strength of the long-term psychophysical character of the current research approach is that it permits the identification of strategic differences (i.e., patterns of consistent responding) among subjects. As annoying as these individual differences are to our abstract theoretical structures, they clearly occur even in pigeons. Whatever Judy's strategy, it did not involve a very broadly defined same-different rule. But in the exception that proves the generalized rule, this bird's consistent failure with photographic stimuli does provide a critical piece of evidence. In particular, it documents that these photographic stimuli were indeed distinct and discriminable from the other four display types, and therefore suitable for verifying the breadth of the remaining birds' conceptual behavior.

GENERAL DISCUSSION

Same-different conceptual behavior in birds

These experiments revealed strong evidence in the majority of the pigeons for same-different concept transfer to two novel types of pictorial stimuli. In Experiment 1, four pigeons readily transferred to novel semi-realistic gray scale renderings of natural objects. In Experiment 2, three pigeons readily transferred to both novel realistic color and gray scale photographs of natural objects. These results are important because they broaden the range of stimulus conditions over which these birds have shown evidence of using an abstract concept. In particular, they show that exemplars drawn from outside of the stimulus domain used for training are also capable of supporting discrimination transfer. It is especially critical to have established this because the recent demonstrations of pigeon same-different conceptual behavior have tested only novel exemplars from within the same class of stimuli as experienced during training (Cook et al., 1995, 1997; Young, Wasserman, & Dalrymple, 1997; Wasserman, Hugart, & Kirkpatrick-Steger, 1995). These new results are a significant step forward in making the case that birds, like primates, are capable of forming and using generalized rules for categorizing stimulus identity and non-identity.

It is important to consider alternatives to such an account, however. Besides classifying same-different relations among component stimulus elements, are there other highly correlated perceptual features in these displays that might more directly and simply account for the discriminative behavior observed in these studies? One frequently suggested alternative is that the pigeons have simply learned to respond to the presence and absence of global spatial discontinuities in the displays. That is, the birds have learned a feature-based approach in which they can detect generalized differences in the spatial patterns or regularities of these displays that are independent of the organization (texture versus visual search), stimulus class (texture, feature, geometric, object, photographic), and specific identity of the stimuli. Some of our earlier research looking at texture perception in pigeons would indicate that they have necessary mechanisms for detecting such a global feature, at least for highly discriminable displays (Cook, 1992a, 1992b, 1993b).

We believe several results argue against this type of account in the present setting. First, the pigeons consistently show a decrement in performance during each transfer in comparison to baseline levels of accuracy (Experiment 1 & 2, Cook, et al., 1997). If a global perceptually-based abstraction of the displays was the key feature, then the specific identity of the individual stimuli shouldn't matter during transfer since the global arrangement remains exactly the same. Further, we have collected evidence that the specific objects or patterns depicted in the object and photographic displays also directly influence accuracy (see the next section on within- versus between-category effects). Thus, the specific identity of the highly variable local components making up these displays is available and used by the pigeons in performing the task. Besides the importance of such local factors, we have found that the specific global organization of the displays as tested here is also not critical to successfully performing the task. Cook et al. (1997) found that these same birds could still perform the task even when the number of individual geometric elements or objects making up the displays was reduced to 3 or 4 items and arranged in different ways. Finally, we have

recently extended our observations to examine performance in a successive same-different task (Cook, Kelly, & Katz, 1998). Such a successive
task removes any spatial discontinuities from the discrimination, and
requires the use of memory to compare the items across time. Using a
go/no-go discrimination, pigeons are presented photographs in succession that are either the same ones (S+) or different from one another
(S-). We have found that this discrimination is easily learned by the
birds and will transfer to novel photographs (see also Young, Wasserman, & Dalrymple, 1997, for a closely related result). Collectively,
these various results argue against any exclusively perceptually-based
feature account of these same-different results. Instead, they suggest that
the pigeons are capable of comparing the specific individual items in the
display across space and time and making relational judgments about
their identity.

Several key questions remain to be addressed. What is the maximum
range of stimuli over which these birds can successfully apply their
same-different rule? What are the underlying mechanisms that encourage or limit the breadth of this conceptual scope? The present evidence
indicates that the range over which this rule can be applied is sufficient
to encompass both color and gray scale photographic stimuli that contrast with their earlier training experiences. For instance, it will now be
of interest to see if this conceptual behavior trained with simultaneous
displays is sufficiently abstract to transfer to successively presented
Same and Different displays. In addition, future tests should examine
this issue by testing for transfer to Same and Different arrangements of
stimuli from other modalities. For instance, cross modal same-different
tests with auditory stimuli (e.g., Shyan et al., 1987) or temporal stimuli
(e.g., Fetterman, 1991) following visual training would further help to
establish the degree of abstractness of their conceptual rule.

These more demanding cross-model tests do have some challenges
associated with them. The most critical is the noted stimulus specificity
of pigeons. If not challenged by large numbers of training exemplars
(Kendrick et al., 1990; Wright et al., 1988; Wasserman & Bhatt, 1992),
for instance, it appears that the initial disposition of these animals is to
learn stimulus-specific response rules (see Wright, 1997, for another
possible factor in this regard). It is this competing tendency to learn
stimulus or context specific attributes that may be the limiting factor on
an animal's conceptual domain. For example, the one bird in the present
experiment that consistently failed to transfer to new displays apparently

did so because the photographs were too distinct from the large number of familiar items that concurrently supported highly flexible discriminative behavior. It seems likely to us that the three "conceptual" birds revealed by the present tests would eventually suffer a similar fate if tested with non-visual stimuli. That is, temporal and auditory stimuli might be judged to be so different from the familiar domain of visual stimuli that they might not support immediate above chance transfer. This reaction to their unfamiliarity might mask, however, any appreciation of their same-different relations as accrued from their prior visual experience. In such cases, a more appropriate transfer design for detecting concept learning might be to look for savings or interference (e.g., Edwards et al., 1983; Zentall & Hogan, 1976) in the subsequent acquisition of auditory or temporal same-different tasks following visual training. A clear goal of future research with pigeons is to better understand how their competing tendencies to be both stimulus-bounded and conceptually-unbounded simultaneously interact to produce avian discriminative behavior.

Implications for picture perception

As mentioned, the studies of conceptual behavior and picture perception in animals have long been scientific siblings. In this tradition, the same-different procedure used here is also an ideal one for studying picture perception. This is because the animals' same-different judgments provide a direct means for studying the perceived similarity among sets of stimulus items. Assuming that contrasting stimulus pairs that are more difficult to discriminate are also perceptually more similar (i.e., they generate fewer *different* responses), one can use the pattern of these choices to infer the nature of the stimulus effectively controlling a discrimination (Blough, 1982; Cook et al., 1997; Sands et al., 1982; Schneider, 1972).

What does our technique reveal about the perception of the various pictorial stimuli introduced in these studies? Consider first the implications of Experiment 1 for the perception of the semi-realistic object displays. The gray scale performance described above suggests that our previous finding of strong control by the color attributes of object displays was not reflective of exclusive control by the latter dimension. Rather, it represents the overshadowing of shared control by shape-related information that can also be extracted from these picture stimuli. Using the birds' reactions to the similarity relations among numerous pairs of these stimuli, our correlational analyses trying to identify a featural basis for this shape-related discrimination revealed that no one simple feature was especially critical. While several factors were significant, in part because of the large number of observations involved, the amount of variance accounted for by each of these features was negligible. Whatever the nature of the shape information, it is likely to be multidimensional, with several features being integrated together at the same time. One such possible multidimensional property is tied to the categorical identity of the objects. Because of this, we were particularly curious to find out if and how an object's category influenced the current discrimination.

The identical question, of course, arises for the photographic displays. Did the category membership of the photographed objects make any difference? The photographic displays are even more interesting than the object displays because of their mixture of foreground figures and background features and the local differences resulting from their combination. Did the pigeons perceive these object figures as being separate from the background or were these images discriminated more as meaningless mixtures of contrasting arrangements of colors and grays? If category membership did have an influence, then it would suggest that the objects in the foreground of the photographs were being segregated from their surrounding ground. This would have important implications for the general issue of object-picture equivalence, since such figural separation is prerequisite to the meaningful recognition of a pictured object. On the other hand, if the object figures were not being differentiated from the ground, then the pigeons would still be able to discriminate the Same and Different relations between these stimuli, but one might not expect the "object's" category membership to have any systematic effect on this judgment. To begin answering such questions, we again examined the perceived similarity relations among the pictorial items, but this time as indexed by their semantic category.

We created one large database that included all past sessions involving picture images (objects and photographs) collected with these birds. As of this writing, we had 640 sessions available for each bird, with approximately 170 fewer sessions testing photographs. Only baseline trials involving pictorial stimuli were selected for this analysis, and any other trials related to an experimental manipulation were removed. For the vast majority of these sessions, the object displays were being created from randomized combinations of 48 color (2256 possible combinations) or 48 gray scale images representing four categories (birds flowers, fish, and humans), and the photographic displays were created from combinations of 32 color (992 combinations) or 32 gray scale images representing six categories (birds, flowers, buildings, dogs, cats, and cars).[1] To judge how a picture's object category influenced performance, we examined the percentage of *different* responses for those Different displays created from objects drawn from within the same object category (e.g., bluejay and cardinal) to those different displays created from objects from different categories (e.g., azalea and parrot; see Figure 4 for photographic examples).

The analysis of this corpus revealed that category membership did make a significant difference in the pigeons' discrimination of both the object and photographic pictures. This was reflected by the fact that within-category Different displays consistently produced fewer *different* reports than between-category Different displays (i.e., pairs of stimuli from the same category resulted in more *same* responses). Table 2 lists the percentage of different responses for color and gray scale photographs and object displays as a function of categorical assignment. It shows that within-category displays consistently resulted in 4-5% fewer different responses than did between-category displays. This was true for both display types and for color and gray scale differences. A repeated measures ANOVA (within vs. between $\times$ display type $\times$ color vs. gray scale) confirmed that the category effect was significant, $F(1, 3) = 25.3$, as was the difference between the color and gray scale formats, $F(1, 3) = 26.1$. Table 3 further shows that this effect existed for each of the four object categories and the six photographic categories.

---

1. Besides category membership, we were also interested in how the pigeons judged the relative similarity of the individual stimuli themselves. Despite the large number of sessions included in the analysis, it was frustratingly difficult to obtain sample sizes adequate for conducting interpretable cluster analyses for the individual stimuli. This is because there were so many different combinations of images and so few Different trials tested per session with each display type (typically 8 color and 8 gray scale trials per session). Consequently, a specific combination of stimuli might only be tested once every two to four months.

Table 2
Percentage of Different responses for photographic and object displays as a function of category assignment

	Within-category	Between-category
Objects		
Gray scale	70.7	75.2
Color	81.7	85.5
Photographs		
Gray scale	71.7	75.5
Color	77.2	82.9

Table 3
Percentage of Different responses for photographic and object displays as a function of category and assignment

	Within-category	Between-category
Object categories		
Fish	70	79.9
Humans	72.8	76.6
Birds	78	79.2
Flowers	75.2	76.9
Photograph categories		
Buildings	69.4	77.5
Dogs	70.9	75.1
Cats	74.1	77.8
Cars	77.8	82.4
Birds	78.3	80.7
Flowers	77	79.9

These observations provide some of the first evidence for the spontaneous categorical organization of pictures by pigeons. This finding is noteworthy because while previous categorization experiments have well documented that pigeons can be explicitly trained to discriminate between natural categories, only one to our knowledge has demonstrated this same type of spontaneous categorical coherence without such training (Astley & Wasserman, 1992). Further note that given the contingencies of the present task, persistent attention to such categorical features was actually punished (e.g., responding *same* to a display with a cardinal and a bluejay). These pigeons were specifically reinforced only for differentiating photographs and objects based on their same-different relations. Despite this, the similarity relations among the items of each category consistently interfered with making this same-different judgment.

That the categorical similarity of the object stimuli was a factor is not too surprising. For these stimuli, the category effect could simply be due to the high similarity of the shapes and/or outlines of these isolated figures. Since the exemplars of perceptual categories have a high degree of family resemblance, one could reasonably expect that their isolated forms would look highly similar to one another. That the same categorical effect was found for the objects in the photographs is far more interesting. While photographs representing objects from the same category likely have a greater total image similarity, this calculation is complicated by the fact that the objects in the photographs were not isolated and appeared on varying backgrounds. As such, it raises the possibility that the birds may have been separating the "object" figure from its surrounding background. Pigeons certainly have the prerequisite perceptual mechanisms for accomplishing this kind of figure/ground separation (Cook, 1992a, 1992b, 1992c, 1993b; Cook, Cavoto, & Cavoto, 1996). While future work will need to more completely examine how much and what type of specific information is being extracted from the photographs, this category-based interference effect is consonant with a potentially object-based reaction to the coherent patterns of light, dark, and colors contained with these complex images.

Increasing attention must be given to this issue of picture and video perception in animals. Besides the important theoretical issues involved, the dramatic increase in video playback as a means to study animal behavior (Adret, 1997; Dittrich & Lea, 1993; Evans & Marler, 1991; McQuoid & Galef, 1993; Patterson-Kane, Nicol, Foster, & Temple, 1997; Shimizu, 1998) demands we gain a greater understanding of picture perception by non-humans. Some of these recent playback experiments have suggested that some animals readily substitute video and picture images as replacements for the real stimuli that normally elicit specific behaviors. To the extent that the original behavior was controlled by the "objectness" of the stimulus (i.e., not simple features), such substitution results on their surface suggest some form of picture-object equivalence.

Given the far easier task of analyzing a still image, however, the present experiments continue to show the inherent difficulty of diagnosing the effective elements from complex natural images. Even with the tantalizing hints of spontaneous categorization in the present work, it is still difficult to say with complete confidence exactly what the birds extracted from these picture stimuli. Much too often the face validity of using complex natural pictures with animals has preempted the systematic search for the underlying dimensions of stimulus control. The necessity and value of such a stimulus-analytic approach, one that carefully and systematically decomposes these stimuli in an attempt to identify their effective basis, cannot be overemphasized. The use of experimenter-generated and controlled synthetic stimuli of varying complexity is one extremely profitable alternative approach to addressing these difficult issues (Cook, 1993a). With the contemporary advent of increasingly sophisticated image software coming into the hands of behavioral scientists, we have never been better positioned to tackle these important perceptual and conceptual issues in animals.

ACKNOWLEDGEMENTS

This research was supported by a grant from the National Science Foundation to R. G. Cook. We thank Jennifer Holtzinger and Erika Cozza for helpful comments on the manuscript. Additional examples of the display types described in this article can be found at the first author's website: http://www.pigeon.psy.tufts.edu/.

REFERENCES

Adret, P. (1997). Discrimination of video images by zebra finches (*Taeniopygia guttata*): Direct evidence from song performance. *Journal of Comparative Psychology, 111,* 115-125.

Astley, S. L., & Wasserman, E. A (1992). Categorical discrimination and generalization in pigeons: All negative stimuli are not created equal. *Journal of Experimental Psychology: Animal Behavior Processes, 18,* 193-207.

Bhatt, R. S., Wasserman, E. A., Reynolds, W. F., Jr., & Knauss, K. S. (1988). Conceptual behavior in pigeons: Categorization of both familiar and novel examples from four classes of natural and artificial stimuli. *Journal of Experimental Psychology: Animal Behavior Processes, 14,* 219-234.

Blough, D. S. (1982). Pigeon perception of letters of the alphabet. *Science, 218,* 397-398.

Cerella, J. (1979). Visual classes and natural categories in the pigeon. *Journal of Experimental Psychology: Human Perception and Performance, 5,* 68-77.

Carter, D. E., & Werner, J. T. (1978). Complex learning and information processing in pigeons: A critical analysis. *Journal of the Experimental Analysis of Behavior, 29,* 565-601.

Cook, R. G. (1992a). Acquisition and transfer of visual texture discriminations by pigeons. *Journal of Experimental Psychology: Animal Behavior Processes, 18,* 341-353.

Cook, R. G. (1992b). Dimensional organization and texture discrimination in pigeons. *Journal of Experimental Psychology: Animal Behavior Processes, 18,* 354-363.

Cook, R. G. (1992c). The visual perception and processing of textures by pigeons. In W. K. Honig & G. Fetterman (Eds.), *Cognitive aspects of stimulus control* (pp. 279-299). Hillsdale, NJ: Lawrence Erlbaum Associates.

Cook, R. G. (1993a). The experimental analysis of cognition in animals. *Psychological Science, 4,* 174-178.

Cook, R. G. (1993b). Gestalt contributions to visual texture discriminations by pigeons. In T. Zentall (Ed.), *Animal cognition: A tribute to Donald A. Riley* (pp. 251-269). Hillsdale, NJ: Lawrence Erlbaum Associates.

Cook, R. G., Cavoto, K. K., & Cavoto, B. R. (1995). Same/Different texture discrimination and concept learning in pigeons. *Journal of Experimental Psychology: Animal Behavior Processes, 21,* 253-260.

Cook, R. G., Cavoto, K. K., & Cavoto, B. R. (1996). Mechanisms of multidimensional grouping, fusion, and search in avian texture discrimination. *Animal Learning and Behavior.*

Cook, R. G., Katz, J. S., & Cavoto, B. R. (1997). Pigeon same-different concept learning with multiple stimulus classes. *Journal of Experimental Psychology: Animal Behavior Processes, 23,* 417-433.

Cook, R. G., Katz, J. S., & Cavoto, B. R. (1998). Processes of visual cognition in the pigeon. In S. Soraci & B. McIlvane (Eds.), *Perspectives on fundamental processes in intellectual functioning, Volume 1: A survey of research approaches* (pp. 189-214). Greenwich, CT: Ablex.

Cook, R. G., Kelly, D. M., & Katz, J. S. (1998, November). Successive two-item same-different discrimination and concept learning in pigeons. Paper presented at the 39th meeting of the Psychonomic Society, Dallas, TX.

Cook, R. G., & Wixted, J. T. (1997). Same-different texture discrimination in pigeons: Testing competing models of discrimination and stimulus integration. *Journal of Experimental Psychology: Animal Behavior Processes, 23,* 401-416.

Cook, R. G., Wright, A. A., & Kendrick, D. F. (1990). Visual categorization in pigeons. In M. L. Commons, R. Herrnstein, S. M. Kosslyn, & D. B. Mumford (Eds.), *Quantitative analyses of behavior: Behavioral approaches to pattern recognition and concept formation* (pp. 187-214). Hillsdale, NJ: Lawrence Erlbaum Associates.

Dittrich, W. H., & Lea, S. E. G. (1993). Motion as a natural category for pigeons: Generalization and a feature-positive effect. *Journal of Experimental Analysis of Behavior, 59,* 115-129.

Edwards, C. A., Jagielo, J. A., & Zentall, T. R. (1983). "Same/different" symbol use by pigeons. *Animal Learning and Behavior, 11,* 349-355.

Evans, C. S., & Marler, P. (1991). On the use of video images as social stimuli in birds: audience effects on alarm calling. *Animal Behaviour, 41,* 17-26.

Fetterman, J. G. (1991). Discrimination of temporal same-different relations by pigeons. In M. L. Commons, J. A. Nevin, & M. C. Davison (Eds.), *Signal detection: Mechanisms, models, and applications* (pp. 79-101). Hillsdale, NJ: Lawrence Erlbaum Associates.

Grant, D. S. (1991). Symmetrical and asymmetrical coding of food and no-food samples in delayed matching in pigeons. *Journal of Experimental Psychology: Animal Behavior Processes, 17,* 186-193.

Herrnstein, R. J., & De Villiers, P. A. (1980). Fish as a natural category for people and pigeons. In G. H. Bower (Ed.), *The psychology of learning and motivation*. New York: Academic Press.

Herrnstein, R. J., & Loveland, D. H. (1964). Complex visual concept in the pigeon. *Science, 146,* 549-551.

Herrnstein, R. J., Loveland, D. H., & Cable, C. (1976). Natural concepts in pigeons. *Journal of Experimental Psychology: Animal Behavior Processes, 2,* 285-302.

Holmes, P. W. (1979). Transfer of matching performance in pigeons. *Journal of the Experimental Analysis of Behavior, 31,* 103-114.

Kendrick, D. F., Wright, A. A., & Cook, R. G. (1990). On the role of memory in concept learning by pigeons. *Psychological Record, 40,* 359-371.

King, J. E. (1973). Learning and generalizations of a two-dimensional sameness-difference concept by chimpanzees and orangutans. *Journal of Comparative and Physiological Psychology, 84,* 140-148.

McQuoid, L. M., & Galef, B. G., Jr. (1993). Social stimuli influencing feeding behaviour of Burmese fowl: a video analysis. *Animal Behaviour, 46,* 13-22.

Oden, D. L., Thompson, R. K. R., & Premack, D. (1990). Infant chimpanzees *(Pan troglodytes)* spontaneously perceive both concrete and abstract same/different relations. *Child Development, 61,* 621-631.

Patterson-Kane, E., Nicol, C. J., Foster, T. M., & Temple, W. (1997). Limited perception of video images by domestic hens. *Animal Behaviour, 53,* 951-963.

Pearce, J. M. (1991). The acquisition of concrete and abstract categories in pigeons. In L. Dachowski & C. F. Flaherty (Eds.), *Current topics in animal learning: Brain, emotion, and cognition* (pp. 141-164). Hillsdale, NJ: Lawrence Erlbaum Associates.

Premack, D. (1978). On the abstractness of human concepts: Why it would be difficult to talk to a pigeon. In S. H. Hulse, H. Fowler, & W. K. Honig (Eds.), *Cognitive processes in animal behavior* (pp. 423-451). Hillsdale, NJ: Lawrence Erlbaum Associates.

Premack, D. (1983). The codes of beast and man. *Behavioral and Brain Sciences, 6,* 125-167.

Robinson, J. S. (1955). The sameness-difference discrimination problem in chimpanzee. *Journal of Comparative and Physiological Psychology, 48,* 195-213.

Robinson, J. S. (1960). The conceptual basis of the chimpanzee's performance on the sameness-difference discrimination problem. *Journal of Comparative and Physiological Psychology, 53,* 368-370.

Sands, S. F., Lincoln, C. E., & Wright, A. A. (1982). Pictorial similarity judgements and the organization of visual memory in the rhesus monkey. *Journal of Experimental Psychology: General, 3,* 369-389.

Santiago, H. C., & Wright, A. A. (1984). Pigeon memory: Same/different concept learning, serial probe recognition acquisition, and probe delay effects on the serial-position function. *Journal of Experimental Psychology: Animal Behavior Processes, 10,* 498-512.

Schneider, B. (1972). Multidimensional scaling of color difference in the pigeon. *Perception and Psychophysics, 12,* 373-378.

Sherburne, L. M., & Zentall, T. R. (1993). Asymmetrical coding of food and no-food events by pigeons: Sample pecking versus food as the basis of the sample code. *Learning and Motivation, 24,* 141-155.

Shimizu, T. (1998). Conspecific recognition in pigeons (*Columba livia*) using dynamic video images. *Behaviour, 135,* 43-53.

Shyan, M. R., Wright, A. A., Cook, R. G., & Jitsumori, M. (1987). Acquisition of the auditory same/different task in a rhesus monkey. *Psychonomic Science, 25,* 1-4.

Thompson, R. K. R., & Oden, D. L. (1996). A profound disparity revisited: Perception judgment of abstract identity relations by chimpanzees, human infants, and monkeys. *Behavioural Processes, 35,* 149-161.

Thompson, R. K. R., Oden, D. L., & Boysen, S. T. (1997). Language-naive chimpanzees (*Pan troglodytes*) judge relations between relations in a conceptual matching-to-sample task. *Journal of Experimental Psychology: Animal Behavior Processes, 23,* 31-43.

Wasserman, E. A., & Bhatt, R. S. (1992). Conceptualization of natural and artificial stimuli by pigeons. In W. K. Honig & J. G. Fetterman (Eds.), *Cognitive aspects of stimulus control* (pp. 203-223). Hillsdale, NJ: Lawrence Erlbaum Associates.

Wasserman, E. A., Hugart, J. A., & Kirkpatrick-Steger, K. (1995). Pigeons show same-different conceptualization after training with complex visual stimuli. *Journal of Experimental Psychology: Animal Behavior Processes, 21,* 248-252.

Wixted, J. T. (1993). A signal detection analysis of memory for nonoccurrence in pigeons. *Journal of Experimental Psychology: Animal Behavior Processes, 19,* 400-411.

Wright, A. A. (1997). Concept learning and learning strategies. *Psychological Science, 8,* 119-123.

Wright, A. A., Cook, R. G., & Kendrick, D. F. (1989). Relational and absolute stimulus learning by monkeys in a memory task. *Journal of the Experimental Analysis of Behavior, 52,* 237-248.

Wright, A. A., Cook, R. G., Rivera, J. J., Sands, S. F., & Delius, J. D. (1988). Concept learning by pigeons: Matching-to-sample with trial-unique video picture stimuli. *Animal Learning and Behavior, 16,* 436-444.

Wright, A. A., Santiago, H. C., & Sands, S. F. (1984). Monkey memory: Same/Different concept learning, serial probe acquisition, and probe delay effects. *Journal of Experimental Psychology: Animal Behavior Processes, 10,* 513-529.

Wright, A. A., Santiago, H. C., Urcuioli, P. J., & Sands, S. F. (1983). Monkey and pigeon acquisition of same/different concept using pictorial stimuli. In M. L. Commons, R. J. Herrnstein, & A. R. Wagner (Eds.), *Quantitative analyses of behavior* (Vol. 4, pp. 295-317). Cambridge, MA: Ballinger.

Young, M. E., Wasserman, E. A., & Dalrymple, R. M. (1997). Memory based same-different conceptualization by pigeons. *Psychonomic Bulletin and Review, 4,* 552-558.

Zentall, T. R., & Hogan, D. E. (1976). Pigeons can learn identity, difference or both. *Science, 30,* 177-186.

Generic perception: open-ended categorization of natural classes

Ludwig Huber

Institute of Zoology, University of Vienna, Austria

Abstract. This review surveys some illustrative experiments on categorization of visual stimuli by animals, preferably pigeons (*Columba livia*). Traditionally, it has been assumed that the ability to categorize stimuli and to extend the classification to novel members of the categories involves conceptualization. In the past, however, pigeon studies suffered from overly simplistic assumptions concerning the perceptual aspects of natural categorization. Recent evidence suggests that the way in which pigeons sort natural categories does not require conceptual abilities, i.e., learning that transcends pictorial memory or learning to attend to the class-characteristic features. We found that pigeons classify visually complex, natural images (male and female human faces) by means of their global properties, which covaried with the semantic content of the categories. The hypothesis proposed here is that natural categories and visual classes are coextensive, i.e., that behavioral and perceptual contingencies are conjointly correlated with environmental dimensions of variance. Hence, the pigeon's ability of open-ended categorization may result from the generic nature of natural categories and natural selection that has equipped animals with considerable adaptations for dealing with the categorization problem in this very sense.

Key words: Evolution, perception, categorization, concepts, polymorphous classes, cognition, representation, pigeon.

Correspondence should be sent to Dr. Ludwig Huber, Institute of Zoology, University of Vienna, Biocenter, Althanstrasse 14, 1090 Vienna, Austria (e-mail: ludwig.huber@univie.ac.at).

> *"When it comes to categorization,*
> *nature clearly has a secret"*
> (Richard Herrnstein, 1985)

INTRODUCTION

Categorization is the most contradictory subject in cognitive science. On one hand, many textbooks of human cognition treat categorization as a complex mental process, or a unique ability that creates a gap between human and nonhuman animals. On the other hand, very few comparative psychologists or ethologists would disagree that animals are equipped, as the result of natural selection, with the ability to navigate in an ever-changing environment, and to respond in an appropriate manner to classes of stimuli rather than to individual examples. A solution to this problem can be found either by means of a theory of categorization that covers all phenomena coming under the title "categorization" or by a terminological clarification. In this chapter, I will argue that much of the current confusion surrounding categorization is due to an anthropomorphic bias, an overestimation of what cognition involves, and a simplified theory of perception.

The study of categorization must begin with the question of how objects, events, or even ideas, are sorted into their proper categories. In its broadest sense, categorization involves treating a set of objects or events as equivalent. According to cognitive psychologists, this grouping is accomplished by putting objects or events into the same pile, calling them by the same name, or assigning them the same mental representation. Ethologists suggest that categorization is accomplished when an animal responds to objects or events in the same manner. Although the behavioral outcome of a categorization task does not reveal anything about the underlying mechanism, it is possible to distinguish between different processes. Neisser (1987), for example, suggested the distinction between perceiving and thinking. Animals perceive values of continuous dimensions as qualitatively distinct because of innate sensory mechanisms that trigger "meaningful" behaviors. Color categories and communicative signals are the most obvious examples of the immediate, effortless and veridical processes that produce perceptual categories. The human mind thinks about its world in a limitless, and often unexpected way. This process is anything but effortless or immediate, and frequently goes wrong.

Considering the wide range of phenomena under study, it is difficult to imagine how these processes can be assigned a common name. Only by specifying the entities to be categorized and the mechanisms by which they are categorized, it can be determined whether the linguistic competencies of humans are the result of an evolutionary predisposition to form elementary perceptual and psychophysical categories (e.g., colors, sounds), or are themselves a prerequisite to categorization. Associative mechanisms are somewhat intermediate between the fixed, innate mechanisms involved in color perception and the linguistic competencies of humans. Sorting objects and events in the world into meaningful categories by detecting their recurrence in the environment despite variations in local stimulus energies, is the basic task of perceptual categorization and does not require abstract representations or symbolic manipulations. The processes of discrimination and generalization are prime candidates for accomplishing this job.

In the experimental psychologist's laboratory, pigeons (*Columba livia*) are the preferred species for research, both on simple discrimination and on more complex categorization, simply because of their convenience as laboratory animals. Furthermore, this bird's lack of language competencies and extraordinary perceptual capacities, render it an ideal model system for investigating perceptual or associative processes (Lea, 1984; Wasserman, 1991). Unlike very few other animals, the pigeon has been studied in great detail in many fields including neurobiology, sensory physiology, ethology, psychophysics, and comparative psychology (Abs, 1983). Current knowledge suggests that non-linguistic categorization is not confined to humans, but originates in the perceptual and associative mechanisms that evolved in order to cope with the fundamental problems of a dynamic world. However, despite more than three decades of research two problems remain: the need to specify the mechanism underlying categorization and to overcome the problem of anthropomorphism.

In this chapter I will address the problem of anthropomorphic bias in categorization research (for a discussion of the mechanisms underlying categorization, see Huber, 1999). Considerable confusion has been created by assigning non-human animals conceptual-like capacities although what counts as a "concept" is by no means a well defined matter. Premack (1983) noted with charcteristic strictness: "*As cognition washes belatedly over the shores of animal learning, there is a tendency to "liberalize" association and to reinterpret it as cognition.*" (p. 361). One means of clarifying this issue is to look more carefully than in the past for alternative explanations. More specifically, instead of "liberalizing" concepts we may investigate whether previous findings can be accounted for in terms of perceptual and associative processes alone.

My null hypothesis is that current evidence does not provide a particularly convincing case for conceptual learning in pigeons, i.e., learning that transcends pictorial memory or learning to attend to the class-characteristic perceptual features. By contrasting what classes pigeons can and cannot discriminate, hypotheses will be formulated regarding: (i) what the perceptual primitives in the pigeon's representation might be, (ii) what combinatorial rules are formed associatively and, as a result, (iii) what research strategies we need for finding them. A recent attempt to apply such a research strategy in our laboratory is presented at the end of the chapter.

Before starting my selective survey of the literature, I would like to make some important points concerning the breadth of its coverage, both in terms of related phenomena and species comparison. First, I will confine my review to *picture classification*. There is a huge body of work concerning the formation of abstract representations, of functional and relational concepts, and transitive inference (reviews in Roitblat & von Fersen; 1992; Roitblat & Meyer, 1995; Vauclair, 1996; Shettleworth, 1998). I do not doubt that all these capacities are related, but an exhaustive discussion would clearly go beyond the aim of the paper. Second, my arguments and conclusions will rest primarily on pigeon research, supplemented occasionally by related findings in monkeys. Because I doubt the usefulness of simultaneously considering findings from different species that resemble one another only superficially, I will leave the interpretation of primate capacities to experts in that field (see reviews in Thompson, 1995; Cheney & Seyfarth, 1990; Hauser, 1996; Tomasello & Call, 1997). Comparing the "intelligence" of taxonomically distant species is by itself a problematic issue (see MacPhail, 1987), as is the tendency to use such comparisons in order to impose a sorting order from pigeons to rats to monkeys to apes and finally to humans. I believe that a better understanding of "Picture perception in animals" can be obtained by focussing on the pigeon, a species known for its remarkably sophisticated visual system (Zeigler & Bischof, 1993; Cook, 1999).

"EVIDENCE" FOR CONCEPT FORMATION

Psychologists have studied categorization for over seventy years. However, only lately has it become a concern for comparative psychologists studying animals. Prior to this, psychology was dominated by the study of the mental capabilities of humans. This anthropocentrism culminated in linguistic determinism, which proposes that, for example, the location of color boundaries in human perception are determined by where language happens to place them (Whorf, 1956). Only a few years after this proposal, Herrnstein and Loveland (1964) created a sensation by reporting experiments in which pigeons successfully sorted visual classes defined by an ordinary human language concept. This experiment was so surprising because it implied that even non-mammalian animals are capable of abstracting information about the semantic content of a category from visual stimuli.

Herrnstein and Loveland (1964) trained pigeons to discriminate between color slides containing people, and slides that were of similar natural scenes but that did not contain people. The slides were shown one at a time, and pecks on a response key were rewarded with food only in the presence of slides containing people. All of the pigeons rapidly learned to classify the two sets of slides, and continued to perform at a high level even when slides containing novel scenes and previously unseen people were presented. The latter finding, and the fact that many different instances of the concept had been used, was taken as evidence that the pigeons performed the classification task by learning a generalized concept rather than by attending to a few simple features or by memorizing individual exemplars by rote.

As a result of this experiment subsequent studies of pigeon categorization adopted a cognitive approach (e.g., Lubow, 1974; Poole & Lander, 1971; Malott & Siddall, 1972; Herrnstein, Loveland, & Cable, 1976; Morgan, Fitch, Holman, & Lea, 1976). However, despite this common cognitivistic inclination, there was no general agreement as to whether the concepts under investigation were acquired by the pigeons during classification training, or were already present before the onset of training as part of the bird's innate repertoire or as the result of pre-experimental experience. It was also not clear to what extent the pigeon's concept matched the concept specified by the experimenter when designing the task. Furthermore, no attempt was made to specify the content and quality of a concept that exists independently of human language. These experiments have been reviewed several times, and do not need to be reviewed again here. It only needs be highlighted that the claim that pigeons possess conceptual abilities is probably rooted in a tendency to trust one's intuition that animals will exhibit unexpected cognitive powers when pushed to their limits.

Despite the 30 years of research that followed Herrnstein and Loveland's seminal experiment and several critical reevaluations of their findings (e.g., Edwards & Honig, 1987; Greene, 1983), the situation is still ambiguous. The veil of uncertainty still surrounds pigeon conceptualization, as does the tendency to report surprising intellectual powers in animals. For example, Porter and Neuringer (1984) described three experiments in which pigeons successfully discriminated between excerpts from famous pieces of classical music (Bach flute music and Hindemith viola music). Following training, the pigeons generalized to excerpts of music of related style (e.g., baroque: from Bach to Buxtehude and Scarlatti; 20th century music: from Hindemith to Carter and Piston). Similarly, Watanabe, Sakamoto, and Wakita (1995) found that pigeons discriminated between color slides of paintings by Monet and Picasso, and thereafter generalized to other impressionists (e.g., from Monet to Cezanne and Renoir) or cubists (e.g., from Picasso to Braque and Matisse). This led Watanabe et al. to conclude that pigeons perceive and think more like humans than is often assumed.

EVIDENCE FOR THE LIMITS OF CONCEPTUALIZATION IN PIGEONS

During the past twenty years, the weakness of the above approach has become apparent as researchers identify the questions unanswered by their predecessors. These questions concern: (1) the crucial aspects or properties of the photographs that enables pigeons to discriminate the experimenter-defined classes, (2) the behavioral criteria for determining whether pigeons form a concept during classification tasks, and (3) whether the concept hypothesis can be indirectly evaluated by training pigeons on artificial tasks that are completely prespecified in terms of their feature content and categorical structure. All three questions have led to a critical assessment of the hypothesis that pigeons are guided by acquired concepts. In the following section, I will review evidence to suggest that pigeons do not meet the neccessary criteria to show true conceptualization.

Spontaneous transfer to novel instances

The first piece of evidence comes from an experiment conducted in Herrnstein's laboratory. This experiment was designed to determine whether pigeons perform the people-concept task by memorizing individual exemplars, or by learning to attend to the critical features of the concept. Greene (1983) found strong evidence suggesting that pigeons learn not only about relevant pictorial aspects when abstracting the people concept, but also about irrelevant pictorial aspects present in the background. This conclusion was based upon a series of tests which examined the contribution of feature memorization to categorization. Prior to this study, experimenters relied upon the transfer test to determine whether the ability to sort training pictures could be extended to novel pictures, in order to provide evidence of conceptualization. However, it is not possible to show that the only thing that novel class instances and previously presented training stimuli have in common are conceptually relevant features. Thus the transfer test may not be able to provide evidence of true conceptualization.

One strategy that a pigeon might use to sort photographs according to the experimenter's category definition is to recognize many instances of a stimulus class together with their psychological consequence (e.g., food or no food). This is accomplished by means of a template memorization mechanism, which is insensitive to feature distribution but stores the whole picture as an unanalyzed array of pixels. Conceptualization transcends this "mindless" machine learning by analyzing the pictorial information present in class instances, and by detecting and extracting the "embedded concept". Perceptual concepts, such as a particular person (SE) in different postures, involve category-relevant features distributed across the feature space in a "coherent" fashion (Greene, 1983). Irrelevant features, such as the landscape in the people pictures, should be arbitrarily distributed so that they do not provide any cues for correct classification. Greene (1983) conducted transfer tests with novel slides involving different mixtures of concept and background. In the crucial test, the new positives were views of SE on backgrounds that belonged to the negative training class. Pigeons classified these ambiguous test slides as negative, and therefore appear to have "misunderstood" the concept task. A final test, involving entirely new positives (e.g., new views of SE in front of new backgrounds), revealed that some information about SE had also been memorized during training. Thus it would appear that Greene's (1983) indirect method of assessing the relative effect of conceptual and irrelevant information in solving a perceptual concept task, provided good evidence of pattern learning rather than feature learning (e.g., Lea, 1984).

Pseudo-concept training

Further evidence that pigeons do not solve perceptual concept tasks by using higher-order concepts was reported by Edwards and Honig (1987). Using the concept "person" to define category membership, they found that pigeons were able to identify and use category exemplars as cues for responding. Edwards and Honig employed a control test, which is commonly regarded as one of the standard procedures for demonstrating category rather than pattern learning. Pseudo-concept training, as it is usually called (Astley & Wasserman, 1992; Herrnstein & De Villiers, 1980; Lea & Ryan, 1990; Wasserman, Kiedinger, & Bhatt, 1988), involves the arbitrary assignment of category and non-category exemplars to positive and negative classes, respectively. The ability to correctly perform this task is interpreted as evidence that animals learned about the individual slides, at least to the extent that the pseudo-classes did not share, by chance, simple pictorial properties. If using a great number of different slides makes this improbable, then learning to discriminate pseudo-classes should be more difficult than learning true categories.

Edwards and Honig's (1987) pigeons performed poorly during pseudo-concept training. This result makes it unlikely that the subjects assigned to the concept group achieved their high level of performance simply by memorizing positive or negative instances. Rather, they appear to have learned about the correlation between concept and reward. The birds also showed a high level of transfer during subsequent generalization tests. However, the question of how the categories were represented during task acquisition remains unanswered. The use of category exemplars as cues for responding is necessary, but not sufficient, evidence for concept abstraction. In fact, Edwards and Honig's (1987) results do not disprove, but are compatible with, Greene's (1983) data which indicates that pigeons remember in detail something about most or all of the available cues in a complex visual display, and not just about the category-relevant cues. The facilitated performance that is observed when category exemplars consistently appear on either reinforced or nonreinforced trials, may be caused by a reduction in the amount of information stored as a result of redundant category features. This interpretation explains the poor performance of subjects in the "Human negative group", i.e., in a true concept task in which reward is associated with the absence, rather than the presence, of a concept. In this case we need only assume that reward serves to direct attention towards the content of positive slides. In contrast, experiments in which all instances are rewarded when the given response is correct, for example in discrete trial simultaneous and successive forced-choice procedures (e.g., Bhatt & Wasserman, 1989; D'Amato & Van Sant, 1988), obtained better transfer performance.

In conclusion, neither Greene (1983) nor Edwards and Honig (1987) found evidence of concept learning in pigeons. Both studies did confirm, however, that pigeons have a remarkable pictorial memory (Vaughan & Greene, 1984; von Fersen & Delius, 1989), and that even in those cases in which something was learned about a concept, category-irrelevant information was also stored. The latter finding may be taken as evidence that pigeons are not capable of true conceptualization. However, this clearly depends upon how a perceptual concept is defined. In any case, it is important to note that these studies also demonstrated the important role of several procedural variables, including (a) the number of exemplars, (b) the quality of exemplars, and (c) the functional significance of a stimulus. Taken together, these findings indicate that other mechanisms, simpler than conceptualization, are at work in the pigeon's brain when it is presented with an experimenter-defined concept task.

Indirect evidence from the conceptual structure

Further indirect evidence that pigeons perceive concepts, if at all, in a different way to how they are perceived by humans comes from studies of the hierarchical structure of categories. There is ample evidence that humans organize their conceptual world into different hierarchical levels. Studies of natural object categorization have confirmed the suggestion by philosophers (e.g., Ryle, 1949; Wittgenstein, 1953) that this hierarchical structure is not the result of a logic device or a consequence of language, but an intrinsic property of natural categories called "family resemblance" (Rosch & Mervis, 1975). For example, the common

Kingfisher (*Alcedo athis*) clearly belongs to the categorical level of birds (Aves), but is also a member of the higher level of animals.

The different levels of kingfisher classification can be distinguished in terms of breadth and therefore in terms of abstractness. Abstractness is a critical property of concepts. If the categories represent conceptual structures rather than perceptual ones, then the ability of non-human animals to classify stimuli in accordance with this hierarchy can be taken as indirect evidence of their conceptual abilities (Premack, 1983). Roberts and Mazmanian (1988) presented pigeons and squirrel monkeys with the above problem. Using a two-alternative forced choice discrimination procedure, the animals were trained to discriminate three types of problems according to their abstractness: a) the common kingfisher from other birds, b) several bird species from other animal classes, and c) animal pictures from non-animal pictures. The outcome of this experiment is rather questionable from the point of view of animal conceptualization, because neither the pigeons nor the monkeys performed in the same manner as human subjects. They were unable to classify stimuli at the intermediate level (b), they experienced initial difficulties at the abstract level (c) – although the monkeys outperformed the pigeons –, and they performed well at the concrete level (a). The pigeons and monkeys behaved in an opposite manner to what would be predicted by the category model of human conceptualiztion. It would appear that the difference between human and non-human animal categorization is a result of the non-human animal's tendency to classify stimuli in terms of similarity rather than abstractness. Alternatively, the lack of isomorphy between human and animal classification behavior in this study may be due to a different knowledge base at the beginning of the experiment. In any case, how abstract, and therefore how conceptual, the pigeons' or the monkeys' classification rules were is not easy to specify.

While field studies (reviewed in Cheney & Seyfarth, 1990) have shown that juvenile vervet monkeys learn to discriminate between birds and other animals (intermediate level), and recent experiments have also provided some evidence that monkeys may succeed at the abstract animal/non-animal categorization level (Fabre-Thorpe, Ghislaine, & Thorpe, 1998), the difference between human and pigeon conceptualization has not been questioned. On the contrary, it has been further supported by comparing the typicality rankings made by pigeons and humans. Cook, Wright, and Kendrick (1990) used line drawings of birds and mammals that had previously been rated by humans on the basis of prototypicality. Despite the fact that the training stimuli were drawn from a small range of typicality ratings, pigeons transferred best to novel exemplars that were similar to the training stimuli. They did not demonstrate superior responding to the prototypical exemplars, which suggests that they were insensitive to the categorical structure generated by the human typicality raters. Alternatively, the pigeons may have memorized the training stimuli and shown orderly generalization in the presence of novel test stimuli, or attended to those aspects of the stimuli that were not included in human concepts. The fact that not only the similarity between training and test stimuli, but also the number of training stimuli, exerted a major influence on transfer behavior "seems most consistent with an instance or exemplar-based representational system" (Cook, Wright, & Kendrick, 1990, p. 210).

Specifying the content of the animal's representation

There are two reasons to doubt that pigeons are capable of forming concepts. First, stimulus generalization from stored training exemplars occurs, and second, stimulus aspects not involved in the target concept exert control over the bird's behavior. However, this conclusion must remain tentative until the critical features that are represented during classification training can be identified. The use of a great number of different class instances, presented in full-color and detail, renders such an a priori specification very difficult.

Only in a few perceptual classification studies investigators have attempted to determine the animal's perceptual code. Roberts and Mazmanian (1988), for example, carried out an item analysis of their animal and non-animal pictures by rating them along 10 different dimensions. With the exception of the eyes – which we now know are biologically relevant for monkeys (but see Abbott, Rolls, & Tovee, 1996; Nahm, Perret, Amaral, & Albright, 1997; Rolls, Treves, Tovee, & Panzeri, 1998) – there was no obvious stimulus aspect that, from the human's point of view, exerted significant control over the pigeons' or monkeys' behavior. In the light of these methodological problems, stating that "*these experiments have demonstrated that monkeys and pigeons can conceptualize at a more abstract level*" (Roberts & Mazmanian, 1988, p. 259) warrants caution. In contrast, recent attempts to study neuronal responses to faces, conspecifics, and objects are currently improving our understanding of the picture perception of the animals under investigation.

Furthermore, analysing animal misidentifications, or judgements that deviate considerably from the human point of view, can reveal other ways in which animals categorize stimuli. Herrnstein and de Villiers (1980), for example, reported that pigeons trained on the concept "fish/non-fish" were unable to classify a close-up view of the head of a fish, which is a rather typical view for humans. Conversely, the pigeons were able to recognize a skate as a fish, whereas humans are not. The authors concluded that the pigeons had formed a sufficiently general concept of fish, although their representation was clearly not equivalent to that formed by humans. D'Amato and Van Sant (1988) had a more serious concern about the similarity of human and animal concepts. They re-evaluated the findings obtained by Schrier and Brady (1987), who investigated the person concept in rhesus monkeys (*Macaca mulatta*), by analyzing misclassifications made on specific slides. They concluded that it is doubtful whether these monkeys used a well-differentiated person concept, since their performance was highly influenced by the total area of the slide occupied by the human. An analysis of the misidentifications made by their own subjects (Capuchin monkeys, *Cebus apella*) led to similar reservations. First, while to a human observer the portrait of a person is an incontestable positive instance of the person concept, this was not the case for monkeys. Second, persistent errors were elicited by non-person slides containing a patch of a reddish color produced, for example, by a piece of watermelon.

The main conclusion that must be drawn from these findings is that the animals may have learned a human-like concept before or during concept training. However, the data do not rule out other possibilities (see also Thompson, 1995). It is very likely that the animals learned to perform the concept discrimination task by using a few feature dimensions that correlated to some extent with the features contained in our well-differentiated concepts. There are two reasons why it is difficult to disprove this statement. First, there is no generally agreed-upon definition of the term "concept" (Chater & Heyes, 1994; Medin & Smith, 1984; Shank, Collins, & Hunter, 1986). Second, the categorical content of naturalized experimental stimuli has not been controlled in studies employing an analytic approach to natural categorization (Astley & Wasserman, 1992; Thompson, 1995). A post-hoc analysis of response rates to slides containing hundreds of full-color photographs, which are then used to infer the feature content of the animals' representation, does not deal with the fundamental problem of correlation. Even if it were possible to predict response rates from a feature model, it could never be ascertained that the features we have identified are the only ones controlling the animals' classification behavior (von Fersen & Lea, 1990).

ARTIFICIAL CATEGORIES

An alternative approach to categorization involves the use of artificial categories. This approach overcomes the correlation problem by constructing artificial categories that are composed of clearly defined stimuli and based upon clearly specified rules regarding how compositional features are distributed within and across classes (see also Jitsumori, 1993, 1994; Lea, Lohmann, & Ryan, 1993; Lea & Ryan, 1990; von Fersen & Lea, 1990). Class exemplars are defined by a small number of independent feature dimensions, none of which are necessary or sufficient for class membership. If animals learn these artificial categorizations, this implies that the prespecified features exerted significant control over their behavior. The advantage of this procedure lies in its analytical strength. However, it is necessary to be cautious when generalizing from these impoverished categories to the complex categories found in nature.

Artificial stimuli

Morgan, Fitch, Holman, and Lea (1976) trained pigeons to discriminate between the letter "A" and the number "2" presented in 18 different typefaces. Alphanumeric characters appear to represent a rather impoverished version of natural visual environments. However, there is at least one aspect of these stimuli that renders their use worthwhile. Alphanumeric stimuli are "polymorphic". The natural environment is a "*network of similarities overlapping and criss-crossing, sometimes overall similarities, sometimes similarities of detail*" (Wittgenstein, 1953, p. 66). By presenting alphanumerical characters in different typefaces, it is possible to simulate the natural phenomenon of generic variation.

Morgan and colleagues found that the pigeons rapidly learned the discrimination. Moreover, they also maintained a high level of performance when the characters were presented in 22 novel typefaces. By introducing dissected and rotated figures, Morgan et al. were able to show that the pigeons achieved such excellent classification behavior, not only because they stored every stimulus as a single template, but also because they extracted topological features. An analysis of the pigeons' generalization performance revealed exactly which features were, and which were not, controlling responding. A feature model which included concrete topological aspects (e.g., apex, vertical lines, right gap) as well as more general aspects (e.g., openness, compactness) achieved a sufficiently accurate description of pigeons' perception of simple forms (e.g., Lea & Ryan, 1983).

In subsequent investigations, the use of sophisticated statistical procedures, such as multi-dimensional scaling and cluster analysis, has led to an improvement not only in research methods but also in the specificity of psychophysical and pattern recognition theories (e.g., Blough & Fanklin, 1985). The artificial stimulus classes used in these experiments have included letters of the alphabet (Blough & Fanklin, 1985; Lea & Ryan, 1983, 1990; Morgan et al., 1976), random dot patterns (Watanabe, 1988), "Caminalcules" (Cerella, 1986), cartoon characters (Cerella, 1980), and line drawings of the human face (Huber & Lenz, 1993, 1996). These stimuli are sufficiently numerous and complex that their similarity creates a meaningful structure. Pigeons cope with these patterns of similarity like a "perceptron" (Cerella, 1986). During the course of learning, they attend to redundant sets of distinctive stimulus aspects, and then form a representation of a large unstructured set of features. Each exemplar is characterized by a subset of these features. Further research is necessary to specify the "ontogeny" of the extracted features, their "capture ratio", and their "relatedness". Feature distinctiveness may be acquired during classification training, their specificity may be relaxed in a new context, and they may not be perceived independently of others. Although we are far from providing a universal feature alphabet for pigeons, the presentation of artificial stimulus classes has proven to be an exceptionally promising research technique for uncovering the basic perceptual processes involved in natural categorization (see review by Cerella, 1982).

Artificial representation of natural stimuli

In later research, two methodological problems with the artificial stimulus approach were addressed. In order to create artificial stimuli that were more closely related to natural categories, researchers used abstract representations of stimuli that were assumed to be of ecological significance to the species under investigation. Two obvious examples of visual stimuli of ecological relevance to pigeons are seeds and other pigeons. Lea and Ryan (1990) used stylized black-and-white drawings of pigeons that were composed of five bipolar features: wings (checkered or gray), neck (striped or gray), beak (light or dark), cere (large or small), and legs (thick or thin). By varying the five bipolar features they were able to create 32 different figures. These figures were then sorted into positive and negative categories according to a polymorphous feature rule. Surprisingly, the four experimental subjects did not achieve a satisfactory level of discrimination. This was because they attended to the wing feature alone, while ignoring all other features. A similar outcome was reported by Lea, Lohman, and Ryan (1993) using "pseudoseeds" as stimuli. Five bipolar features were created, and food was signaled by figures that contained at least three of these features. The subjects failed to attend equally to all features, relying instead on only two to four.

The pigeon's failure to take full advantage of the entire feature space of abstract versions of natural stimuli, and to extract all relevant information in order to cope with the categorization problem, can be interpreted as a general weakness of feature analysis theory (cf. Watanabe, Lea, & Dittrich, 1993). However, it is possible that the use of stimuli and features that are of unequal salience to the pigeon may have affected their classification performance. The well-documented effects of selective attention and/or overshadowing may be the proximate reasons for the pigeon's failure. Thus there is no reason to doubt the usefulness of the feature strategy in natural classification *per se*. However, we cannot hope to match the structure of natural classes every time we create simplified and idealized categorization tasks. Furthermore, we cannot assume that the pigeon's brain operates like a general-purpose computer. It is more likely that it is predisposed to detect specific sets of natural feature dimensions.

The fact that a small set of features recurs in a large set of otherwise different instances does not mean that pigeons use these features to classify stimuli. Significant correlations between these feature dimensions and the animal's responding may be caused by obscure features that are by themselves correlated with the features under investigation. Fortunately, some years ago we were able to create a polymorphous categorization task using artificial stimuli that allowed us to determine all features that pigeons would need to solve the categorization problem (Huber, 1995; Huber & Lenz, 1993, 1996).

In our experiments, there were five basic requirements for the selection of stimuli. They were that the stimuli should (a) be composed of a few features that could be easily manipulated, (b) not have any background features, (c) be separable along their feature dimensions, (d) be of equal salience, and (e) have no obvious pre-experimental significance. We used schematic line drawings of human faces, or "Brunswik faces", as experimental stimuli. The feature dimensions were based upon simple graphic elements (e.g., lines, circles), and varied according to their length or distance. Representative examples of these faces are shown in Figure 1. The four feature dimensions can be labeled as "Area above the eyes" (BROW), "Distance between the eyes" (EYE), "Length of the nose" (NOSE), and "Area below the mouth" (MOUTH). It could be determined a priori how pigeons would perceive these figures. However, the manipulation of the above-mentioned features generated a four-dimensional feature space in which each stimulus had its own distinctive position, and there was no other dimension along which the stimuli could vary. With this setup, the experimenter knows which features the subject must use in order to solve the discrimination problem.

By exactly specifying the type of feature variation, it is possible to specify the class definition. Huber and Lenz (1993) attempted to test the variably weighted feature rule (Lea & Ryan, 1990). This is a variant of feature learning theory wherein the relevant feature dimensions acquire an equal amount of control over classification performance during the course of learning. The appropriate way to investigate this ability is to employ a polymorphous class rule (see above). In our 1993 study, we varied the four feature dimensions in three steps, from small to large, and assigned each step an arbitrary number. For example, a small nose was assigned a value of −1, a large nose a value of +1, and an intermediate length nose a value of zero. Applying this logic to the four dimensions created 81 different faces. In the two most extreme cases, one face contained four features all assigned the value −1, and another face contained four features all assigned the value +1. These faces are

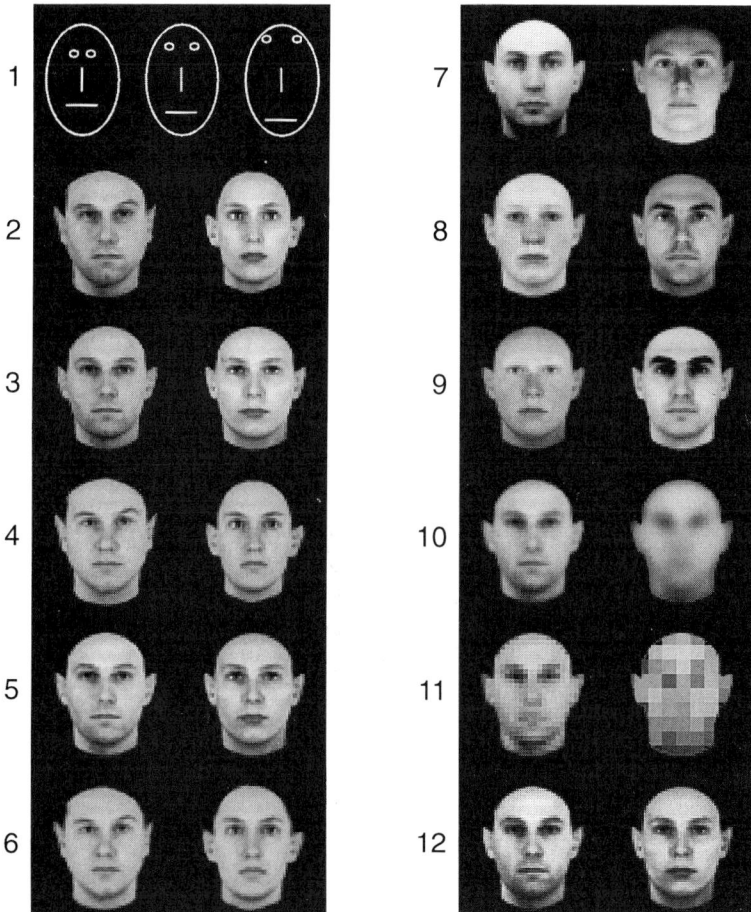

Figure 1. Examples for the different types of stimuli used in Huber and Lenz (1993, 1996), Troje et al. (1999), and Huber et al. (submitted); see body of article.
(Further details and the entire set of test stimuli used in Huber et al. can be seen at http://www.pigeon.psy.tufts.edu/avc/huber/).

depicted in Figure 1 on the left and right sides, respectively. The middle face contains four features all assigned the value zero. Decisions about whether a particular face belongs to the positive or negative class are made by summing across the four feature values. In this experiment, the pigeons were rewarded for pecking in the presence of any face with a feature of values greater than zero, and not rewarded for pecking in the presence of any face with a feature sum less than zero. All 19 faces with a feature sum of zero were dropped from the experiment.

The remaining 62 faces were readily sorted by the pigeons into their respective classes. The classification performance and transfer ability exhibited by the three pigeons used in this experiment were equivalent to those of Herrnstein's pigeons. At the beginning of a new training set the pigeons showed no signs of confusion, even when previously unseen stimuli were presented. It would appear that the pigeons were able to decipher the perceptual code, which signaled the presence or absence of food. Subsequent feature analysis revealed that during training, they learned to attend equally to all four feature dimensions and to combine this information in a way that matched the experimenter's class rule. This resulted in an ordered relationship between the sum of the feature values of a particular face and the rate of responding it elicited.

These findings provide support for both the variably weighted feature model (Lea & Ryan, 1983, 1990) and the feature theory of categorization (Lea, 1984). They are also consistent with predictions derived from the Rescorla and Wagner (1972) model of classical conditioning, and classical network models such as Selfridge's (1959) Pandemonium model.

In a second study (Huber & Lenz, 1996), we continued to use Brunswik faces, but altered the class structure. The aim of this study was to test the prototype theory of categorization. It was necessary to substantially increase the number of faces. This was achieved by assigning each feature nine, rather than three, different values, thus creating 6561 different faces. The boundary between positive and negative classes was defined by a threshold distance from a "prototypical" face. These manipulations created a very confusing and demanding stimulus space that appeared to be accurately divided only by a quite sophisticated categorization mechanism. Although we never believed that this task would require true concept formation, successful performance, as it was shown by a small subset of our pigeon subjects, does shed some light upon this theory.

If pigeons solve a task that is extremely difficult for humans, who possess sophisticated conceptual tools, and which does not fit into the common notion of concepts, we might be more likely to accept that some very powerful but also very different mechanism is at work in this bird. From a mechanistic point of view, the task only requires the pigeon to average across all four feature dimensions and measure the similarity between this "central tendency" and any incoming stimulus. This strategy is consistent with a "distance to prototype model" (Reed, 1972), and also with a "generalization-from-stored-exemplars" model (Pearce, 1994). The prototype effect, which occurs when the prototypical stimulus is classified with superior accuracy, can then be explained either by its correspondence to the central tendency or by a peak shift effect. In any case, both explanations, in addition to the simple feature model, offer no place for the possession or formation of concepts that transcend the perceptual level (see also Mackintosh, 1995, for a similar conclusion in humans).

Furthermore, all of the above-mentioned findings from the pigeon laboratory can be simulated and extended by using connectionist or neural network techniques (see for instance Roitblat & von Fersen, 1992). For example, Shanks (1991) described how a simple network can simulate classification behavior by implementing the delta rule, which is formally equivalent to the Rescorla and Wagner (1972) theory of associative learning in animals. However, the problem with computer simulation is that it appears to be too flexible to predict, rather than to only correlate with, the performance of a particular species on a given classification task. For instance, although Shanks implemented a network as a sort of prototype account, the network had no difficulty also showing exemplar effects (Shanks, 1991).

It is quite possible that past research conducted in the experimental psychologist's laboratory only touched upon the natural conditions for pigeon classification. According to Watanabe et al.'s (1993) pessimistic review, there are two alternative explanations for this; either feature analysis has no chance of working effectively under natural conditions, or researchers have misunderstood the structure of natural concepts. In the remainder of this chapter, I will describe some of the critical features of natural categories, and how a simple creature might cope with them.

NATURAL CATEGORIES

The putative nature of our inferences about the perceptual code formed by pigeons in any given task can be demonstrated by a survey of the relevant literature. Researchers have been too hasty in drawing the conclusion that categorization is based upon simple aspects of form, rather than of color, texture, motion, or any statistical information inherent in natural scenes (Cerella, 1982). For decades feature analysis has been seriously underspecified at the perceptual level (Watanabe et al., 1993). Consequently, it has fallen into disgrace even among the original proponents of feature theory (e.g., Lea & Ryan, 1990). This means that the limits of our experimental subjects may be determined by the limits in our understanding. Before describing some unduly neglected feature dimensions that may be important in the natural visual environment, I will consider graphic variation as it occurs in nature.

"Hidden" perceptual differentiation

One of the most important theoretical issues in studies of perception is the concept of similarity. According to Herrnstein (1990), similarity is not equivalent to indiscriminability but an evolutionary adaptation to the natural variation in the appearance of objects. In Herrnstein's (1990) taxonomy of categorization levels, natural classes are open-ended and defined by their functional status rather than by their physical variation. However, it is conceivable that perceptual and behavioral contingencies are jointly correlated with environmental dimensions of variance. As Cerella (1979) suggests, visual classes and natural categories may be co-extensive.

Cerella arrived at this conclusion following a very clever and fortuitous set of experiments conducted in Herrnstein's laboratory at Harvard (Cerella, 1979). Four pigeons were trained to discriminate 40 examples of silhouettes of leaves of white oak trees from 40 examples of tree leaf patterns from other deciduous trees (e.g., elms, maples, tulip-trees, sassafras). After the pigeons achieved a criterion level of performance, a second sample of 40 white oak leaves was substituted for the first set, for a single test session. The pigeons not only learned to distinguish between the leaf patterns of oak and non-oak trees, they also recognized completely novel instances of the oak class without any signs of disturbance. The pigeons also transferred to test instances of oak leaf patterns following exposure to a single training instance, as readily as they did following exposure to multiple training instances.

Subsequent examination of whether the pigeons learned about the oaks, the non-oaks, or both revealed that classification ability was based primarily upon stimulus information abstracted from the oak leaf patterns. Spontaneous generalization occurred to other instances of oak leaf patterns, even if the pigeons had only been exposed to a single instance of oaks, and in the absence of any contrasting negatives. Finally, in order to examine the possibility that the oak leaves were learned in detail, Cerella trained four naive pigeons to discriminate between 40 oak leaves that were assigned to the "positive" category and 40 oak leaves that were assigned to the "negative" category. Even after 100 sessions, the pigeons were unable to sort these two stimulus sets. Furthermore, even though two birds eventually responded to differences between some of the oak instances, they generally responded more to the common characteristics of the oak leaves, and this response interfered with the required discrimination.

The results of this study suggest that pigeons are able to perceive the instances of a natural category as similar and the non-instances as dissimilar, even if this interferes with learning about reinforcement contingencies. This ability enables pigeons to generalize spontaneously to novel class instances, to distinguish instances of other classes without effort, and to confuse class instances despite continued discrimination training. According to Cerella, these classes are perceptually self-evident, i.e., their perceptual and functional boundaries are coextensive. We may therefore assume that natural categories can be described in a way that reflects their generic relationships despite individual variation in instances. Whatever these class aspects are, we must also assume that perceptual systems like the pigeon's are not only able to detect them, but are also evolutionarily preadapted to perceiving them. Categorization in this sense is an inferential process. It is not a matter for learning theorists, but for biologists studying the correspondence between perceptual systems and the actual distribution of reinforcement in the environment.

The partitioning of the natural environment into functionally relevant categories is a crucial adaptation means of virtually every perceptual system. This is fully consistent with other evolutionary predispositions that guide perception, particularly in cases in which individual experience is not yet available or incomplete. Examples include Gestalt perception, object constancy, and color perception. Animals use species-specific predispositions to focus attention upon the characteristics of objects and events, and thereby reduce the natural environment to classes that predict their effect on, or value to, the organism. Examples include young birds that discriminate between the songs of a conspecific and an alien species and monkeys that categorize their vocal repertoire. The biological significance of these behaviors is evident, although the mechanisms by which the organism transcends innate programs is not (Marler, 1982).

Sources of natural variation

When is it justifiable to speak about natural categories rather than about variations in the appearance of objects? The distinction between natural categories and natural objects is a matter of degree rather than of kind. Natural objects vary as the result of (a) the different physical conditions under which they are perceived, (b) physical changes occurring to the object over time, and (c) their generative history, which is determined by more general sets of information.

The last of these sources of variation is particularly noteworthy in this context. Living entities, or the products of living entities, are generated on the basis of a general program such as genetic information. During development, variations occur due to different sorts of perturbations. There is variation in virtually every generative event, at every level (e.g., reproduction, execution), as the result of eternal physical laws such as the second law of thermodynamics. Given this natural variation in stimulation, organisms at any level of complexity can be expected to have a means of identifying relevant objects despite variations in detail, perspective, and background. This ability has been well described in the literature, but has seldom been related to categorization. Object constancy, as it is called, is regarded as the most pervasive, although the most basic, ability of perceptual systems. It has been studied by psychophysicists interested in the function of sense organs, but not by psychologists or psycholinguists interested in the inferential processes of the brain. Despite this scientific paradox, object constancy should be viewed not only as a complicated achievement of nature, but also as a prerequisite to, or even foundation for, visual abstraction and categorization (Weiskrantz, 1985).

Natural classes are comprised of (living) *objects* that vary along one or more dimensions due to variations in a common "Bauplan". These variations are not stochastic, but follow several more or less specifiable lines. Mutations of genetic information are for the most part small, and if they are not maladaptive, then they are in very few cases neutral and in fewer cases still adaptive. As a result of constraints upon variation caused by the high level of organization inherent in biological systems, only very few sources of variation are "open". The result of biological variation and evolutionary change is radiation or continuous divergence starting from a common origin. Illustrative examples are shown in Figure 2.

Natural classes can be viewed as hierarchical fields of similarities, generated genealogically by variations in genetic information (Riedl, 1987). Taxonomists faced with harmonic-divergent fields of similarities among plants and animals (see the radiation of the mammalian forehand in Fig. 2), have tried to develop a system that reflects the genealogical paths along which these taxa have moved during evolution. Long before scientists were able to use more direct methods such as genetic finger-printing to assess the relationships between taxa, taxonomists success-fully systematized the world of biological creatures. The reason for this astonishing human achievement may lie in gestalt perception, or in the ability to sort polymorphous, multi-dimensional fields of similarities according to their underlying system of variation (Lorenz, 1974). This, in my view, is one of the perceptual, rather than inferential, capabilities that must be studied when we examine pigeon categorization.

There is no doubt that the instantaneous recording of a reinforcing event and the stimulus signaling its recurrence is an important function of the visual system. If the animal's perceptual code is to be adaptive it must reflect the actual distribution of reinforcement. In nature, the ap-pearance of a reinforcing event is often tied to taxonomic units, and this is the critical information. Is it possible to determine the critical infor-mation that is specific to natural classes? In the above example of oak leaf silhouettes, it is conceivable that the lobe pattern of oak leaves was encoded by the pigeons (Cerella, 1982). As a local feature it is shared with other oak trees, but is distinctive relative to the leaves of other genera. Failures of specificity and of generality at different taxonomic levels are caused by the fact that not all graphic characteristics are encoded by the visual system. For example, the pigeons were unable to

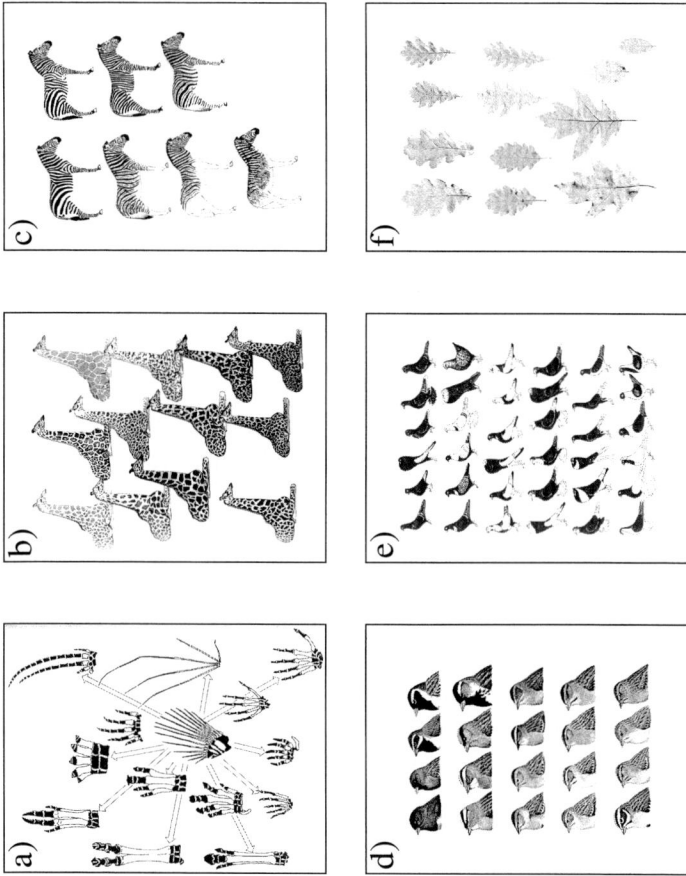

Figure 2. Examples of natural object classes. (a) Radiation of the bony forehand in vertebrates (from Riedl, 1987); (b) different morphogenetic types of giraffes; (c) different species of the zebra; (d) members of the sparrow family; (e) different races of pigeons; (f) leaf examples from different oak species.

record the individual lobe patterns of oak leaves in order to divide up the oak class.

Pattern recognition theory supplies a broad spectrum of visual domains in which critical information might be conveyed. Natural patterns offer a lot more possibilities than hitherto considered. In this sense "hidden" information may be encoded by a natural system that can effectively sort natural categories. The possibility that a pigeon makes use of texture, motion, color, and lower-order statistics was seldom regarded as an alternative to higher-order concepts in categorization experiments. On the contrary, researchers have been guided by the idea *"that discriminating persons from non-persons, for example, is a more difficult task than discriminating red from green"* (Lea, 1984, p. 264). Indeed, until the suggestion that some thoroughly abstruse single common feature (at the extreme) or a set of linearly separable features is involved in categorization is proven, *"no one is obliged to take the suggestion seriously"* (p. 267).

The role of texture and shape in natural categorization

We have taken the suggestion seriously in an attempt to investigate the influence of some very basic feature domains in the classification of natural classes (Troje, Huber, Loidolt, Aust, & Fieder, 1999). According to the ecological approach to perception (Gibson, 1979), any investigation should start by seeking to adopt the animal's eye view. Given the pigeon's exceptional color perception and orientation abilities, it seemed worthwhile to study basic stimulus aspects other than shape. Stimulus attributes can be subdivided at a basic level by distinguishing between the information carried by the spatial arrangement of structural elements contained in natural images, and the information carried by their particular appearance. In computer graphics, the terms "shape" and "texture" are used to refer to this division. We will use the term "texture" very broadly here to cover all aspects of the color or gray-level map of an object. This definition, unlike previous more restrictive definitions, does not rule out considering first-order object properties such as average luminance and chromaticity.

Recently, the differential contribution of shape and texture has been investigated in studies of the classification of human faces (Beymer & Poggio, 1996; Troje & Buelthoff, 1996; Troje & Vetter, 1998; Vetter &

Troje, 1997). To my knowledge, no attempt has ever been made to investigate the pigeon's ability to use the texture domain relative to the shape domain, particularly in complex visual tasks. One reason for this neglect may be difficulty finding appropriate stimulus material and separating the two stimulus domains. In order to control and quantify the amount of texture information that exerts control over the pigeon's responding, it is necessary to present the bird with stimuli containing this aspect alone, i.e., the information that remains if a stimulus item is normalized with respect to its shape, and vice versa when quantifying shape information.

The technical advances made by computer vision researchers in the development of representations or models of human faces (Beymer & Poggio, 1996; Vetter & Troje, 1997) enabled us to design a categorization experiment for pigeons that meets the following three criteria. First, by using the concept "sex" as the categorization criterion, we were able to present true natural categories. Male and female faces reflect polymorphous stimulus variation. These categories can be discriminated by humans (Bruce, Burton, Hanna, Healey, Mason, Coombes, Fright, & Linney, 1993), who may possess evolutionary predispositions in this respect, and also by neuronal networks (Troje & Vetter, 1998). Second, human faces are very complex visual objects. Their shape and texture provide a source of variation that is rich enough to simulate categorization problems present in the natural environment. Finally, in contrast to humans, pigeons are unlikely to be preadapted to recognize the sex of a human person from its face. We may thus study their ability to learn, rather than to apply, this complex visual class definition.

The training procedure was based on the go/no-go successive discrimination paradigm. In the presence of a positive stimulus, pigeons were required to peck repeatedly at a clear-perspex key in order to earn food. In the presence of a negative stimulus, pigeons were required to withhold pecking. These trials were never followed by food. Successful classification was defined as a high pecking rate in the presence of positive class members, and zero or a low pecking rate in the presence of negative class members. This procedure allowed us to measure classification ability not only in terms of session performance, but also in terms of individual stimuli. By averaging over many such stimuli during asymptotic performance, we were able to conduct a detailed feature analysis and to make precise predictions about how the subject solved the categorization problem.

Computer models of human faces were derived from 3-D laser scans of the heads of university students (Fig. 1). In all, 200 such faces were used. The faces were free from accessories, men were shaven, and the hair of the head was removed digitally. A correspondence-based representation of the computer faces allowed the two basic kinds of information inherent in natural objects, namely, the surface and the spatial properties, to be separated. A detailed description of the procedures applied to create the correspondence-based representation is given in Vetter and Troje (1997) and Troje and Vetter (1998).

Briefly, the representation included the correspondence between two images for every pixel location, which was established through gradient based optical flow algorithms. For all 200 faces, the correspondence to a reference face (a prototype) was calculated. The resulting images are described by a single vector containing an ordered list of color and x/y values as two separate components (Beymer & Poggio, 1996). The first part of the vector, called the "texture component", is an ordered list of the values (color or gray-scale) of corresponding pixels relative to the reference image. (The use of the term "texture" is in accordance with its meaning in computer graphics, where the texture of an object is meant to be its color or gray-level map. Note that this meaning includes first-order statistical properties such as average luminance or average chromaticity.) The shape vector is an ordered list of the disparities, or the x/y locations of corresponding features relative to the reference image.

By combining the average "texture" of all faces with the individual form we derived "shape-only" faces, i.e., faces that could only be discriminated by making use of information about shape. "Texture-only" faces were derived by combining the average shape of all faces with the individual texture, i.e., faces that could only be discriminated by making use of information about texture. In the first experiment we investigated how pigeons recognize the sex of faces when presented with either shape or texture information, and compared their performance with pigeons that were presented with the original stimuli that contained both feature domains (Fig. 1, rows 2-4). In training we used 100 images, those of 50 men and 50 women. The transfer test involved the intermixed presentation of the remaining 100 faces.

The results were surprisingly clear. Only those pigeons that had texture information available succeeded. Those subjects presented with texture-only faces or the original stimuli, showed excellent acquisition, although the latter group reached a slightly higher asymptotic level.

Shape-only pigeons showed poor discrimination. Only a small subset of these birds achieved a significant, but low, learning level.

These results suggest that (a) pigeons prefer to extract information about texture rather than shape, (b) pigeons use these features to quickly solve a complex visual categorization task, and (c) it is very unlikely that they were learning the faces by rote. When the pigeons were subsequently presented with 100 previously unseen faces, the successful birds classified them without the slightest sign of confusion (Fig. 3, upper row).

Inspection of those faces that were most accurately classified suggests that the overall intensity of the texture-only faces and the overall size of the shape-only faces provided a strong cue for categorization. Quantifying these measures revealed that the male faces were, on average, darker and larger than the female faces. We computed the partial correlation between pecking rate and either average intensity or average size and found that intensity explained a large proportion of the variance in the classification behavior of most pigeons. For both groups trained with faces that contained the texture information, the Spearman rank correlations between pecking rate and average intensity were highly significant (averaged across 16 pigeons: absolute $rs = 0.593$ for male faces, absolute $rs = 0.588$ for female faces). However, despite these high correlations, more direct evidence that the pigeons relied upon these global stimulus aspects was required. This involved presenting pigeons with test faces that were ambiguous with respect to intensity or size information (Fig. 1, rows 5 and 6).

Texture-only pigeons were shown male faces rescaled to an intensity that corresponded to the average intensity of female training faces, and vice versa for female faces. Shape-only pigeons were shown male faces at a size that corresponded to the average size of female training faces, and vice versa for female faces. As predicted, transfer ability was substantially disrupted (Fig. 3, lower row). However, while the texture-only pigeons showed some signs of positive classification, pecking in the shape-only group was reversed. Discrimination, if any, of the sex classes was thus controlled by average size when only shape information was available. If only texture information was available, discrimination was much easier. The average intensity of the faces was the main, but not the only, controlling factor. The performance of pigeons trained on the original stimuli containing the complete information revealed that they were able to combine both sorts of information. Their transfer ability was greatly affected by presenting "shape-only" stimuli, but only slightly affected by presenting "texture-only" stimuli (Fig. 3, lower-left panel).

ORIGINAL   TEXTURE   SHAPE

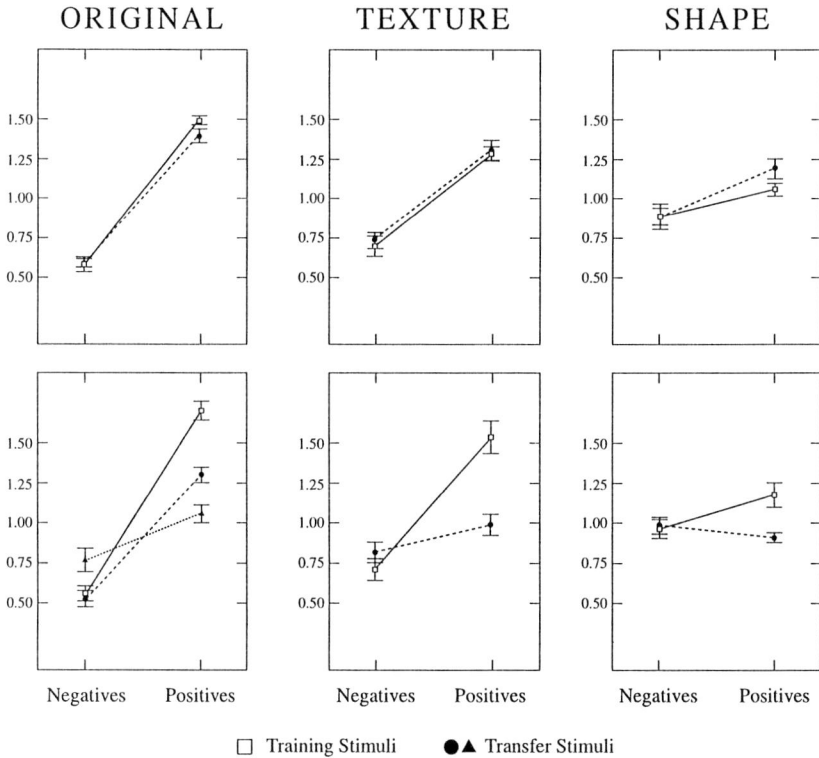

☐ Training Stimuli   ●▲ Transfer Stimuli

Figure 3. Pecking rates on positive and negative training stimuli (empty symbols) as well as positive and negative test stimuli (filled symbols).
The upper row shows the transfer performance of each training group confronted with 100 novel images presented in the same version as in training. The left diagram of the lower row shows the transfer performance of the Original group confronted with novel texture-only as well as novel shape-only stimuli. Finally, the Texture (middle) and Shape (right) groups were presented with ambiguous stimuli with respect to average intensity and average size, respectively. Pecking rates were computed by dividing the pecking rate by the average over all pecking rates measured from the same bird during the current 40-trial session. Each data point contains the averaged data of 8 subjects.

Subsequent experiments were conducted in order to determine the residual information used by the texture-only pigeons, and also to investigate how pigeons classify faces when the average intensity of "texture-only" faces is normalized (Huber, Troje, Loidolt, Aust, & Grass, submitted). Although the pigeons ($N = 11$) experienced considerable difficulty, they eventually solved this problem. Discriminant function analysis was used to determine the physical dimensions that separate male and female faces in this impoverished stimulus space. The resulting canonical discriminant function is a linear combination of the original variables (the principal components) chosen in such a way that it reflects sex differences as much as possible. Using a stepwise procedure, we found that the second principal component gives the maximum possible *F*-ratio in a one-way analysis of variance for the variation within and between groups. Interestingly, a correlation between response rates and the eigen values of the first 20 principal components revealed that only the first three components gained significant control over responding in most of the 11 subjects. Even more important, the highest correlations were found with the second component (averaged across 11 pigeons: absolute *r*s = 0.30 for male faces, absolute *r*s = 0.62 for female faces).

In order to understand what stimulus aspects these principal components (PC) represent, we generated virtual faces that were arranged along these dimensions but several standard deviations away from the mean in both directions. These "supernormal" faces show that the first PC represented the brightness gradient from the top to the bottom of the face, the second PC represented color differences, and the third PC represented shading patterns (Fig. 1, rows 7-9). In order to determine whether these stimulus aspects influenced responding, we introduced the supernormal faces into normal training sessions. Spontaneous classification followed the predicted pattern, irrespective of the sex of these virtual faces. Support for the importance of color, in contrast to other more subtle texture aspects, came from those tests in which faces were substantially destroyed by Gaussian and mosaic filters (Fig. 1, rows 10-11). Classification ability remained high over a wide range of distortions.

The difference in color between male and female faces (males tend to be more red, females tend to be more green and blue) was found to be a more important classification cue than overall brightness. However, it is important to keep in mind that we presented trichromatic computer images to animals that possess a tetra- or a pentachromatic visual system (see review in Varela, Palacios, & Goldsmith, 1993). Thus, it cannot be determined how the pigeons perceived the colors of the faces, what cone types were involved, or what type of information arrived at the higher brain centers. We can only emphasize that color played an important role in allowing the birds to discriminate between male and female faces, as shown by their poor performance on the grayscale test. Furthermore, the high correlation between the rgb-values or the second principal component (two descriptions of our manipulations in the three-dimensional color space) and the pecking rate on individual images indicated that some equivalent information controlled the pigeons' pecking behavior. Note that the correlational nature of such an analysis is an inherent problem in purely behavioural studies. *"Even if we can predict response rates exactly from a feature model, we can never be sure that the features we identify are the ones the birds are responding to; instead they may be responding to some linearly equivalent set"* (von Fersen & Lea, 1990, p. 70).

In a later experiment, we trained four naive pigeons on a black-and-white version of the texture-only/brightness-normalized task (Fig. 1, row 12). The subjects experienced considerable difficulty. Their final level of performance was only slightly better than that of the "shape-only" pigeons in the first experiment, although their transfer ability was quite good. Their classification strategy was based upon the extraction of stimulus aspects that were originally less important than color: the vertical brightness gradient which is relatively sharp in male faces due to the beard shadow but smooth in female faces, and subtle shading aspects such as deep eyes and massive eyebrows in male faces.

In conclusion, by using the complex natural classes of male and female human faces we were able to show that pigeons can perform a "concept" task very well. However, when their behavior was analyzed more closely it became necessary to propose a more mundane explanation than conceptualization. Pigeons learned to attend to those stimulus aspects that most perfectly divided up the classes in the multidimensional feature space. Extraction of the relevant information occurred on an individual basis, although the ability to do this is clearly an adaptation of the visual system. By using the principal components as face variables, and by applying discriminant function analysis in order to detect the strongest physical discriminants, we showed that the pigeons were able to track these cues in changing situations. Average brightness, color, size, and shading were used as cues, in this order of preference.

However, despite this general trend we found individual differences in the combination of cues and in their weightings. Given the pigeon's exceptional visual capabilities, particularly with respect to color perception (Varela et al., 1993) and the detection and discrimination of small differences in the spatial distribution and intensity of achromatic light (Hodos, 1993), this result is not really surprising. But it led us to claim even more strongly that feature learning might be the primary mechanism underlying picture categorization, rather than learning by rote or by the formation of concepts.

Two findings suggest that it is reasonable to generalize these results. First, Lubow (1974) reported that pigeons were able to form "higher-order concepts" by discriminating 80 black and white aerial photographs on the basis of their content of man-made objects. However, after examining the slides that were either significantly responded to or significantly avoided, he concluded that the pigeons had learned to extract simple invariants such as the presence of straight lines or the contrast between dark and light areas. Second, we are currently re-examining Herrnstein and Loveland's (1964) experiments on the superordinate "people concept" to determine whether discrimination is even based here upon "low-level" features. In a sample of 80 snapshots of everyday scenes which did or did not contain people, we were able to detect a physical measure that varied unequally across the two classes. For instance, the number of pixels in the blue spectrum (about 400 nm) differed between the classes to an extent that made significant discrimination possible. The same was also true for a number of measures derived from the co-occurrence matrix. These differences may be an artifact of the selection of experimental stimulus sets. However, this applies to most experiments conducted in the past, except perhaps single-presentation studies using several hundreds, or even several thousands, of stimuli (e.g., Wright, Cook, Rivera, Sands, & Delius, 1988).

Recent advances in computer vision, which attempt to understand the "naturalness" of natural scenes, have made substantial progress in uncovering the global aspects that correlate with semantic or superordinate categories (Field & Brady, 1997; Schaaf & Hateren, 1996). For example, instances belonging to either outdoor or indoor scenes, artificial or natural environments, and urban scenes or landscapes, are similar by means of a common global organizational regularity (Schyns & Oliva, 1994). These regularities give rise to characteristic features in the power spectrum that can be exploited by both human and artificial classifiers. Recent studies have revealed that basic predominant features extracted from the orientation distribution at various spatial scales provide enough discrimination information for scene classification (Guerin-Dugue, Bernard, & Oliva, 1998). It remains to be specified whether pigeons are sensitive to these metrics. This current empirical weakness notwithstanding, the "bottom line" is that we cannot a priori claim to present superordinate concepts if we have not exhausted the investigation of the underlying interclass similarities.

CONCLUSION

Current knowledge regarding the physical dimensions that covary with the relevant classes in the pigeon's visual world is too vague to allow any strong and coherent claims to be made. With respect to this species' ability to discriminate visual classes, at least at a concrete level, available evidence does not force us to assume that pigeons form concepts. Given the pigeon's enormous potential for picture memorization and the ability of these birds to discriminate complex visual classes through perceptual shaping and associative integration, interpreting existing research as evidence of concept formation would be misleading.

This somewhat conservative interpretation of the pigeon's visual classification abilities is based on current evidence and on attempts to study natural classification. Following Monen, Brenner, and Reynaerts (1998), we have focussed on *ecological* classes rather than on *synthetic* classes, the latter being defined by the human experimenter using some arbitrary or semantic distinctions. Because we are primarily interested in the integration of perceptual and associative abilities, I have also excluded classification studies that used individual (ontogenetically acquired) or collective (phylogenetically acquired) concepts. Surely, it would be foolish to assert that pigeons are incapable of other, perhaps more cognitive learning abilities (see for instance Cook, 1999; Delius, Siemann, Emmerton, & Xia, in press).

As noted at the beginning of this chapter, the sometimes "sloppy" manner in which animal concepts are discussed deserves attention because it distracts from the true capacities of the species under investigation. According to Mackintosh (in press), animals may represent classes of stimuli in three rather distinct ways: (i) *pictorially,* as arrays or configurations of features or elements defined in their own absolute values (called "imaginal" representations by Premack, 1983); (ii) *abstractly,* as relations between two or more arrays; and (iii) *symbolically,* as relations between relations. There is ample evidence that pigeons form pictorial representations, but only weak evidence that they form abstract representations, and no evidence that they form symbolic representations. Some birds (such as ravens and parrots) and most primates have been shown to be capable of abstract but not symbolic representation, while apes are most probably able to form symbolic representations.

The difference between pictorial and abstract representation in pigeons is currently a much disputed issue (see Delius et al., in press). This point is well-illustrated by attempts to teach pigeons the relational concepts "same/different" and "symmetry". For example, Wasserman, Hugart, and Kirkpatrick-Steger (1995) claimed to have obtained strong evidence of same/different conceptualization in pigeons because the birds in their study showed good transfer to arrays of novel icons. However, Young and Wasserman (1997) found that pigeons' performance in this task was controlled by the degree of entropy inherent in the stimulus arrays. Furthermore, despite earlier claims that pigeons form symmetry concepts (Delius & Habers, 1978; Delius & Nowak, 1982), we recently found this ability to be severely limited (Huber, Aust, Michelbach, Ölzant, Loidolt, & Nowotny, in press).

The formation of relationships between stimuli may depend not only on abstract properties but also on reinforcement contingencies. For example, Delius and coworkers recently made a strong case for equivalence formation in pigeons (Delius, Jitsumori, & Siemann, in press). In some sense (Lea, 1984), the grouping of stimuli according to their training history (e.g., always paired with reward or non-reward, see Vaughan, 1988) rather than their similarity may be interpreted as the formation of a functional concept. However, given that only pigeons with extensive training (over 100 reversals in Vaughan, 1988; negative results in Bhatt & Wasserman, 1989; von Fersen & Lea, 1990) established an equivalence between the class members, it would completely suffice to explain these results in terms of mediated or secondary generalization (Keller & Schoenfeld, 1950).

Nevertheless, some authors continue to describe pigeons' behavior in equivalence procedures in terms of conceptualization. For example, Wasserman, DeVolder, and Coppage (1992) trained pigeons to group pictures of cars and flowers into one class while concurrently grouping pictures of chairs and people into another. Since such joint category learning cannot be explained in terms of similarity, it is reasonable to speak of the formation of nonsimilarity-based or superordinate concepts, each comprised of two basic-level categories. It remains to be determined, however, whether superordinate concepts in humans are established on the basis of mediated generalization alone or whether verbalization is critical in establishing behavioral inferences.

In the human literature, concept learning has traditionally been regarded as the bastion of analytic and abstract thinking. Concepts are stable, context-free resources that mediate transfer, irrespective of whether they take on the form of prototypes, schemata, frames, diagnostic rules, or even differential habits (Jacoby & Brooks, 1984). However, this view underwent a significant conceptual shift towards a nonanalytical cognitive framework, as the result of growing evidence suggesting that generalization is based upon the similarity between new events and past events (for a review, see Medin & Smith, 1984). Despite this, humans asked to categorize artificially constructed stimulus classes behave in a purely associative manner (Mackintosh, 1995). If similarity alone were sufficient to keep the notion of a concept alive, it would undoubtedly be used to explain anything surprising or admirable about the conceptual abilities of humans. However, in a number of contexts, human categorization has been found to be more like problem solving than attribute or template matching. Therefore, there is good reason in human psychology to dismiss similarity as a sufficient or adequate categorization principle in favor of a "deeper" principle (Medin, 1989). In order to give human concepts life, coherence, and meaning, many psychologists now propose that the organization of concepts is knowledge-based and driven by theories about the world (Murphy & Medin, 1985).

In the same line, critics of the cognitivistic approach to animal behavior research emphasize that concepts have not been successfully separated from natural language, and hence do not provide good leads in terms of appropriate theoretical tools and empirical methods (Chater & Heyes, 1994). For example, concepts corresponding to natural language terms cannot be applied to nonlinguistic animals, and do not allow for empirical research in mere behavioral terms. The notion that some patterns of animal categorization correspond to human concepts does not necessarily imply that the content or structure of the animal and human concepts are identical. Language concepts are often grounded in theoretical constructs and thus cannot be viewed as being clustered together in an appropriate perceptual feature space.

Consider the following two examples. The concept "LIFE" cannot be understood on the basis of the optical arrays reflected from the surface of its members, but requires knowledge about key features such as "reproduction" and "self-organization". Obviously, pigeons cannot be assumed to have access to this critical information and therefore cannot be assumed to successfully categorize between still pictures of animate and inanimate objects unless the picture samples of each category resemble each other to some degree. Such intersimilarities may be an artefact of the experimenter's picture selection, especially if the sample size is small or has uncovered global picture properties like orientation preference in the power spectra (see above). The same argument applies to the pigeons' discrimination between paintings of Monet and Picasso (Watanabe et al., 1995). In this example, we do not believe that the pigeons proved themselves to be clever art historians, but rather demonstrated very efficient perceptual capacities (see also Monen et al., 1998).

Outside of the experimental psychologist's laboratory, categorization research has employed a wide range of species, functional contexts, and research methods. One of the most famous examples is the study of alarm calls in vervet monkeys (Cheney & Seyfarth, 1990). Vervet monkeys give and respond to six different calls in the presence of six different types of predators. With respect to the Roberts and Mazmanian (1988) study mentioned above, it is interesting to note that young vervet monkeys can distinguish between birds and other animals. However, because observations in the wild are not sufficiently reliable indicators of the extent to which young monkeys acquire conceptual behavior through learning or maturation, they will not render careful laboratory experiments and accounts in purely perceptual and associative terms superfluous. "*Perhaps exemplars of real birds that fly and sing, for example, would make a difference in how subjects categorize animals*" (Tomasello & Call, 1997, p. 117).

Thus it would appear that after three decades of research, it is not clear how best to understand conceptualization in nonlinguistic agents (Chater & Heyes, 1994). The same conclusion may apply to research on animal communication, relational concepts, and cognitive ethology. Linguistic discontinuity, rather than the inability to cope with categorical problems in nature, is the evolutionary answer for comparative psychologists attempting to close the cognitive gap between animals and man. Animal concept research will reach a dead end if it continues to interpret non-human categorization abilities in terms that cannot be freed from a linguistic or meta-theoretical base.

The consequence is a return back to nature. In order to clear up the muddy waters of animal cognitivism, we must understand that evolution has equipped animals with adaptations for dealing with categorization problems in nature. This approach requires that we investigate (a) the sensory-physiological, neuronal, and behavioral predispositions of the species under study, (b) the means by which reinforcement shapes the polymorphous description of natural classes, and (c) the perceptual dimensions that covary with natural classes. Only in this sense may categorization be viewed as the groundwork of cognition (Harnad, 1987), a study in its own right, without denying human competencies.

REFERENCES

Abbott, L. F., Rolls, E. T., & Tovee, M. J. (1996). Representational capacity of face coding in monkeys. *Cerebral Cortex, 6*, 498-505.

Abs, M. (Ed.) (1983). *Physiology and behaviour of the pigeon.* London: Academic Press.

Astley, S. L., & Wasserman, E. A. (1992). Categorical discrimination and generalization in pigeons: All negative stimuli are not created equal. *Journal of Experimental Psychology: Animal Behavior Processes, 18*, 193-207.

Beymer, D., & Poggio, T. (1996). Image representations for visual learning. *Science, 272*, 1905-1908.

Bhatt, R. S., & Wasserman, E. A. (1989). Secondary generalization and categorization in pigeons. *Journal of the Experimental Analysis of Behavior, 52*, 213-224.

Blough, D. S., & Fanklin, J. J. (1985). Pigeon discrimination of letters and other forms in texture displays. *Perception and Psychophysics, 38*, 523-532.

Bruce, V., Burton, A. M., Hanna, E., Healey, P., Mason, O., Coombes, A., Fright, R., & Linney, A. (1993). Sex discrimination: how do we tell the difference between male and female faces? *Perception, 22*, 131-152.

Cerella, J. (1979). Visual classes and natural categories in the pigeon. *Journal of Experimental Psychology: Human Perception and Performance, 5*, 68-77.

Cerella, J. (1980). The pigeon's analysis of pictures. *Pattern Recognition, 12*, 1-6.

Cerella, J. (1982). Mechanisms of concept formation in the pigeon. In D. J. Ingle, M. A., Goodale & R. J. W. Mansfield (Eds.), *Analysis of visual behavior* (pp. 241-259). Cambridge, MA: MIT Press.

Cerella, J. (1986). Pigeons and perceptrons. *Pattern Recognition, 19*, 431-438.

Chater, N., & Heyes, C. (1994). Animal concepts: Content and discontent. *Mind and Language, 9*, 209-246.

Cheney, D. L., & Seyfarth, R. M. (1990). *How monkeys see the world.* Chicago, IL/London: University of Chicago Press.

Cook, R. G. (Ed.) (1999). *Avian visual cognition.* World Wide Web (http://www.pigeon.psy.tufts.edu/ avc).

Cook, R. G., Wright, A. A., & Kendrick, D. F. (1990). Visual categorization by pigeons. In M. L. Commons, R. J. Herrnstein, S. M., Kosslyn & D. B. Mumford (Eds.), *Behavioral approaches to pattern recognition and concept formation* (Vol. 8, pp. 187-214). Hillsdale, NJ: Erlbaum.

D'Amato, M. R., & Van Sant, P. (1988). The person concept in monkeys (*Cebus apella*). *Journal of Experimental Psychology: Animal Behavior Processes, 14*, 43-55.

Delius, J. D., & Habers, G. (1978). Symmetry: Can pigeons conceptualize it? *Behavioral Biology, 22,* 336-342.

Delius, J. D., Jitsumori, M., & Siemann, M. (in press). Stimulus equivalencies through discrimination reversals. In C. Heyes & L. Huber (Eds.), *Evolution of cognition.* Cambridge, MA: MIT Press.

Delius, J. D., & Nowak, B. (1982). Visual symmetry recognition by pigeons. *Psychological Research, 44,* 199-212.

Delius, J. D., Siemann, M., Emmerton, J., & Xia, L. (in press). Cognitions of birds as products of evolved brains. In G. Roth & M.F. Wullimann (Eds.), *Brain evolution and cognition.* New York: Wiley.

Edwards, C.A., & Honig, W. K. (1987). Memorization and "feature selection" in the acquisition of natural concepts in pigeons. *Learning and Motivation, 18*, 235-260.

Fabre-Thorpe, M., Ghislaine, R., & Thorpe, S. J. (1998). Rapid categorization of natural images by rhesus monkeys. *Neuroreport, 9*, 303-308.

Field, D. J., & Brady, N. (1997). Visual sensitivity, blur, and the source of variability in the amplitude spectra of natural scenes. *Vision Research, 37,* 3367-3383.

Gibson, J. J. (1979). *The ecological approach to visual perception.* Boston, MA: Houghton Mifflin.

Greene, S. L. (1983). Feature memorization in pigeon concept formation. In M. L. Commons, R. J. Herrnstein, & A. R. Wagner (Eds.), *Discrimination processes* (Vol. 4, pp. 209-229). Cambridge, MA: Ballinger.

Guerin-Dugue, A., Bernard, P., & Oliva, A. (1998). Search for scale-space salient orientations in real-world scenes. *Perception, 27* (Suppl.), 151.

Harnad, S. (1987). *Categorical perception. The groundwork of cognition.* Cambridge, MA: Cambridge University Press.

Hauser, M. D. (1996). *The evolution of communication*. Cambridge, MA: MIT Press.

Herrnstein, R. J. (1985). Riddles of natural categorization. In L. Weiskrantz (Ed.), *Animal intelligence* (Vol. 7, pp. 129-144). Oxford: Clarendon Press.

Herrnstein, R. J. (1990). Levels of stimulus control: A functional approach. *Cognition, 37*, 133-166.

Herrnstein, R. J., & De Villiers, P.A. (1980). Fish as a natural category for people and pigeons. In G. H. Bower (Ed.), *The psychology of learning and motivation* (Vol. 14, pp. 59-95). New York: Academic Press.

Herrnstein, R. J., Loveland, D. H., & Cable, C. (1976). Natural concepts in pigeons. *Journal of Experimental Psychology: Animal Behavior Processes, 2*, 285-302.

Hodos, W. (1993). The visual capabilities of birds. In H. P. Zeigler & H.-J. Bischof (Eds.), *Vision, brain, and behavior in birds* (pp. 63-776). Cambridge, MA: MIT Press.

Huber, L. (1995). On the biology of perceptual categorization. *Evolution and Cognition, 1*, 121-138.

Huber, L. (1999). Visual categorization in pigeons. In R. G. Cook (Ed.), *Avian visual cognition: World Wide Web* (http://www.pigeon.psy.tufts.edu/avc).

Huber, L., Aust, U., Michelbach, G., Ölzant, S., Loidolt, M., & Nowotny, R. (in press). Limits on symmetry conceptualization in pigeons. *Quarterly Journal of Experimental Psychology*.

Huber, L., & Lenz, R. (1993). A test of the linear feature model of polymorphous concept discrimination with pigeons. *Quarterly Journal of Experimental Psychology, 46B*, 1-18.

Huber, L., & Lenz, R. (1996). Categorisation of prototypical stimulus classes by pigeons. *Quarterly Journal of Experimental Psychology, 49B*, 111-133.

Huber, L., Troje, N. F., Loidolt, M., Aust, U., & Grass, D. (submitted). Natural categorization through multiple feature learning in pigeons.

Jacoby, L. L., & Brooks, L. R. (1984). Nonanalytic cognition: Memory, perception, and concept learning. *The Psychology of Learning and Motivation, 18*, 1-47.

Jitsumori, M. (1993). Category discrimination of artificial polymorphous stimuli based on feature learning. *Journal of Experimental Psychology: Animal Behavior Processes, 19*, 244-254.

Jitsumori, M. (1994). Discrimination of artificial polymorphous categories by rhesus monkeys (*Macaca mulatta*). *Quarterly Journal of Experimental Psychology, 47B*, 371-386.

Keller, F. S., & Schoenfeld, W. N. (1950). *Principles of psychology*. New York: Appleton-Century-Crofts.

Lea, S. E. G. (1984). In what sense do pigeons learn concepts? In H. L. Roitblat, T. G. Bever, & H. S. Terrace (Eds.), *Animal cognition* (pp. 263-276). Hillsdale, NJ: Lawrence Erlbaum Associates.

Lea, S. E. G., Lohmann, A., & Ryan, C. M. (1993). Discrimination of five-dimensional stimuli by pigeons: Limitations of feature analysis. *Quarterly Journal of Experimental Psychology, 46B*, 19-42.

Lea, S. E. G., & Ryan, C. M. E. (1983). Feature analysis of pigeons' acquisition of concept discrimination. In M. L. Commons, R. J. Herrnstein, & A. R. Wagner (Eds.), *Discrimination processes* (Vol. 4, pp. 263-276). Cambridge, MA: Ballinger.

Lea, S. E. G., & Ryan, C. M. E. (1990). Unnatural concepts and the theory of concept discrimination in birds. In M. L. Commons, R. J. Herrnstein, S. M. Kosslyn, & D. B. Mumford (Eds.), *Quantitative analysis of behavior* (Vol. 8, pp. 165-185). Cambridge, MA: Ballinger.

Lorenz, K. (1974). Analogy as a source of knowledge. *Science, 185,* 229-234.

Lubow, R. E. (1974). High-order concept formation in the pigeon. *Journal of the Experimental Analysis of Behavior, 21,* 475-483.

Mackintosh, N. J. (1995). Categorization by people and pigeons: The twenty-second Bartlett memorial lecture. *Quarterly Journal of Experimental Psychology, 48B*, 193-214.

Mackintosh, N. J. (in press). Abstraction and discrimination. In C. Heyes & L. Huber (Eds.), *Evolution of cognition*. Cambridge, MA: MIT Press.

Macphail, E. M. (1987). The comparative psychology of intelligence. *Behavioral and Brain Sciences, 10,* 645-695.

Malott, R. W. & Siddall, J. W. (1972). Acquisition of the people concept in pigeons. *Psychological Reports, 31,* 3-13.

Marler, P. R., (1982). Avian and primate communication: The problem of natural categories. *Neuroscience and Biobehavioral Reviews, 6,* 87-94.

Medin, D. L. (1989). Concepts and conceptual structure. *American Psychologist, 44,* 1469-1481.

Medin, D. L., & Smith, E.E. (1984). Concepts and concept formation. *Annual Review of Psychology, 35,* 113-138.

Monen, J., Brenner, E., & Reynaerts, J. (1998). What does a pigeon see in a Picasso? *Journal of the Experimental Analysis of Behavior, 69,* 223-226.

Morgan, M. J., Fitch, M. D., Holman, J. G., & Lea, S. E. G. (1976). Pigeons learn the concept of an "A". *Perception, 5,* 57-66.

Murphy, G. L., & Medin, D. L. (1985). The role of theories in conceptual coherence. *Psychological Review, 92,* 283-285.

Nahm, F. D. K., Perret, A., Amaral, D. G., & Albright, T. D. (1997). How do monkeys look at faces? *Journal of Cognitive Neuroscience, 9,* 611-623.

Neisser, U. (1987). *Concepts and conceptual development. Ecological and intellectual factors in categorization*. Cambridge, MA: Cambridge University Press.

Pearce, J. M. (1994). Discrimination and categorization. In N. J. Mackintosh (Ed.), *Animal learning and cognition* (pp. 109-134). San Diego, CA: Academic Press.

Poole, J., & Lander, D. G. (1971). The pigeon's concept of pigeon. *Psychonomic Science, 25,* 157-158.

Porter, D., & Neuringer, A. (1984). Music discriminations by pigeons. *Journal of Experimental Psychology: Animal Behavior Processes, 10,* 138-148.

Premack, D. (1983) Animal cognition. *Annual Review of Psychology, 34,* 351-362.

Reed, S. K. (1972). Pattern recognition and categorization. *Cognitive Psychology, 3,* 382-407.

Rescorla, R., & Wagner, A.R. (1972). A theory of Pavlovian conditioning. Variations in the effectiveness of reinforcement and nonreinforcement. In A. H. Black & W. F. Prokasy (Eds.), *Classical conditioning II: Current research and theory* (pp. 64-99). New York: Appleton-Century-Crofts.

Riedl, R. (1987). *Begriff und Welt. Biologische Grundlagen des Erkennens und Begreifens.* Berlin, Hamburg: Parey.

Roberts, W. A., & Mazmanian, D. S. (1988). Concept learning at different levels of abstraction by pigeons, monkeys, and people. *Journal of Experimental Psychology: Animal Behavior Processes, 14,* 247-260.

Roitblat, H. L., & Meyer, J.-A. (Eds.) (1995). *Comparative approaches to cognitive science.* Cambridge, MA: MIT Press.

Roitblat, H. L., & von Fersen, L. (1992). Comparative cognition: Representations and processes in learning and memory. *Annual Review of Psychology, 43,* 671-710.

Rolls, E. T., Treves, A., Tovee, M. J., & Panzeri, S. (1998). Information in the neuronal representation of individual stimuli in the primate temporal visual cortex. *Journal of Computational Neuroscience, 4,* 309-333.

Rosch, E., & Mervis, C. B. (1975). Family resemblances: Studies in the internal structure of categories. *Cognitive Psychology, 7,* 573-605.

Ryle, G. (1949). *The concept of mind.* London: Hutchinson.

Schaaf, A., & Hateren, J. H. (1996). Modelling the power spectra of natural images: Statistics and information. *Vision Research, 36,* 2759-2770.

Schrier, A. M., & Brady, P. M. (1987). Categorization of natural stimuli by monkeys (*Macaca mulatta*): Effects of stimulus set size and modification of exemplars. *Journal of Experimental Psychology: Animal Behavior Processes, 13,* 136-143.

Schyns, P. G., & Oliva, A. (1994). From blobs to boundary edges: Evidence for time and spatial scale scene recognition. *Psychological Science, 5,* 195-200.

Selfridge, O. G. (1959). Pandemonium: a paradigm for learning. In *Mechanisation of thought processes: Proceedings of a Symposium held at the National Physical Laboratory* (pp. 513-526). London: HM Stationery Office.

Shank, R. C., Collins, G. C., & Hunter, L. E. (1986). Transcending inductive category formation. *Behavioral and Brain Sciences, 9,* 639-686.

Shanks, D. R. (1991). Categorization by a connectionist network. *Journal of Experimental Psychology: Learning, Memory, and Cognition, 17,* 433-443.

Shettleworth, S. (1998). *Cognition, evolution and behavior.* New York, Oxford: Oxford University Press.

Thompson, R. K. R. (1995). Natural and relational concepts in animals. In H. L. Roitblat & J.-A. Meyer (Eds.), *Comparative approaches to cognitive science* (pp. 175-224). Cambridge, MA: MIT Press.

Tomasello, M., & Call, J. (1997). *Primate cognition.* New York, Oxford: Oxford University Press.

Troje, N., & Buelthoff, H. (1996). Face recognition under varying poses: The role of texture and shape. *Vision Research, 36,* 1761-1771.

Troje, N. F., Huber, L., Loidolt, M., Aust, U., & Fieder, M. (1999). Categorical learning in pigeons: The role of texture and shape in complex static stimuli. *Vision Research, 39,* 353- 366.

Troje, N., & Vetter, T. (1998). Representations of human faces. In C. Taddei-Ferretti & C. Musio (Eds.), *Downward processing in the perception representation mechanism* (pp. 189-205). Singapore: World Scientific.

Varela, F. J., Palacios, A. G. & Goldsmith, T. H. (1993). Color vision of birds. In H. P. Zeigler & H.-J. Bischof (Eds.), *Vision, brain, and behavior in birds* (pp. 77-98). Cambridge, MA: MIT Press.

Vauclair, J. (1996). *Animal cognition. An introduction to modern comparative psychology.* Cambridge, MA/London: Harvard University Press.

Vaughan, W. J. (1988). Formation of equivalence sets in pigeons. *Journal of Experimental Psychology: Animal Behavior Processes, 14,* 36-42.

Vaughan, W., & Greene, S. L. (1984). Pigeon visual memory capacity. *Journal of Experimental Psychology: Animal Behavior Processes, 10,* 256-271.

Vetter, T., & Troje, N. (1997). Separation of texture and shape in images of faces for image coding and synthesis. *Journal of the Optical Society of America A, 14,* 2152-2161.

von Fersen, L., & Delius, J. D. (1989). Long-term retention of many visual patterns by pigeons. *Ethology, 82,* 141-155.

von Fersen, L., & Lea, S.E. (1990). Category discrimination by pigeons using five polymorphous features. *Journal of the Experimental Analysis of Behavior, 54,* 69-84.

Wasserman, E. A. (1991). The pecking pigeon: A model of complex visual processing. *Contemporary Psychology, 36,* 605-606.

Wasserman, E. A., DeVolder, C. L., & Coppage, D. J. (1992). Non-similarity-based conceptualization in pigeons via secondary or mediated generalization. *Psychological Science, 3,* 374-379.

Wasserman, E. A., Hugart, J. A., & Kirkpatrick-Steger, K. (1995). Pigeons show same-different conceptualization after training with complex visual stimuli. *Journal of Experimental Psychology: Animal Behavior Processes, 21,* 248-252.

Wasserman, E. A., Kiedinger, R. E. & Bhatt, R. S. (1988). Conceptual behavior in pigeons: Categories, subcategories, and pseudocategories. *Journal of Experimental Psychology: Animal Behavior Processes, 14,* 235-246.

Watanabe, S. (1988). Failure of visual prototype learning in the pigeon. *Animal Learning and Behavior, 16,* 147-152.

Watanabe, S., Lea, S. E. G., & Dittrich, W. H. (1993). What can we learn from experiments on pigeon concept discrimination? In H. P. Zeigler & H.-J. Bischof (Eds.), *Vision, brain, and behavior in birds* (pp. 351-376). Cambridge: MIT Press.

Watanabe, S., Sakamoto, J., & Wakita, M. (1995). Pigeons' discrimination of painting by Monet and Picasso. *Journal of the Experimental Analysis of Behavior, 63,* 165-174.

Weiskrantz, L. (1985). *Animal intelligence.* Oxford Psychology Series No. 7. Oxford: Clarendon.

Whorf, B. L. (1956). *Language, thought and reality.* Cambridge, MA: MIT Press.

Wittgenstein, L. (1953). *Philosophical investigations.* New York: Macmillan.

Wright, A. A., Cook, R. C., Rivera, J. J., Sands, S. F. & Delius, J. D. (1988). Concept learning by pigeons: Matching-to-sample with trial-unique video picture stimuli. *Animal Learning and Behavior, 16,* 436-444.

Young, M. E., & Wasserman, E. A. (1997). Entropy detection by pigeons: Response to mixed visual displays after same-different discrimination training. *Journal of Experimental Psychology: Animal Behavior Processes, 23,* 157-170.

Zeigler, H. P., & Bischof, H.-J. (Eds.) (1993). *Vision, brain, and behavior in birds.* Cambridge, MA: MIT Press.

Picture perception in primates:
The case of face perception

Olivier Pascalis,[1] Odile Petit,[2] Jun H. Kim,[3]
and Ruth Campbell[4]

1. *The University of Sheffield, UK*
2. *Université Louis Pasteur, Strasbourg, France*
3. *University of Washington, Seattle, WA, USA*
4. *University College London, UK*

Abstract

This paper reviews studies of processing of monkey-images by non-human primates of same and different species. We describe some ethological approaches to primate cognition that have a bearing on this. We then review the literature on experimental studies of conspecific and face perception in non-human primates in order to clarify those aspects of the image which may be processed by monkeys, with implications for human visual processing of such stimuli. The aim of the review is to provide a general overview, with methodological comments, of behavioural studies in this field.

Key words: Face, perception, primate.

Correspondence should be sent to Olivier Pascalis, Department of Psychology, The University of Sheffield, Psychology Building, Sheffield S10 2TP, UK (e-mail: O.Pascalis@Sheffield.ac.uk).

INTRODUCTION

One of the perceptual abilities that primates other than humans need to have in order to function effectively is the ability to identify individuals within the group, and to interpret their expressions and intentions. In humans, face-processing abilities underpin such functions (Bruce & Young, 1998). If it can be established that all primates show similar face processing abilities, that would suggest a common evolutionary route for this important ability and possibly for visual cognition more generally. In humans, pictures are used to test these skills and our knowledge of visual recognition in non-human primates has also been established using still images such as photographs or slides. The use of pictures is technically important because such displays permit control and principled investigation of image qualities such as brightness, contrast, spatial frequency, and so on. However they do not help in answering the most important question of all: what does the picture represent to the animal?

One way to approach this question has used cross-modal perception. If an animal can map haptic knowledge of an object to its visual characteristics, so that it can recognise by eye an object presented by touch (or vice-versa), that would suggest that the animal's behavioural response to a picture extends beyond the image to other characteristics of the object represented. The data on this in primates are contradictory. For example, whereas Davenport and Rogers (1971) found chimpanzees (*Pan troglodytes*) can recognise haptically learned objects from pictures, Winner and Ettlinger (1979) did not. Malone, Tolan, and Rogers (1980) explored this ability in a single rhesus macaque (*Macaca mulatta*): only after long training could their subject perform correctly on a cross-modal task. Developmental data have been more consistent. Gunderson (1983) showed that 4-week-old infant pigtail macaques visually recognised a pacifier that they learned orally before. Gunderson, Rose, and Grant-Webster (1990) showed that 4-week-old monkeys can also recognise visually an object that they learned haptically.

A second approach has been to study categorisation. As suggested by Zayan and Vauclair (1998), categorisation "implies that subjects have detected some invariant properties of unique objects that are being represented". If monkeys who are able to categorise real objects are then tested with pictures, and can categorise them appropriately, that would suggest that non-human primates perceive the pictured object as a representation of, or equivalent to, the real one. The data obtained here are also confused. For example, whereas Sands, Lincoln, and Wright (1982) showed that rhesus monkeys can distinguish the categories of fruit/ monkey/human on slides, Vauclair and Fagot (1996) found that Guinea baboons (*Papio papio*) tested this way have limited categorical abilities. D'Amato and Van Sant (1988) showed that capuchin monkeys (*Cebus apella*), could categorise two types of complex scenes in pictures: one category included scenes with humans (*Homo sapiens*) and another those without. They first concluded that these monkeys had a concept of "human" from pictures, but a detailed analysis showed that the categorisation could have been made on a different basis (reddish coloration of one set of slides) than that intended by the authors (see Zayan & Vauclair, 1998, for a review of categorisation in non-human primates).

To date, then, cross-modal matching and categorisation have failed to indicate clearly what a primate perceives from a picture. This failure could sometimes be a consequence of the use of human categories which are inappropriate for use by non-human primates. Some studies have therefore tried to use pictures of greater relevance and salience to the species investigated. The complexity of social organisation and inter-individual communication in all primates, including humans, implies recognition and distinction of conspecifics. The recognition of the species or group is also clearly indicated from observation of homogeneous social groups (see below). From such evidence, species recognition (within-species individuation and species identification more generally) may be a very good candidate domain in which to explore and evaluate cognitive skills such as picture perception in the non-human primate. It is in this area that we can be reasonably sure that the animal subject's behaviour with respect to a picture (of a face or face and body of another individual, or group of individuals) is representative of the animal's cognition more generally and not just its response to an image projected on a screen.

The present article will, firstly, outline some ethological approaches to primate cognition that have a bearing on this issue, and then review the literature on conspecific and face perception in non-human primates as conducted within an experimental tradition. We will try to link this review to some studies of face processing in humans. The review is, however, selective. We will not report in detail on the neurobiology of face processing in which research on primate neural systems has figured (see, e.g., Tovée & Cohen-Tovée, 1993), but we will refer to some of the developmental literature since, in monkeys as in humans, specific experience with different stimulus arrays and different individuals may shape perceptual and recognition skills.

In the review that follows we are also careful to distinguish between discrimination, where there is behavioural evidence that the subject has made a perceptual distinction between stimuli or classes of stimuli, and recognition, where there is behavioural evidence that a stimulus event has been registered as familiar, tagged as such, and elicited a specific, familiarity-based response. As far as we can tell there are no single studies conclusively demonstrating that recognition has been achieved when it is defined in this stringent way. However, such a demonstration necessarily requires converging evidence from several sources and it is possible that the weight of converging evidence from similar and from different paradigms may convince the reader that (strong) recognition has indeed been achieved in some cases.

ETHOLOGY

Non-human primates must recognise the features of the environment where they live, to behave in the most appropriate way according to that environment. We will distinguish between the physical environment and the social one.

Knowledge of physical environment

In their home range, non-human primates eat seasonal food which is located in special places. From one year to the next, location of food is quite identical, but types of food change according to the seasons. Non-human primates must remember food locations from one year to another to forage efficiently.

Menzel tested Japanese macaques (*Macaca fuscata*) with native akebi fruit (*Akebia trifoliata*) which is highly preferred food. The fruit was presented to monkeys from approximately four weeks before, until about 6 weeks after the time when ripe akebi fruit was available in the home range (Menzel, 1991). When presented with pieces of akebi fruit, Japanese macaques ate them and then investigated distant trees containing akebi vines, even at times of year when the naturally occurring akebi fruit was not ripe. These vines could not have been visible to the animals at the outset of their travel. Reacting animals were older than 3 years and hence old enough to have eaten the fruit in previous seasons (Menzel, 1991). Foraging after presentation of akebi fruit is extended to the *Akebia quinata*, vines which suggests a plant categorisation by monkeys.

Knowledge of social environment

We will consider the three kinds of individuals of the social environment of a non-human primate: predators, members of other social groups of non-human primates, and members of its own group.

Recognition of predators. Wild-born rhesus monkeys showed fear reactions when they were confronted with snakes, models, or toy snakes (Mineka, Davidson, Cook, & Keir, 1984). Individuals born in captivity showed a fear reaction only after seeing their wild-born conspecific reacting fearfully to the snake or the model (Mineka et al., 1984). A pile of food with a fear object on the top (plastic model of a snake or alligator) was presented to a group of chimpanzees (Menzel, 1971). Animals stared at the pile and "mobbed" it by throwing sticks, slapping with a hand and jumping back, or hanging over the object by a tree and "tree shaking" (Menzel, 1971). Boesch (1991) observed the use of sticks by chimpanzees against a wild living leopard. Kortlandt tested different groups of chimpanzees with a stuffed leopard: animals were observed displaying threats, harassing and mobbing it, or throwing big sticks towards the "false" leopard (for further details, see Kortlandt, 1994).

So, non-human primates recognise predators and emit alarm calls when encountering them in their natural environment. According to recognition, it is interesting to note that some species are able to distinguish between predators in the wild. Zuberbühler, Noë, and Seyfarth (1997) report that male diana monkeys (*Cercopithecus diana diana*) display different alarm calls corresponding to different predators. Analysis of alarm calls given to leopards (*Panthera pardus*) and crown hawk eagles (*Stephanoaetus coronatus*) showed that they differed according to a number of acoustic parameters. When playing the two call variants to different diana monkey groups, conspecifics responded to them as though the original predator was present (Zuberbühler et al., 1997). Vervet monkeys (*Cercopithecus aethiops*) present the same pattern by emitting different alarm calls according to different predators (Struhsaker, 1967). Experiments conducted with leopard, snakes, or vervet silhouettes elicit alarm calls from captive vervet monkeys in contrast with goose or eagle silhouettes (Brown, Kreiter, Maple, & Sinnott, 1992).

When infant vervets first begin giving alarm calls, they often make "mistakes" and give alarms to species that pose no danger to them (Cheney & Seyfarth, 1990). Adult vervet monkeys give eagle alarm calls almost exclusively to raptors (family *Falconidae*). Within this class, they give alarm calls most often to the vervets' two confirmed predators, martial and crowned eagles. Juveniles are less selective but more likely to give alarm calls to raptors than to nonraptors. Infants are the least selective and do not distinguish between these two broad classes of birds. Nevertheless, infants give eagle alarm calls only to birds and things in the air (a falling leaf) (Cheney & Seyfarth, 1990).

Vervet monkeys can respond to the alarm calls of other species as well. Play-back experiments lead to results that support the view that vervet monkeys treat superb starling (*Spreo superbus*) alarms as relatively precise signals (Cheney & Seyfarth, 1990). Red colobus (*Procolobus badius*) follow groups of Diana monkeys and use their alarm calls to escape to the predation pressure from chimpanzees (Noë & Bshary, 1997).

Although the monkeys do recognise and respond to the different alarm calls given by birds, non-primate mammals, and other non-human primates, they appear to ignore the visual and behavioural cues associated with some predators. Apparently, they do not recognise the relationship between a python and its track, nor do they understand that a carcass in a tree indicates a leopard's proximity (Cheney & Seyfarth, 1990).

Recognition of other groups of non-human primates. Different groups of the same species can live in the same area with different territories. Inter-group encounters can then occur. In vervet monkeys, when the members of one group first spot another group, they give a loud, trill-like vocalisation called *wrr*, which apparently functions to inform members of their own group and to warn members of the neighbouring group that they have spotted (Cheney, 1987; Cheney & Seyfarth, 1990). Play-back experiments were designed to examine whether monkeys can recognise the members of other groups by voice alone. When a call was played from an inappropriate territory (call of A-group from B-group territory), vervets responded more strongly than to a call which was played from the true range of the vocaliser's group. Therefore, vervets seemed to associate the vocalisations of individual members of other groups with those groups' territories (Cheney & Seyfarth, 1990).

Recognition of different individuals. In social groups of non-human primates, individuals are very often ranked from subordinate to dominant. These ranks result from agonistic interactions which lead to a winner and a loser. When several such interactions have the same stable outcome, one individual is dominant over the other one. This real dominance could be expressed in a formal way by individuals (de Waal, 1982): the subordinate could avoid the incoming dominant individual or displays its submissive silent bared-teeth towards him. For the subordinate animal, this is the recognition of his lower status and of the other individual dominance (de Waal & Luttrell, 1985).

In social groups, kin and non-kin individuals are interacting. When infant and juvenile vervets scream during rough play, their mothers often run to support them. This behaviour suggests that females can distinguish among the calls of different individuals (Cheney & Seyfarth, 1990). In a play-back experiment, Cheney and Seyfarth (1980) played the scream of a 2-year-old juvenile to its mother and two control females who also had offspring in the group. They found that mothers consistently looked towards or approached the speaker for longer durations than did control females, indicating that they recognise the voice of their offspring.

After a conflict, former opponents could have a non-aggressive contact: this post-conflict contact is called reconciliation (de Waal & van Roosmalen, 1979) and was studied in several species (see Kappeler & Van Schaik, 1992, for a review). When studying reconciliation in captive patas monkeys (*Erythrocebus patas*), York and Rowell (1988) found that unrelated animals contacted the kin of their former opponents almost twice as often following a fight as during control periods (i.e., without previous conflict). The same pattern is observed in other species (Cheney & Seyfarth, 1989, for vervet monkeys; Judge, 1991, for pig-tailed macaques, *Macaca nemestrina*; Aureli & van Schaik, 1991, and Das, Penke, & Van Hooff, 1997, for longtailed macaques, *Macaca fascicularis*).

Recognition of the relationships. The preceding results show that non-human primates recognise nonetheless the type of relationship they have with other group members, but that they are also conscious of the relationship which exists between two other group members even if they are not involved in the relationship themselves (Hinde, 1983).

When Cheney and Seyfarth (1980) played the scream of a 2-year old juvenile to its mother and two control females, they found that the mother recognised the voice of her offspring by looking at and approaching the speaker, but they noted that the control females looked at the mother. By associating particular screams with particular juveniles, and these juveniles with particular adult females, the control females behaved as if they recognised the kinship relations that existed among other group members (Cheney & Seyfarth, 1990). Dasser (1988) conducted a study on a group of 40 captive longtailed macaques. She trained two females to press a response button when two slides of pairs of individuals were presented: females were rewarded when they chose a mother-offspring pair against an unrelated pair of individuals. Subjects correctly selected the mother-offspring pair in all tests even when the offspring was a male or a female, an infant, a juvenile, or an adult (Dasser, 1988).

Finally, monkeys seem not only to recognise the relationships of others but also to compare relationships, judging some to be similar and others to be different (Cheney & Seyfarth, 1990).

EXPERIMENTAL STUDIES

Ethological studies have demonstrated that non-human primates can categorise their species and their predators, and can recognise individuals within their community and their relationship with a specific individual. Such findings cannot be replicated directly in the laboratory with real objects and real individuals. Here, picture studies come into their own, and allow us to infer some of the cognitive processes whereby an animal perceives another as friend or foe, kin or non-kin. These are summarised in Table 1.

Species discrimination

Real-life recognition of species is salient and efficient in many primates, so this is an obvious area in which to conduct lab-based picture-

Table 1
Summary of the authors, species studies, and results of experimental studies using picture on either species discrimination or face discrimination in nonhuman primates

Authors	Species	Task	Results
Boysen & Berntson (1989)	Chimpanzee *Pan troglodytes*	Heart rate	Heart rate varies among the expression of the face presented.
Bruce (1982)	Longtailed macaque *Macaca fascicularis*	Concurrent discrimination	There is discrimination among individuals from their species but no inversion effect.
Dasser (1987)	Longtailed macaque	Simultaneous discrimination and matching-to-sample	Recognition of wellknown individuals on slides.
Demaria & Thierry (1988)	Stumptailed macaque *Macaca arctoides*	Looking time	Greater looking time for their species.
Dittrich (1990)	Longtailed macaque	Visual discrimination	No inversion effect for facial line drawing.
Dittrich (1994)	Longtailed macaque	Visual discrimination	Face is important in conspecific recognition.

Table 1 (continued)

Authors	Species	Task	Results
Fujita (1987)	Japanese macaque *Macaca fuscata*, rhesus macaque *Macaca mulatta*, Bonnet macaque *Macaca radiata*, Pigtail macaque *Macaca nemestrina*, Stumptailed macaque	Duration of lever-pressing to see a picture	Macaques visually discriminate their conspecifics from close species based on the still image of them.
Fujita (1993)	Pigtailed macaque	Duration of lever-pressing to see a picture	Species preference. The head may be relatively more important than the other features.
Fujita & Watanabe (1995)	Sulawesi macaque	Fixation time to the stimulus	Discrimination among several macaque species.
Humphrey (1974)	Rhesus macaque	Habituation, dishabituation	Discrimination of conspecifics observed. Discrimination of individuals from a different species occurred only after experience.
Keating & Keating (1982)	Rhesus macaque	Eye tracking	Human and monkey faces are scanned in the same way.

Table 1 (continued)

Authors	Species	Task	Results
Kim, Gunderson & Swartz (1999)	Pigtailed macaque	Visual paired comparison task	Infant monkeys recognize faces of own species only.
Nahm, Perret, Amaral & Albright (1997)	Rhesus macaque	Eye tracking	Scanning of conspecific or human face is identical: internal features and eyes are the most important.
Overman & Doty (1982)	Rhesus macaque and human *Homo sapiens*	Matching-to-sample	Recognition across species is possible on picture. Inversion effect is also present in monkeys.
Parr, Dove & Hopkins (1998)	Chimpanzee	Sequential matching-to-sample	Chimpanzees show inversion effect for human and chimpanzee faces but not for car or capucin.
Pascalis & Bachevalier (1998)	Rhesus macaque and human	Visual paired comparison task	Recognition for conspecifics but not for individuals from another species.
Phelp & Roberts (1994)	Squirrel monkey *Saimiri sciureus* and human	Delayed matching-to-sample	Recognition across species and inversion effect are observed.

Table 1 (continued)

Authors	Species	Task	Results
Rosenfeld & Van Hoesen (1979)	Rhesus macaque	Two choice visual discrimination	There is discrimination among individuals of their own species. No inversion effect.
Sands, Lincoln & Wright (1982)	Rhesus macaque	Same/different	Monkeys process face as a category.
Swartz (1983)	Pigtailed macaque	Habituation, dishabituation	Discrimination of faces of different species which disappears if faces are inverted.
Tomonaga, Itakura & Matsuzawa (1993)	Chimpanzee	Matching task	Chimpanzees show no inversion effect for human and chimpanzee faces
Vermeire & Hamilton (1998)	Rhesus macaque	Go/nogo	Greater inversion effect for faces with the right hemisphere than with the left.
Wright & Roberts (1996)	Rhesus macaque and human	Same/different	Inversion effect for human faces only.
Yoshikubo (1985)	Rhesus macaque	Visual discrimination	Rhesus discriminate pictures with or without an individual on it.

processing experiments. Many studies have explored species discrimination. Most have used preferential choice or looking tasks in which it is assumed that a subject will look longer at a portrait of a conspecific than at that of another species member (a "stranger").

Fujita (1987), using a preferential procedure, compared portrait preference in different macaque species (*Macaca fuscata, Macaca mulatta, Macaca radiata,* and *Macaca arctoides*), exploring the extent to which different species showed conspecific preference. The animal learned to press a lever to show a picture on a screen. The picture remained on for as long as the subject held the lever down. Using this simple method it was possible to assess the time spent looking at a picture of a conspecific compared with one from a different species. In this task, it is assumed that habituation will be achieved more quickly (i.e., there will be reduced looking time) with a picture of a different species member, because it is less attractive to the looker. With the exception of the stumptailed macaques, Fujita found that monkeys showed conspecific preference. Most of the subjects can discriminate conspecifics by picture and prefer to look at them than to look at a macaque of a different species.

What of the "discrepant" stumptailed macaque (*Macaca arctoides*)? Using a different task in which they recorded the duration of viewing the screen when slides of the conspecific or other species were projected, Demaria and Thierry (1988) found that stumptailed macaques also looked longer at their conspecific rather than at other species. The methodological differences between the two studies should be noted: Fujita's monkeys had to hold a lever down, requiring some exertion and sustained motor control, and the task required mastery of a learned association. Arctoides may differ from other macaque species studied in their ability to learn the lever-press task rather than in perceptual discrimination. The second difference is in the stimuli; Demaria and Thierry's slides showed a single individual with a neutral background, whereas on Fujita's slides several individuals were presented at the same time with various backgrounds. A third difference is that Fujita's subjects were about 20 years of age whereas Demaria and Thierry's monkeys were young adults. The age difference could also explain differences in outcome between the studies. Any of these differences could explain the discrepancy between the two studies.

Again using the lever-press task, Fujita (1993) showed that pigtailed macaques preferred to look at the conspecific than at Japanese macaques. Fujita and Watanabe (1995) also found that Sulawesi macaques prefer to look at their conspecifics than at other species.

Fujita's studies demonstrated that preference for pictures of one's own species is common in different macaque species. Do monkeys have access to the *concept* of "species" or "us" from pictures? Yoshikubo (1985), using a reinforcement procedure, showed that rhesus macaques can learn to distinguish pictures with and without rhesus monkeys on them. The animals were shown a series of slides. Pictures with rhesus present were reinforced on button-press, while pictures without monkey were not reinforced. Similarly, rhesus macaques quickly learned to discriminate pictures of rhesus from pictures of Japanese macaques. This study suggests that recognition of conspecifics in pictures can be reliably indexed in rhesus monkeys – however, this is not conclusive evidence that the monkeys were using the cue intended by the experimenter. The monkeys might have been using some relatively low level discrimination cue, such as colouring or specific areas of pigmentation characteristic of the species, in order to make the distinction between the two groups – the study contained no control for this.

Conspecific discrimination

Humphrey (1974), using a habituation task, showed that rhesus monkeys can distinguish different individuals from within their own species – but not between individuals from other non-primate species. In this study the monkey had to learn to press a button for a picture or a blank screen (successive holds on the button produced the two stimuli in a strict alternation) shown for a 100-second session. Preference for the picture was calculated as the ratio of the total time spent with the picture to the total time spent with both stimuli. After a 200-second period of presentation of a picture A, a new picture B was introduced for a second 200-second session. The experimental variable was in the type of image shown. This could either be that of an individual from the same species or from another species. Dishabituation was observed for own species, but not for other species. This general pattern generalises to other species; moreover, it may not be limited to low-level image qualities of the individual shown. Thus, it seems reasonably safe to conclude that macaques are able to distinguish between individuals of the same species.

These images were, as far as we know, of *unfamiliar* individuals, who were unknown to the monkey subjects prior to test.

Can monkeys use their real-life knowledge of an individual in recognising his image? Dasser (1987) used a simultaneous discrimination task in which animals learned to respond to one of a pair of pictures of different individuals from their group. A second test (the transfer test) was then given, using different views of the same animal. Longtailed macaques learned the transfer task when tested in this way – but only for own-species images. While this test used images of familiar individuals, it did not directly test recognition of those individuals as known conspecifics. Boysen and Berntson (1989) used heart-rate as a measure of familiarity (it increases with familiarity) in a single chimpanzee. This animal showed reliable heart rate changes when shown pictures of known and unknown individuals. This technique has been used extensively with human infants, as well as with neurological patients, and can be a reliable measure of familiarity. It would be useful to see this demonstration replicated using larger numbers of animal subjects and reasonably larger numbers of images.

Given that several monkey species do reliably distinguish both species and individuals within (their own) species, what visual cues are they using? Fur color, body shape, tail length (or their presence or absence) may all be important: is there evidence suggesting that one or other of these cues is more important – or does the monkey make use of all the cues together? Fujita (1993) showed that pigtailed macaques preferred to look at their conspecifics rather than at Japanese macaques. The preference pattern was diluted when either the head, or the head and the tail, were removed from the picture. This suggests the head is most useful for the task. In the same way, the face was found to be important in conspecific discrimination by longtailed macaques (Dittrich, 1994). It should be noted that this study used linedrawings, not halftone images.

The importance of the face in same-species recognition is not too surprising. Humans possess a neural mechanism specialised for the processing of faces (Sergent, McDonald, & Zuck, 1995; Haxby, Ungerleider, Horwitz, Rapoport, & Grady, 1995), and a number of studies using single-cell recording techniques indicate that such a specialised system seems also to be present in non-human primates. Lesion, cell-recording, and brain-imaging experiments in humans have revealed specific cortical areas in the ventral part of the occipito-temporal junction which are involved in face processing and recognition (see, for a review, Tovée &

Cohen-Tovée, 1993). Likewise, electrophysiological studies in non-human primates have demonstrated neurones in the superior temporal sulcus of the inferior temporal cortex which discharge specifically to face stimuli. These cells respond to a variety of photographs of human and monkey faces, as well as to the recognition of specific individuals, facial emotional expressions, and facial orientations (Desimone, 1991; Perret, Mistlin, Chitty, Smith, Potter, Broennimann, & Harries, 1988; Rolls, 1984). What is still unclear is the extent to which the human face-processing sites are neuro-anatomically homologous with the "face areas" in the monkey brain.

Can monkeys recognise an individual face in a picture? Do they process it in the same way as a real face?

Discrimination of individual faces

Sands et al. (1982) used a same/different task in which sequentially presented pictures were compared to each other in a pair-wise fashion. The errors made by the animals (rhesus) suggested a categorisation split: human or monkey faces versus fruits or flowers.

Rosenfeld and Van Hoesen (1979) showed that the rhesus monkey can use pictures of faces as discriminative stimuli in a two-choice visual discrimination task. Varying the size and orientation of the face had little effect, suggesting the monkeys were seeing the face "as a face" rather than using low-level image qualities of the display on which to base their discrimination. Keating and Keating's findings (1982) also suggest that rhesus monkeys are processing face pictures as real faces. When viewing face stimuli, rhesus monkeys spent more time scanning the internal than the external features of a face, as has been reported for normal human observers (Nahm, Perret, Amaral, & Albright, 1997). In this study, rhesus monkey inspection patterns for unknown faces suggested the eyes were more important than any other area – again this reflects findings with human subjects (Ellis & Shepherd, 1975).

Overman and Doty (1982) measured rhesus monkeys' emotional responses to different categories of pictures. Monkeys differentiated images of monkey and human faces from other classes of visual stimuli.

Facial inversion

In humans, the vertical orientation of the face is salient to its processing. Inverted faces are less efficiently processed than upright faces (Yin, 1969). Sensitivity to vertical orientation is not observed to this extent for pictures of other objects (Ellis & Shepherd, 1975; Philips & Rawles, 1979), and therefore sensitivity to inversion has been widely used as a "marker" for skilled (i.e., human-like) face processing ability. Sensitivity to inversion is usually measured as the difference between upright and inverted face processing scores. Such difference measures are, themselves, not unproblematic and there can be a range of interpretative problems that arise from this. Also, there is argument concerning what exactly is reflected in inversion sensitivity for faces. Does it mean that faces are generally processed holistically by skilled observers, and that this is orientation sensitive (Farah, Tanaka, & Drain, 1995), or does it mean that the configuration of features – the relation between the disposition of specific face features – is orientation sensitive (Diamond & Carey, 1986)? While the latter view suggests that faces are indeed "special", the former may not: holistic processing may be engaged when any set of patterns with varied internal structure/external contour shape are well learned for discrimination. There are further considerations. Learned patterns of low spatial frequency are generally more vulnerable to inversion than high spatial frequency patterns. Inversion effects may be predicted to the extent that the facial image (typically a photographic halftone) is processed in terms of its low SF components (dominating in the right hemisphere in humans) rather than high SF ones (see, e.g., Sergent, 1982).

To what extent is *monkey* face-processing sensitive to inversion? If it is, we may propose that it shares similar mechanisms (and possibly a similar neural substrate) to human face processing. Rosenfeld and Van Hoesen (1979) found no inversion disruption for face discrimination in rhesus monkeys in their forced-choice task. Bruce (1982) found also no inversion effect in longtailed macaques, using a concurrent discrimination task with pictures of monkey faces of the same species as stimuli. Dittrich (1990) found no inversion effect in longtailed macaques. In this study, the stimuli were line drawings designed to study discrimination of facial expression. Under these conditions, high SF components dominate (see above) and also the expression task may require different processing mechanisms than those for recognition. Tomonaga, Itakura, and

Matsuzawa (1993) taught one chimpanzee to associate a sign to 3 HF and 3 MF. Once learning was correct, they presented the faces upside-down: this did not impair performance. This failure to find an inversion effect may reflect (1) small numbers of stimuli, (2) failure to achieve over-learning, and (3) a single subject cannot be used to draw negative conclusions. Indeed, several other studies have successfully demonstrated an inversion effect in monkeys. First, Overman and Doty (1982) using a match-to-sample task found a significant decline in performance when rhesus monkeys viewed inverted human and rhesus faces but no inversion effect for scenes. More recently, using a match-to-sample task, Phelps and Roberts (1994) found an inversion effect in human subjects and a squirrel monkey (*Saimiri sciureus*), but this inversion effect appeared only for human faces and not for monkey faces or scenes. However, only one monkey was used in that experiment and the monkey faces were not from the subject's own species. Given the findings reported above concerning intraspecies discrimination in other species, it is not surprising that no inversion effect was found. A more recent report of the inversion effect in both humans and rhesus monkeys (Wright & Roberts, 1996), using three monkey subjects, seemed to confirm the earlier finding. However, since the stimuli were still those of monkeys of other species it is relatively unsurprising that this study, too, found no inversion effects for the monkey subjects. By contrast, Parr, Dove, and Hopkins (1998) tested chimpanzees' discrimination of faces of chimpanzees, brown capuchins (*Cebus apella*), humans, and cars in upright and inverted orientations. They found an inversion effect for both human and chimpanzee faces but not for capuchin faces nor cars. Vermeire and Hamilton (1998) have explored face processing in rhesus monkeys with surgically separated hemispheres (callosal-sectioned or "split-brain" preparations). They found a greater inversion effect for conspecific faces in the right than in the left hemisphere. This pattern is also found in callosal-sectioned human subjects and suggests similar mechanisms underlie rhesus and human face processing as far as independent hemispheric functioning is concerned.

Overall, while monkeys can discriminate their conspecifics from a face picture, the effect of stimulus inversion is still somewhat uncertain: inversion effects can sometimes be demonstrated; they tend to be strongest for own-species members, but can sometimes extend to faces of other species too. However, much depends on the task, as well as the stimuli and the species tested (see Vermeire & Hamilton, 1998, for further discussion).

Face discrimination across species

Most mammalian faces share similar display characteristics. The disposition of the features of the face, two eyes, a nose and a mouth arrayed vertically about a central axis on the front of the head, is common to all of them. Several studies of face recognition in non-human primates have used human faces as well as other non-human primate species than that of the subject. The idea underlying these tests is that a *common face template* may underpin face processing in primates. Campbell, Pascalis, Coleman, Wallace, and Benson (1997) suggested that humans perceive monkey faces in terms of human characteristics, albeit distinctive ones. Other studies have explored human and monkey performance on identical tasks using both human and monkey faces.

Pascalis and Bachevalier (1998) used a paired-comparison task administered to both humans and monkeys. In this task, the subject was first exposed to a visual stimulus and allowed to passively explore it during a familiarisation period. After a brief delay, during which the subject's view of the stimulus was prevented, the subject was confronted with the familiarised stimulus presented together with a new one, for two successive retention periods. The position of the stimuli on the screen was reversed to minimise left/right looking preference. Sensitivity to familiarity (recognition) was inferred from the subject's tendency to fixate the novel stimulus for longer during the retention periods. They found that human subjects showed this pattern for individual human faces but not for monkey faces, while the opposite was true for monkeys. It may be argued that a reason for species-specificity in this study could be differential expertise in the two subject groups. This argument is weakened by the fact that these monkeys were handreared by humans. Pascalis, Coleman, and Campbell (1997) investigated upright and inverted face recognition in human subjects, for human, bovine, and monkey faces using both a forced-choice matching task and a visual paired comparison task ("just look at the pictures"). Subjects in the forced-choice task had to make an explicit recognition response, which was not required in the visual paired comparison task. For forced-choice recognition, human subjects showed an inversion effect for human and for monkey faces, but not for those of cows. This was not the pattern found for the visual-paired comparison task. Here, only human faces showed (a) a preference effect and (b) inversion sensitivity. This suggests that while human subjects can make use of a primate or human face template in explicit categorisation and recognition of non-human, primate faces, they only do this when instructed to do so. Under normal viewing conditions, without instruction, they do not spontaneously engage the processing system that is used to recognise (detect familiarity) in individual (human) primates.

The infant monkey

The last report (above) raises the question of the role of experience in the ability to process and recognise conspecific pictures. Few developmental studies have addressed this topic.

The first question is: At what age do monkeys respond behaviourally to socially relevant stimuli in a similar way to adults? Infant rhesus macaques raised in a nursery were found to avert their gaze in response to human and monkey faces at a mean age of 10.3 days and lip-smack at a mean age of 12.2 (Mendelson, 1982). Both these responses are normal monkey submissive reactions to faces. However, lack of a non-face control stimulus does not eliminate the possibility that the monkeys were responding to the test situation and not the particular stimuli. In another gaze aversion experiment, Mendelson, Haith, and Goldman-Rakic (1982) found that one-week-old infant rhesus monkeys did not differ in their visual fixation of pictures of monkey faces looking at them and faces looking away. However, at 3 and 7 weeks of age, infant monkeys looked longer at faces looking away than faces looking at them. These data correspond well with the age at which rhesus infants begin to show gaze-aversion and lip-smacking.

Work by Sackett (1966) suggests that neither social experience nor learning are necessary for infant monkeys to respond to socially relevant stimuli in species-typical ways. Sackett (1966) reared 8 infant rhesus macaques in isolation from birth to 9 months. The monkeys never saw another monkey during this period and did not see a human after the first 5 to 9 days of life. From day 14, the monkeys were presented with coloured slides of monkeys engaged in various social activities such as threat, fear, and play. They were also presented with coloured slides of non-monkey objects such as geometric patterns, trees, a living room, and an adult human female. After the first 30 days, the monkeys inspected the monkey stimuli more than the pictures of objects or the picture of the adult female human. Pictures of threatening monkeys and infants produced more exploratory and play responses, and higher motor activity than any other pictures. From day 80 to day 120 the frequency of fear, withdrawal, and disturbance behaviours rose in the monkeys whenever the threat picture was displayed. In line with the ethological framework of that time, the author suggested that infant monkeys are born with prepotent responses to certain classes of visual stimuli and that some aspects of social communication may lie in innate releasing mechanisms.

In a separate study, the same stimuli were presented to 3 rhesus macaque groups with different rearing histories to determine the effects of social experience in monkeys' preference for social and nonsocial stimuli (Sackett, 1965). Subjects in group 1 were reared in the jungle (5-year olds), monkeys in group 2 (3.5-year olds) were reared in the laboratory with mother and peers, and monkeys in group 3 (3.5-year olds) were raised in total isolation from birth to one year. The sexually experienced jungle-reared monkeys visually explored slides with sexual content more than monkeys in groups 2 and 3. The isolate monkeys showed more exploration of non-monkey pictures and pictures without social communication content than with socially relevant pictures. The isolates also showed fewest exploration responses to pictures with 2 animals and pictures depicting fear and threat. Monkeys from all the rearing conditions displayed species-appropriate behavioural responses to the threat pictures, but the type of behaviour shown varied with the rearing condition. Both the laboratory-reared and isolate monkeys displayed a high frequency of submitting and withdrawal responses. Jungle-reared monkeys, on the other hand, displayed threat behaviours in response to the threat pictures.

Redican, Kellicut, and Mitchell (1971) studied 6 juvenile rhesus macaques' preference for viewing slides of different facial expressions. Faces of infant, juvenile, and adult rhesus macaques displaying different facial expressions – threat, grimace, lipsmack, plain face, and yawn – were used. The juvenile macaques' response rate did not differ for facial expressions of infant or adult. However, they showed a reduction of responses for juvenile grimace and threat face slides. It is interesting that the juvenile macaques only showed differential response to threat and grimace pictures for juvenile faces and not infant or adult faces. This finding is similar to Sackett's (1966) finding that infant monkeys responded most strongly to infant pictures.

It is possible that responsiveness to social stimuli may be influenced by the importance of the social context perceived by the monkey or it could be that individuals have a "sense of how they look" from their own action patterns: this too could be involved in imitative behaviours (i.e., Meltzoff & Moore, 1977, 1997) and lead to strongest imitation of most similar models.

Another way of studying monkeys' responses to socially relevant information is through videotape presentations. The major difference between slides and color videotapes, apart from the presence of movement, which is a potent elicitor of behaviour in its own right, is that a more comprehensive repertoire of threat or other social communicative behaviours can be shown. Six male and six female juvenile bonnet macaques (*Macaca radiata*) were shown color videotape recordings of a passive female, a passive male, and a threatening male (Plimpton, Swartz, & Rosenblum, 1981). All the stimulus animals were unfamiliar adult bonnet macaques. The subjects were observed in the presence of their mother and another juvenile-mother dyad. The monkeys showed the greatest contact with their mother when presented with the videotape of the threatening male. Furthermore, subjects lipsmacked more to the video of the threatening male than the passive male or female. Juvenile monkeys also approached the female videotapes more than the male videotapes. Social information delivered as a video can result in socially appropriate responses by juvenile macaques. Infant and juvenile monkeys behaviourally responded to social pictures on slides and videotapes as if they were in front of real conspecifics, suggesting that they responded to the two-dimensional representation *as if* it was a real event.

Given that adult monkeys process conspecific faces effectively from pictures, a second developmental question of interest is how do infant monkeys process pictures of faces at different periods of development? Human infants show peripheral scanning of faces at one month of age, moving to more internal scanning of faces at two months of age (Maurer & Salapatek, 1976; Haith, Bergman, & Moore, 1978). Using the corneal reflection technique, Mendelson (1982) found that infant rhesus macaques scanned both the internal and external features of a picture of an infant monkey's face and they found no developmental change during the first 7 weeks of life. Nevertheless, the part of the face given the most attention by the infant monkey was the region of the eyes and near the ear. Scanning patterns by infant monkeys for adult faces, whether of their own or other species have not yet been reported. When given a choice between viewing line-drawings of monkey faces with normal arrangement of facial features (e.g., eyes, mouth, nose) and faces with the facial features scrambled, 2.5- to 10-week-old infant pigtailed macaques preferred to look at the normal line-drawings of a face (Lutz, Lockard, Gunderson, & Grant, 1998). This preference for normal line-drawings of faces over scrambled faces is also seen in human infants (Johnson, Dziurawiec, Bartrip, & Morton, 1992). Using a habituation-dishabituation paradigm, 3-month-old pigtailed macaques were tested for discrimination of adult female faces of three different species: pigtailed, longtailed, and stumptailed (Swartz, 1983). The infants only had experience with conspecific (pigtailed) peers. Based on gross physical features, the pigtailed and longtailed macaques are more similar in appearance compared to the stumptailed macaque, which has a distinctive appearance compared to the other two species. The pigtailed macaques were able to discriminate between individual faces for all three macaque species. Infant pigtailed macaques did not demonstrate discrimination when the faces were presented upside down.

Species discrimination has also been tested by observing infant monkeys' preference patterns for faces of different species. Using the procedure used for adult monkeys described previously, Fujita (1987, 1993) tested Japanese and rhesus macaques' preference for slides of several macaque species (Japanese, rhesus, pigtailed, bonnet, longtailed, and stumptailed). Both mother-reared and lab-reared rhesus infants preferred to view the rhesus pictures over pictures of other macaque monkeys (Fujita, 1987, 1993). While mother-reared Japanese macaques preferred viewing Japanese macaque faces, lab-reared Japanese macaques preferred viewing rhesus macaques over their own species. It is not clear why lab-reared Japanese macaques prefer to view rhesus macaques over Japanese macaques. Fujita suggested that rhesus have a hard-wired preference for their own species, while Japanese macaques have a more flexible preference that is influenced by experience. The general pattern of results, however, shows that infant monkeys, like adults, can discriminate their own species from a picture. Recently, Kim, Gunderson, and Swartz (1999) using a visual paired comparison task showed that infant monkeys (pigtailed macaques) present a novelty preference for a face that is presented in a new orientation than the one used during the familiarisation only for their own species.

Biological insult can impair the ability to recognise faces (prosopagnosia in humans). Longtailed macaque infants exposed to methylmercury were deficient in visual recognition memory for pictures of monkey faces compared to controls who were not exposed to the teratogen (Gunderson, Grant-Webster, Burbacher, & Mottet, 1988). It must be pointed out that the pictures of monkey faces were not of conspecifics, but a closely related species, the pigtailed macaques.

Rodman, Scalaidhe, and Gross (1993) compared the response properties of single neurones in the inferior temporal cortex of rhesus macaques of different ages, ranging from 5 weeks to 7 months and to adult monkeys. For awake monkeys, the percentage of cells responsive were similar in infants and adults. However, the response magnitude of single neurones was lower in the infants compared to adults. In addition, infant cells had longer and more variable firing latencies. Both infant and adult monkeys had neurones that responded selectively to faces, geometric patterns, and shapes. This study may demonstrate the early specialisation for faces in monkeys.

Human infants

In human infants, several studies have shown than during the first week of life, newborns look longer at their mother's than at a stranger's face (Field, Cohen, Garcia, & Greenberg, 1984; Bushnell, Saï, & Mullin, 1989; Pascalis, de Schonen, Morton, Deruelle, & Fabre-Grenet, 1995). Bushnell (1982) showed that 2-month-old infants preferred to look at a picture of their mother's face rather than that of a stranger; Barerra and Maurer (1981) found the same results at three months of age. From the age of 4 months, infants recognise their mother's face even when the outer head contour is masked (de Schonen, de Diza, & Mathivet, 1986). More recently, using a High Amplitude Sucking technique, Walton, Bower, and Bower (1992) observed that the preference for the mother's face by newborns extended to videotapes of faces. These studies suggest that the discrimination of a significant other person, from picture alone, is well established very early in life.

To our knowledge, only one study has explored cross-species face discrimination in human infants. Nelson (1993) recorded Event Related

Potentials in 9-month-old infants when viewing novel and familiarised monkey faces. Distinctive ERP waveforms were found for the familiar compared with the nonfamiliar faces.

DISCUSSION

The first part of this review reported a number of observational studies in natural habitats showing the extent to which different primate species categorise events in their world. The key finding was that salient events or actors, essential to effective social function and hence to survival, are efficiently discriminated and remembered. Thus, for example, Cheney and Seyfarth (1990) showed that monkeys give alarm calls to different predators, and each of these alarm calls evokes qualitatively different escape responses. Calls given to leopards cause monkeys to run into trees, while calls given to eagles cause monkeys to look up in the air. When testing animals experimentally, the question of stimulus pertinence is paramount, as is the association between the perception of a picture and the required reaction to it. Anderson (1998) noted that experiments using social stimuli have established the basic efficacy of social stimuli as reward. Photographs, moving images, and mirrors have proven to be effective "social" stimuli in preference tests. Anderson also concluded that there is suggestive evidence for primates' ability to understand the representational aspects of many two-dimensional stimuli.

Dasser (1987) has pointed out that there are some response biases that need to be borne in mind in interpreting several experiments. "Preference" for social partners and relatives may reflect the emotional "pull" these significant others exert, compared with a more reluctant response to a display depicting a potentially threatening actor or event. Under these conditions, "failure to respond" differentially may be misinterpreted. Therefore, a high proportion of correct choices (i.e., of correct individuals) suggests that the subjects' responses met the requirement of the experiment, and thus Dasser concluded that two-dimensional pictures of familiar monkeys can be used as representations of the real animals in experiments requiring conceptual performance.

The present review shows that many species of non-human primate can distinguish conspecifics from members of another species and also that they can show distinctive patterns of preference suggesting that they recognise unfamiliar individuals as members of their own species from pictures. What sorts of association do they make to these images? This should inform us more about the extent to which "recognition" can be inferred from their behaviour.

In a matching-to-sample task designed by Dasser (1987), longtailed macaques successfully associated slides of overlapping body parts of a stimulus animal with a slide of the entire animal; the subjects were able to use information that they learned during everyday interactions to identify a subject either as a whole or in part. Individual recognition was possible on non-facial cues.

Such experiments need to be replicated in other species, and further studies should determine which stimuli other than faces are amenable to manipulation as images.

The material reviewed here also suggests that face-recognition ability in non-human primates can be reliably and validly tested using images (pictures or slides). On the whole, non-human primates appear to process faces in a way similar to that used by humans. For example, internal parts of familiar faces are more salient than outer parts for adult primates (Keating & Keating, 1982). The face inversion effect is however still controversial in monkeys (Overman & Doty, 1982; Wright & Roberts, 1996) but not in apes (Tomonaga et al., 1993; Parr et al., 1998). Monkeys' face-processing ability would be more appropriately tested if experimenters took care to use pictures from the subject's species and use several, converging, tasks to control for methodological problems.

Cheney and Seyfarth (1990) have suggested that monkeys may also create in their minds a number of representations that describe different sorts of social relationship: mother-offspring relationship, relationship among kin, and friendship between males and females. When considering their data and results of Dasser's experiments (see p. 896 for further details), they assume that animals recognise some similarity between their own close bonds and the close bonds of others. That is, some primates, at least, have the capacity for a degree of empathy and the perception of intention. Dasser (1988) concluded that one mechanism underlying the complex social structure of a non-human primate group may be the ability of its members to categorise group members, individual by individual. If this is the case, face *recognition* skills should vary with the social complexity of the primate group. Expression and intention-reading skills may be similarly affected.

This review has focused on what happens when monkeys and apes view images of faces. The purpose has not been to provide a theoretical analysis of these studies but to explore the findings in relation to their methodological and theoretical adequacy. In principle, the further use of such material should allow us to explore some deeper aspects of cognition and its roots – including the perception of intention and the understanding of "other minds" in non-human primate species.

REFERENCES

Anderson, J. R. A. (1998). Social stimuli and social rewards in primate learning and cognition. *Behavioural Processes, 42,* 159-175.

Aureli, F., & van Schaik, C. P. (1991). Post-conflict behaviour in longtailed macaques (*Macaca fascicularis*): I. The social events. *Ethology, 89,* 89-100.

Barerra, M. E., & Maurer, D. (1981). The perception of facial expressions by the three-month-old. *Child Development, 52* (1), 203-206.

Boysen, S. T., & Berntson, G. G. (1989). Conspecific recognition in the chimpanzee (*Pan troglodytes*): cardiac responses to significant others. *Journal of Comparative Psychology, 103,* 215-220.

Boesch, C. (1991). The effects of leopard predation on grouping patterns in forest chimpanzees. *Behaviour, 117,* 220-242.

Brown, M. M., Kreiter, N. A., Maple, J. T., & Sinnott, J. M. (1992). Silhouettes elicit alarm calls from captive Vervet monkeys. *Journal of Comparative Psychology, 106,* 350-359.

Bruce, C. (1982). Face recognition by monkeys: absence of an inversion effect. *Neuropsychologia, 20,* 515-521.

Bruce, V., & Young, A. W. (1998). *In the eye of the beholder.* Oxford: Oxford University Press.

Bushnell, I. W. R. (1982). Discrimination of faces by young infants. *Journal of Experimental Child Psychology, 33,* 298-308.

Bushnell, I. W. R., Saï, F., & Mullin, J. T. (1989). Neonatal recognition of the mother's face. *British Journal of Developmental Psychology, 7,* 3-15.

Campbell, R., Pascalis, O., Coleman, M., Wallace, S. B., & Benson, P. J. (1997). Are faces of different species perceived categorically by human observers? *Proceedings of the Royal Society, B 264,* 1429-1434.

Cheney, D. M. (1987). Interactions and relationships between groups. In B. B. Smuts, D. L. Cheney, R. M. Seyfarth, R. W. Wrangham, & T. T. Struhsaker (Eds.), *Primate societies.* Chicago, IL: University of Chicago Press.

Cheney, D. M., & Seyfarth, R. M. (1980). Vocal recognition in free-ranging vervet monkeys. *Animal Behaviour, 28,* 362-367.

Cheney, D. M., & Seyfarth, R. M. (1989). Redirected aggression and reconciliation among vervet monkeys, *Cercopithecus aethiops. Behaviour, 110,* 258-275.

Cheney, D. M., & Seyfarth, R. M. (1990). *How monkeys see the world.* Chicago, IL: University of Chicago Press.

D'Amato, M. R., & Van Sant, P. (1988). The person concept in monkeys (*Cebus apella*). *Journal of Experimental Psychology: Animal Behavior Processes, 14,* 43-55.

Das, M., Penke, Z., & van Hooff, J. A. R. A. M. (1997). Affiliation between aggressors and third parties following conflicts in longtailed macaques (*Macaca fascicularis*). *International Journal of Primatology, 18,* 159-181.

Dasser, V. (1987). Slides of group members as representations of the real animals (*Macaca fascicularis*). *Ethology, 76,* 65-73.

Dasser, V. (1988). A social concept in Java monkeys. *Animal Behaviour, 36,* 225-230.

Davenport, R. K., & Rogers C. M. (1971). Perception of photographs by apes. *Behaviour, 39,* 318-320.

Demaria, C., & Thierry, B. (1988). Responses to animal stimulus photographs in stumptailed macaques (*Macaca arctoides*). *Primates, 29,* 237-244.

de Schonen, S., de Diaz, G., & Mathivet, E. (1986). Hemispheric asymmetry in face processing in infancy. In H. D. Ellis, M. A. Jeeves, F. Newcombe, & A. Young (Eds.), *Aspects of face processing.* Dordrecht: Martinus Nijhoff Publisher.

Desimone, R. (1991). Face-selective cells in the temporal cortex of monkeys. *Journal of Cognitive Neuroscience, 3,* 1-8.

de Waal, F. B. M. (1982). *Chimpanzee politics.* London: Jonathan Cape.

de Waal, F. B. M., & Luttrell, L. M. (1985). The formal hierarchy of rhesus macaques: an investigation of the bared-teeth display. *American Journal of Primatology, 9,* 73-85.

de Waal, F. B. M., & van Roosmalen, A. (1979). Reconciliation and consolation among chimpanzees. *Behavioral Ecology and Sociobiology, 5,* 55-66.

Diamond, R., & Carey, S. (1986). Why faces are and are not special: an effect of expertise. *Journal of Experimental Psychology: General, 115,* 107-117.

Dittrich, W. (1990). Representation of faces in longtailed macaques (*Macaca fascicularis*). *Ethology, 85,* 265-278.

Dittrich, W. (1994). How monkeys see others: discrimination and recognition of monkeys' shape. *Behavioural Processes, 33,* 139-154.

Ellis, H. D., & Shepherd, J. W. (1975). Recognition of upright and inverted faces in the left and right visual fields. *Cortex, 11,* 3-7.

Farah, M., Tanaka, J., & Drain, H. M. (1995). What causes the face inversion effect. *Journal of Experimental Psychology: Human Perception and Performance, 21,* 628-634.

Field, T. M., Cohen, D., Garcia, R., & Greenberg, R. (1984). Mother-stranger face discrimination by the newborn. *Infant Behavior and Development, 7,* 19-25.

Fujita, K. (1987). Species recognition by five macaques monkeys. *Primates, 28,* 353-366.

Fujita, K. (1993). Role of some physical characteristics in species recognition by pigtail monkeys. *Primates, 34,* 133-140.

Fujita, K., & Watanabe, K. (1995). Visual preference for closely related species by Sulawesi macaques. *American Journal of Primatology, 37,* 253-261.

Gunderson, V. M. (1983). Development of cross-modal recognition in infant pigtail monkeys (*Macaca nemestrina*). *Developmental Psychology, 19,* 398-404.

Gunderson, V. M., Grant-Webster, K., Burbacher, T., & Mottet, N. (1988). Visual recognition memory deficits in methylmercury exposed *Macaca fascicularis* infants. *Neurotoxicology and Teratology, 60,* 119-127.

Gunderson, V. M., Rose, S. A., & Grant-Webster, K. S. (1990). Cross-modal transfert in high- and low-risk infant pigtailed macaque monkeys. *Developmental Psychology, 26,* 576-581.

Haith, M. M., Bergman, T., & Moore, M. J. (1978). Developmental changes in visual scanning of face and nonface patterns by infants. *Science, 198,* 853-855.

Haxby, J. V., Ungerleider, L. G., Horwitz, B., Rapoport, S. I., & Grady, C. L. (1995). Hemispheric differences in neural systems for faces working memory: a PET rCBF study. *Human Brain Mapping, 3,* 68-82.

Hinde, R. A. (1983). *Primate social relationships*. Oxford: Blackwell Scientific Publications.

Humphrey, N. K. (1974). Species and individuals in the perceptual world of monkeys. *Perception, 3,* 105-114.

Itakura, S. (1992). Sex discrimination of photographs of humans by chimpanzee. *Perceptual and Motor Skills, 74,* 475-478.

Johnson, M. H., Dziurawiec, S., Bartrip, J., & Morton, J. (1992). The effects of movement of internal features on infants' preferences for face-like stimuli. *Infant Behavior and Development, 15,* 129-136.

Judge, P. G. (1991). Dyadic and triadic reconciliation in pigtailed macaques (*Macaca nemestrina*). *American Journal of Primatology, 23,* 225-237.

Kappeler, P. M., & van Schaik, C.P. (1992). Methodological and evolutionary aspects of reconciliation among primates. *Ethology, 92,* 51-69.

Keating, C. F., & Keating, E. G. (1982). Visual scan patterns of rhesus monkeys viewing faces. *Perception, 11,* 211-219.

Kim, J. H., Gunderson, V. M., & Swartz, K. S. (1999). Humans all look alike: cross-species face recognition in infant pigtailed macaque monkeys. Paper presented at the Biennial Meeting of the Society for Research in Child Development, Albuquerque.

Kortlandt, A. (1994). Naturalistic primate research: Flourishing but losing momentum? In B. Thierry, J. R. Anderson, J.-J. Roeder, & N. Herrenschmidt (Eds.), *Current primatology, Vol. 1, Ecology and evolution* (pp. 133-141). Strasbourg: Université Louis Pasteur.

Lutz, C. K., Lockard, J. S., Gunderson, V. M., & Grant, K. S. (1998). Infant monkeys' visual responses to drawings of normal and distorted faces. *American Journal of Primatology, 44,* 169-174.

Malone, D. R., Tolan, J. C., & Rogers, C. M. (1980). Cross-modal matching of objects and photographs in the monkey. *Neuropsychologia, 18,* 693-697.

Maurer, D., & Salapatek, P. (1976). Developmental changes in the scanning of faces by young infants. *Child Development, 47,* 523-527.

Meltzoff, A. N., & Moore, M. K. (1977). Imitation of facial and manual gestures by human neonates. *Science, 198,* 75-78.

Meltzoff, A. N., & Moore, M. K. (1997). Explaining facial imitation: A theoretical model. *Early Development and Parenting, 6,* 179-192.

Mendelson, M. J. (1982). Visual and social responses in infant rhesus monkeys. *American Journal of Primatology, 3,* 333-340.

Mendelson, M. J., Haith, M. M., & Goldman-Rakic, P. S. (1982). Face scanning and responsiveness to social cues in infant rhesus monkeys. *Developmental Psychology, 18,* 222-228.

Menzel, C. R. (1991). Cognitive aspects of foraging in Japanese monkeys. *Animal Behaviour, 41,* 397-402.

Menzel, E. W., Jr. (1971). Communication about the environment in a group of young chimpanzees. *Folia Primatologica, 15,* 220-232.

Mineka, S., Davidson, M., Cook, M., & Keir, R. (1984). Observational conditioning of snake fear in rhesus monkeys. *Journal of Abnormal Psychology, 93,* 355-372.

Nahm, F. K. D., Perret, A., Amaral, D. G., & Albright, T. D. (1997). How do monkeys look at faces? *Journal of Cognitive Neuroscience, 9,* 611-623.

Nelson, C. A. (1993). The recognition of facial expressions in infancy: behavioral and electrophysiological evidence. In B. de Boysson-Bardies, S. de Schonen, P. Jusczyk, P. MacNeilage, & J. Morton (Eds.), *Developmental neurocognition: Speech and face processing in the first year of life* (pp. 165-178). Dordrecht: Kluwer Academic Publishers.

Noë, R., & Bshary, R. (1997). The formation of red colobus-diana monkey associations under predation pressure from chimpanzees. *Proceedings of the Royal Society, B 264,* 253-259.

Overman, W. H., & Doty, R. W. (1982). Hemispheric specialization displayed by man but not macaques for analysis of faces. *Neuropsychologia, 20,* 113-128.

Parr, L. A., Dove, T., & Hopkins, W. D. (1998). Why faces may be special: evidence of the inversion effect in chimpanzees. *Journal of Cognitive Neuroscience, 10,* 615-622.

Pascalis, O., de Schonen, S., Morton, J., Deruelle, C., & Fabre-Grenet, M. (1995). Mother's face recognition by neonates: a replication and an extension. *Infant Behavior and Development, 18,* 79-85.

Pascalis, O., & Bachevalier, J. (1998) Face recognition in primates: a cross species study. *Behavioural Processes, 43,* 87-96.

Pascalis, O., Coleman, M., & Campbell R. (1997). Face recognition across different species: effects of inversion and instruction. *Society for Neuroscience Abstracts, 821-4, 2112.*

Perrett, D. I., Mistlin, A. J., Chitty, A. J., Smith P. A. J., Potter, D. D., Broennimann, R., & Harries, M. (1988). Specialized face processing and hemispheric asymmetry in man and monkey: evidence from single unit and reaction time studies. *Behavioural Brain Research, 29,* 245-258.

Phelps, M. T., & Roberts, W. A. (1994). Memory for pictures of upright and inverted primate faces in humans (*Homo sapiens*), squirrel monkeys (*Saimiri sciureus*) and pigeons (*Columba livia*). *Journal of Comparative Psychology, 108,* 114-125.

Philips, R. J., & Rawles, R. E. (1979). Recognition of upright and inverted faces: a correlational study. *Perception, 8,* 577-583.

Plimpton, E. H., Swartz, K. B., & Rosenblum, L. A. (1981). Responses of juvenile bonnet macaques to social stimuli presented through color videotapes. *Developmental Psychobiology, 14,* 109-117.

Redican, W. K., Kellicut, M. H., & Mitchell, G. (1971). Preferences for facial expressions in juvenile rhesus monkeys (*Macaca mulatta*). *Developmental Psychology, 5,* 539.

Rodman, H. R., Scalaidhe, S. P. O., & Gross, C. G. (1993). Response properties of neurons in temporal cortical areas of infant monkeys. *Journal of Neurophysiology, 70,* 1115-1136.

Rolls, E. T. (1984). Neurons in the cortex of the temporal lobe and in the amygdala of the monkey with responses selective for faces. *Human Neurobiology, 3,* 209-222.

Rosenfeld, S. A., & Van Hoesen, G. W. (1979). Face recognition in the rhesus monkey. *Neuropsychologia, 17,* 503-509.

Sackett, G. P. (1965). Response of rhesus monkeys to social stimulation presented by means of colored slides. *Perceptual and Motor Skills, 20,* 1027-1028.

Sackett, G. P. (1966). Monkeys reared in isolation with pictures as visual input: evidence for an innate releasing mechanism. *Science, 154,* 1468-1473.

Sands, S. F., Lincoln, C. E., & Wright, A. A. (1982). Pictorial similarity judgments and the organization of visual memory in the rhesus monkey. *Journal of Experimental Psychology: General, 111,* 369-389.

Sergent, J. (1982). About face: left hemisphere involvement in processing physiognomies. *Journal of Experimental Psychology: Human Perception and Performance, 8,* 1-14.

Sergent, J., MacDonald, B., & Zuck, E. (1995). Structural and functional organization of knowledge about faces and proper names: a PET study. In M. Moscovitch & C. Umilta (Eds.), *Conscious and nonconscious information processing: Attention and performance, Volume XV* (pp. 204-228). Cambridge, MA: MIT Press.

Struhsaker, T. (1967). Auditory communication among vervet monkeys. In S. Altmann (Ed.), *Social communication among primates* (pp. 281-324). Chicago, IL: University of Chicago Press.

Swartz, K. B. (1983). Species discrimination in infant pigtailed macaques with pictorial stimuli. *Developmental Psychobiology, 16,* 219-231.

Tomonaga, M., Itakura, S., & Matsuzawa, T. (1993). Superiority of conspecific faces and reduced inversion effect in face perception by a chimpanzee. *Folia Primatologica, 61,* 110-114.

Tovée, M. J., & Cohen-Tovée, E. M. (1993). The neural substrate of face processing models: a review. *Cognitive Neuropsychology, 10,* 505-528.

Vauclair, J., & Fagot, J. (1996). Categorization of alphanumeric characters by Guinea baboons: within- and between-class stimulus discrimination. *Cahiers de Psychologie Cognitive/Current Psychology of Cognition, 15,* 449-462.

Vermeire, B. A., & Hamilton, C. A. (1998). Inversion effect for faces in split-brain monkeys. *Neuropsychologia, 36,* 1003-1014.

Walton, G. E., Bower, N. J. A., & Bower T. G. R. (1992). Recognition of familiar faces by newborns. *Infant Behavior and Development, 15,* 265-269.

Winner, E., & Ettlinger, G. (1979). Do chimpanzees recognize photographs as representation of objects? *Neurospychologia, 17,* 413-420.

Wright, A. A., & Roberts, W. A. (1996). Monkey and human face perception: Inversion effects for human faces but not for monkey faces or scenes. *Journal of Cognitive Neuroscience, 8,* 278-290.

Yin, R. K. (1969). Looking at upside-down faces. *Journal of Experimental Psychology, 81,* 141-145.

York, A. D., & Rowell, T. E. (1988). Reconciliation following aggression in patas monkeys (*Erythrocebus patas*). *Animal Behaviour, 36,* 502-509.

Yoshikubo, S. (1985). Species discrimination and concept formation by rhesus monkey (*Macaca mulatta*). *Primates, 26,* 285-299.

Zayan, R., & Vauclair, J. (1998). Categories as paradigms for comparative cognition. *Behavioural Processes, 42,* 87-99.

Zuberbühler, K., Noë, R., & Seyfarth, R. M. (1997). Diana monkey long-distance calls: messages for conspecifics and predators. *Animal Behaviour, 53,* 589-604.

What is the evidence for an equivalence between objects and pictures in birds and nonhuman primates?

Joël Fagot, Julie Martin-Malivel, and Delphine Dépy

CNRS, Marseille, France

Abstract

This paper examines the way birds and nonhuman primates process pictures of objects. After having defined three main modes of picture perception that might occur in animals (independence, confusion, and equivalence), we review the literature providing direct evidence in favor of these three possible modes of processing. This review reveals that experimental evidence for object/picture equivalence is weak and often inconsistent in birds, and even in nonhuman primates. It also underlines the role of several experimental factors in picture processing modes.

Key words: Equivalence, perception, picture, primate, representation.

Correspondence should be sent to Joël Fagot, CNRS-CRNC, 31 Chemin Joseph Aiguier, 13402 Marseille Cedex 20, France (e-mail: fagot@lnf.cnrs-mrs.fr).

INTRODUCTION

This paper examines the way birds and nonhuman primates, the most commonly studied animal subjects in laboratories of comparative psychology that work on visual perception, process pictorial representations of real objects, such as pictures of non-living objects or social partners. Since the initial work by Herrnstein and Loveland (1964) on concept formation in pigeons, pictures have become one of the favored types of experimental stimuli to assess a variety of cognitive phenomena in animals, including spatial representation, social cognition, viewpoint consistency, serial list learning, and the neural bases of object perception. Determining how animals process pictures is thus particularly important for several scientific domains of comparative psychology and neuroscience.

The main advantage of pictures compared to more simple artificial stimuli (e.g., simple geometrical forms) is that they share many characteristics with the real objects they represent. This similarity gives pictures an apparent ecological validity, and in principle may make it possible to infer some of the properties of real-object processing in natural settings. With the development of recent computer technologies, pictures have also become convenient laboratory stimuli because they are easy to alter in controlled ways and to reproduce within and accross experiments. However, use of pictures as experimental stimuli has a cost: like real three-dimensional (3D) objects, pictures are polymorphous and it is often difficult to identify which aspects of the pictures control the behavior.

Pictures are both complex in their physical structure and ambiguous with respect to their representational content. On the one hand, objects and their pictures have several characteristics in common, for instance in terms of luminance variation or shape. On the other hand, the correspondence between the objects and their pictures is necessarily limited, and pictures lack some important characteristics of the actual objects, such as motion or 3D cues. In short, pictures have only some of the characteristics of actual objects, and there is a necessary discrepancy between real objects and their pictures.

Given the dual nature of pictures, it is reasonable to assume that animals process pictorial stimuli in various possible ways, depending, for instance, on their experience with the pictures or on the quality of the image. For the sake of our discussion, we propose to distinguish three main modes of picture perception which might occur in animals.

The first possible way animals might follow to discriminate pictures is to process them as combinations of features or patterns, regardless of their representational content. In this context, no association is made by the animals between the real objects and their pictures (although such associations might exist in the experimenter's mind), and the processing of the pictorial stimulus is independent of the processing of the real object. Because this mode of picture processing is unrelated to the representational content of the pictures, we will call it the *independence* mode of picture processing.

A second possible mode of picture processing implies a confusion between the object and its picture. In this context, the picture and the natural object are processed in exactly the same way, because they are not distinguished from each other. In the animal's view, the picture is the same as the real object. This is the *confusion* mode of picture processing.

In the third mode, the animal may associate the real objects with their pictures, while being perfectly aware that the picture is different from the real object. In the animal's view, the picture is a representation of the actual object, not the object itself. This mode of processing will be called the *equivalence* mode.

The proposed classification into three modes of processing is intuitively obvious. It is also experimentally approachable. The *independence* mode of processing might be ruled out when the animal exibits some kinds of overt or cover behavioral responses that might be expected to be elicited by the object depicted in the picture but not by non-representative stimuli (e.g., when the animal expresses social behaviors when shown pictures of conspecifics). The *confusion* mode can be demonstrated when the behavioral response is relevant for the real objects but not for pictures of those objects (e.g., grabbing and eating a picture of a food item). Demonstration of the *equivalence* mode of processing would imply that the subject continue to exhibit object-related behaviors in situations in which the confusion between the object and its image is no longer possible, for instance due to some degradations of the image (e.g., use of a line drawing).

In the remainder of this chapter, we shall review the literature on the perception of still images that provides information about the possible use of the above three modes of processing by animals (for a review on the perception of moving images, see Lea & Dittrich, this issue). Surprisingly, probably because there has been a long-lasting belief that animals perceive pictures as we do (i.e., as a representation of real objects), relatively few studies have directly tested and analysed the possibility that animals establish some associations between objects and their pictures. In parallel, pictures have often been used in the literature for different scientific purposes, for instance to study conceptual abilities or social cognition. Because the literature is too large to be presented in this chapter, the present review will be selective in two respects.

First, a rapid inspection of the literature reveals that pictures have mostly been presented in picture-to-picture transfer procedures. In general, this type of experiment has shown that pigeons or monkeys can sort pictures in a manner consistent with what humans would do on a conceptual basis, and generalize to an extent that cannot be the result of chance to previously unseen pictures depicting the same classes of objects as the original stimulus sets (e.g., Herrnstein & Loveland, 1964). Studies employing the picture-to-picture transfer procedure will not be considered in this chapter, because it is almost impossible with this procedure to reject the hypothesis that positive transfers are due to stimulus generalization from specific components or features of previous instances (see Huber, this issue; D'Amato & Van Sant, 1988).

Second, complementary to the use of a picture-to-picture procedure, several studies have employed a habituation-dishabituation procedure (e.g., Swartz, 1982). In our view, this procedure is a particularly interesting tool for revealing discrimination between sets of pictures. However, one serious limitation of this procedure is that it tells little about which aspect(s) of the picture control(s) discrimination, because it is very difficult – if not impossible – to determine whether animals process some particular physical dimensions of the pictures, such as their texture or their color (*independence* mode), or consider instead their representational content (*confusion* or *equivalence* modes). Work based on the habituation-dishabituation paradigm will also be omitted in this chapter because of its limited heuristic value in the current discussion.

Several other procedures have the potential to provide more direct information on the possible associations between objects and their pictures. These include object-to-picture transfer tests, the manipulation of the subject's exposure to the objects depicted in the pictures, the analysis of spontaneous overt and covert reactions to pictures, inter-modal matching, and priming. In this chapter, we shall focus our attention on the findings obtained using these procedures. This review will underline the role of several experimental factors in picture processing modes, and will reveal that experimental evidence for *equivalence* in animals is still weak and often inconsistent.

PICTURE-TO-OBJECT AND OBJECT-TO-PICTURE TRANSFERS

The first possibility for verifying associations between objects and their pictures is to assess performance in situations involving training in discriminating real objects, followed by transfer tests using the pictures of those objects, or *vice versa*. In the animal literature, this procedure has mostly been employed with pigeons (e.g., Cabe, 1976; Trillmich, 1976; Lumsden, 1977; Watanabe, 1993), although, occasionally, object-to-picture transfer tests have also been conducted with nonhuman primates (e.g., Zimmermann & Hochberg, 1970; Martin-Malivel, 1998).

Cabe (1976) trained pigeons to discriminate two simple objects: a white rectangle and a white cross. After discrimination training, performance was generalized to black and white photographs of the two objects and to their silhouettes, but not to their line drawings. In this experiment, the birds perceived the objects from a single point of view, and the pictures showed the objects in the same orientation as in training. It is likely that this procedure facilitated transfer and possibly confusion between the objects and their pictures.

In an effort to verify whether object-to-picture transfers can occur across viewpoints, Lumsden (1977) trained pigeons to discriminate a real object (S+) from two others (S-) presented in a standardized orientation. After training, the pigeons generalized their performance across viewpoints in a transfer test involving the real objects or their cutout photographs. Unfortunately, no statistical analyses were provided in this paper, which prevents any conclusion on the issue of viewpoint consistency and picture-object equivalence.

Watanabe (1993) recently published a more extensive study on picture-object equivalence in pigeons. The birds learned to categorize objects (object group) or their pictures (picture group) either on a food versus nonfood basis (concept group), or on arbitrary experimenter-defined basis (pseudo-concept group). Afterwards, picture-to-object or object-to-picture transfers were assessed. The transfer was two-directional, but it was limited to the concept group. The author concluded that generalization across presentation modes did not occur in a systematic way, which suggests that pictures cannot be used as realistic stimuli in any experimental context. Watanabe (1993) further proposed that classification on a natural-concept basis is required for generalization. Should we accept this conclusion? Examination of the training stimuli suggests that conceptualization might not have been the critical variable in this task. It appears, for instance, that the food objects (various types of grain) were more homogeneous in shape (and often smaller) than the non-food objects. Assuming that the pigeons learned this invariant characteristic, consideration of stimulus size or shape might have allowed positive transfers, without recognition of the real 3D objects.

Contrary to Watanabe's (1993) proposal concerning the role of natural concepts in object-picture equivalence, object-to-picture transfers were observed by Delius (1992) in pigeons in a categorization task based on the analysis of stimulus forms, rather than on a natural concept. This study involved discrimination between spherical and non-spherical objects. The pigeons generalized with both black and white photographs and drawing of the objects, although transfer with pictures gave rise to lower performance than transfer with novel real objects. Noticeably, pigeons did worse on transfer with color photographs than with black and white photographs. According to Delius (1992), the difference was a reflection of the fact that color photographs are matched to human trichromatic vision, which is inadequate for pigeons whose vision is pentachromatic. Color photographs are probably poor or false color representations of real objects for pigeons, a limitation often disregarded in the literature (but see Delius and Lea & Dittrich, this issue).

Other experiments on object-to-picture transfers have used conspecifics as discrimination stimuli. Again, the results are inconsistent. Trillmich (1976) presented pictures of conspecifics to budgerigars. The birds had to move towards the S+ picture which was displayed at one extremity of a Y-shaped maze. After task acquisition, when the live budgerigars actually depicted in the pictures were used instead of the pictures, significant transfer of performance was observed. Unfortunately, only one bird was tested in this condition. It is thus impossible to determine whether the subject associated the birds with their pictures or showed individual preferences for the S+ stimuli.

Using more subjects in each experimental condition ($N = 10$), Dawkins (1996) examined whether hens preferred flockmates rather than unfamiliar hens as feeding companions. A preference for familiar birds was found, but the bias disappeared when the real animals where replaced by their photographs. Dawkins (1996) explained her results by noting that a close-up inspection of the real animal is important for social recognition, but that close-up inspections reveal the artificial nature of the pictures. If this is true, then pictures can be used as social stimuli only in species for which recognition can be achieved from distant views of individuals.

Other experiments on object-to-picture transfers have been conducted with monkeys and apes. In infant rhesus monkeys, Zimmermann and Hochberg (1970) showed transfer in an experiment that suffered from the same limitations as Cabe's (1976), because it involved two very simple, artificial geometrical stimuli perceived under restricted exposure.

Using more stimuli than Zimmerman and Hochberg (1970), we looked at whether baboons were capable of associating objects with their pictures (Martin-Malivel, 1998). To do so, we developed a computerized go/no-go task requiring joystick manipulation to respond. Two conditions were proposed in our experiments: the "real-object" and the "picture" conditions. In the real-object condition, one object was randomly selected from a stimulus pair and then stuck on the center of a computer screen. To receive a food pellet, the baboons had to move the joystick when the real object corresponded to S+, and to refrain from moving it when it corresponded to S-. In the picture condition, real-size color images of the same objects as in the real-object condition were displayed on the screen. Again, the animal had to move the joystick when the image showed S+, and to refrain from moving it when it showed S-.

In the first experiment, four baboons were trained to discriminate two objects in a stimulus pair (e.g., a pencil vs. a clothespin). After they performed at the 90% correct level over 100 consecutive trials, transfer of learning was assessed using pictures of the same two objects. The variable of interest was the number of correct responses on the first 10 non-reinforced trials of the transfer test. This procedure involving an initial learning phase followed by a transfer phase was replicated four times with a novel pair of objects each time. Individual results for each transfer test are shown in Figure 1. One animal exhibited two instances of significant transfer, another exhibited only one significant transfer,

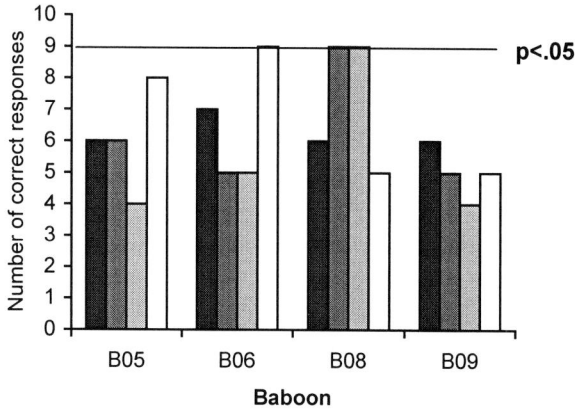

Figure 1. Individual numbers of correct responses during the four object-to-picture transfer tests conducted with each baboon.
Each transfer test is represented by a vertical bar. On the basis of a two-tailed binomial test ($p < .05$), transfers were considered significant when there were more than 8 correct responses during the 10 transfer trials (from Martin-Malivel, 1998).

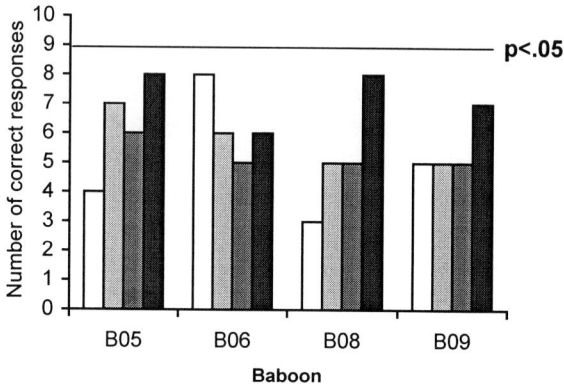

Figure 2. Individual numbers of correct responses during the four picture-to-object transfer tests conducted with each baboon.
On the basis of a two-tailed binomial test ($p < .05$), transfers were considered significant when there were more than 8 correct responses during the 10 transfer trials (from Martin-Malivel, 1998).

and the remaining two failed to show any significant evidence of transfer. This first experiment thus provided some arguments for an association between the objects and their picture, but in only two of the four baboons.

In the next experiment using four novel pairs of objects, pictures were presented in the learning phase, and transfer was assessed with the real objects. None of the baboons showed positive transfer in this picture-to-object condition (see Figure 2), suggesting that associations between objects and their pictures are easier in the object-to-picture condition than in the picture-to-object condition. A third experiment compared the object-to-picture and picture-to-object conditions using the same experimental design. For each baboon, there were two transfer tests per condition. The results were significant for only 2 of the 8 tested transfers in the object-to-picture condition. There was not a single case of significant transfer in the picture-to-object condition. The fact that the transfer was one-directional rules out the possibility that the pictures were processed in the *confusion* mode, but suggests instead that the baboons occasionally processed the pictures in the *equivalence* mode, and that this mode of picture processing requires previous exposure to the real objects. Note, however, that this mode was not available to every baboon, since one baboon never transferred above the chance level in the three experiments. Moreover, for those animals exhibiting significant transfers, transfers were observed for very few stimulus pairs.

Additional evidence for object-to-picture associations in nonhuman primates can be found in studies on chimpanzees, a species more closely related to humans. Tanaka (1996) trained chimpanzees to match one part of a 2-part object with its other part, as in matching a plastic box with its lid. The objects belonged to several categories, and each category was comprised of a two-part object, a container, and a tool. The chimpanzees were first trained in several combinations of within-category matching, as in matching the tool with the container of the same category. The learning criterion was reached in only one of the two chimpanzees tested. When later tested in an object-to-picture transfer test, the successful chimpanzee correctly matched the objects and their pictures on a categorical basis, even when the matched combination had never been presented in Experiment 1. Although picture-object matching occurred on a categorical basis, this study does not allow us to reject the hypothesis that the chimpanzee confused the objects and their pictures. It does demonstrate, however, that categorical relations learned with real objects may be transferred to pictorial representations of the same objects. Tanaka's (1996) results are reminiscent of earlier observations by Hayes and Hayes (1953), who showed that a chimpanzee could match real objects with pictures of objects belonging to the same category as the sample objects.

In short, object/picture transfer tests have failed to provide any clear-cut evidence for the equivalence mode of picture processing. Some studies have revealed associations between the objects and their pictures (e.g., Delius, 1992; Martin-Malivel, 1998) while others have failed to find such associations (e.g., Dawkins, 1996) or have demonstrated instead that such associations may only emerge in some experimental contexts (e.g., Watanabe, 1993). Interestingly, the strongest transfers have been the result of the use of objects with invariant physical properties, such as shape properties (Delius, 1992; Watanabe, 1993), or when the animals had little opportunity to perceive the objects from different points of view (e.g., Cabe, 1976). These studies may demonstrate either the processing of some of the objects' distinctive characteristics also shared by the pictures, or alternatively, that the pictures were processed in the *confusion* mode.

EXPERIMENTAL MANIPULATION OF THE FAMILIARITY OF OBJECTS DEPICTED IN PICTURES

If animals associate the real object with their picture, then familiarity with an object depicted in a picture should facilitate picture discrimination. Some studies have assessed the effect of familiarity using pictures of real objects. For example, Watanabe (1997) trained pigeons to discriminate pictures of a familiar object (i.e., a feeder) from pictures of an unfamiliar object (i.e., a mug). Some pigeons were trained with the familiar object as S+, while for others, S+ was the unfamiliar object. A generalization test using views of the same two objects from unusual viewpoints followed training. Only those pigeons trained with the familiar object as S+ showed viewpoint consistency. Does this result demonstrate some form of equivalence between objects and their pictures? In this study, the familiar stimulus had a uniformly gray color that remained invariant whatever the viewpoint, whereas the color of the unfamiliar stimulus varied with orientation. We suspect that such a bias facilitated transfer in the feeder S+ group compared to the S- group. Control experiments are thus needed to draw firm conclusions on the effect of stimulus familiarity in this task.

Another way of testing the effect of stimulus familiarity is to see if animals discriminate views of familiar places faster or better than views of unfamiliar places. Wilkie, Willson, and Kardal (1989) took this approach. They trained two groups of pigeons to discriminate pictures of sites. For one group, the two sets of pictures depicted unfamiliar locations. For the other half ("homing group"), one set represented homing locations and the other showed unfamiliar places. The homing pigeons were significantly better at transfer tests than the other birds, although the effect was weak. It was limited to the first three transfer tests, and was not significant when the all transfer tests were pooled. Interestingly, Wilkie et al. (1989) reported that, due to inclement weather, the homing group ceased to have outdoor experience with the real locations after the third transfer test, which suggests that a vivid recollection of the real place is needed to associate places and their pictures. In agreement with Wilkie et al. (1989), Kendrick (1992) also reported that the pigeons with homing experience at a specific location were better than naive animals on transfer tests involving views of that location.

Cole and Honig (1994) provided more contrasted data on the possible effect of exposure to objects shown in pictures. Their pigeons discriminated pictures of two ends of a room. One set of pictures was the positive set, associated with food delivery. The other set was negative. After discrimination training, the birds had to find food in the real room. For half of the subjects (i.e., the congruent transfer group), the food was hidden at the end of the room shown in the positive slides during initial training. For the other half (i.e., the incongruent transfer group), the food was located at the end of the room shown in the S- pictures. The congruent transfer group reached the learning criterion faster than the incongruent group (Experiments 1 and 2), suggesting that the pigeons in the congruent group processed pictures as representations of the real environment. However, this conclusion is weakened by the results of a third experiment showing the lack of a significant transfer from the real-world environment to the pictures.

Although Wilkie et al. (1989), Kendrick (1992), and to some extent, Cole and Honig (1994) suggested that birds recognize locations in pictures, some negative results also exist. Dawkins, Guilford, Braithwaite, and Krebs (1996) looked at whether outdoor experience at a location affects the ability to categorize slides of the location vs. other (unknown) locations. Prior to testing, four pigeons had the opportunity to visit one homing location which was later presented on slides during testing. The other four birds visited irrelevant locations. There was no effect of outdoor experience on either acquisition or transfer. Negative evidence for an effect of object familiarity in pigeons was also provided by Gray (1987, cited by Dawkins et al., 1996), who demonstrated that homing experience did not facilitate discrimination learning or generalization with pictures of geographical locations.

Taking a different approach, Lechelt and Spetch (1997) examined the types of landmarks used for spatial localization when the pigeon had to find some hidden food in an open field or peck a tactile screen at the location of the food on a pictorial representation of the field. Some pigeons were trained to search for the real food and then tested with the pictures, while others were trained and tested in the reverse order. Moreover, for half of the birds, the spatial arrangement of the landmarks was held constant across the real and pictorial conditions, whereas for the remaining birds, the spatial arrangement was switched when the birds were transferred between tasks. There was no evidence of significant transfer between the real-word (open field) and the pictorial conditions, and changes in the spatial arrangement did not affect transfer performance. The authors concluded that "birds solved the touch-screen task on the basis of the 2-D spatial relationships, rather than on the basis of 3-D spatial relationships extracted from the images".

In summary, some of the experiments reported in this section suggest that animals develop some associations between real-world objects and their pictures, and that such associations more readily develop when the animal is exposed to the real-word stimulus. Unfortunately, the available data suffer from the same limitation as in picture/object transfer experiments, because there is no way of knowing whether the animals confused the real-world and pictorial stimuli (*confusion* mode) or processed the pictures as representations of the real-word stimuli (*equivalence* mode).

SPONTANEOUS EMOTIONAL AND NON-EMOTIONAL
RESPONSES TO PICTURES

Animals may produce overt or covert emotional responses to the representational content of pictures. For instance, Boysen and Berntson (1986) showed that pictures of familiar caregivers accelerated the heart rate of chimpanzees, compared to pictures of strangers or other familiar individuals. An accelerated heart-beat response was also reported when pictures of agonistic conspecifics were shown (Boysen & Berntson, 1989). These results indicate that chimpanzees are able to recognize humans and emotional expressions of conspecifics in pictures, and react emotionally to these humans or partners. Emotional reactions to pictures are not restricted to apes. Macaques exhibit social reactions like lip-smacking and teeth chattering when shown pictorial faces (Perrett & Mistlin, 1990) and make threat gestures, vocalizations, and threatening movements when presented with pictures of emotional objects (Wright, 1989). Also, pigeons were found to attack photographs of conspecifics or taxidermically stuffed pigeons during agonistic periods, in the same way as they do when attacking live conspecifics (Looney & Cohen, 1974).

Emotional reactions to pictures reveal that some associations exist for these animals between real objects and their pictures, and then rule out the *independence* mode as a possible mode of picture processing. Still, do they show *confusion* or *equivalence* as defined above? One would expect emotional reactions to be stronger in the *confusion* than in the *equivalence* mode, because in the former the animal confuses the picture and its object. However, pictures may evoke emotional reactions in humans, even when we are aware that the visual stimulus is a picture (e.g., Lang, Bradley, & Cutherbert, 1998). Emotional responses to pictures thus provide few arguments to clearly distinguish these two processing modes.

Bovet and Vauclair (1998) demonstrate that analyzing the spontaneous behavioral responses to pictures can help make a clearer distinction between the *confusion* and *equivalence* modes. Their study on category learning involved two baboons that were WGTA-trained to discriminate food from non-food objects, and then tested with cutout or whole photos (i.e., pictures with a uniform background) of the objects. Of particular interest for our purposes here were the controlled experiments conducted after the initial tests. During these tests, both the cutouts and whole pictures were presented at an arm's distance from the animals, and any possible attempt to grab the pictures was recorded. Noticeably, there was no attempt at all to grab the whole pictures or the cutouts of the non-food objects. The baboons, however, showed a significant bias for grabbing the cutouts of food objects (Experiment 2C). Because the object-background relation was more realistic in the cutouts than in the whole pictures (for the cut-outs, the backgrounds were not in the same plane as the object), this result reveals that the baboons confused the objects and their cutouts. In support of the *confusion* mode of processing, the frequency of grabbing responses decreased when the experimenter rotated the cutouts in front of the animal prior to giving it the chance to grab them (Experiment 2D). Very likely, the rotation of the cutouts revealed the flatness of the pictures which could no longer be confused with the real food objects.

Similar observations were made by Fagot and Fujita (unpublished data). In this study, squirrel monkeys were trained to grab food objects presented by the experimenter, and to avoid grabbing non-food objects. After six days of training, food and non-food objects were replaced by their real-size color pictures (on a white background), and any attempt to grab them was recorded in a transfer test. Not only did the monkeys reach for the pictures of the food items; they also brought them to their mouths in an attempt to eat them. On several instances, pictures of pieces of an orange or sunflower seeds were brought to the mouth and the animals made peeling gestures. These observations unambiguously demonstrate that the animal confused the real objects and their pictures.

LANGUAGE STUDIES

Some stronger evidence for *equivalence* between pictures and objects has been obtained in language studies involving apes. Unfortunately, observations in this domain are often anecdotal because of the small number of observations and the necessarily small number of subjects. It was nevertheless reported that Wicky, a home-raised chimpanzee, could sort photographs of chimpanzees and humans into two piles, and place her own photograph on the human pile (Hayes & Nissen, 1971). Similarly, Koko, a language-trained gorilla recognized herself and signed her name on photographs (Patterson, 1978; cited by Anderson, this issue).

Matsuzawa (1990) and Itakura (1994) recently reported more extensive observations of this type. In their study, a chimpanzee named "Ai" was trained to label familiar human individuals or familiar chimpanzees using letters of the alphabet. After training, Ai could correctly label pictures (Matsuzawa, 1990) and line drawings (Itakura, 1994) of the same individuals. The line drawings were perceptually very different from the actual humans, thereby showing that performance with these stimuli was based on *equivalence* because it is very unlikely that the apes confused the actual humans and their pictorial representations. Although some other studies involving non-linguistic chimpanzees suggest that they recognize objects in pictures (e.g., Boysen & Berntson, 1986), it remains to be determined whether it was the language-training itself or the intensive training in associating the pictures and the objects that facilitated the *equivalence* mode of picture processing.

INTER-MODAL TRANSFER TESTS
INVOLVING PICTURES

One potentially powerful procedure for studing object-picture associations is to test the ability to match pictures and objects when the real objects are explored by touch only. Although the issue of inter-modal integration has been explored in several papers involving primates (e.g., Cowey & Weiskrantz, 1975), very few studies in this field have used pictures as visual stimuli.

One such study was conducted with two chimpanzees and one orangutan (Davenport & Rogers, 1971). The apes could match the pictures with the real objects inspected by touch, suggesting that they did recognize the objects in the pictures (see also Davenport, Rogers, & Russell, 1975). Unfortunately, Winner and Ettlinger (1979) replicated this experiment with chimpanzees and failed to find any evidence of tactual-object/picture matching. The same animals could match the haptic and visual percepts of the real objects. According to these authors, the successful apes in Davenport and Roger's study may have used an uncontrolled stimulus dimension (size) as a discrimination cue. Winner and Ettlinger concluded from their experiments that (for the chimpanzee) "the photographs were meaningless 2-dimension objects". They further added that "the chimpanzees did not realize that a photograph is a visual stimulus that must be read" (p. 419).

Interestingly, however, two rhesus macaques, which are from a lower primate species than chimpanzees, were found to be successful at matching pictures with haptically explored objects (Malone, Tolan, & Rogers, 1980; Tolan, Rogers, & Malone, 1981). Matching in these animals was not immediate, but required an initial training period in which the objects to explore by touch were available to vision at the same time as their pictures. As noted by Malone et al. (1980), this procedure might have helped the animals associate the objects and pictures. Further work is thus needed to clarify the conditions under which photographic recognition does (or does not) occur in these primate species.

INTER- AND INTRA-MODAL PRIMING STUDIES

Priming effects occur when identification of a stimulus is facilitated (or altered) by prior exposure to a related stimulus. Because priming effects can occur within a single modality (e.g., when the prime and target are both visual stimuli) or between modalities (e.g., when the prime is an auditory stimulus and the target is a visual one), the priming procedure is probably one of the best procedures for disentangling the role of perceptual and cognitive factors in picture processing, and for unambiguously demonstrating implicit recognition of pictured objects. One merit of priming experiments is that inter-modal priming effects, if any, cannot be due to the processing of invariant physical cues, and therefore should reflect recognition of the objects in the pictures.

Unfortunately, although priming effects have been studied in pigeons (e.g., Blough, 1991) and non-human primates (e.g., Hopkins, Morris, & Savage-Rumbaugh, 1991) for different purposes, to the best of our knowledge, this procedure has been used in only a few studies on picture perception (e.g., Brodbeck, 1997; Martin-Malivel & Fagot, in preparation). Brodbeck (1997) showed that categorization by pigeons of partially occluded pictures of cars or cats was facilitated when the positive stimulus served as the prime in previous trials. This result is reminiscent of the results obtained by Jitsumori, Wright, and Shyan (1989), who found an effect of proactive interference in a monkey during a picture categorization task (see also Sands, Lincoln & Wright, 1982). Although the above studies demonstrate that the processing of some pictures may affect the processing of others, they do not indicate whether such an interference occurs on a perceptual basis, due to the presence of some invariant features in pictures belonging to the same categories, or on a more abstract basis, due to the recognition of the pictured objects.

In our laboratory, we conducted three experiments on inter-modal and intra-modal priming in baboons (Martin-Malivel & Fagot, in preparation). Four baboons were initially trained to categorize 40 pictures of humans and 40 pictures of baboons, presented in random order. The baboons moved a joystick ("go" response) or refrained from moving it ("no-go" response) depending on the category (human or baboon) to which the target image belonged. The digitized pictures of humans and baboons had identical backgrounds, because they were all taken in an enclosure for baboons. The target picture was preceded by a prime image which also depicted either humans or baboons and was displayed for 120 ms. When subjects reached a criterion of 80 percent correct responses during one session of 80 trials, a transfer test was proposed with 80 novel photographs (40 per category) taken using the same procedure as for initial training. The baboons systematically failed to perform above the chance level in this transfer test. Their scores ranged from 50 to 67 percent correct. This poor performance contradicts previous observations that animals (e.g., Herrnstein & Loveland, 1964; Schrier & Brady, 1987) can generalize categorization rules by the first presentation of novel pictures. This difference may have been caused by the presentation of prime stimuli prior to the target.

In order to have baboons solve the task on a categorical basis rather than by rote learning, they were then re-trained and re-tested with novel target pictures of humans and baboons until they all performed above chance on the first presentation of novel pictures. Four transfer tests were needed to achieve this performance level. The experimental test was proposed immediately after the fourth transfer test.

During the test, novel pictures were used as prime and target stimuli. In one experimental condition, referred to as the "same" condition, the prime belonged to the same category as the target. It was thus a picture of the "baboon" category if the target showed one or more baboons, or a picture of the human category if the target showed one or more humans. In another condition, the "different" condition, the prime and the target pictures were from two different categories. For comparative purposes, four humans were tested using the same priming procedure as for baboons.

Individual response time results are reported in Figure 3 for both baboons and humans. Three of the four baboons had shorter response

times in the "same" than in the "different" condition. This priming
effect was replicated in three of the four human subjects, the fourth one
showing a nonsignificant trend ($p < .06$) for positive priming. What
could be the origin of these priming effects? Do they demonstrate some
form of implicit or explicit recognition of humans (or baboons) in pictures? Or do the priming effects reflect the processing of some invariant
stimulus cues, such as shape or color, shared by the prime and target
pictures belonging to the same category?

One way to assess these two possibilities is to test for inter-modal
priming. We conducted one experiment on inter-modal auditory-visual
priming, and a complementary one on visual-auditory priming. The auditory stimuli in these two experiments were one of two possible words
pronounced by humans, or one of two possible social vocalizations of
baboons (screaming, contact calls). As before, the visual stimuli were
pictures of humans and pictures of baboons. The two experiments were
conducted with both humans and baboons.

The experiment with auditory primes revealed significant effects for
three of the four human participants (see Figure 4). Response times were
shorter when primes and targets were selected from the same (human or
baboon) category than when they were from a different category. This
priming effect was found in only one of the four baboons. Similarly, the

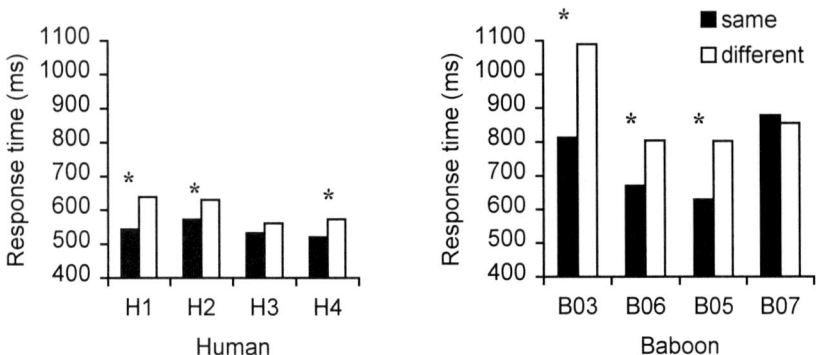

Figure 3. Intra-modal (visual-visual) priming experiment.
Left: Mean response time of the four human participants when the prime and
target stimuli belonged to the same category (black bars) or to different categories (empty bars). Right: Results of the four baboons tested under the same
conditions as humans (* = $p < .05$).

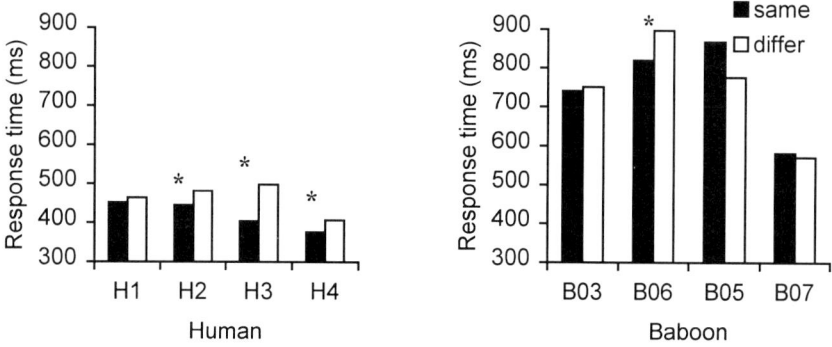

Figure 4. Inter-modal (auditory-visual) priming experiment.
Left: Mean response time of the four human participants when the auditory primes and the visual targets belonged to the same category (black bars) or to different categories (empty bars). Right: Results of two baboons tested under the same experimental conditions as humans (* = p < .05). Note that significant priming effects emerged in three of the four human participants, but in only one of the four baboons.

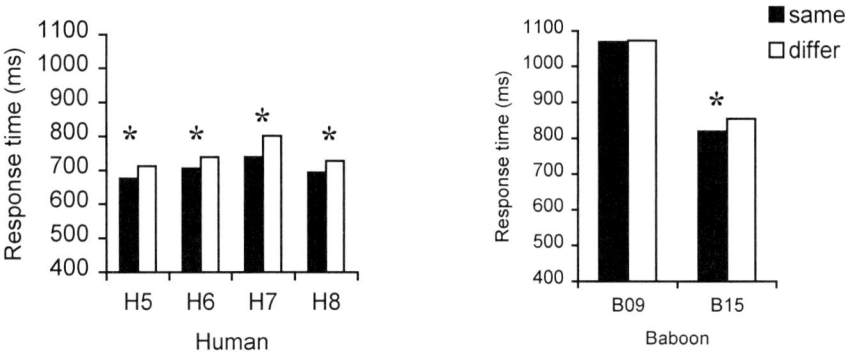

Figure 5. Inter-modal (visual-auditory) priming experiment.
Left: Mean response time of the four human participants when the visual primes and auditory targets belonged to the same category (black bars) or to different categories (empty bars). Right: Results of four baboons tested in the same conditions as humans (* = p < .05).

experiment using visual primes and auditory targets gave rise to significant priming effects in all four humans, but in only one of the two baboons (Figure 5). Again, for the human or baboon subjects showing priming effects, response times were faster when the prime and targets were from the same category than when they were from different categories.

In short, our research demonstrated that intra- and inter-modal priming can be found in both humans and baboons. Interestingly, intra-modal (visual-visual) priming effects emerged in our tasks more readily than inter-modal (visual-auditory, auditory-visual) ones. This result suggests that interference effects observed in categorical tasks involving pictures (e.g., Jistumori et al., 1989) reflect the processing of some basic invariant features of the stimuli, rather than a unique consideration of the representational content of the pictures. In more general terms, inter-modal priming demonstrates that baboons "see" some sort of correspondence between real humans and baboons and their pictures. Because the inter-modal procedure allows us to reject the hypothesis that pictures are processed in the *independence* mode, we are inclined to conclude that baboons process pictures in either the *confusion* or *equivalence* mode. Unfortunately, our procedure does not allow for a clearcut distinction between the *confusion* and *equivalence* hypotheses. Finally, remember that inter-modal priming effects occurred in some but not all the baboons. Why only some baboons underwent these priming effects remains unclear to us. On the basis of our previous experiments on object-to-picture transfers (see above), we presume that the baboons exhibiting no inter-modal priming effects did not recognize the humans or baboons in the pictures. A necessary conclusion to draw from these three experiments is thus that we should not take for granted the fact that animals, even monkeys, systematically recognize objects in pictures.

GENERAL DISCUSSION

This chapter examined the hypothesis that birds and nonhuman primates are able to associate pictures with the real-word objects they depict. To this end, we proposed a distinction between three main modes of picture processing, and then reviewed the studies providing direct evidence in favor of these modes.

A first and very immediate conclusion which derives from this review is that there is relatively little available data on the issue of picture-object correspondence in animals. Clearly, this issue has not been regarded as a crucial one, although pictures have very commonly been used as experimental stimuli in animal cognition studies. Yet determining how animals see pictures, and the factors affecting that processing, is a logical prerequisite to interpreting experimental data obtained through picture presentation. For instance, what is the significance of the literature on natural concepts (which mainly uses pictures) if the demonstration is still to be made that animals perceive some correspondence between natural objects and their pictorial representations? Similarly, what conclusion can be drawn from studies on social cognition that use pictures of conspecifics, if it remains to be demonstrated that the pictures represent social partners for the animals.

The problem it that there is no good reason to assume that animals perceive pictures as representations of real things. Even in humans, pictures are not always treated as representations of real objects. Adults from cultures with little exposure to pictures do not necessarily process photographs as we (Asian or Western people familiarized with pictures) do (e.g., Deręgowski, 1989; see also Deręgowski, this issue). In human newborns, the ability to associate objects and their pictures also develops during ontogeny (Slater, Rose, & Morrison, 1984). Thus, picture processing depends not only on the physical characteristics of the pictures, but also on the characteristics of the perceivers, such as the functional properties of their visual system and their degree of experience with pictorial representations. Experimenters working with animals (mostly in the cognitivist tradition) have often neglected to consider that pictures might not be treated by their subjects as representations of real objects, and consequently, they have rarely tested this hypothesis in experimental contexts.

The available studies on the issue of picture-object associations have provided unconclusive evidence in support of the hypothesis that animals systematically perceive some equivalence between pictures and real-world stimuli, even when the object or scene depicted in the photograph is familiar (e.g., Dawkins et al., 1996). Interestingly, several animal studies have successfully identified which physical aspects of the stimuli were processed in certain picture discrimination tasks. For instance, in one of our studies, we found that baboons discriminated human faces by considering variations in facial contour, rather than the internal structure of the face (Martin-Malivel & Fagot, submitted). In another study (D'Amato & Van Sant, 1988), Cebus monkeys were found to rely on the presence of a reddish color to sort person and non-person slides. This type of result demonstrates that the representational content of the pictures did not control discrimination behavior. It thus suggests an *independence* mode of picture processing, rather than a *confusion* or *equivalence* mode. It should be noted, however, that identification of the physical stimulus property that controls discrimination does not rule out the possibility that the animal is also sensitive to the representational content of the picture, at least implicitly. This assertion raises the very difficult question of whether the *independence* hypothesis should be accepted, based on the demonstration that animals process some physical stimulus cues as identified by experimental manipulation.

Although limited in number, other studies in the literature have demonstrated that animals are capable of associating objects with their pictures. This conclusion can be drawn, for instance, from recordings of emotional responses to the presentation of conspecifics in pictures (Boysen & Berntson, 1986) or from studies on inter-modal priming (Martin-Malivel & Fagot, in preparation). A close examination of these studies showing associations between objects and their pictures suggests the following remarks:

1) Very few studies have unambiguously demonstrated that animals process pictures in the *equivalence* mode. The most convincing demonstration of the *equivalence* mode was obtained in tests of language-trained apes (e.g., Itakura, 1994).

2) Most studies showing associations between objects and their pictures do not allow us to clearly distinguish between the *equivalence* and *confusion* modes of picture processing (e.g., studies on object-picture transfer).

3) Some of these studies, however, have demonstrated that the pictures were processed in the *confusion* mode. This phenomenon occurred for both birds (e.g., Looney & Cohen, 1974) and nonhuman primates (e.g., Bovet & Vauclair, 1998).

4) Several stimulus factors appear to support the *confusion* mode of picture processing. Among these factors are stimulus simplicity and the perception of objects from a single, restricted point of view (e.g., Cabe, 1976).

5) There are noticeable differences across individuals in the capacity to associate objects and pictures (see our experiments on inter-modal

priming). Interindividual differences have demonstrated that the ability to associate pictures and objects is not uniformly distributed within a group of subjects, nor within a species, and depends for a large part on individual factors.

6) It is likely that there are also differences across species in the ability to match objects and pictures. To the best of our knowledge, there is as yet no clear-cut demonstration of the *equivalence* mode of picture processing in birds.

As a general conclusion, while there is now convincing evidence that animals can recognize objects in pictures, evidence for *equivalence* (and to some extent *confusion*) remains weak and contradictory. We believe that such a conclusion is not trivial and has both methodological and theoretical implications for comparative cognition research. On the theoretical side, understanding picture-object relationships is an interesting way to learn about abstract and symbolic functioning in animals. For instance, the literature suggests that monkeys and prosimians often express social behaviors in front of a mirror, whereas apes express self-directed behaviors. Self-directed behaviors are usually taken as evidence that apes alone are capable of self-recognition (see Anderson, this issue). It is possible that such behavioral differences in front of a mirror are not necessarily related to self-recognition abilities *per se*, but derive instead from the fact that only apes are capable of processing their mirror image in the *equivalence* mode. Indeed, processing the mirror image in the *confusion* mode implies that the mirror image be perceived as a "real" animal different from the perceiver. Alternatively, processing the image in the *equivalence* mode, i.e., as a pictorial representation rather than as a real objet, is a necessary prerequisite for matching the internal representation of the self to the external mirror image. On the more practical side, our review recommends maximum caution when pictures are employed as substitutes of real-world objects in experimental contexts. It also suggests more serious consideration of the issue of object-picture equivalence in the near future. Undoubtedly, the field of animal cognition, and to some extent that of the neurosciences, will benefit from the promotion of this issue as one of the main and most important topics now to be investigated in animals.

REFERENCES

Blough, P. M. (1991). Selective attention and search images in pigeons. *Journal of Experimental Psychology: Animal Behavior Processes, 17,* 292-8.

Bovet, D., & Vauclair, J. (1998). Functional categorization of objects and of their pictures in baboons (*Papio anubis*). *Learning and Motivation, 29,* 309-322.

Boysen, S. T., & Berntson, G. G. (1986). Cardiac correlates of individual recognition in the chimpanzee (*Pan troglodytes*). *Journal of Comparative Psychology, 100,* 321-324.

Boysen, S. T., & Berntson, G. G. (1989). Conspecific recognition in the chimpanzee (*Pan troglodytes*): Cardiac responses to significant others. *Journal of Comparative Psychology, 103,* 215-220.

Brodbeck, D. R. (1997). Picture fragment completion: Priming in the pigeon. *Journal of Experimental Psychology: Animal Behavior Processes, 23,* 461-468.

Cabe, P. A. (1976). Transfert of discrimination from solid objects to pictures by pigeons: A test of theoretical models of pictorial perception. *Perception and Psychophysics, 19,* 545-550.

Cole, P. D., & Honig, W. K. (1994). Transfer of a discrimination by pigeons (*Columbus livia*) between pictured locations and the represented environments. *Journal of Comparative Psychology, 108,* 189-198.

Cowey, A., & Weiskrantz, L. (1975). Demonstration of cross-modal matching in rhesus monkeys, *Macaca mulatta. Neuropsychologia, 13,* 117-120.

D'Amato, M. R., & Van Sant, P. (1988). The person concept in monkeys (*Cebus apella*). *Journal of Experimental Psychology: Animal Behavior Processes, 14,* 43-55.

Davenport, R. K., & Rogers, C. M. (1971). Perception of photographs by apes. *Behaviour, 39,* 318-320.

Davenport, R. K., Rogers, C. M., & Russell, I. S. (1975). Cross-modal perception in apes: Altered visual cues and delay. *Neuropsychologia, 13,* 117-120.

Dawkins, M. S. (1996). Distance and social recognition in hens: Implications for the use of photographs as social stimuli. *Behaviour, 133,* 663-680.

Dawkins, M. S., Guilford, T., Braithwaite, V. A., & Krebs, J. R. (1996). Discrimination and recognition of photographs of places by homing pigeons. *Behavioural Processes, 36,* 27-38.

Delius, J. D. (1992). Categorical discrimination of objects and pictures by pigeons. *Animal Learning and Behavior, 20,* 301-311.

Deręgowski, J. B. (1989). Real space and represented space: Cross-cultural perspectives. *Behavioral and Brain Sciences, 12,* 51-119.

Gray, E. M. (1987). *Visual recognition of landmarks in the homing pigeon.* MSc thesis, Harvard-Radcliffe Colleges, Cambridge, MA.

Hayes, C., & Nissen, C. H. (1971). Higher mental functions of a home-raised chimpanzee. In A. M. Schrier & F. Stollnitz (Eds.), *Behavior of nonhuman primates* (Vol. 4, pp. 59-115). New York: Academic Press.

Hayes, K. J., & Hayes, C. (1953). Picture perception in a home-raised chimpanzee. *Journal of Comparative and Physiological Psychology, 46,* 470-474.

Herrnstein, R. J., & Loveland, D. H. (1964). Complex visual concept in the pigeon. *Science, 146,* 549-551.

Hopkins, W. D., Morris, R. D., & Savage-Rumbaugh, E. S. (1991). Evidence for asymmetrical hemispheric priming using known and unknown warning stimuli in two language-trained chimpanzees (*Pan troglodytes*). *Journal of Experimental Psychology: General, 120,* 46-56.

Itakura, S. (1994). Recognition of line-drawing representations by a chimpanzee (*Pan troglodytes*). *The Journal of General Psychology, 121,* 189-197.

Jitsumori, M., Wright, A. A., & Shyan M. R. (1989). Buildup and release from proactive interference in a rhesus monkey. *Journal of Experimental Psychology: Animal Behavior Processes. 15,* 329-337.

Kendrick, D. F. (1992). Pigeon's concept of experienced and non-experienced real-world locations: Discrimination and generalisation across seasonal variation. In W. K. Honig & J. G. Fetterman (Eds.), *Cognitive aspects of stimulus control* (pp. 113-134). Hillsdale, NY: Lawrence Erlbaum Associates.

Lang, P. J., Bradley, M. M., & Cutherbert, B. N. (1998). Emotion and attention: Stop, look, and listen. *Cahiers de Psychologie Cognitive/Current Psychology of Cognition, 17,* 99-1020.

Lechelt, D. P., & Spetch M. L. (1997). Pigeons' use of landmarks for spatial search in a laboratory arena and in digitized images of the arena. *Learning and Motivation, 28,* 424-445.

Looney, T. A., & Cohen, P. S. (1974). Pictorial target control of schedule-induced attack in white carneaux pigeons. *Journal of Experimental Analysis of Behavior, 21,* 571-584.

Lumsden, E. A. (1977). Generalization of an operant response to photographs and drawings/silhouettes of a three-dimensional object at various orientations. *Bulletin of the Psychonomic Society, 10,* 405-407.

Malone, D. R., Tolan, J. C., & Rogers, C. M. (1980). Cross-modal matching of objects and photographs in the monkey. *Neuropsychologia, 18,* 693-697.

Martin-Malivel, J. (1998). Existe-t-il une équivalence entre l'objet et sa représentation photographique chez le babouin (*Papio papio*)? *Primatologie, 1,* 249-268.

Martin-Malivel, J., & Fagot, J. (submitted). Inversion effects in the processing of pictures of human faces by baboons (*Papio Papio*).

Matsuzawa, T. (1990). Form perception and visual acuity in a chimpanzee. *Folia Primatologica, 55,* 24-32.

Patterson, F. G. (1978). Conversation with a gorilla. *National Geographic,* 438-465.

Perrett, D. I., & Mistlin, A. J. (1990). Perception of facial characteristics by monkeys. In W. C. Stebbins & M. A. Berkley (Eds.), *Comparative perception: vol. 2. Complex signals* (pp. 187-215). New York: John Wiley & Sons.

Sands, S. F., Lincoln, C. E., & Wright, A. A. (1982). Pictorial similarity judgement and the organization of visual memory in the rhesus monkey. *Journal of Experimental Psychology: General, 111,* 369-389.

Schrier, A. M., & Brady, P. M. (1987). Categorization of natural stimuli by monkeys (*Macaca mulatta*): Effects of stimulus set size and modification of exemplars. *Journal of Experimental Psychology: Animal Behavior Processes, 13,* 136-143.

Slater, A., Rose, D., & Morrison, V. (1984). Newborn infants' perception of similarities and differences between two- and three-dimensional stimuli. *British Journal of Developmental Psychology, 2,* 287-294.

Swartz, K. B. (1982). Species discrimination in infant pigtail macaques with pictorial stimuli. *Developmental Psychobiology, 16,* 219-231.

Tanaka, M. (1996). Information integration about object-object relationships by chimpanzees (*Pan troglodytes*). *Journal of Comparative Psychology, 110,* 323-335.

Terrace, H. S. (1993). The phylogeny and ontogeny of serial memory: List learning by pigeons and monkeys. *Psychological Science, 4,* 162-169.

Tolan, J. C., Rogers, C. M., & Malone, D. R. (1981). Cross-modal matching in monkeys: Altered visual cues and delay. *Neuropsychologia, 19,* 289-300.

Trillmich, F. (1976). Learning experiments on individual recognition in budgerigars (*Melopsittacus undulatus*). *Zeitschrift für Tierpsychologie, 41,* 372-395.

Watanabe, S. (1993). Object-picture equivalence in the pigeon: An analysis with natural concept and pseudoconcept discriminations. *Behavioural Processes, 30,* 225-232.

Watanabe, S. (1997). An instance of viewpoint consistency in pigeon object recognition. *Behavioural Processes, 39,* 257-261.

Wilkie, D. M., Willson, R. J., & Kardal, S. (1989). Pigeons discriminate pictures of a geographic location. *Animal Learning and Behavior, 17,* 163-171.

Winner, E., & Ettlinger, G. (1979). Do chimpanzees recognize photographs as representations of objects? *Neuropsychologia, 17,* 413-420.

Wright, A. A. (1989). Memory processing by pigeons, monkeys and people. In G. H. Bower (Ed.), *The psychology of learning and motivation* (Vol. 23, pp. 25-70). New York: Academic Press.

Zimmermann, R. R., & Hochberg, J. (1970). Responses of infant monkeys to pictorial representations of a learned visual discrimination. *Psychonomic Science, 18,* 307-308.

Reshaping neuronal representations
of visual scenes through attention

Stefan Treue and Julio C. Martinez Trujillo

University of Tübingen, Germany

Abstract

The sensory systems supply the information that is used to build a representation of our external world. However, the amount of information provided by highly evolved sensors such as the eyes of higher animals, exceeds the nervous system's capacity. Attention serves as one of the main selection mechanisms that allows these animals and humans to concentrate processing resources on the most relevant information. Here we review selected findings and present some of our own data in macaques about how this selection process effectively and often without the individual's awareness prevents irrelevant information from reaching later stages of processing.

Key words: Attention, contrast, illusions, electrophysiology, monkey, visual cortex, motion.

Correspondence should be sent to Stefan Treue, Cognitive Neuroscience Laboratory, Sektion für Visuelle Sensomotorik, Department of Neurology, University of Tübingen, Auf der Morgenstelle 15, 72076 Tübingen, Germany (e-mail: treue@uni-tuebingen.de).

> Everyone knows what attention is. It is the taking possession by the mind, in clear and vivid form, of one out of what seems several simultaneously possible objects or trains of thought. Focalization, concentration, of consciousness are of its essence. It implies withdrawal from some things in order to deal effectively with others.
>
> (William James, 1890,
> *The Principles of Psychology*)

Our senses are the design of eons of evolution. They have evolved not primarily to give us *accurate or complete* information about the world but to supply us with *useful* information. This distinction might seem subtle since information is normally only useful if it is accurate. But the difference between accurate and useful information becomes particularly obvious if we consider the role of attention. Attention is an important part of everyday life. We use it to concentrate on aspects of our sensory input that we deem worthy of further processing. Without such a selection process our sensory systems would be inundated with information. Instead, only a small fraction of the information received by our sensory organs reaches awareness. This small fraction does not represent an accurate representation of the world but rather is the result of the application of two processes, namely, the attentional selection and the attentional weighing of sensory input.

The purpose of this chapter is to present a few examples of how attention shapes the internal representation of the external world generated from the information supplied by our sensory organs. Obviously this cannot be an exhaustive treatment of this issue but rather it is a collection of examples from psychophysics and physiology, that concentrates on the role of attention in the *visual* system.

The chapter should give the reader a sense of how attentional modulation enhances the representation of attended elements of our world and suppresses information from unattended stimuli. The studies presented here will also show that some of these attentional processes are hidden from conscious experience, leaving us to underestimate attention's influence on everyday perception.

"THE WORLD AS OUTSIDE MEMORY"

We normally are aware of the effort of attending, i.e., of concentrating our attention on a particular sensory detail and experiencing the *increase* in detailed information obtained from attended features. The latter is introspectively the main reason for directing attention in the first place. What we are much less aware of is the *loss* of information from unattended aspects of a visual scene. This loss should degrade our internal representation of our environment. But while we generally concentrate on just a few details of any given scene we still feel that our internal representation has information about many details to which we never paid attention.

In a series of experiments O'Regan, Rensink, and their colleagues investigated the richness of internal representations of the visual environment and the role of attention in creating and maintaining those representations. For this purpose they developed a "flicker" paradigm (Rensink, O'Regan, & Clark, 1997, 1999). Subjects were asked to detect the difference between two still images of a scene. The images alternated continuously until the observer responded and was then asked to verbally describe the change.

Figure 1 shows the basic paradigm and examples of the image pairs used. The difference between the images could be in an aspect of central interest (Fig. 1b) or of marginal interest (Fig. 1c) to the viewer, and the changed object or feature could either be missing from one image, change colors between images, or change locations. In all cases, subjects had great difficulty detecting changes of marginal interest, requiring on average about 11 seconds (17 image alternations) before identifying the change. Changes of central interest were identified quicker (even though they were on average 20% smaller in area) but still required about 5 seconds (7 image alternations). These difficulties did not exist because the changes were too small to be noticeable: when the measurements were repeated with the blanks between images removed, the identification of both central and marginal interest changes occurred in less than 2 image alternations, requiring only about one second.

One might argue that the flicker paradigm, i.e., the rapid alternation of still images, is an artificial situation that is a poor representation of real-world experiences of the visual scene and tells us little about the richness of our internal representation of the real environment. This argument has been addressed in experiments where the changes occurred during eye blinks while viewing a picture (O'Regan, Deubel, Clark, & Rensink, 1999a) and using motion picture sequences (Levin & Simons, 1997) where changes were introduced at the moment of a camera cut. Again, subjects had a great deal of trouble noticing even large changes in salient objects. Similar results have been obtained with groups of isolated objects rather than whole scenes (Zelinsky, 1997) and with still image changes in the absence of blank intervals but accompanied by the brief appearance of several small patches covering parts of the image ("mudsplash" experiment, O'Regan, Rensink, & Clark, 1999b).

All these experiments combine the changes subjects are asked to detect, with transients in the visual input, either through whole image changes (such as in the blank intervals of the flicker paradigm, the occlusion of the images by an eye blink, or the movie cuts) or through other large changes in the image (as in the "mudsplash" experiment). If these transients are removed, as when presenting the flicker paradigm without the blank intervals, the changes become immediately apparent.

O'Regan and others have interpreted these results as evidence against a detailed internal representation of the visual environment. Rather, given that the physical environment is generally fairly stable, evolution seems to have opted for using "the world as an outside memory" (O'Regan, 1992). A memory or detailed representation is only built up for attended aspects of or objects in the visual scene. To detect changes in this environment, a system that pre-attentively notices changes in the visual scene and attracts attention, i.e., detailed analysis to the corresponding locations has been developed. But note that even at attended locations changes can go unnoticed, as observed by O'Regan and his

Figure 1. Flicker paradigm.
Panel A shows the prototypical sequence of images in a flicker paradigm. A pair of images (I' and I'') is each shown twice in rapid alternation with blank frames. The duration of individual image presentations is 240 ms and 80 ms for the blank intervals. The sequence is repeated until the subject reports the difference between image I' and I''.
Panel B shows an example of an image pair with a difference in an aspect of central interest (the helicopter seen through the window), while panel C shows an image pair with a difference in an aspect of marginal interest (the railing in the background). In both of these examples, the position of the object was changed but other changes were also used in the experiments.

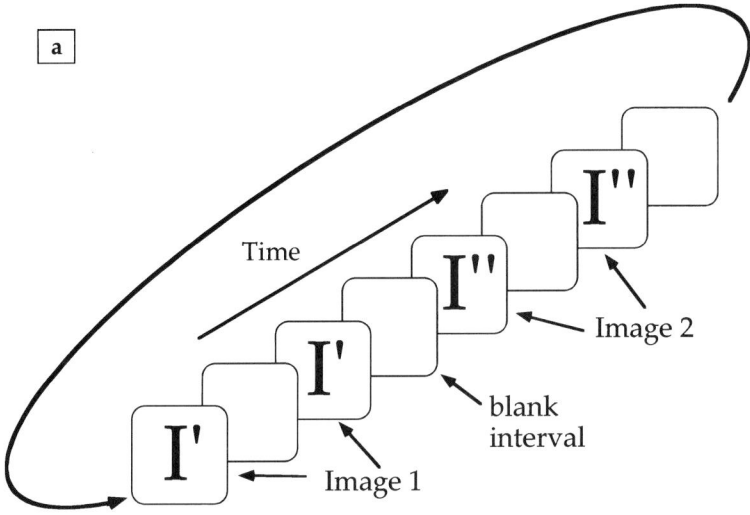

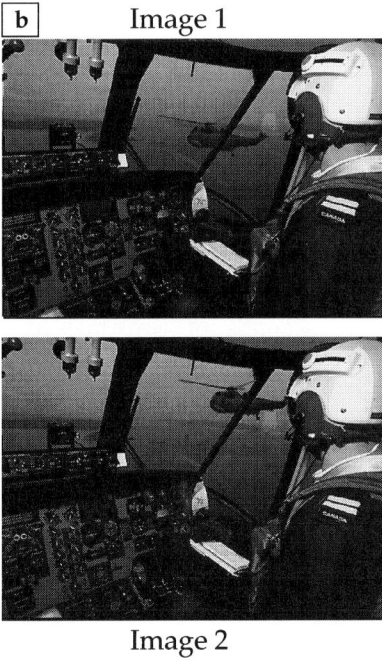

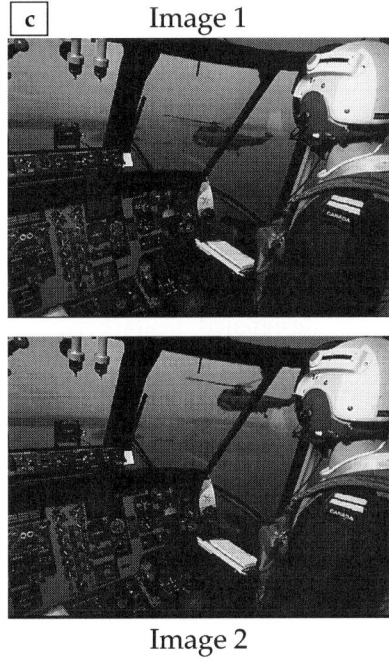

colleagues (O'Regan et al., 1999). They monitored the subjects' gaze positions, i.e., which part of the image they were foveating, during experiments where scene changes were applied during blinks. In almost 50% of the cases, subjects were looking (and therefore most likely attending) within 1° of the change at the moment the change occurred. This suggests that even at the attended location, attention is directed at only a subset of the features (form, color, motion, etc.) at that location.

In summary, these experiments suggest that a large proportion of the visual information received by the eyes is not processed, and that the visual system combines an automatic system for detection of transients with the illusion of a rich and detailed internal representation of our environment.

ATTENTION AS A NON-UNITARY PROCESS

The experiments described above might support the notion of a single "spotlight of attention" that is directed towards the current area of interest in the visual field. While many studies support such a notion (Eriksen & St. James, 1986), and demonstrate that this locus of attention can be moved rapidly and independently of any eye movements (Saarinen & Julesz, 1991), information from outside this region of focal attention can be processed beyond the simple detection of transients. Pylyshyn and his colleagues demonstrated the ability to track several items moving among identically-shaped distractors (Pylyshyn & Storm, 1985). In their experiments, subjects fixated a central fixation point and were presented with ten identical moving white X's one to five of which were designated as targets. After several seconds of Brownian-like, pseudo-random movement, a marker was flashed at the location of one X and the subjects had to respond if the X was a target. The accuracy of responding to target flashes (and of withholding responses to flashes at distractor locations) decreased as the number of targets increased, but was above 80% even for 5 targets. Additional experiments demonstrated that an increased size of the focus of attention encompassing all tracked objects could not be the basis of this phenomenon, since subjects were not more sensitive to changes in items lying within the polygon formed by the targets compared to changes in items outside the polygon. While Pylyshyn and his colleagues argued that the indexing and tracking of objects is a *pre*-attentive process, they were also able to show that attention can be allocated to multiple locations. They designed an experiment using the line-motion illusion reported by Hikosaka, Miyauchi, and Shimojo (1991). The illusory line motion phenomenon occurs when attending to a location induces the perception of motion of a line that is presented with that location as one endpoint. In a typical experiment, a spatial cue is presented first, in order to draw the subjects' attention to its location. Then, after a brief inter-stimulus interval the line is presented all at once, but instead of perceiving that the complete line appeared instantaneously, subjects reported that the line was "drawn" starting at that end of the line closest to the cued location. Pylyshyn and Storm (1985) presented a ring of cues around a fixation point and after the cues were taken away, a line was presented connecting the fixation point to either a cue location or to a location halfway between two neighboring cue locations. The line illusion was observed significantly less frequently in the latter case, suggesting that attention was only allocated to cued locations. The strength of the effect diminished as the number of cues increased, supporting Pylyshyn's notion that there is a limited number of loci that can be indexed.

ATTENTIONAL BLINKS

While the studies discussed above support the role of attention in selecting stimuli that compete for processing resources, there is also a body of evidence that attention operates over time too. Most notable in this context is the attentional blink or dwell time, so called because it involves the loss of information processing abilities for a brief period of time after the appearance of an attentionally demanding stimulus (Weichselgartner & Sperling, 1987; Raymond, Shapiro, & Arnell, 1992; Duncan, Ward, & Shapiro, 1994; Shapiro, Arnell, & Raymond, 1997). Similar to what happens in eye blinks, the "blindness" created by the attentional blink is not readily noticed introspectively. Figure 2 shows a classical paradigm and exemplary results. Subjects are asked to perform either two (dual-task) or just the second of two tasks (single-task) during the rapid serial visual presentation (RSVP) of individual stimuli. Figure 2b shows the results from an experiment where the RSVP consisted of a stream of random individual black letters. Target 1 was the only white letter in the stream and target 2 (if present) was an X (not used as a distractor or as target 1). Subjects were asked to report, after a trial, if an

X had been included in the RSVP, and in the dual task, subjects had to additionally report which white letter had been presented. Figure 2b plots the proportion of correct decisions in target 2 detection in the single task (upper curve, filled circles) and dual-task (lower curve, empty triangles) paradigms. The detection of the X was highly reduced when it appeared within about 500 ms after the white letter (target 1). The single task data showed that the RSVP per se did not cause this drop in performance since the single task curve showed no corresponding drop for short target 1-target 2 separations. These results were interpreted as evidence that attention-demanding tasks (such as identifying the white letter) interfere with the allocation of attention to a task occurring up to several hundred ms after the first task.

Figure 2. Attentional blink paradigm.
Panel A shows the prototypical sequence of images in an RSVP experiment designed to demonstrate the "attentional-blink". Here, letters were presented foveally in rapid succession on a computer monitor. Each letter was shown for 53 ms with 67 ms of blank screen between individual letter presentations. The dots are intended to indicate that a variable number of distractors could be presented before Target 1, between Target 1 and Target 2, and after Target 2. The distractor and Target 1 could be any letter other than an "X". Target 1 was the only white letter. Target 2 was an "X" and was present in half of the trials. In the single-task condition, subjects had to state after each series of letters whether an "X" had been present ("target 2 task"). In the dual-task condition, they also had to report which white letter was presented.
Panel B plots the mean correct response rate for 7 subjects in the target 2 task, i.e., judging whether a letter "X" was among the letters presented. Half of the trials contained this letter (always after the target 1 letter), and the other half included another letter in its place. Performance was plotted for trials containing the "X" as a function of its onset asynchrony (SOA) relative to target 1. The upper curve (solid circles) is the performance for the single-task experiments, i.e., when subjects did not have to identify target 1. The lower curve (empty triangles) plots the performance in the dual-task experiments. Error bars denote 95% confidence intervals around the means. The difference between the two curves (shaded area) is the loss in detectability of target 2 caused by performing the target 1 task, i.e., the "attentional blink".

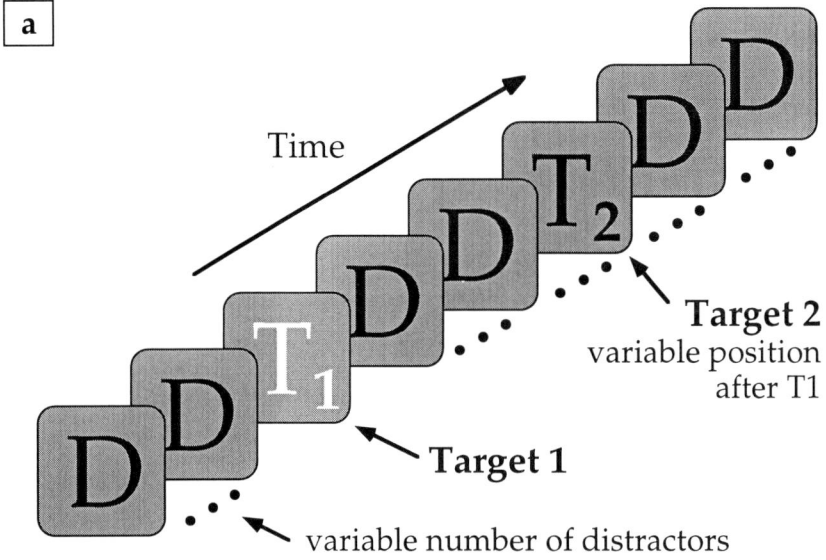

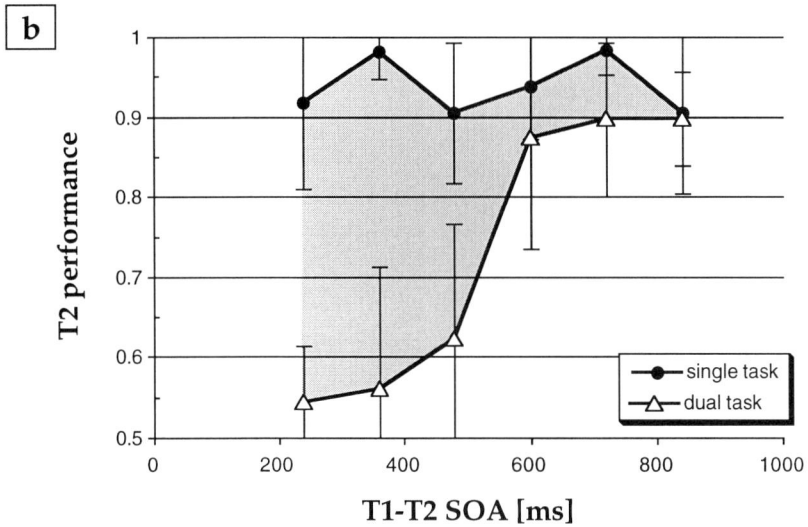

The attentional blink is not restricted to letter tasks or the exact RSVP paradigm shown in Figure 2. Recent experiments have shown that presenting just two motion stimuli or a motion stimulus and a letter in rapid succession (each followed by a mask) also results in an attentional blink (Krope, Treue, & Husain, 1998). Thus, in time, just as in space, attention seems to be needed for visual information to be processed, and conversely, in the absence of allocation of attention to a stimulus, that stimulus appears not to reach higher levels of processing.

PHYSIOLOGICAL CORRELATES OF ATTENTIONAL MODULATION

All of the effects of attention described above share the loss of processing of unattended features. What are its possible physiological correlates? Rensink and O'Regan's work suggests that the impression of a rich and detailed internal representation of our environment is an illusion, and that detailed information is only processed from the few attended features in our environment. This ever-changing weighing and selection mechanism does not seem to occur at the front end of the visual system. Our retinas offer a fairly homogenous and detail-rich matrix of information that, while being influenced by the eccentricity of the stimulation, does not seem to reflect an attentional selection process.

Traditionally, studies on the neuronal encoding of signals in the visual system have concentrated on sensory aspects, i.e., on how stimulus properties are encoded in the firing rates of neurons. This has lead to the recognition that visual information processing to a large extent reflects a hierarchical system of cortical areas that extract increasingly complex information from the sensory signals arising in the retinas via a bottom-up process. More recently an increasing number of studies have addressed non-sensory, top-down influences on visual information processing. They have shown that, in addition to purely sensory processing, representations in the visual cortex can be profoundly influenced by the organism's behavioral state, of which attention is an important component (e.g., Moran & Desimone, 1985; Treue & Maunsell, 1996). The interplay between bottom-up sensory information and top-down effects of attention is likely to be an important aspect of cortical processing.

Here we will present one example of such attentional modulation, based on our work on attentional influences on visual motion processing in the macaque monkey cortex. We shall show that there are neuronal phenomena that could be the basis of the selective processing of visual information demonstrated in the psychophysical studies outlined above. Specifically we shall attempt to demonstrate the neuronal correlate of the invisibility of unattended aspects of the visual environment. We shall first review experiments demonstrating a neuronal correlate of attentional modulation, and then we shall suggest a way of transposing those attentional modulations into the sensory domain.

Attentional modulation of neuronal responses is a change in a neuron's firing rate as a function of the attentional state of the animal. To show such changes one has to make sure that they are not generated accidentally by changes in the sensory properties of the stimulation. Our experiments therefore always compare experimental conditions in which the sensory stimulation is identical but the attentional state of the animals is changed. Because the location of a stimulus on the retina is an important sensory parameter, all our experiments require the animal to maintain fixation on a stationary fixation point throughout the trials. This is monitored at a high resolution using the scleral search coil technique, and will insure that the receptive field of a given neuron remains at the same location in visual space.

We recorded responses from neurons in the middle temporal (MT) and medial superior temporal (MST) visual areas in the superior temporal sulcus of two behaving macaque monkeys using standard extracellular recording techniques (for additional details and methods, see Treue & Maunsell, 1996; Treue & Martinez Trujillo, 1999). Both areas contain a high proportion of direction-selective cells, and their sensory responses to moving stimuli have been studied extensively (for a review, see Logothetis, 1994). These cells show a tuned response to the direction of motion inside their receptive field, i.e., the response is strongest when the motion is in the cell's preferred direction and falls monotonically as the direction diverges from the preferred one, reaching a minimum for motion 180° from the preferred direction. These direction-tuned responses are thought to be the substrate of the visual system's encoding of motion information. They are generally bell-shaped and well fitted by a Gauss function (Snowden, Treue, & Andersen, 1992). Combining two moving stimuli inside the receptive field generally evokes a response approximated by the average of the responses evoked by the individual motions (Snowden et al., 1991; Recanzone, Wurtz, & Schwarz, 1997). Here we review experiments that have demonstrated that attention enables the visual system to overcome this equipotent influence of various stimuli on neuronal responses.

The stimuli were two random dot patterns (RDP) made up of small bright dots moving within a stationary virtual aperture on an otherwise dark computer monitor in front of the animal. Each trial began with the appearance of a small fixation cross on the screen (see Figure 3). After the monkey had foveated this cross, in two thirds of the trials (the "attend-in" trials) a single moving RDP (the "cue") appeared somewhere on the screen. The animal responded by touching a lever which caused the cue pattern to disappear. Within a few hundred milliseconds, two moving RDPs appeared, one (the "target") at the cued location and the other (the "distractor") right next to it. Both the target and the distractor started to move continuously at the same speed. One RDP (the "null pattern") always moved in the direction opposite to the cell's preferred direction, the 'anti-preferred' or 'null' direction, while the other RDP (the "tuning pattern") moved in one of 12 possible directions chosen to cover the range of possible directions evenly (0, 30, 60, ..., 300, 330°, with 0° denoting the preferred direction). Both the target and distractor positions were chosen such that the two stimuli were inside the receptive field of the cell under study. The animal's task was to attentionally track the target and to release the lever quickly when it transiently increased its speed or changed its direction. Since the change occurred after a random amount of time, the animal had to maintain attention on the target for the whole time. Sometimes the distractor changed first, but a response of the animal to that change ended the trial without a reward, providing a strong incentive for the animal to respond to changes in the target only. In the remaining third of the trials (the "attend-out" trials) the cue stimulus was a small square appearing on top of the fixation cross.

Figure 3. Time course and stimulus layout of the experimental conditions used in the physiology experiments.
A trial started with the fixation acquisition phase. By foveating the fixation cross (FC) the monkey initiated the trial. This caused the appearance of one of three possible cues (a moving random dot pattern and one of two possible locations, or a colored square on top of the fixation cross) for 250 ms, indicating to the monkey the task for the selective attention phase. After a blank

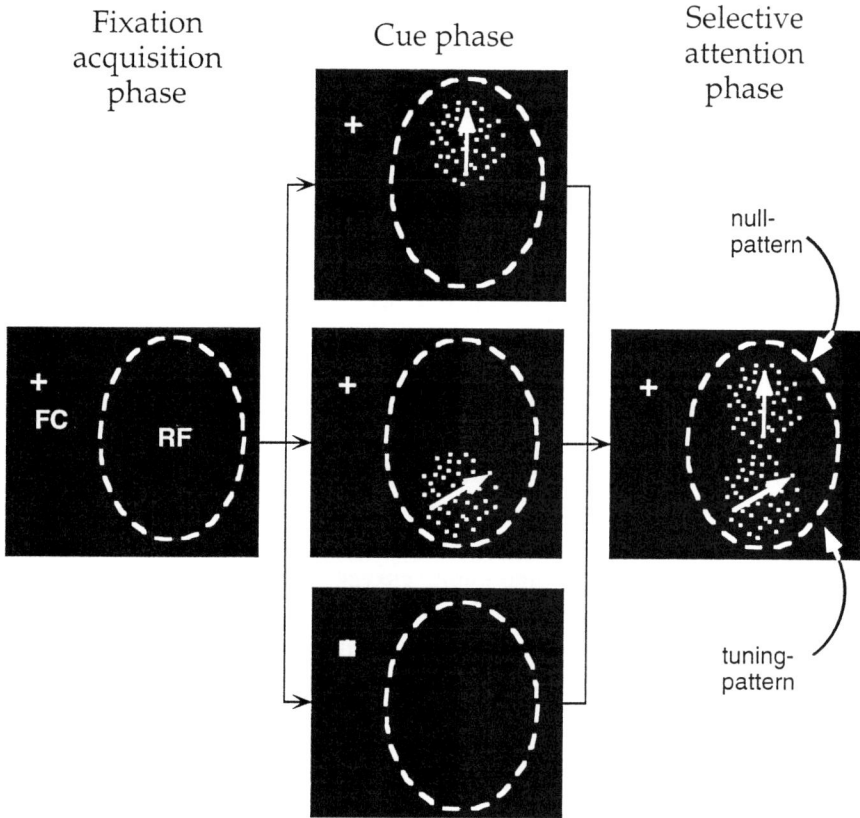

Fixation acquisition phase — Cue phase — Selective attention phase

null-pattern

FC RF

tuning-pattern

interval of 400 ms (during which only the fixation cross was on the screen) the selective attention phase, in which two moving random dot patterns were presented inside the receptive field, started. After a random interval of 500 to 3000 ms the luminance of the fixation point ("attend-out" trials) or the direction or speed of the target pattern changed (in the "attend-in" trials). Responding to this change (but not to changes in the other pattern) within a few hundred milliseconds triggered a reward for the animal. Throughout the trial, the animal had to maintain its gaze on the fixation cross.

The white arrows symbolize the direction of motion of the random dot pattern. Neither they nor the dashed ellipse denoting the receptive field (RF) were actually shown on the monitor. The tuning pattern could move in one of twelve directions, whereas the null pattern always moved in the cell's null-direction (upward in this example, but chosen individually for every cell). Random dot patterns where matched to the cell's preferred speed and positioned at about equipotent locations in the receptive field.

This served as an instruction to the animal to respond to a subtle luminance change on this square. The attend-out trials also included the presentation of the two moving RDPs inside the receptive field. They included the attention-demanding task of detecting the luminance change to control the animal's attention. Without such a task the animal would be free to attend to whatever stimulus it pleased without the experimenter's knowledge.[1]

Throughout every trial, the animal had to maintain its gaze on the fixation cross. Only those portions of correctly completed trials before any RDP had changed were analyzed. This ensured that all trial periods analyzed represented identical sensory stimulations. By using tuning patterns moving in different directions, we were able to modulate the response of a given neuron. Since this sensory modulation was recorded for three attentional conditions, we were able to determine both the effect of moving the "spotlight of attention" into the receptive field as well as shifting it from the null pattern to the tuning pattern on the sensory responses.

Figure 4 presents the three tuning curves recorded from a typical MT neuron under these three attentional conditions. Like most cells we encountered, this neuron showed an intermediate level of response during the attend-out trials. When attention was switched into the receptive field, responses increased if the tuning pattern was the target and decreased if the null pattern (moving downward for this cell) was the target. These changes are a neuronal correlate of spatial attention. Attention seems to be able to reduce the influence of the unattended stimulus, thus increasing responses if the inhibitory null pattern is suppressed and decreasing responses when the tuning pattern is suppressed. On average we found a 31% increase over the attend-out responses when the target was the tuning pattern, and a 27% reduction in responses (i.e., of the sensory modulation) when the target was the null pattern. While this is a substantial change in neuronal responses that clearly demonstrates that

---

1. The exact task an animal is performing outside the receptive field can influence the response of the neuron to a stimulus inside the receptive field, demonstrating that attention does not only operate within the receptive field (for details, see Treue & Martinez Trujillo, 1999). Attending to a color change at the fixation point is the most neutral condition and was therefore chosen for the experiments presented here.

the neural representations in MT and MST are influenced by the behavioral significance of the stimuli in the receptive field and not only by their sensory properties, the suppression of the unattended patterns seems far from complete.

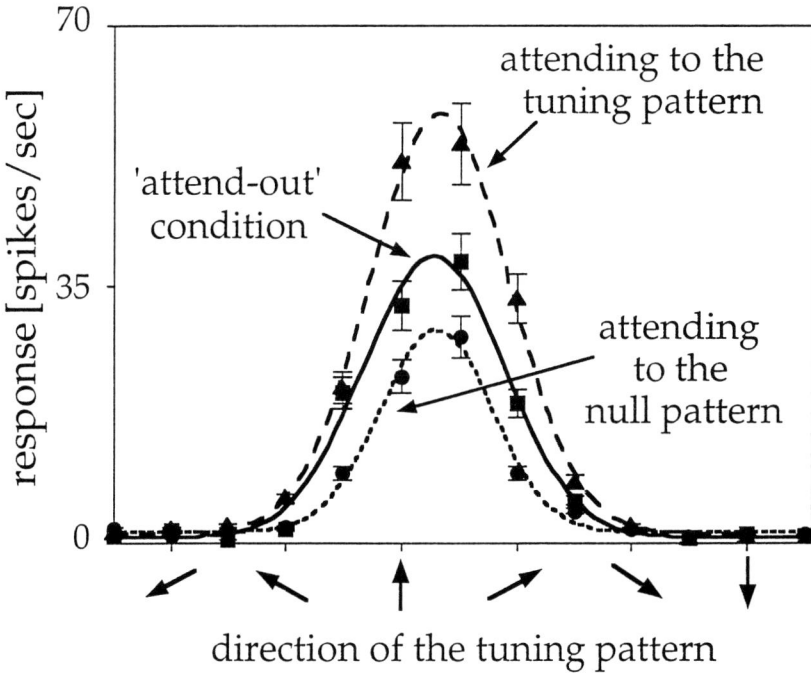

Figure 4. Example of the attentional modulation of an MT cell between the three attentional conditions used.
The solid line is a Gauss function fit over the responses of a neuron to various directions of motion of the tuning pattern when the animal was cued to respond to a luminance change at the fixation point. Similarly the other lines represent fits over the responses using the identical stimuli inside the receptive field but with the animal directing its attention into the receptive field, either to the tuning pattern (dashed line, direction of tuning pattern is shown along the x-axis) or to the null pattern (dotted line, for this cell the null pattern moved downward). Clearly, directing attention to the tuning pattern increased responses (by about 50% for this neuron), whereas directing attention to the null pattern decreased responses (by about 30%).

"TITRATING" THE ATTENTIONAL MODULATION
WITH CHANGES IN CONTRAST

It is difficult to establish the level of neuronal response suppression that would correspond to the psychophysical effects of attention discussed above. The psychophysical experiments suggest that unattended stimuli become largely invisible. By attempting to translate the attentional suppression we observed into a measure of stimulus visibility, we were wondering whether the attentional modulation could be mimicked by a reduction in stimulus visibility in the absence of changes in the attentional state. In our physiological experiments described above, we determined how much a change in attentional state could change a neuron's firing rate. Now we tried to determine if and how much of a change in stimulus visibility would create the same modulation in the absence of a change in attentional state.

As discussed above, attention seems to suppress the influence of unattended stimuli. Therefore the flattened tuning curve observed when the animal was attending to the null pattern (dotted curve in Figure 4) might reflect the reduced influence of the unattended tuning pattern that supplies the sensory modulation. We therefore attempted to mimic this attention effect with a reduction in the luminance of the corresponding stimulus. More specifically, we recorded neuronal responses in a variant of the attend-out condition used before. The only difference was that we reduced the luminance levels of the tuning pattern in an attempt to create response levels that resembled the ones recorded in the corresponding attend-in conditions, i.e., when the null pattern was the target. Thus the

Figure 5. Attentional titration experiment: Effect of attention and of reducing luminance on the response of one MT cell (the same as shown in Figure 4).
The top panel replots the attend-out responses and the responses when the animal was attending to the null pattern from the previous figure. The middle and bottom panels replot the attend-in curve from the top panel, i.e., with 100% luminance (the brightest luminance that could be achieved on our monitor) of both stimuli, and also show the responses in attend-out conditions where the luminance of the tuning pattern was reduced (to 6.6% and 1% of the maximal luminance, respectively). The data shows that the reduction of luminance lowered the height of the cell's tuning curve. Around a luminance of 7% the attend-out tuning curve is similar to the attend-in tuning curve derived at full luminance.

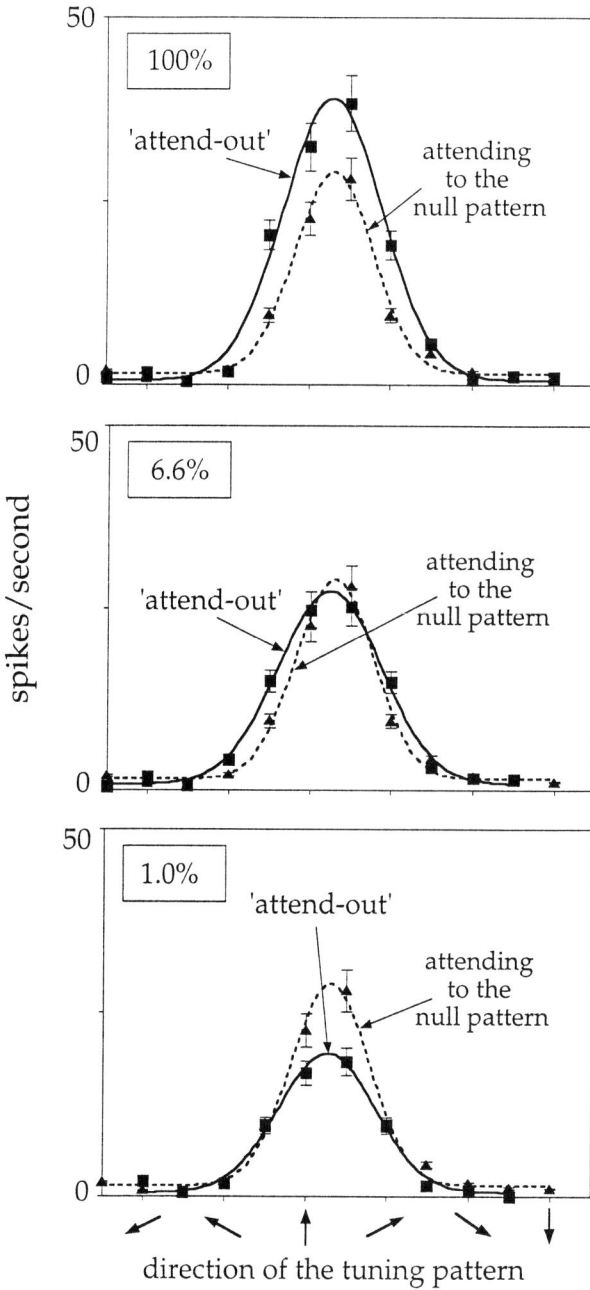

direction of the tuning pattern

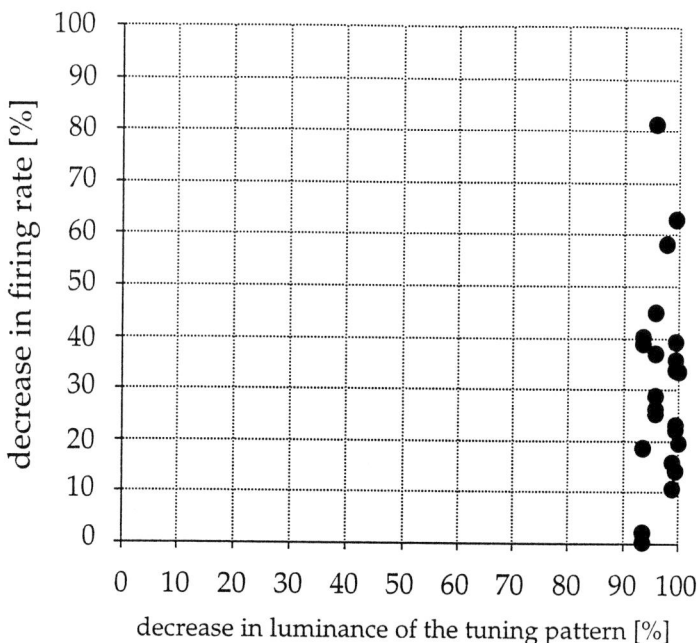

Figure 6. Scatter plot of attentional modulation and contrast modulation at the titration point for all cells.

The x-axis represents the luminance reduction that is necessary (in the absence of a shift of attention) to achieve the same response modulation as the one caused by attention. A large x-value represents a cell where the tuning pattern's luminance had to be reduced so much that it became almost invisible. The y-axis represents the attentional modulation, i.e., the reduction in response when the animal attended to the null pattern inside the receptive field vs. when attention was directed outside the receptive field (in this comparison all patterns have 100% luminance). A large y-value represents a cell with a strong attentional modulation. For example, a point with an x-value of 95% and a y-value of 25% represents a cell whose firing rate decreased by 25% when the animal directed its attention (but not its gaze) from the fixation point to the null pattern inside the receptive field. To achieve the same 25% reduction in firing rate while the animal kept attending to the fixation point, the luminance of the tuning pattern had to be reduced by 95%, i.e., to 5% of the value used for the previous measurement. All data points fell on the far right of the graph, indicating that luminance reductions of more than 90-95% were needed to equal the effect of directing attention towards the null pattern and away from the tuning pattern. This was true even for cells where the response modulation evoked by directing attention from outside the receptive field (solid curve in Fig. 4) to the null pattern inside the receptive field (dotted curve in Fig. 4) was small.

luminance of the tuning pattern was reduced so as to decrease the attend-out firing rate to the level observed when the target was the null pattern and both RDPs had full luminance.

Figure 5 shows the results with this approach for one neuron. In the three panels we replotted the tuning curve for the attend-in condition with the null pattern as the target (dashed tuning curve). The first panel also shows the response in the attend-out condition with both RDPs at full luminance (solid tuning curve). This condition is the same as the one shown in Figure 4. As demonstrated there, the attend-out condition led to a larger response, presumably because the processing of the tuning stimulus was not suppressed (as in the attend-in condition) and therefore was able to strongly modulate the response. The other two panels show the tuning curve in the attend-out condition with reduced levels of luminance (reduced to 6.6% and to 1.0% of the full luminance) on the tuning pattern, in an attempt to mimic the suppressing effect of attention on the processing of the tuning pattern when the null pattern was behaviorally relevant. The responses decreased with decreasing luminance until they fell below the levels of the attend-in tuning curve in the bottom panel. This means that for this neuron, the attentional modulation of switching from the attend-out condition to the target being the null pattern caused a reduction in distractor luminance of about 93%. We call the corresponding luminance level the titration point. A reduction in luminance of more than 90% makes the dots in the tuning pattern so dim that it becomes almost invisible. Figure 6 shows the *attentional* modulation (corresponding to panel 1 in Figure 5) and the *luminance* modulations necessary to match it for the 23 cells we recorded.

SUMMARY AND DISCUSSION

Our physiological data demonstrate that it is possible to create changes in neuronal firing rate by changing the sensory properties of the visual input that are virtually indistinguishable from the changes caused by different attentional conditions. Furthermore these data show that attentional suppression of unattended stimuli, even when it results in only moderate changes in firing rate (average suppression of about 30% in the experiments presented here), can represent large changes (luminance reduction needed to reach the titration point of more than 90%) in the effective visibility of the unattended stimuli.

These findings are clearly consistent with similar results from experiments in areas along the temporal visual pathway (Reynolds & Desimone, 1997) and with the effects observed psychophysically. The psychophysical and physiological studies discussed here all point to a powerful influence of attention on the processing of sensory information. The same is true for a large number of studies using functional brain imaging techniques, all of which support the claim that without the allocation of attention, stimuli loose much of their ability to activate even sensory neurons, i.e., neurons that are considered sensory because they can be strongly modulated by sensory changes in the stimulus. These attentional effects in the sensory cortex and the similarity of attentional and sensory influences on neuronal firing rate might even suggest that the two aspects share neuronal mechanisms.

The convergence of data recorded in awake macaque monkeys regarding the influence of attention on the processing of visual information, and the data collected from human subjects using functional brain imaging and psychophysical methods, strongly suggest that even though selective attention is a complex cognitive function, it is not only present in humans but can be demonstrated in primates and presumably other animals. This suggests that monkeys and humans share an important and advanced aspect of visual information processing, allowing us to gain important insight into human vision through the study of non-human primates. Inversely, it seems reasonable to expect that scene perception in animals shows the same constraints imposed by attention as demonstrated in the flicker-paradigm and attentional-blink experiments in humans.

ACKNOWLEDGEMENTS

This work was supported by a grant from the MWF of Baden-Württemberg and the DFG. JCMT is a fellow of the Graduiertenkolleg Neurobiologie, Tübingen. We thank Dr. Rensink for supplying examples of the images used in their study.

REFERENCES

Duncan, J., Ward, R., & Shapiro, K. (1994). Direct measurement of attentional dwell time in human vision. *Nature, 369,* 313-315.

Eriksen, C. W., & St. James, J. D. (1986). Visual attention within and around the field of focal attention: A zoom lens model. *Perception and Psychophysics, 40,* 225-240.

Hikosaka, O., Miyauchi, S., & Shimojo, S. (1991). Focal visual attention produces motion sensation in lines. *Investigative Ophthalmology and Visual Science (Supplement), 32,* 716.

Krope, K., Treue, S., & Husain, M. (1998). An attentional blink for visual motion perception. *Perception (Supplement), 27,* 35.

Levin, D. T., & Simons, D. J. (1997). Failure to detect changes to attended objects in motion pictures. *Psychonomic Bulletin and Review, 4,* 501-506.

Logothetis, N. K. (1994). Physiological studies of motion input. In A. T. Smith & R. J. Snowden (Eds.), *Visual detection of motion* (pp. 177-216). New York: Academic Press.

Moran, J., & Desimone, R. (1985). Selective attention gates visual processing in the extrastriate cortex. *Science, 229,* 782-784.

O'Regan, J. K. (1992). Solving the "real" mysteries of visual perception: the world as an outside memory. *Canadian Journal of Psychology, 46,* 461-488.

O'Regan, J. K., Deubel, H., Clark, J. J., & Rensink, R. A. (1999). Picture changes during blinks: Looking without seeing and seeing without looking. *Visual Cognition* (in press).

O'Regan, J. K., Rensink, R. A., & Clark, J. J. (1999). "Mudsplashes" cause blindness to large scene changes. *Nature, 398,* 34.

Pylyshyn, Z. W., & Storm, R. W. (1985). Tracking multiple independent targets: evidence for a parallel tracking mechanism. *Spatial Vision, 3,* 179-197.

Raymond, J. E., Shapiro, K. L., & Arnell, K. M. (1992). Temporary suppression of visual processing in an RSVP task: An attentional blink? *Journal of Experimental Psychology: Human Perception and Performance, 18,* 849-860.

Recanzone, G. H., Wurtz, R. H., & Schwarz, U. (1997). Responses of MT and MST neurons to one and two moving objects in the receptive field. *Journal of Neurophysiology, 78,* 2904-2915.

Rensink, R. A., O'Regan, J. K., & Clark, J. J. (1997). To see or not to see: The need for attention to perceive changes in scenes. *Psychological Science, 8,* 368-373.

Rensink, R. A., O'Regan, J. K., & Clark, J. J. (1999). On the failure to detect changes in scenes across brief interruptions. *Visual Cognition, 7,* 127-145.

Reynolds, J. H., & Desimone, R. (1997). Attention and contrast have similar effects on competitive interactions in macaque area V4. *Society for Neuroscience Abstracts,* 302.

Saarinen, J., & Julesz, B. (1991). The speed of attentional shifts in the visual field. *Proceedings of the National Academy of Sciences, USA, 88,* 1812-1814.

Shapiro, K. L., Arnell, K. M., & Raymond, J. E. (1997). The attentional blink. *Trends in Cognitive Sciences, 1,* 291-296.

Snowden, R. J., Treue, S., Erickson, R. E., & Andersen, R. A. (1991). The response of area MT and V1 neurons to transparent motion. *Journal of Neuroscience, 11,* 2768-2785.

Snowden, R. J., Treue, S., & Andersen, R. A. (1992). The response of neurons in areas V1 and MT of the alert rhesus monkey to moving random dot patterns. *Experimental Brain Research, 88,* 389-400.

Treue, S., & Maunsell, J. H. R. (1996). Attentional modulation of visual motion processing in cortical areas MT and MST. *Nature, 382,* 539-541.

Treue, S., & Martinez Trujillo, J. C. (1999). Feature-based attention influences motion processing gain in macaque visual cortex. *Nature, 399,* 575-579.

Weichselgartner, E., & Sperling, G. (1987). Dynamics of automatic and controlled visual attention. *Science, 238,* 778-780.

Zelinsky, G. J. (1997). Eye movements during a change detection search task. *Investigative Ophthalmology and Visual Science (Supplement), 38,* S373.

Picture perception in animals
J. Fagot (Ed.)

Visual cues for attention following
in rhesus monkeys

Erika N. Lorincz, Christopher I. Baker,
and David I. Perrett

University of St Andrews, Scotland

Abstract

It is now well established that great apes follow human gaze direction. Despite physiological evidence showing cells in macaque temporal cortex sensitive to direction of eye gaze, there has been little evidence in non-ape species of similar abilities. The aim of this study was to investigate, at a behavioural level, whether monkeys can use static gaze, head, and body cues of conspecifics to interpret the direction of attention of others. We recorded the looking behaviour of 2 rhesus monkeys elicited by the presentation of photographs of conspecifics directing their attention in space. With photos of monkey stimuli whose head and body were oriented in different or similar directions, we found that the head but not the body was used by the monkey subjects to orient their own attention. With photos of monkey faces oriented to the camera while gaze was averted left, right, up or down, we demonstrated that monkeys are able to spontaneously follow gaze of conspecifics. With photos of monkey heads oriented 45 degrees to the right or left, attention following was stronger when the gaze direction was consistent with the head

Correspondence should be sent to E.N. Lorincz or D. I. Perrett, School of Psychology, University of St Andrews, Scotland, KY16 9JU (e-mail: ell@st-andrews.ac.uk or dp@st-andrews.ac.uk).

orientation than when the eyes were directed towards the observer. Our studies show that both head orientation and eye gaze influence the observer's orienting responses.

Key words: Gaze following, attention direction, looking behaviour, facial cues, rhesus monkeys.

INTRODUCTION

One of the primary cognitive mechanisms enabling human social interaction and communication is the ability to follow the attention direction of others (Baron-Cohen, 1994). For instance, to understand where, and hence at what, an individual is looking, visual cues such as gaze direction, head position and/or body posture can be used to orient the observer's attention towards the same place of interest in the environment. There is increasing behavioural and physiological evidence suggesting that this ability to follow attention is present in non-human species, including great apes (e.g., Povinelli & Eddy, 1996a; Itakura & Tanaka, 1998), monkeys (Emery, Lorincz, Perrett, Oram, & Baker, 1997; Tomasello, Call, & Hare, 1998) and dogs (Miklósi, Polgárdi, Topál, & Casányi, 1998). The nature and relative importance of the visual cues supporting this ability, however, remain confused. Some authors do not discriminate between the cues available to subjects (eyes, head, or body posture) and the different conjunctions of these cues. In natural situations the evidence available from different cues may not be congruent. For example, the head may be oriented in one direction but the eye gaze may be in a different direction.

The terms attention following, gaze following, and joint attention have often been used interchangeably but may be considered different yet related abilities (Emery et al., 1997). Here, attention following will be considered as the general ability of one individual to follow the direction of attention given by any body cue (e.g. gaze, head, or body posture) from a second individual to a position in space. In this study, gaze refers more specifically to eye gaze, i.e., the orientation of the eyes. Joint attention requires the additional process of combining the attention of both individuals onto a common object or focus of attention and can be considered a triadic interaction (Emery et al., 1997).

Human infants begin to follow attention as early as 3-4 months of age as long as the direction of attention is specified by at least the head direction of the adult (Scaife & Bruner, 1975; Vecera & Johnson, 1995; D'Entremont, Hains, & Muir, 1997). More complex attention following responses emerge in older infants (6-18 months) with the use of the eyes to locate accurately the focus of another's attention (Butterworth & Jarrett, 1991; Moore & Corkum, 1998). By two years of age, children begin to be able to use eye gaze direction to infer desires of others (Lee, Eskritt, Symons, & Muir, 1998). Finally, by the age of 4 years, they can accurately follow gaze when eye cues are presented in an impoverished context such as drawing (Baron-Cohen, 1994).

In non-human primates, visual signals including gaze may play a central role in social interaction. They can provide information about emotional state (e.g., threat includes eye contact, submission includes gaze aversion), the direction of attention (Chance, 1962; Perrett & Mistlin, 1990; Emery et al., 1997) and the intention of actions (Jellema, Baker, Wicker, & Perrett, 1999). Monitoring cues to the direction of attention may allow an individual to gain information about the location of food and predators, social dominance and mating behaviour (Menzel & Halperin, 1975; van Schaik, van Noordwijk, Warsono, & Surtiono, 1983). Attentional cues containing directional information like gaze, head and body posture could be the foundation of referential communication and participate in the process of vicarious learning (Mineka, Davidson, Cook, & Keir, 1984; Emery & Perrett, 1999; Perrett, 1999).

There is evidence that great apes have the ability to use such a referential aspect of focus of attention. For instance, in a problem solving experiment where a gorilla needed to request help from a human experimenter in order to reach a goal, the gorilla alternately looked between the goal (object of attention) and the eyes of the experimenter (Gómez, 1990). In the same fashion, attention following abilities seem to be used as a subterfuge to create false belief in conspecifics, for instance to gain food "safely", in what has been called "tactical deception" (Whiten & Byrne, 1988). For example, an individual will look in the opposite direction of the food he/she covets, to attract the attention of a second individual away from the food. Humans and great apes may share cognitive mechanisms through which gaze following and shared attention act as precursors to the development of theory of mind (Baron-Cohen, 1994). Alternatively, gaze following may more simply be a quasi-orienting-reflex that allows a social individual to orient to important events (Povinelli & Eddy, 1996; Moore & Corkum, 1994; Friesen & Kingstone, 1998; Langton & Bruce, 1999).

Chimpanzees and orang-outans will follow the direction of attention of humans (Povinelli & Eddy, 1994, 1996a, 1996b, 1997; Itakura, 1996; Itakura & Tanaka, 1998) and conspecifics (Tomasello et al., 1998). Cues manipulated include orientation of the head and eyes and the use of gestures (e.g., pointing). In the majority of studies, movement is involved in the attentional cues (e.g., head and eyes turning in a particular direction) and multiple cues are presented. For example, Povinelli and Eddy (1994, 1996a, 1996b) found that young chimpanzees will follow the attention direction of humans when specified by movement of the head and eyes or movement of the eyes alone. Similarly, Itakura and Tanaka (1998) found that chimpanzees and an orang-outan were able to use experimenter-given cues in an object-choice task, including tapping, gazing (head and eyes), pointing, gazing alone, and glancing (eyes alone). At the start of each trial the experimenter was looking at the mid-point between the two objects and therefore all cues also included a movement component. The ability to follow attention is seen in chimpanzees even when the focus of attention of the experimenter is located behind the subject or beyond an opaque object (Povinelli & Eddy, 1996a, 1997).

In monkeys, there is conflicting evidence for attention following. In object-choice tasks, capuchin and macaque monkeys failed to use conjoint head and gaze orientation of a human experimenter to guide their responses although they could learn to use gestural cues such as pointing (Anderson, Sallaberry, & Barbier, 1995; Anderson, Montant, & Schmitt, 1996). One capuchin, however, after 120 trials with sequential introduction of different cues, learned to use combined head and gaze orientation (Itakura & Anderson, 1996). Itakura (1996) reported that non-ape species (including macaques and capuchins) failed to follow attention direction specified by conjoint movement and orientation of the head and eyes.

In all of these studies in monkeys, the stimulus for attention following was the experimenter. In experiments with a conspecific as the stimulus, attention following has been observed (Emery et al., 1997; Tomasello et al., 1998). For example, Emery et al. (1997) analysed the spontaneous behaviour (looking behaviour) of 2 rhesus macaques during the presentation of a video-film of conspecifics directing their attention towards one of two identical objects. Cues specifying the direction of attention included orientation of the head and body with some movement. Both monkey subjects inspected the target location (object or position attended by the stimulus monkey) more than the distracter (nonattended object or position). Tomasello et al. (1998) showed that four species of monkeys (rhesus, pigtail and stumptail macaques, and sooty mangabeys) followed the attention direction of conspecifics onto a distal object (although pigtail macaques failed to show evidence of attention following with more stringent criteria). Cues specifying the direction of attention in this experiment included orientation of the head and eyes of the stimulus monkey and any associated movement.

The studies of attention following described in monkeys have manipulated many different visual cues to attention direction (i.e., body posture, head, gaze, and any associated motion). It is not clear whether monkeys can make use of eye gaze signals alone to determine the direction of attention in extra-personal space.

There is clear evidence showing that monkeys process gaze signals directly addressed to them. Indeed monkeys as young as 3 months of age exhibit a variety of expressions (appeasement, fear, etc.) to faces depending on whether the stimulus face makes eye contact or not (Redican, Kellicutt, & Mitchell, 1971; Keating & Keating, 1982; Mendelson, Haith, & Goldman-Rakic, 1982; Perrett & Mistlin, 1990). Such studies show that monkeys react to gaze signals of an agent when the agent directly looks at the observer (that is, when the agent's attention was directed at the observer itself).

At the neurophysiological level there is evidence for the coding of attention direction, even when specified by eye gaze alone. Cells responsive to face stimuli in the temporal cortex and amygdala of macaque, have been found that are sensitive to the eye region and to gaze direction (Leonard, Rolls, Wilson, & Baylis, 1985; Perrett, Smith, Potter, Mistlin, Head, Milner, & Jeeves, 1985; Perrett, Harries, Mistlin, Hietanen, Benson, Bevan, Thomas, Ortega, Oram, & Brierly, 1990; Perrett et al., 1993; Perrett & Mistlin, 1990; Brothers & Ring, 1993). In particular, in the superior temporal sulcus, cells are found responsive to particular face and body orientation and views (Wachsmuth, Oram, & Perrett, 1994; Perrett et al., 1985). Rather than coding the geometric features of different facial views, some of these cells code the attention direction. These cells show response generalisation across different views, orientations, and postures of the body and head as long as the available cues suggest that attention is maintained in a given direction

(Perrett, Hietanen, Oram, & Benson, 1992; Perret et al., 1985, 1990, 1993; Walsh & Perrett, 1994). Particular populations of cells code for attention directed towards the observer, other populations code for attention directed to locations in extra-personal space (e.g., up, left, or right). For these cell populations, visual information from different origins (body, head, and gaze) is combined in a compatible manner. If a cell responds to gaze left, the same cell may respond to the left profile view of the face when the eyes are not visible, or to the left profile view of the body if the head is occluded from sight (Perrett et al., 1985; Wachsmuth et al., 1994). In combining the cues, for some cells the eye direction takes priority over the head direction and the head direction over the body direction (Perrett et al., 1985, 1990, 1992; Jellema et al., 1999). In other cases the information from the eyes, face, or body make independent contributions, with no particular priority. These physiological results indicate extensive neural processing of cues to the attention direction of others. Within these cues it would appear that eye gaze cues have a powerful role, so it is surprising that there is no behavioural evidence for pure gaze processing in monkeys.

In the present study we investigated the spontaneous reactions of macaques (in terms of looking behaviour) to static images of conspecifics directing their attention in space. The pattern of eye movements and duration of fixations on static images have been widely used as measures of preference and perceptual development (Humphrey, 1974; Keating & Keating, 1982; Mendelson et al., 1982; Wilson & Goldman-Rakic, 1994; Emery et al., 1997). Such studies show that monkeys respond to photographic images of social stimuli in a manner similar to natural real stimuli (e.g., Perrett & Mistlin, 1990). Monkeys discriminate between images of human, monkey, and schematic faces from non-face stimuli (Keating & Keating, 1982) and differentiate between pictures of different animal species and between individuals of the same species (Humphrey, 1974; Rosenfeld & Van Hoesen, 1979; Dittrich, 1994). Furthermore, monkeys respond differentially to images of facial expressions with species typical emotional responses such as vocalisation and lip smacking (Redican et al., 1971; Sackett, 1966; Mendelson et al., 1982; Perrett & Mistlin, 1990).

The current study assesses the relative importance of different visual cues to attention direction. The three cues for attention direction manipulated were orientation of the head, body posture, and eye gaze. Since static images were used, movement was not available as a cue for the direction of attention. The first experiment investigated the relative importance of head and body orientation. In some cases the head and body orientation of the stimulus monkey were in the same direction (compatible cues), whereas in other stimuli head and body orientation were in different directions (incompatible cues). We predicted that subjects would follow the attention direction given by the orientation of the head when there was a conflict between the orientation of the head and body. The second experiment investigated the ability to follow eye gaze alone. The stimuli consisted of static, frontal view of macaque heads with the eyes orientated in different directions (up, down, left, or right). We predicted that subjects would follow the gaze direction and look more frequently in the direction given by the gaze than in the other directions. The final experiment investigated the interaction between head orientation and gaze direction. The stimuli showed macaque heads oriented 45 degrees to the right or left with the eyes either directed in the same direction or at the observer. We predicted that the subjects would be more likely to follow attention when the head and gaze direction were consistent.

METHOD

Subjects

The subjects were two male rhesus macaques (Terry and Steve, 4 and 6 years old, respectively) born and reared in a social colony of conspecifics. During the experimental period the subjects were housed individually but in visual and auditory contact with other macaques. The subjects had previously seen slides as well as video-film of humans, conspecific monkeys and other animals and had participated in an earlier study on gaze following (Emery et al., 1997). Both subjects were also involved in concurrent electrophysiological studies. All experiments were performed under appropriate UK Home Office Licenses and were regulated by the University of St Andrews Animal code of Practice.

Set-up and testing

The subject faced a rectangular white screen (222 by 183 cm) situated 450 cm away onto which stimuli were projected in a darkened room using a slide projector (Kodak Ektapro 5000). The screen contained 5 embedded LEDs used for calibration of the eye position. The LEDs were located at the screen centre and at the middle of each edge of the screen.

The looking behaviour of the subject was recorded with an infrared camera mounted inside a box attached to the front of the primate chair (see for details Hietanen & Perrett, 1993). The stimuli were viewed through a liquid crystal shutter (Screen Print Technology – rise time < 15 ms) under computer control. A further camera mounted above the head of the subject recorded the test stimuli projected on the screen. A time and frame code was added to the image from the first camera (VITC time-code generator and frame counter – Horita VG50) and the output sent to 2 separate video recorders. A video record of eye position and a time code were recorded on one recorder (Akai VHS VS – 603EK). A record of the eyes and the time code was mixed (Panasonic VHS video mixer, WJAVE7) with the record of the test stimuli and recorded on a second recorder (Panasonic NV – FS200B).

Before each testing procedure, the eye movements were calibrated. The monkeys had been previously trained to perform a colour discrimination task dependent on the colour of an LED. Licks during the presentation of a green LED were rewarded with fruit juice whereas licks during the presentation of a red LED were discouraged with no reward or a mildly aversive saline solution. A 500 ms tone was sounded before the illumination of the LED, lasting 3 s. The colour of the LED was varied in a pseudo-random order under computer control. For calibration, the LED at each position was presented at least twice. Then, the LEDs were turned off and the tone was presented on its own to habituate any behavioural tendency to search for LED lights on the screen.

Test stimuli and procedure

The stimuli were colour slides of monkeys taken with a Nikon camera (F-801). The monkeys were attracted to look intently in one direction (left, right, up, down, or at the camera) by presenting interesting stimuli (e.g., hand puppets or fruit) at the desired location.

Experiment 1: Head and body cues. Photographs of individual monkeys were taken through a glass window in a colony room. The monkeys in the photographs were looking either to the right or to the left. Orientation of the head and body varied across the photographs. In some photographs, the head and body were oriented in the same direction (e.g., body left, head left; Figure 1a), whereas in others the head and body were oriented in different directions (e.g., body left, head right; Figure 1b). Eye gaze direction was always compatible with head direction. The photographs were digitised with a flatbed scanner (Epson GT-6500) and the background cropped to leave a centrally positioned stimulus monkey. The stimulus slides were made out of these pictures (resolution, 1900 by 1400 pixels at 24-bit colour).

The image of the monkey stimulus was displayed at the same height as the subject. The size of the head and body stimuli ranged from 6.4 to 10.2 degrees of visual angle.

The stimuli were presented on 20 trials (10 compatible head and body cues, 10 incompatible head and body cues), each of 3 s duration, and an inter-trial period of approximately 10 s. The trials were blocked into 5 sessions. Each session included 2 randomly selected compatible and 2 incompatible head and body slides interspersed with trials with non-test slides. The sessions were run at intervals of 2-3 days and were preceded by calibration trials. Presenting few stimuli on a given day was designed to avoid habituation.

Experiment 2: Gaze direction cues. Photographs were taken of the two monkey subjects seated in a primate chair. Black material was used to restrict the camera view to the head only. Photographs were taken of a frontal face view of the head with the eyes directed in the four cardinal directions (up, down, left, and right; Figure 2). The size of the head stimuli ranged from 6.7 to 7 degrees of visual angle.

Experiment 2 included 12 trials per condition, each trial of 5 s duration, and 10 s inter-trial intervals. The trials were blocked into 3 sessions containing one trial of each the 4 eye directions.

Experiment 3: Head and gaze direction cues. Photographs were taken of the head rotated 45 degrees away from the camera to give left and right half-profile views. In the "Head = Gaze" condition, the gaze was compatible with the head (e.g., head and eyes looking left, Figure 3a) and in the "Head ≠ Gaze" condition, the gaze was directed at the camera (i.e., eye contact, Figure 3b). The size of the head stimuli ranged from 9.8 to 11.3 degrees of visual angle.

Figure 1. Examples of the head and body stimuli used in Experiment 1. (a) head and body oriented in the same direction, i.e., left; (b) head and body oriented in different directions, i.e., body left, head right.

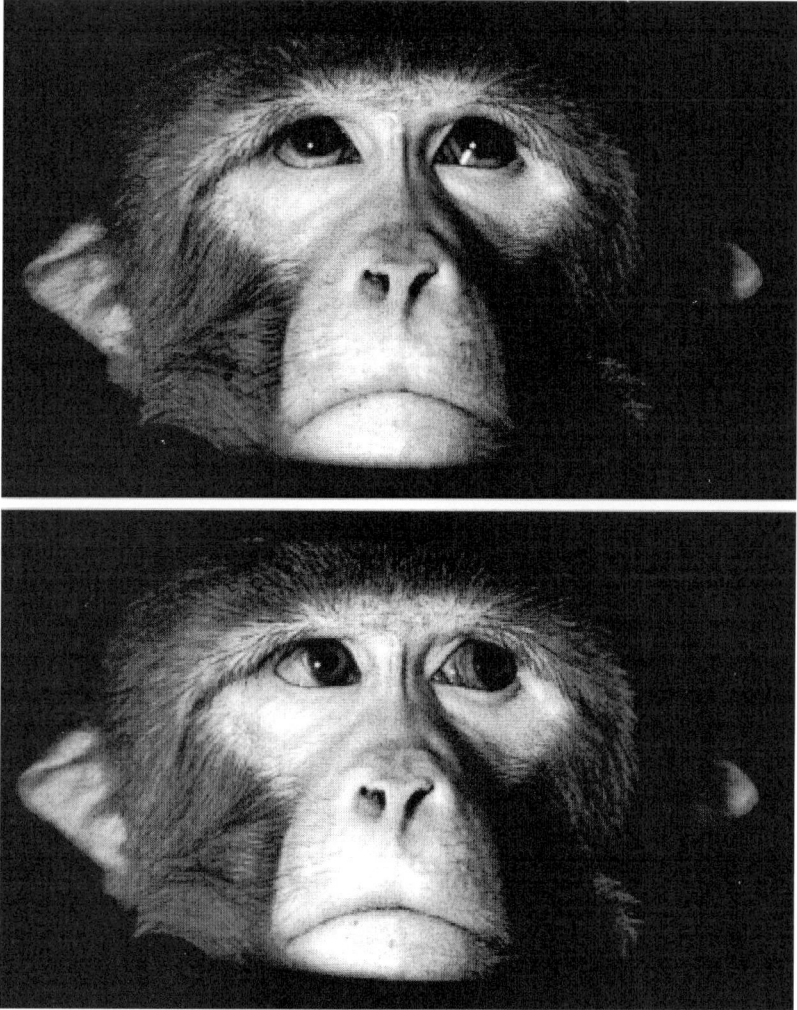

Figure 2. Examples of the gaze stimuli used in Experiment 2. Photographs of frontal face view of one of the monkey subjects with eyes directed up (a) and right (b).

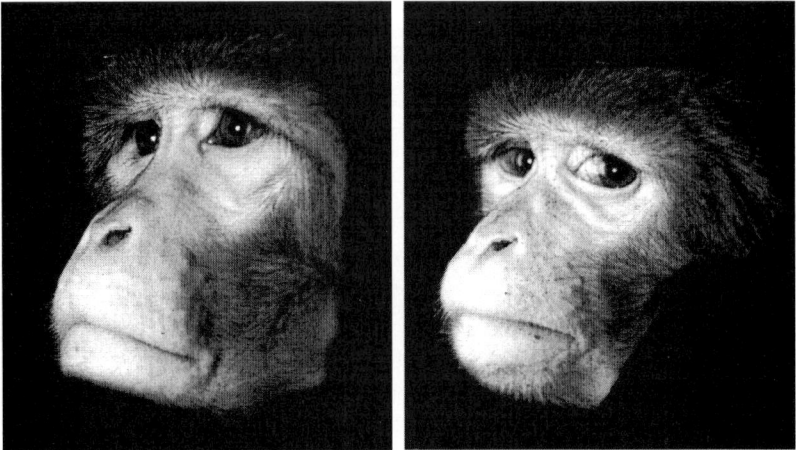

Figure 3. Examples of head and gaze stimuli used in Experiment 3. (a) "Head = Gazes" condition, head and gaze direction are compatible and oriented left. (b) "Head ≠ Gaze" condition, head and gaze direction are incompatible; the head is directed left while the gaze is directed to the camera or observer.

Experiment 3 included 12 trials per condition, each trial of 5 s duration with 10 s inter-trial intervals. Experiment 3 was split up into 6 sessions of 4 trials equally mixing the two conditions ("Head = Gaze" and "Head ≠ Gaze").

Evaluation of performance

The video of the subject's eyes only (including time code) was shown on a monitor with a distance between the centre of the pupils of 40 cm. The duration and position of fixations made by the subjects were recorded. Fixations are defined as a glance to one position of the screen with the eyes remaining static for at least 2 frames (80 ms). Inspections are defined as the sum of fixations of one area of the screen without intervening fixations of other areas. The duration of each inspection was defined as the cumulative number of video frames the subject spent at one area.

For Experiments 1 and 3, the screen was divided into 4 exclusive areas (following Emery et al., 1997). In these experiments the stimulus monkey was depicted directing attention in one of two peripheral directions (left and right). The target area (T) was defined as the position to which the head of the stimulus monkey pointed. A distracter area (D) was defined as an area of equivalent size in a position laterally opposite the target area. The area around the stimulus monkey was denoted (M) and all other areas on the screen and beyond were defined as elsewhere (E) (Figures 4a and 4c).

For Experiment 2, the screen was divided into five areas: 4 peripheral quadrants of equal area (up, down, right, and left) and a central area occupied by the stimulus monkey (M). In this experiment the stimulus monkey was depicted directing attention in one of these 4 quadrants. The quadrant attended by the stimulus-monkey is referred to as the target area (T), the opposite quadrant as the anti-target area (AT) and the 2 remaining quadrants as clockwise (C) and anti-clockwise (AC) to the target area (Figure 4b).

The analysis of the eye position consisted of attributing a judgement of which of these areas the subject was looking for each fixation. During the initial "blind analysis", attributions were simply made to areas labelled left, right, M, and E for Experiments 1 and 3, and quadrants labelled left, right, up and down, or M, for Experiment 2. Subsequently the areas and quadrants were re-coded.

From the score sheet, the mean number of inspections and fixations made on each of the four or five positions (depending of the experiment) as well as the duration of the inspections (calculated from the frame count) were calculated for each condition in the three experiments.

Data analysis

Previous studies have used either the duration of looking, or the position of looking. Our methods allow quantification of both the duration of inspection and the spatial distribution of inspection (Emery et al., 1997). Since these measures can yield different results we present an analysis of both measures.

The data from both subjects were analysed for the number of inspections and for the duration of inspections using a multi-factorial ANOVA. As the data on the number of inspections and duration of inspections

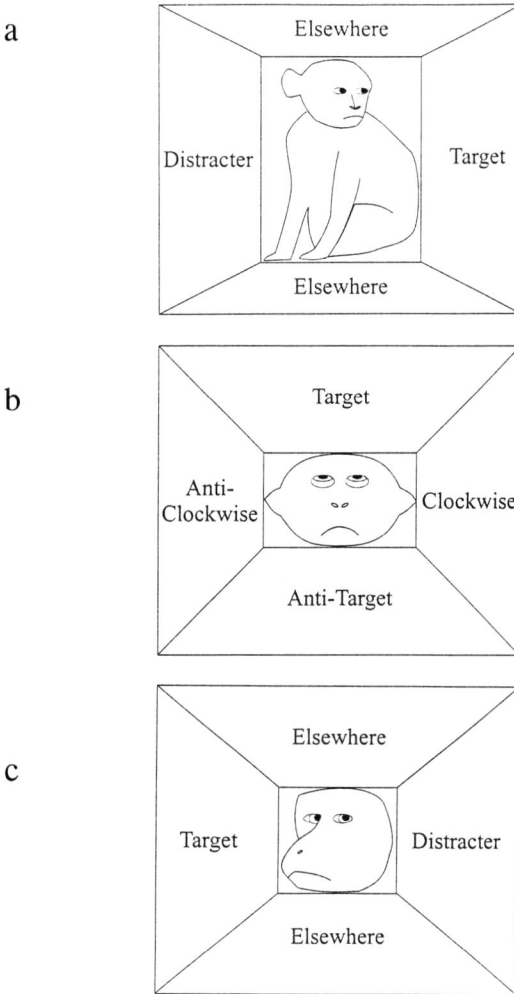

Figure 4. Areas delimited in judgements of subject's fixations. (a) Experiment 1: "Head right and body left"; (b) Experiment 2: "Eyes up"; (c) Experiment 3: "Head ≠ Gaze".

A stimulus monkey attending to a target area occupied the central position of the screen. In experiments 1 and 3 (a and c), the target quatrand located either left or right of the stimulus monkey was given by the head direction, its mirror position determined the distracter area and the remaining areas were defined as elsewhere. In experiment 2, the quadrant opposite the target was labelled as anti-target, and the two remaining quadrants were labelled clockwise and anti-clockwise to the target area (b).

were not distributed normally but followed roughly a Poisson distribution, they were transformed using $\sqrt{(x+1)}$ before undergoing the ANOVAs. Post-hoc testing was performed using the Fisher's Protected Least-Significant Difference test (PLSD, Snedecor & Cochran, 1980).

For Experiment 1, a three-way ANOVA was performed on the total number of trials, with subjects, compatibility (head and body compatible/incompatible) and eye position (T, D, M, and E) as main factors. Experiment 3 was analysed similarly with a three-way ANOVA of the total number of trials, with subjects, eye/head compatibility, and position as factors.

For Experiment 2, a two-way ANOVA was carried out on the duration of inspection at a given position on each trial. The factors were subjects and position (M, T, AT, C, and AC). Another two-way ANOVA with subjects and quadrants as factors was dedicated to check that the subjects watched equally each quadrant. It was carried out on the total time spent in each quadrant (up, down, right, and left) regardless of their status (T, AT, C, and AC).

For each experiment, the frequency of inspections of the target position was compared to that expected by chance using the Binomial test. For Experiments 1 and 3, the number of inspections made of the target and distracter positions was compared to an expected probability of 0.5 (i.e., 50% of inspections should be made of the target position and 50% of the distracter position if inspection was random). For Experiment 2, the number of inspections of the Target quadrant (T) divided by the total number of inspections made of all 4 peripheral quadrants (T, AT, AC, and C) was compared to an expected probability of 0.25. After inspections of the central monkey stimulus have been excluded, one expects 25% of the remaining inspections to be in each of the 4 peripheral quadrants if inspections were made at random.

Analysis was made of the "first" fixation made of either the T or D positions for Experiments 1 and 3 (and of T, AT, C, or AC for Experiment 2) after the monkey subject had looked at the stimulus monkey. For each subject, this analysis compared the proportion of trials where the "first" fixation was made on T position against the expected probability (Experiments 1 and 3, $p = 0.5$; Experiment 2, $p = 0.25$). In Experiments 1 and 3, if the monkey subject did not look during a trial at either the target or the distracter position after watching the stimulus monkey (e.g., looking only at the monkey and/or the elsewhere positions), the trial was discounted from the analysis of "first" fixation.

A single scorer, "blind" to the stimulus conditions, performed the analysis. The inter-observer reliability was assessed with a second scorer (also "blind" to the stimulus conditions) independently analysing eye position from the video records of 12 trials in Experiment 2. The 2 scorers exhibited significant agreement (Cohen's kappa statistic $K = 0.564$, $p < 0.001$) on their ratings of the sequence of 132 fixations assigned to the 5 positions (left, right, up, down, and stimulus monkey).

EXPERIMENT 1: HEAD AND BODY CUES

Results

The sequence of inspections produced at the appearance of the slide always began by a fixation of the monkey or the elsewhere positions, with fixation of the monkey being more likely to occur (respectively for monkey and elsewhere positions: Terry: 13 M/7 E; Steve: 11 M/9 E). Fixations of the monkey were always of longer duration than fixations elsewhere (mean number of frames; Terry: 24.4 M, 2.9 E; Steve: 26.8 M, 3.4 E). Fixations in the elsewhere positions were always followed by a fixation of the monkey position. For most trials, the "first" fixation of the target or distracter positions immediately followed the initial fixation of the monkey (Terry: 15/18; Steve: 17/17).

Both subjects made a greater number of inspections of the target position than of the distracter position (Figure 5). The number of inspections made of the target position expressed as a fraction of the total number of inspections made of target or distracter positions across all trials was 17/22 for Terry (Binomial test, $p < 0.009$) and 28/39 for Steve ($p < 0.005$). Analysis of the "first" fixation on target or distracter also showed that both subjects were more likely to look first at the target than distracter position (Terry: 14/18, $p < 0.015$; Steve: 14/17, $p < 0.006$).

The three-way ANOVA with subject, compatibility, and position as main factors showed a significant main effect of position on the number of inspections made, $F(3, 3) = 35.5$, $p = 0.008$, which relates, among other things, to a significantly greater number of inspections of the target than of the distracter ($p < 0.05$). Although for both monkeys there was a greater difference for the inspections made to the target compared to those made to the distracter in the incompatible body and head cue

Head and body cues

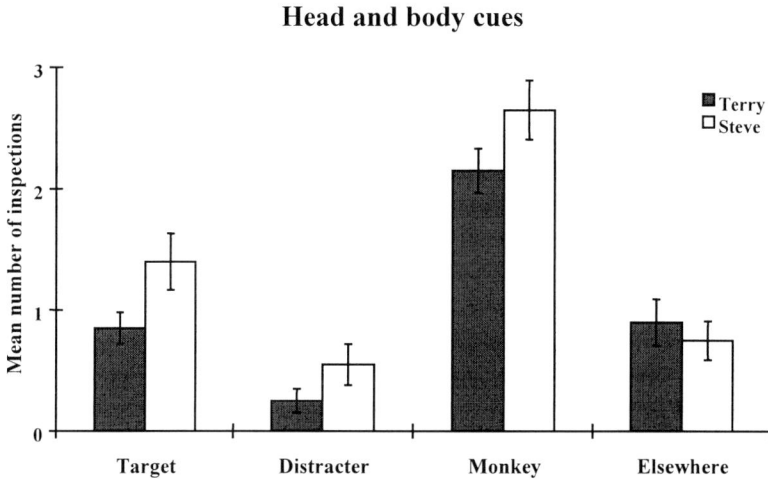

Figure 5. Number of inspections for head and body stimuli. Mean number of inspections (+/- SEM) made per trial of each stimulus position (target, distracter, monkey, and elsewhere). Each bar gives the average across 20 trials for Terry (grey) or Steve (white).

condition than in the compatible body and head cue condition, this variation was not significant as reflected by a non-significant interaction between compatibility and position, $F(3, 3) = 2.04$, $p = 0.29$. There was no significant main effect of compatibility, $F(1, 1) = 0.01$, $p = 1.00$, or subjects, $F(1, 36) = 2.91$, $p = 0.10$, and no interactions between the main effects (subjects and compatibility: $F(1, 36) = 3.16$, $p = 0.08$; subjects and position: $F(3, 108) = 1.56$, $p = 0.20$; subjects, compatibility, and position: $F(3, 108) = 1.82$, $p = 0.15$).

The average duration of inspections (total number of frames) of each position per trial was analysed using a three-way ANOVA. There was a significant main effect of position, $F(3, 3) = 30.99$, $p = 0.009$. Post-hoc tests showed that this was due to a longer time spent looking at the monkey's position over the other positions ($p < 0.05$ each comparison) and that the average time spent looking at the target was not significantly greater than that for the distracter ($p > 0.05$). Of less importance, there was a significant interaction between subjects and position, $F(3, 108) = 2.80$, $p < 0.05$, the "Elsewhere" position being looked at for longer by Terry than by Steve. There was no significant main effect of subjects, $F(1, 36) = 0.67$, $p = 0.42$; compatibility, $F(1, 1) = 0.05$, $p = 0.87$. There were no interactions between subjects and compatibility, $F(1, 36) = 1.19$, $p = 0.28$, compatibility and position, $F(3, 3) = 0.99$, $p = 0.50$, or between subjects, compatibility, and position, $F(3, 108) = 1.17$, $p = 0.32$.

Discussion

The results replicate the finding of Emery et al. (1997) that rhesus monkeys spontaneously follow the direction of attention of other monkeys. In the present experiment the sight of a static image of a monkey oriented to the left or right was sufficient to trigger the two observing subjects to look at a position aligned with the direction of attention demonstrated by the stimulus monkey. This result was evident for the analysis of the number of inspections and the position of initial fixations. Throughout these analyses, compatibility had no effect on the pattern of inspection: the subjects inspected a position indicated by the orientation of the head of the monkey stimuli. The alignment of the body in the stimuli made no impact on the pattern of fixation. Thus the subjects followed the head direction of the stimulus monkey and ignored the body direction.

Although this experiment failed to find evidence that body posture influences attention following in macaque monkeys, this does not mean that the body is uninformative about attention direction. Physiological evidence indicates that body posture may provide information about direction of attention (see Perrett et al., 1992) or the intentionality of an action (Jellema et al., 1999).

EXPERIMENT 2: GAZE CUES

Results

Both monkeys made more inspections of the target quadrant than of any of three remaining quadrants (Figure 6). The fraction of inspections of the target quadrant out of inspections of all 4 quadrants was greater than expected by chance ($p = 0.25$; Terry: 21/54, $p < 0.017$; Steve:

22/48, $p < 0.0014$). The sequence of inspections produced at the appearance of the slide always began by a fixation on the monkey's position for all trials with Steve, and on all but one trial for Terry. Analysis of the "first" fixations of peripheral quadrants on each trial also showed that both monkeys initially looked at the target quadrant more frequently than other quadrants ($p = 0.25$; Terry: 8/12, $p < 0.003$; Steve: 7/12, $p < 0.014$).

Gaze cues

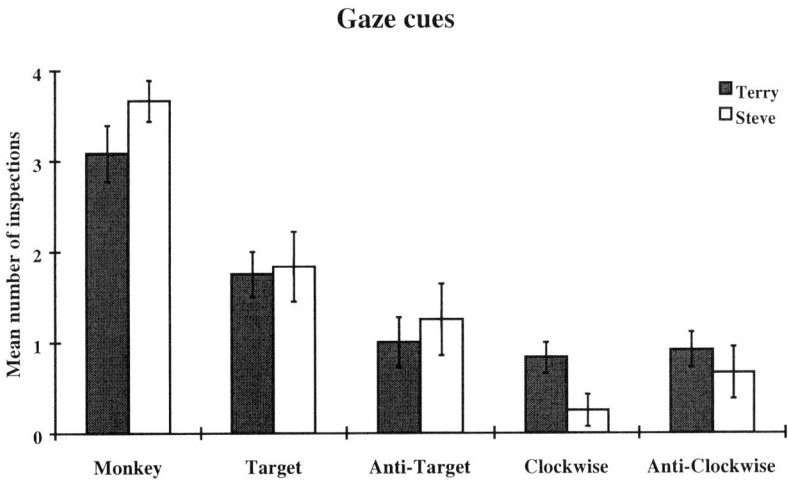

Figure 6. Number of inspections for eye gaze stimuli. Mean number of inspections (+/- SEM) made per trial of each stimulus position (monkey, target, anti-target, clockwise, and anti-clockwise). Each bar represents the average across 12 trials for Terry (grey) or Steve (white).

The analysis of the duration of inspection confirms this result. A two-way ANOVA (subjects and position of gaze as main factors) reported a significant main effect of positions, $F(4, 4) = 11.2$, $p < 0.02$, which reflected in part a greater time spent in inspecting the target quadrant than on any of the three other quadrants ($p < 0.05$). Each of the remaining quadrants (AT, C, and AC) was watched for an equal duration ($p > 0.05$). Of less interest, there was a significant main effect of subjects, $F(1, 22) = 4.36$, $p = 0.049$. The interaction between subjects and position was not significant, $F(4, 88) = 1.67$, $p = 0.16$, which confirmed that both monkeys followed the same observational pattern.

A second two-way ANOVA with subjects and quadrants as main factors was performed which showed that there was no existing bias in duration spent within any particular direction as there was no significant main effect of quadrants, $F(3, 3) = 3.11$, $p = 0.19$, and no subject and quadrant interaction, $F(3, 66) = 1.09$, $p = 0.36$. There was a significant main effect of subjects, $F(1, 22) = 5.30$, $p = 0.03$.

Discussion

Previous studies of attention following have rarely differentiated between head and gaze cues. To date, there is in fact no evidence for attention following in monkeys using cues derived solely from the orientation of the eyes. With natural (conspecific) stimuli it becomes almost impossible to control gaze and head cues independently. With human experimenters acting as stimuli, gaze direction is easier to control, yet monkeys fail to use human gaze as a visual cue in discrimination learning experiments. The use of static photographs allows the role of gaze cues from conspecifics to be assessed unambiguously. The results of Experiment 2 are clear and by each of the measures used (number of inspections, duration of inspection, and "first" fixation) the subjects followed the direction of eye gaze displayed by the stimulus monkeys.

Analysis revealed no bias for overall inspection time in particular quadrants. Thus we can conclude that eye gaze cues can guide attention following in the vertical or horizontal plane.

EXPERIMENT 3: HEAD AND GAZE CUES

The sequence of inspections produced at the appearance of the slide always began by a fixation on the monkey's position for Steve. Terry was also more likely to begin a trial by a fixation on monkey than on elsewhere position ("Head = Gaze": 10 M/2 E; "Head ≠ Gaze": 7 M/5 E). The fixations in the elsewhere sectors were always of shorter duration than fixations on the monkey (mean number of frames, "Head = Gaze": 8.5 M, 4.5 E; "Head ≠ Gaze": 6.1 M, 3.6 E) and were always followed by a fixation on the monkey position. The "first" fixation of the target or distracter positions followed the initial fixation of the monkey on 17/23 trials for Terry and 11/24 trials for Steve.

For "Head = Gaze" stimuli with the head and gaze pointing left or right, the two monkeys made more inspections of the target than of the distracter position (Figure 7a). This difference was not significant when each subject's data were analysed separately (Terry: 27/45, $p = 0.12$; Steve: 30/49, $p = 0.08$), but the target position was inspected more frequently than expected by chance when the results from both monkeys are combined (57/94, $p < 0.02$). Analysis of the "first" fixation of the target and distracter positions failed to reveal a difference between target and distracter positions when data were analysed separately by subject (Terry: 6/11, $p = 0.5$; Steve: 8/12, $p = 0.19$) or combined (14/23, $p = 0.11$).

For "Head ≠ Gaze" stimuli where the face was presented in half profile with the eyes looking back at the camera, analysis of the number of inspections (Figure 7b) revealed that neither subject inspected the target more than the distracter position (Terry: 17/34, $p = 0.57$; Steve: 22/36, $p = 0.12$; combined 39/70, $p = 0.15$). Analysis of the "first" fixation of the target and distracter positions failed to reveal differential fixation of the target and the distracter positions (Terry: 6/12, $p = 0.61$; Steve: 9/12, $p = 0.07$; combined 15/24, $p = 0.08$).

The number of inspections and their duration were analysed for both subjects by a three-way ANOVA (subjects, eye/head compatibility and positions as main factors) of both inspection number and duration showed a significant main effect of position: $F(3, 3) = 37.15$, $p < 0.01$; $F(3, 3) = 14.53$, $p < 0.03$, respectively. A post-hoc analysis showed that inspection duration was increased for the target position compared to the distracter position ($p < 0.05$). There was a significant interaction of eye/head compatibility and position for number of inspections, $F(3, 3) = 17.80$, $p = 0.02$. The difference between the number of inspections made of target and distracter positions was greater for stimuli with eyes averted than with eye contact. More inspections were made in the "Elsewhere" category for stimuli with eye contact than eyes averted. This interaction between position and eye/head compatibility was also significant for inspection duration, $F(3, 3) = 10.02$, $p < 0.05$. Post-hoc analysis replicated the greater difference between target and distracter positions for the eyes averted stimuli. For both inspection number and duration, there was no main effect of subjects, $F(1, 44) = 0.85$, $p = 0.36$; $F(1, 44) = 0.04$, $p = 0.84$, or head/eye compatibility, $F(1, 1) = 49.17$, $p = 0.09$; $F(1, 1) = 3.78$, $p = 0.30$, and other interactions were non-significant (subjects and head/eye compatibility: $F(1,$

44) $= 0.02$, $p = 0.88$; $F(1, 44) = 0.35$, $p = 0.56$; subjects and position: $F(3, 132) = 1.07$, $p = 0.36$; $F(3, 132) = 1.03$, $p = 0.38$; subjects, head/eye compatibility, and position: $F(3, 132) = 0.14$, $p = 0.93$; $F(3, 132) = 0.16$, $p = 0.92$).

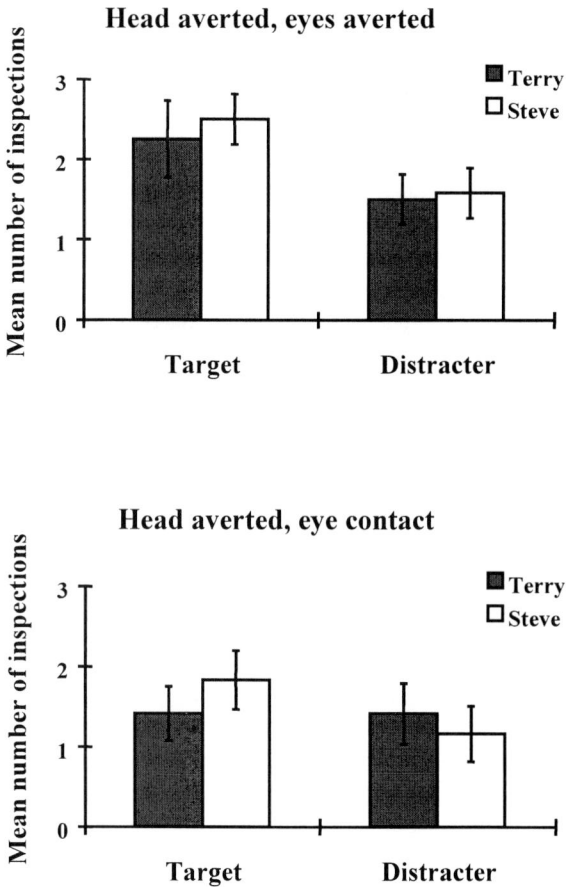

Figure 7. Number of inspections for the head and gaze stimuli. Mean number of inspections (+/- SEM) per trial made of the target and distracter positions for "Head = Gaze" stimuli with head and gaze directed laterally (upper) and for "Head ≠ Gaze" stimuli with head directed laterally and gaze at the observer (lower). Each bar represents the average number of inspections over 12 trials for Terry (grey) or Steve (white).

Discussion

Experiment 3 utilised stimuli with head turned to the left or right and the eyes oriented in the same direction or looking back at the camera and observer. Attention following was predicted for stimuli with both the head and gaze oriented compatibly and directed laterally. As predicted, the ANOVA of inspection duration and inspection frequency indicated that these stimuli did provoke attention following.

For stimuli with the head turned laterally but eyes directed at the observer, we predicted less attention following than for stimuli with both eyes and head directed laterally. Stimuli with eye contact should fail to elicit pronounced attention following to lateral positions for the following reason. If the gaze is the most important index of attention direction, then the stimulus monkey can be considered to be attending in the direction of the observer, and therefore there is no reason for the observer to look to a lateral position. The observer may simply maintain attention on the face. In line with the prediction above, this bias towards the target position was significantly less marked with the eye contact stimuli than with stimuli where the gaze was turned laterally.

In summary, Experiment 3 demonstrates that monkeys show a stronger tendency to follow attention when both the head and gaze are directed to same position than when they are directed to different positions. This confirms the findings of Experiments 1 and 2: both head and gaze cues contribute to attention following.

GENERAL DISCUSSION

Static vs. dynamic stimuli

Studies of attention following that employ live stimuli invariably include movement as a cue for the attention direction. In our previous study we used dynamic video sequences of other conspecific monkeys (Emery et al., 1997). With these realistic and complex stimuli, there was clear evidence of attention following for rhesus monkeys (Emery et al., 1997). The present study confirms and extends this result by defining the visual cues that are and are not essential for attention following behaviour. The present work shows that dynamic cues are not necessary to elicit attention following in macaques. Each of the three experiments reported here demonstrates that the two monkey subjects are behaviourally responsive to static 2-D pictorial images of other monkeys. The subjects' spontaneous reaction to the images shown was to direct their own gaze (and attention) to match the direction of attention of the monkey in the 2-D image. Static postural information is thus sufficient to drive attention following, and while eye, head, and body movements accompany the orienting behaviour of one monkey, these dynamic cues are not necessary to trigger orienting responses in an observing monkey.

Object of attention

In our current study there was no object of attention: the stimulus monkey was depicted with gaze and/or head oriented in one direction but there was no object located in this direction. Attention following in this experiment (and in the initial phase of our previous experiment, Emery et al., 1997) occurs despite the absence of an object. This lack of an object of attention contrasts with most other studies of attention following (e.g., Itakura & Tanaka, 1998). The mechanisms required to follow the direction of attention of another may be simpler than the mechanisms required to follow attention to the object of another's attention, i.e., joint attention (Emery et al., 1997).

Attention following to a spatial position is a sensible strategy because the object of another's attention may not always be visible: it may be occluded from the observer's sight (e.g. a predator hidden from the observer's line of sight). Alternatively, the focus of attention may be ambiguous because there are several candidate objects coincident with the direction of attention of the other individual. In these cases attention following to a rough spatial area can be adaptive because it can lead to the observer being more ready to react to the particular object of the other's interest, for example as soon as it moves into sight.

Cues for attention following

Experiment 1 showed that attention following is influenced by head direction but not body orientation. Experiment 2 showed that eye gaze cues alone could trigger attention following. Experiment 3 confirmed that head and gaze direction influences attention following.

Physiological studies of visual processing by macaque monkeys indicate that body orientation and posture can form a visual cue to the direction of attention or intentions of others (Perrett et al., 1992; Wachsmuth et al., 1994; Jellema et al., 1999). The current study failed to find evidence that body posture influences attention following in macaque monkeys. There are other situations in which the role of the body might be more apparent. For example, when the body posture is clearly visible but the head is occluded from sight or the head direction is ambiguous. The use of stimuli depicting these situations could provide behavioural evidence that the body can act as a visual cue to direction attention.

We have revealed a partial hierarchy in the importance of cues to attention direction. Visual cues from head posture are more important than cues from body posture. The data from Experiment 3 are consistent with the gaze being more important than the head, since changing the gaze direction with constant head direction reduced the tendency for the subjects to follow the head direction. Such data are also consistent with the head and gaze making independent contributions to the control of attention following. To obtain more definitive results on the relative importance of head and gaze, it would be more appropriate to use stimuli where the head and gaze point in different directions and neither are oriented towards the observer. We can conclude from the current experiment that attention following is controlled by both the head and gaze cues and that these are more important than body cues.

Picture perception and social behaviour

As predicted by previous studies, photographic presentations elicit interest of the monkey subjects. Indeed, both subjects were most likely to look initially at the monkey's position at the appearance of the slide, although the tone previously associated with centrally presented stimuli may have biased the subjects' initial inspections to the central area of the projection screen. Subjects also exhibited, at the beginning of the experiment, facial expressions such as lipsmacking at the sight of the monkey stimulus. The lack of behavioural response to the photographic stimuli, particularly in the eye contact configuration (Experiment 3), may simply reflect the loss of behavioural relevance from stimulus repetition. Such a habituation process when the behavioural reinforcement is absent has been reported previously, even from an early age (Sackett, 1966;

Rosenfeld & Van Hoesen, 1979). The fact that emotional responses did not persist for a long period might indicate, however, that subjects perceived the stimuli as pictures rather than real conspecifics, although it remains questionable whether monkeys have knowledge of the representational nature of the picture. Nevertheless, the use of pictures provided a valid substrate for this study, as monkey subjects were able to follow attention displayed by the monkey stimulus. Care was taken to avoid habituation by the infrequent use of test stimuli and the inclusion of other control stimuli.

Attention following has been suggested to be a non-cognitive process where body cues are associated with a quasi-orienting reflex. If so, such a reflex should not need the contextual richness of a social environment (Povinelli & Eddy, 1996; Moore & Corkum, 1994; Langton & Bruce, 1999). In support of this idea, Friesen and Kingstone (1998) show that human subjects are faster at detecting a target when they have been previously primed with a simple line drawing face looking in the direction where the target will appear. Sensitivity to face patterns is also observable in newborn humans using a line drawing face (Goren et al., 1975; Johnson et al., 1991), and infants of 4 months old begin to discriminate eyes contact from gaze averted (Vecera & Johnson, 1995). Despite such sensitivity to the eye region, it is only at 18-24 months old that human infants will co-orient to another individual's gaze regardless of the format (realistic, 2D/3D) of the face or the familiarity of the cue giver (Butterworth & Jarrett, 1991; Anderson & Doherty, 1997; Corkum & Moore, 1998; Lee et al., 1998). Moreover, the faculty to determine reliably and accurately gaze direction from photographs is even not fully achieved at 4 years old in humans (Anderson & Doherty, 1997). Some forms of gaze processing, e.g., identifying whether another individual is making eye contact or not, and attention shifting may be reflexive (innate), as such capacities do not depend upon the richness and the realism of the representation. By contrast, attention following processes, which require the emission of a learned motor response (co-orientation), appear to rely upon multiple developmental factors and the fidelity of the representation (occurring minimally for schematic displays). Interpreting social information, such as attention direction, from a picture may require a greater degree of complexity in the visual and conceptual processing compared to detecting eye contact. Detailed understanding of others (e.g., comprehending desires and intentions) may depend even more on contextual information and social interaction with the other.

ACKNOWLEDGEMENTS

This research was supported by grants from the Fyssen Foundation and Singer-Polignac Fondation of France to E. Lorincz and the Human Frontier Science Program to D. Perrett. C. Baker was supported by St Leonard's College and the School of Psychology, University of St Andrews. We thank T. Jellema for comments on an earlier version of the manuscript. Some of the results reported here were presented in abstract form (Lorincz et al., 1998).

REFERENCES

Anderson, J. R. & Doherty, M. J. (1997). Preschoolers' perception of other people's looking: Photographs and drawings. *Perception, 26,* 333-343.

Anderson, J. R., Montant, M., & Schmitt, D. (1996). Rhesus monkeys fail to use gaze direction as an experimenter-given cue in an object-choice task. *Behavioural Processes, 37,* 47-55.

Anderson, J. R., Sallaberry, P., & Barbier, H. (1995). Use of experimenter-given cues during object-choice tasks by capuchin monkeys. *Animal Behaviour, 49,* 201-208.

Baron-Cohen, S. (1994). How to build a baby that can read minds - cognitive mechanisms in mindreading. *Cahiers de Psychologie Cognitive/Current Psychology of Cognition, 13,* 513-552.

Brothers, L., & Ring, B. (1993). Mesial temporal neurons in the macaque monkey with responses selective for aspects of social stimuli. *Behavioural Brain Research, 57,* 53-61.

Butterworth, G., & Jarrett, N. (1991). What minds have in common is space: spatial mechanisms serving joint visual attention in infancy. *British Journal of Developmental Psychology, 9,* 55-72.

Chance, M. R. A. (1962). An interpretation of some agonistic postures: the role of cut-off acts and postures. *Symposium of the Zoological Society of London.*

Corkum, V., & Moore, C. (1998). The origins of joint visual attention in infants. *Developmental Psychology, 34,* 28-38.

D'Entremont, B., Hains, S. M. J., & Muir, D. (1997). A demonstration of gaze following in 3- to 6-month olds. *Infant Behavior and Development, 20,* 569-572.

Dittrich, W. (1994). How monkeys see others: discrimination and recognition of monkeys' shape. *Behavioural Processes, 33,* 139-154.

Emery, N. J. Lorincz, E. N. Perrett, D. I. Oram, M. W., & Baker, C. I. (1997). Gaze following and joint attention in rhesus monkeys (*Macaca mulatta*). *Journal of Comparative Psychology, 111,* 1-8.

Emery, N. J., & Perrett, D. I. (1999). How can studies of the monkey brain help us understand "theory of mind" and autism in humans. In S. Baron-Cohen et al. (Eds.), *Understanding other minds. 2: Perspectives from autism and cognitive neuroscience.* Oxford: Oxford University Press (in press).

Gómez, J. C. (1990). Visual behaviour as a window for reading the mind of others in primates. In A. Whiten (Ed.), *Natural theories of mind* (pp. 197-207). Oxford: Blackwell.

Goren, C. C., Sarty, M., & Wu, P. Y. K. (1975). Visual following and pattern discrimination of face-like stimuli by newborn infants. *Pediatrics, 56,* 544-549.

Hietanen, J. K., & Perrett, D. I. (1993). Motion sensitive cells in the macaque superior temporal polysensory area. I. Lack of response to the sight of the animal's own limb movement. *Experimental Brain Research, 93,* 117-128.

Humphrey, N. K. (1974). Species and individuals in the perceptual world of monkeys. *Perception, 3,* 105-114.

Itakura, S. (1996). An exploratory study of gaze-monitoring in nonhuman primates. *Japanese Psychological Research, 38,* 174-180.

Itakura, S., & Anderson, J. R. (1996). Learning to use experimenter-given cues during an object-choice task by a capuchin monkey. *Cahiers de Psychologie Cognitive/Current Psychology of Cognition, 15,* 103-112.

Itakura, S., & Tanaka, M. (1998). Use of experimenter-given cues during object-choice tasks by chimpanzees (*Pan troglodytes*), an orangutan (*Pongo pygmaeus*), and human infants (*Homo sapiens*). *Journal of Comparative Psychology, 112,* 119-126.

Jellema, T., Baker, C. I., Wicker, B., & Perrett, D. I. (1999). Neural representation for the perception of the intentionality of hand actions. *Brain and Cognition* (in press).

Johnson, M. H., Dziurawiec, S., Ellis, H., & Morton, J. (1991). Newborns' preferential tracking of face-like stimuli and its subsequent decline. *Cognition, 40,* 1-19.

Keating, C. F., & Keating, E. G. (1982). Visual scan patterns of rhesus monkeys viewing faces. *Perception, 11,* 211-219.

Lee, K., Eskritt, M., Symons, L. A., & Muir, D. (1998). Children's use of triadic eye gaze information for mind reading. *Developmental Psychology, 34,* 525-539.

Langton, S. R. H., & Bruce, V. (1999). Reflexive visual orienting in response to the social attention cues of others. *Visual Cognition* (in press).

Leonard, C. M., Rolls, E. T., Wilson, F. A. W., & Baylis, G. C. (1985). Neurons in the amygdala of the monkey with responses selective for faces. *Behavioural Brain Research, 15,* 159-176.

Friesen, C. K., & Kingstone, A. (1998). The eyes have it! Reflexive orienting is triggered by non-predictive gaze. *Psychonomic Bulletin and Review, 5,* 490-495.

Mendelson, M. J., Haith, M. M., & Goldman-Rakic P. J. (1982). Face scanning and responsiveness to social cues in infant rhesus monkeys. *Developmental Psychology, 18,* 222-228.

Menzel, E., & Halperin, S. (1975). Purposive behavior as a basis for objective communication in chimpanzees. *Science, 189,* 652- 654.

Miklósi, Á., Polgárdi, R., Topál, J., & Casányi, V. (1998). Use of experimenter-given cues in dogs. *Animal Cognition, 1,* 113-121.

Mineka, S., Davidson, M., Cook, M., & Keir, R. (1984). Observational conditioning of snake fear in rhesus monkeys. *Journal of Abnormal Psychology, 93,* 355-372.

Moore, C., & Corkum, V. (1994). Social understanding at the end of the 1st year of life. *Developmental Review, 14,* 349-372.

Moore, C., & Corkum, V. (1998). Infant gaze following based on eye direction. *British Journal of Developmental Psychology, 16,* 495-503.

Perrett, D. I. (1999). A cellular basis for reading minds from faces and actions. In M. Hauser & M. Konishi (Eds.), *Behavioural and neural mechanisms of communication.* Cambridge, MA: MIT Press (in press).

Perrett, D. I., Harries, M. H., Mistlin, A. J, Hietanen J., Benson, P. J., Bevan, R., Thomas, S., Ortega, J., Oram, M., & Brierly, K. (1990). Social signals analysed at the single cell level: someone's looking at me, something touched me, something moved. *International Journal of Comparative Psychology, 4,* 25-50.

Perrett, D. I., Hietanen, J. K., Oram, M. W., & Benson, P. J. (1992). Organization and functions of cells responsive to faces in the temporal cortex. *Philosophical Transactions of the Royal Society of London: Biological Sciences, 335,* 23-30.

Perrett, D. I., & Mistlin, A. J. (1990). Perception of facial characteristics by monkeys. In W. C. Stebbins & M. A. Berkley (Eds.), *Comparative perception* (Vol. II, pp. 187-215). New York: John Wiley and Sons Ltd.

Perrett, D. I., Oram, M. W., & Wachsmuth, E. (1993). Understanding minds and expression from facial signals: Studies at the brain cell level. In *2nd IEEE International Workshop on Robot and Human Communication* (pp. 3-12). Tokyo: Ro-man.

Perrett, D. I., Smith, P. A. J., Potter, D. D., Mistlin, A. J., Head, A. S., Milner, A. D., & Jeeves, M. A. (1985). Visual cells in the temporal cortex sensitive to face view and gaze direction. *Proceedings of the Royal Society of London B, 223,* 293-317.

Povinelli, D. J., & Eddy, T. J. (1994). The eyes as a window: What young chimpanzees see on the other side. *Cahiers de Psychologie Cognitive/ Current Psychology of Cognition, 13,* 695-705.

Povinelli, D. J., & Eddy, T. J. (1996a). Chimpanzees: joint visual attention. *Psychological Science, 7,* 129-135.

Povinelli, D. J., & Eddy, T. J. (1996b). What young chimpanzees know about seeing. *Monographs of the Society for Research in Child Development, 61,* Serial No. 247.

Povinelli, D. J., & Eddy, T. J. (1997). Specificity of gaze-following in young chimpanzees. *British Journal of Developmental Psychology, 15,* 213-222.

Redican, W. K., Kellicutt, M. H., & Mitchell, G. (1971). Preferences for facial expressions in juvenile rhesus monkeys (*Macaca Mulatta*). *Developmental Psychology, 5,* 539.

Rosenfeld, S. A., & Van Hoesen, G. W. (1979). Face recognition in the rhesus monkey. *Neuropsychologia, 17,* 503-509.

Sackett, G. P. (1966). Monkeys reared in isolation with pictures as visual input: evidence for an innate releasing mechanism. *Science, 154,* 1468-1473.

Scaife, M., & Bruner, J. S. (1975). The capacity for joint visual attention in the infant. *Nature, 253,* 265-266.

Snedecor, G. W., & Cochran, W. G. (1980). *Statistical methods* (7th Edition). Ames, IO: Iowa State University Press.

Tomasello, M., Call, J., & Hare, B. (1998). Five primate species follow the visual gaze of conspecifics. *Animal Behaviour, 55,* 1063-1069.

van Schaik, C, P., van Noordwijk, M. A., Warsono, B., & Surtiono, E. (1983). Party size and early detection of predators in Sumatran forest primates. *Primates, 24,* 211-221.

Vecera, S. P., & Johnson, M. H. (1995). Gaze detection and the cortical processing of faces: evidence from infants and adults. *Visual Perception, 2,* 101-129.

Wachsmuth, E., Oram, M. W., & Perrett, D. I. (1994). Recognition of objects and their component parts: responses of single units in the temporal cortex of the macaque. *Cerebral Cortex, 4,* 509-522.

Walsh, V., & Perrett, D. I. (1994). Visual attention in the occipitotemporal processing stream of the macaque. *Cognitive Neuropsychology, 11,* 243-263.

Whiten, A., & Byrne, R. W. (1988). The manipulation of attention in primate tactical deception. In R. W. Byrne & A. Whiten (Eds.), *Machiavellian intelligence: Social expertise and the evolution of intellect in monkeys, apes and humans* (pp. 211-223). Oxford, UK: Oxford University Press.

Wilson, F. A. W., & Goldman-Rakic, P. S. (1994). Viewing preferences of rhesus-monkeys related to memory for complex pictures, colors and faces. *Behavioural Brain Research, 60,* 79-89.

Primates and representations of self

James R. Anderson

University of Stirling, Scotland

Abstract

Some approaches to the study of nonhuman animals' self-representations are outlined. The responses of nonhuman primates to a variety of external representations of self are then reviewed, including reflections in mirrors, televised images, photographs, shadows, and moving computer screen cursors controlled by the primate's hand. Contrasts between species in the ability to infer self from these external representations are presented, which typically means members of the great apes, capable of self-recognition, contrasted with other nonhuman primates which show little or no understanding of the duality of these external visual representations of themselves. An original experiment on self-recognition in monkeys is proposed, based on experience with mirrors and matching-to-sample of photographs of non-overlapping body parts of familiar individuals.

Key words: Self-recognition, mirror, television, video, shadow, joystick, photographs, monkeys, great apes.

Correspondence should be sent to Dr. James R. Anderson, Department of Psychology, University of Stirling, Stirling FK9 4LA, Scotland (e-mail: jra1@stir.ac.uk).

INTRODUCTION

What kinds of representations do nonhuman animals have of themselves? Are they mindless organisms, responding unthinkingly if at times flexibly to environmental events, with little or no conscious appreciation of those events or of themselves as agents in the environment? Or are they sentient in the way humans are, with self-representations which allow them to contemplate alternative events, states, and courses of action? These questions, reflecting the extreme animals-as-automats and animals-as-fully-sentient philosophies of Descartes and some animal rights advocates, respectively, focus attention on the extent to which animals are aware of themselves as both subjects and objects, and as feeling, memorising, representing, evaluating, planning individuals (see Vauclair, 1996; Rogers, 1997). The present paper reviews one small subset of the ongoing research effort devoted to elucidating animals' cognitive processes: studies of nonhuman primates' understanding of representations of themselves. While small in terms of number of publications within the huge literature on learning and cognition in animals, or even in nonhuman primates, this area of research stands out by virtue of the fact that it directly addresses primates' understanding of themselves, rather than how they encode and organise information pertaining to environmental resources or social relationships (although such processes may impact importantly upon the individual's sense of self). The human concept of self is recognised as multifaceted and central to much of human behaviour (Neisser, 1988; Mitchell, 1994; Parker, Mitchell, & Boccia, 1994; Hart & Karmel, 1996), and evidence that some nonhuman primates share at least some of the more advanced facets of self-consciousness with humans has been presented in the debate over ethical aspects of humans' treatment of their nearest evolutionary relatives (Cavalieri & Singer, 1993; Fouts, 1997).

How nonhuman primates (hereafter referred to simply as "primates") view themselves has been studied most extensively through their reactions to visual representations of themselves, i.e., reflections, televised images, and photographs. What is known about primates' reactions to these stimuli as well as some other kinds of external representations of the self will be described and the implications of the data for primates' understanding of self will be discussed. I will also describe a study which has yet to be done but which, I believe, might effectively counter the objections that are most frequently raised with regard to experiments on self-recognition in monkeys.

INTERNAL AND EXTERNAL REPRESENTATIONS

Thus the focus here is on the question of self-recognition in response to *external* representations of the self. This is not to deny the validity of other approaches to understanding the processing of self-relevant stimuli in primates, including those which emphasise *internal* representations. Indeed, self-recognition of an external representation of oneself is impossible without a corresponding internal representation. In other words, in order to self-recognise, an organism must be capable of second-order representation.

Among the studies aimed at understanding internal representations are those by neurophysiologists, involving single-cell recording from various regions of the brain. This approach has identified neural units sensitive to self-related events such as being touched or gazed at (e.g., Perrett et al., 1990). One class of neurons recently discovered in the monkey prefrontal cortex fires when the monkey performs an action and in response to another individual performing a similar action (Gallese, Fadiga, Fogassi, & Rizzolatti, 1996; Rizzolatti, Fadiga, Gallese, & Fogassi, 1996). So-called "mirror" neurons such as these might form part of a neural substrate for imitation of motor acts, which in turn appears to be related to self-recognition ability (e.g., Hart & Fegley, 1994; Mitchell, 1997). However, the behavioural evidence regarding imitative evidence in monkeys is largely negative, suggesting that these primates do not match their own actions with those of another individual in a precise or intentional way (see Visalberghi & Fragaszy, 1990, for a review, and Mitchell & Anderson, 1993, for an example). Great apes, on the other hand, do show some ability to imitate, although the extent and limits of the ability are disputed (e.g., Whiten & Custance, 1996; Tomasello, 1996). At present there is little information from neurophysiological studies which might throw light on the origins or the nature of species differences in self-awareness.

Another behavioural approach to studying animals' internal representations of themselves involves the use of operant techniques to explore their discriminations between ongoing or recently performed behaviours. This approach has been taken with rodents, birds, and cetaceans

(Beninger, Kendall, & Vanderwoff, 1974; Shimp, 1982; Mercado, Murray, Uyeyama, Pack, & Herman, 1998), and holds considerable potential as a window onto how animals monitor self-produced motor acts. For example, dolphins were rewarded if they either repeated a recently performed action (Mercado et al., 1998), or if they innovated, i.e., did not repeat a previously performed action (Pryor, Haag, & O'Reilly, 1969). There is a lack of similar work in nonhuman primates, but Iversen, Ragnarsdottir, and Randrup (1984) and Louboungou and Anderson (1987) trained monkeys to alter the form of operantly condi-tioned self-scratching responses from one trial to the next, demonstrat-ing vervet and macaque monkeys' ability to hold a representation of a recently performed act in working memory. More studies along these lines could provide insight into the upper limits of primates' ability to monitor their own behavioural repertoires.

As pointed out by Hart and Karmel (1996), one facet of the experi-ence of self in humans is the construction of coherent notions about the self, including representations about the self's typical physical appear-ance, intelligence, social relationships, and so on. The first of these, concerning the individual's view of his or her own typical physical appearance, is perhaps the easiest to explore in nonverbal primates. It has been explored mainly through assessing their understanding of one type of external representation of self, namely, their reflection in a mirror.

RESPONSES TO MIRRORS IN PRIMATES

Gallup (1968) drew attention to the fact that in the presence of a mirror, any visually capable organism is literally an audience to its own behaviour. Individuals of most species show social responses towards their reflection, treating the image as an unfamiliar or a familiar con-specific to be threatened, appeased, tested, affiliated with, played with, or ignored, depending on environmental and organismal factors (Gallup, 1968, 1975, 1987; Anderson, 1984a, 1994a). The most intriguing find-ing to emerge from studies of mirror-image responses in primates con-cerns the division of this mammalian order into two groups of species: those for which the reflection comes to be understood as an external rep-resentation of the self, and those for which the social stimulus properties of the reflection continue to predominate. The former group consists exclusively of the great ape family: bonobos, chimpanzees, gorillas, and orangutans; evidence for self-recognition in the presence of a mirror exists for individuals of all four species. The latter group comprises prosimians, monkeys (including marmosets, tamarins, squirrel and capuchin monkeys, macaques, baboons), and the so-called "lesser" apes, the gibbons. More than twenty species of monkeys and gibbons have so far been tested for mirror self-recognition, with no convincing evidence for self-recognition emerging in any of these primates. It seems reasonable to infer that all other species in the latter genera would be unlikely to make the transition from social responding to their reflection to understanding that the image is an external representation of the self, given their structural and behavioural similarities with those species already tested.

Mirror self-recognition in great apes

The first experimental demonstration of mirror self-recognition in nonhuman primates was by Gallup (1970), who reported spontaneous use of the reflection to inspect otherwise invisible body parts in chimpanzees, and positive responses by the same apes on what has become known as the mark test. After a relatively rapid extinction of social responses towards their reflections, individually housed chimpanzees began to show spontaneous self-exploration, including acts such as visually and/or tactually examining inside the mouth or other normally visually inaccessible body regions (e.g., head, ano-genital region), while monitoring the activity in the mirror and apparently using the reflection to guide their movements.

Although such self-directed activities strongly suggested that the chimpanzees had overcome their initial tendency to treat the image as a conspecific and to use the image to focus on their own visual appearance, Gallup (1970) complemented these observations with the mark test. The reasoning was as follows: if the chimpanzees recognise themselves, then they should exploit their understanding of the reflection to investigate an experimentally made change to their appearance. Each chimpanzee was anaesthetised, and while it was unconscious a red mark was painted on one side of the brow ridge and on the opposite ear, using an odourless, nonirritant dye. Several hours later, after the chimpanzee had recovered from the anaesthetic, an observation period was conducted during which any touches to the marked areas were recorded. The frequency of touches was low, indicating that the chimpanzee was not aware of the marks. Then the mirror was reintroduced and the same observation procedure followed. This time, the number of touches to the marked regions of the head increased dramatically, typically with the chimpanzee monitoring its reflection while touching the marks and then looking and sometimes sniffing at its fingers, as if to obtain more information about the change to its physical appearance.

These positive results on the mark test constituted important confirmatory evidence for self-recognition in chimpanzees. This finding has since been replicated in several laboratories, and researchers have extended use of the basic procedure to address issues such as the effects of early social experience, the developmental emergence, and patterns of distribution of mirror self-recognition in chimpanzees (Gallup, McClure, Hill, & Bundy, 1971; Lin, Bard, & Anderson, 1992; Povinelli, Rulf, Landau, & Bierschwale, 1993). Although some authors have questioned the significance of the reports of self-recognition in chimpanzees, for example based on the failure of some chimpanzees to show it (Swartz & Evans, 1994) or on methodological grounds (Heyes, 1994, 1998), the quantitative and visual documentary evidence for self-recognition in chimpanzees is compelling (Gallup, Povinelli, Suarez, Anderson, Lethmate, & Menzel, 1995; Serre & Anderson, 1995; Povinelli, Gallup, Eddy, Bierschwale, Engstrom, Perilloux, & Toxopeus, 1997; Anderson, 1997). Why certain apparently normal chimpanzees do not show some or any signs of self-recognition remains an unresolved issue, but this does not diminish the importance of the finding that many chimpanzees clearly do correctly perceive and actively use this external representation of the self in much the same way as humans might do to check their visual appearance.

Convincing signs of mirror self-recognition have also been described in orangutans (Lethmate & Dücker, 1973; Suarez & Gallup, 1981; Miles, 1994), and more recently in bonobos (Walraven, van Elsacker, & Verheyen, 1995; Westergaard & Hyatt, 1994; see Anderson, 1997, for cinematographic evidence). The picture regarding the remaining great ape species, the gorillas, is less clear. Several attempts to find self-recognition in gorilla have failed (Ledbetter & Basen, 1982; Suarez & Gallup, 1981; Shillito, Gallup, & Beck, 1999), whereas affirmative recent observations have been described in two individuals (Patterson & Cohn, 1994; Swartz & Evans, 1994). An older observation comes from

Hoyt (1941, cited in Mitchell, 1999): a human-reared gorilla closely inspected a new tooth in front of a mirror (but then attacked the reflection). These observations on other great apes are of interest not only because they extend the range of primate species known to possess the capacity for mirror self-recognition, but also because they have provided the basis for some original theorising about the evolutionary processes leading to the current, uneven distribution of self-awareness as expressed through self-recognition (Gallup, 1991, 1997; Povinelli, 1994; Povinelli & Cant, 1995).

Absence of mirror self-recognition in prosimians and monkeys

While interest in mirror self-recognition in great apes has largely shifted from establishing the phenomenon towards the phylogenetic and developmental psychological implications of the findings, self-recognition research on other primate species continues to chase evidence that prosimians, monkeys, or gibbons are able to self-recognise. It is not for lack of effort that researchers have failed to find self-recognition in monkeys (Anderson, 1984a; Gallup, 1987). The following methods have all been used in attempts to find self-recognition in monkeys: sequential marking, shaping of mirror-mediated self-directed responses, early and extensive exposure to mirrors, physical access to large and to portable mirrors, multiple mirrors producing an array of reflections, paired or group access to mirrors, training on mirror-mediated manual searching, increasing the salience of the change to the subject's physical appearance, and varying mirror locations. Anderson and Gallup (1999) give more details of failed attempts.

One of the most intriguing aspects of this line of research is the finding that monkeys can learn to recognise and use reflected environmental information, despite showing no signs of self-recognition. Anderson (1986) reported that macaques learned to use a reflection to search manually for food which could only be seen in the mirror (see Marchal & Anderson, 1993, for a similar demonstration in capuchin monkeys), and Itakura (1987) trained Japanese macaques to press 4-key sequences on a 12-key panel which could only be viewed in a mirror. Despite their impressive mirror-mediated performance, these monkeys gave no convincing signs that they recognised themselves. Instead of being based on self-recognition, their performance appears to reflect a sophisticated visuo-spatial learning in which recognition of the active hand as being their own hand is not necessary. In fact, what the monkeys are doing is an extension of the behaviour of turning around to look directly at something first seen in the mirror, which occurs in many nonhuman species and in human infants before they pass the mark test (Anderson, 1984a, b).

There have been odd claims that monkeys have met one or two criteria for self-recognition (Boccia, 1994; Thompson & Boatwright-Horowitz, 1994; Hauser, Kralik, Botto-Mahan, Garrett, & Oser, 1995), but in no case does the evidence stand up to scrutiny or meet the basic requirement of reliability (Gallup, 1994; Anderson & Gallup, 1997, 1999). In contrast to the lack of evidence for mirror-guided self-directed behaviour in monkeys is an abundance of evidence that monkeys perceive their reflection as if it were another monkey, albeit one with some unusual behavioural properties. The following social phenomena have all been observed in monkeys in the presence of a mirror: overt social responses, spontaneous recovery of social responses following a change in mirror location, attenuation of the isolation-rearing syndrome, attenuation of separation-induced agitation, and social facilitation of ingestive behaviour (Anderson, 1994a).

In fact it has been suggested that the social stimulus properties of mirrors may be strong enough to obstruct the emergence of self-recognition in monkeys, especially in view of the social significance and arousal – inducing properties of the direct eye-gaze which is normally a consequence of a monkey looking at its own reflection. However, in an explicit attempt to reduce social arousal arising from direct eye contact with the conspecific in the mirror, Anderson and Roeder (1989) presented a group of capuchin monkeys with two vertical mirrors outside the cage, converging in such a way as to preclude the possibility of direct eye contact with the reflection. Behavioural observations confirmed a much-reduced social content in reactions to this mirror arrangement, but no signs of self-recognition were shown by the monkeys. (Shillito et al., 1999, recently used an angled mirrors condition with gorillas, but obtained no evidence of self-recognition.) In another attempt to overcome monkeys' natural aversion to close-range eye contact with a conspecific, Thomspon and Boatwright-Horowitz (1994) used water deprivation to train a macaque to engage in prolonged bouts of eye-contact with its reflection, but again the procedure did not lead to self-recognition.

To summarise, the observation of a range of social phenomena in monkeys in the presence of mirrors, coupled with the lack of signs of self-recognition despite many creative attempts to show it, provides support for the view that there is a cognitive division between self-recognising great apes and non-self-recognising monkeys (Gallup, 1982, 1987; Anderson, 1994a; Anderson & Gallup, 1999).

TELEVISION AND VIDEO

Videotape is a valuable research tool in the study of self-recognition because researchers can present a subject with a live representation of itself on a video monitor, i.e., analogous to its mirror image, or in delayed mode in which contingency cues have been eliminated. Various studies of human infants' responses to video have involved presentation of live-self, delayed-self, live-other, or delayed-other sequences, in succession or simultaneously, with or without the addition of a critical stimulus such as a mark on the subject or a probe stimulus appearing in the background (e.g., Papousek & Papousek, 1974; Amsterdam & Greenberg, 1977; Lewis & Brooks-Gunn, 1979; Bigelow, 1981). Behavioural measures have included visual preference, imitation, contingency testing, self-conscious behaviour, and turning around to check a probe stimulus appearing on the screen. In general, these studies have found that recognition of one's own televised (or videotaped) image by human infants emerges at around the same time as mirror self-recognition.

Surprisingly, television/video has not been used much to assess self-recognition in other primates. Savage-Rumbaugh and Rubert (1986) described spontaneous uses of their own live televised images by two chimpanzees in ways which indicate self-recognition, such as watching while making unusual lip movements, and looking inside the mouth with the aid of a torchlight. Eddy, Gallup, and Povinelli (1996) studied chimpanzees' ability to distinguish between their own reflection and video images of other chimpanzees. They found overall greater evidence of contingent facial and body movements and self-exploratory acts in the presence of a mirror, but they did not include a self-videotape condition. A final study to be mentioned regarding chimpanzees' understanding of their televised images is by Menzel, Savage-Rumbaugh, and Lawson (1985), who found that chimpanzees could use a televised image of their hand to visually guide a manual search for a target, also visible only on the video monitor. This image-guided behaviour was maintained across experimental modifications of the image including rotation and inversion.

Responses to televised images also constitute some of the evidence for self-recognition in gorillas, although it is weak evidence. Law and Lock (1994) presented two pairs of zoo-housed gorillas with videotapes of unfamiliar gorillas, the gorillas themselves filmed the previous day, and live televised images of themselves. They observed a number of self-exploratory acts with the live image, such as touching the face and looking inside the mouth. Also, while fixating the screen, one gorilla moved out of the way of a barrel rolling towards her from behind and thus visible on screen. The authors are prudent with regard to whether the gorillas could be said to self-recognise, but they call for a reevaluation of the position of this great ape in the self-recognition debate. There do not appear to be any systematic studies of responses to televised images of self in the other two species of great apes, bonobos and orangutans, although Tobach, Skolnick, Klein, and Greenberg (1997) included videoclips of the subjects themselves in the stimuli they presented to a zoo-housed group of orangutans, to little effect.

There have been no explicit attempts to discover self-recognition in monkeys through the use of televised or video images. However, Washburn, Gulledge, and Rumbaugh (1997) recently found that when rhesus monkeys selected combined food and videoclip rewards for performing joystick-based computer tasks, the monkeys preferred to view a clip of themselves compared to one of a roommate or an unfamiliar conspecific. While the basis and significance of the reported preference is not clear, the authors point out that development of computer and video techniques might lead to new approaches to studying self-recognition.

PHOTOGRAPHS

The development of human infants' ability to recognise pictorial representations of themselves was included in Lewis and Brooks-Gunn's (1979) study, along with mirror and video self-recognition. While delayed video sequences of self are devoid of contingency cues, they can still contain motion cues which present the observer with changing perspectives and information about idiosyncratic postural adjustments, gait, etc. Photographs do neither, as the subject is fixed in one pose. Lewis and Brooks-Gunn (1979) measured visual fixation, affect, and spontaneous vocalisations in response to photographs of self and others, with age and sex of other controlled. They also assessed verbal identification of photographs, and concluded that reliable self-recognition in photographs tends to be slightly delayed compared to self-recognition in a mirror or on video.

There is some evidence that great apes can recognise pictorial representations of themselves. One interesting example is that of the human-raised chimpanzee Viki, who while sorting photographs of chimpanzees and humans into two piles unhesitatingly placed her own photograph on the "human" pile (incidentally also expressing something about her concept of self; this chimpanzee also self-preened in front of a mirror; Hayes & Nissen, 1971). The sign-language trained gorilla Koko apparently recognises and labels herself in photographs (Patterson, 1978). More recently, a chimpanzee trained to use symbolic labels for individuuals appropriately transferred the symbols to label pictures of the individuals, including herself (Itakura, 1992).

Without giving the subject some way to label and thus identify photographs, it would be difficult to obtain unambiguous evidence for self-recognition with this type of external representation. It may be possible to obtain behavioural discrimination between photographs of self and others, but this of course is not sufficient evidence that a stimulus is recognised as a representation of oneself. Instead, discrimination could simply indicate different degrees of familiarity with, or interest in, the stimuli (see Legerstee, Anderson, & Schaffer, 1998, for a recent example in young human infants). Tobach et al. (1997) observed a zoo-housed adult female orangutan shift repeatedly back and forth between a mirror and a life-sized portrait of herself in preference to portraits of the other members of the group. On the basis of this they called for further exploration of the relationship between responses to the mark test for self-recognition and self-portrait viewing, but overall viewing patterns of the portraits gave little useful information.

There is a substantial amount of evidence suggesting that monkeys recognise pictorial representations of other monkeys. They show impressive face recognition abilities even across varying views, and they also respond to several categories of pictures (infants, adults, threat faces, fear faces) with specific social displays (Anderson, 1994b, 1998). But there is no evidence in the literature that monkeys recognise photographs of themselves, and the possibility does not even appear to have received serious study. Wilcoxon, Meier, Orlando, and Paulson (1969) reported that members of a captive group of rhesus monkeys produced operant responses preferentially for the projection of slides of themselves compared to other scenes. However the data were combined for all members of the group and all forty stimulus slides, so it is impossible to know whether individual monkeys responded preferentially for their own picture, and even if this occurred, the difference could be accounted for parsimoniously in terms of differential familiarity of the stimuli.

SHADOWS AND WATER

One's shadow is a natural, external representation of the one's body. Its form and dimensions may vary with climatic and temporal factors, as well as with individual factors such as age-related physical changes and clothing, but the source of the shadow remains the same, i.e., it is "attached" to one's own body. Cameron and Gallup (1988) extended self-recognition research in humans by analysing the development of 1-3-year-old children's ability to correctly identify the source of their own shadows. They did this through the use of a probe stimulus (the shadow of an object appearing near the infant's own shadow), the imitation of shadow "puppets", and a shadow recognition task involving attempts to explore a hat which appeared on the head of the infant's shadow. While turning to look directly at the probe stimulus was observed from approximately 13 months of age and attempts to imitate shadows around 6 months later, shadow self-recognition appeared only after 25 months and occurred in the majority of children only after 3 years of age. Thus, compared to the richer external representations of self such as from mirrors, video and photographs, shadows are recognised later.

Huxley (1941, cited in Mitchell, 1999) reported that a 1.5-year-old gorilla traced the outline of his shadow on a wall. A young language-trained chimpanzee liked to interpose his body between a movie projector and the screen, and pretend that his shadow chased the chimpanzees in the film. When outdoors, he moved in unusual ways while monitoring his shadow (Savage-Rumbaugh, Shanker, & Taylor, 1998). However, only one controlled study has addressed the issue of shadow recognition in great apes. Boysen, Bryan, and Shreyer (1994) presented a 2.8-year-old and an 8-year-old chimpanzees with tasks equivalent to those used by Cameron and Gallup (1988). Only the older chimpanzee was judged to pass criterion for shadow recognition on the hat task, while both chimpanzees passed the other two tasks on approximately half or less of the trials conducted. The authors point out that the chimpanzees' lack of attention or interest was a problem during the running of the trials.

Based on what is already known about self-recognition with good quality visual representations and the modest findings of Boysen et al. (1994), it is a reasonable assumption that mirror self-recognising great apes may also perceive their shadow a representation of themselves. In contrast, there is no reason to believe the same is true for monkeys. Like another form of visual feedback about the self, namely, reflections in water, shadows apparently come to be ignored by monkeys through repeated exposure and habituation from an early age. Petit and Thierry (1994) report that a 6-year-old male Guinea baboon behaved aggressively towards his own clearly defined vertical shadow on four separate occasions, with visual and vocal threats and lunges. A 3-year-old male in the same group also engaged in a bout of barkscreaming against his own shadow for 30 seconds. The 6-year-old was also seen to threaten his own reflection in a pool of water. A pet gorilla also hit out at his own reflection in water (Benchley, 1947), which is interesting in view of the debate surrounding the evidence for self-recognition in this ape. Such incidents strongly suggest social properties of shadows and reflections in water, which may persist, possibly in latent form, despite a more general, long-term habituation.

JOYSTICK-CONTROLLED CURSOR MOVEMENTS

A significant recent advance in comparative psychology has been the development of techniques employing joystick-based computer tasks (or "games") to assess a variety of learning and cognitive processes in primates including chimpanzees, baboons, macaques, capuchins, and squirrel monkeys. Many of the tasks used involve producing a collision between the cursor, which moves according to the subject's manipulation of the joystick, and a stationary or moving target on the screen, target movements not being under control of the subject (cf. Vauclair & Fagot, 1993). The movements of the cursor can be seen as an abstract representation of the subject's hand movements. Several authors have advocated using the behaviour of controlling a cursor on a computer monitor via a joystick as a means of assessing the individual's sense of self. Rumbaugh, Richardson, and Washburn (1989) suggested that the ability to distinguish between the cursor (controlled by the subject) and the target (not controlled by the subject) required the same cognitive components as self-recognition, and predicted that joystick-experienced monkeys might be more likely to display mirror self-recognition than other monkeys (a prediction yet to be supported by data). Heyes (1994) points out that pursuit tracking video tasks require that the subject visually monitor the screen while using the cursor position "as a source of novel, displaced, visual feedback on the position of its hand" (p. 916), and argues for a relationship between such performance and self-recognition, while Vauclair (1996) presents the use of video-tasks as a potential alternative to mirror-guided reaching tasks. All of these authors suggest that the kinaesthetic-visual matching involved in cursor-controlling joystick manipulations shares underlying mechanisms with mirror self-recognition, in which visual-kinaesthetic matching surely plays a fundamental role (Mitchell, 1993).

In the most explicit employment of a joystick paradigm to assess what they refer to as aspects of the "preconceptual self", Joergensen, Suomi, and Hopkins (1995) compared capuchin monkeys and chimpanzees on several video-tasks. The comparison is particularly interesting in view of the fact that capuchin monkeys and chimpanzees share many similarities in terms of biology and behaviour. These behavioural similarities extend to performance on a number of laboratory tasks of learning and cognition, although there appear to be also important differences concerning particularly imitation, understanding of cause-effect relations, and especially mirror self-recognition (see Visalberghi & Fragaszy, 1990; Anderson, 1996; Visalberghi, 1997).

Joergensen et al. (1995) first assessed the monkeys' and chimpanzees' acquisition of two elementary video tasks, known as SIDE and CHASE. The chimpanzees generally outperformed the capuchins, especially on more difficult versions of the tasks, but there were no fundamental differences in the two species' ability to complete the tasks. The authors then introduced a second cursor which appeared at the same time as the one controlled by the subject. When this second cursor moved, it was controlled by the computer and not by the subject. Now, the subject had to distinguish which of the two cursors it was responsible for moving. Overall, only chimpanzees correctly completed a majority of trials in this new condition. Also, the capuchins' performance was adversely affected when the computer-controlled cursor followed a "smart" path on its way to colliding with the target, whereas the chimpanzees were not affected by whether the competing cursor moved smartly or randomly. Thus while the chimpanzees, like human children and adults also tested by the authors, recognised which image they controlled on the screen, capuchin monkeys appeared not to recognise which image they controlled or else they were unable to use their knowledge appropriately. Further clarification is awaited regarding the relationship between the type of self-knowledge required to perform video tasks and the self-knowledge required to recognise more conventional external representations of self such as mirrors or televised images. In the meantime, instead of providing an alternative means of demonstrating self-recognition in monkeys, the most relevant data currently available from the joystick paradigm provide further support for a cognitive distinction between monkeys and apes in terms of "self-recognition".

FUTURE DIRECTIONS

There is no reason to believe that interest in nonhuman animals' knowledge of themselves will diminish in the foreseeable future. Concerning the primates, the growing evidence for some sort of cognitive divide between the few species that appear capable of self-recognition and the vast majority that do not, is unlikely to dilute interest in the issue; indeed it is more likely to stimulate further research. What does seem likely to diminish, however, is the search for self-recognition using mirrors or their televised equivalents with the focus on spontaneous and mark test-induced self-directed responding using the reflection or televised image. Gallup's brilliantly simple and far-reaching mirror method is bound to be complemented and possibly ultimately replaced by new developments in visual technology. As mentioned earlier, the use of video to assess self-recognition in primates has been underused compared to its role in the study of the ontogeny of self-recognition in human infants. Video methods have been better used to explore visual self-recognition in cetaceans (Marten & Psakaros, 1995) than in primates, and it is to be expected that this imbalance will eventually be reduced. Video is also particularly well suited for assessing the salience of visual feedback from self-produced movements, having the advantage of allowing the precise regions of the body shown, viewing angles and directional congruence to be varied systematically (e.g., Bahrick & Watson, 1985; Rochat & Morgan, 1995). Only the study by Menzel et al. (1985) on mirror- and video-guided hand movements in chimpanzees comes close to this approach with nonhuman primates.

Further developments in the use of computer-based video tasks with primates may also lead to new insights into animals' understanding of self. Washburn et al. (1997) have speculated about using a combination of video and computer technologies to create virtual marks which will move with the primate as it views itself. Conceivably, the technique could also be extended to investigate self-recognition based on an external representation in the form of biological motion, using only virtual points of light on strategic parts of the body of the subject and of other individuals on an otherwise dark screen. It is also likely that the study of self-recognition in photographs will undergo computer-mediated changes, as the technology for systematically altering, combining, and averaging digitalised images of facial or other characteristics becomes more widely used, along with subjects controlling their own selection of configurations.

What directions are left for self-recognition studies using on the simpler technologies of mirrors or photographs? Gallup (1991) has argued that comparative self-recognition research using mirrors has run its course and should give way to other approaches to exploring primate cognition, especially in the domain of social cognition. On the other hand, Anderson (1994a) has called for continuing the search for self-recognition, pointing out the possibility of stimulus presentation formats interacting with species or individual factors in ways that are yet to be explored. To conclude, I describe a self-recognition experiment which has not yet been carried out. Combining two "old" stimuli from self-recognition research, namely, mirrors and pictures, the experiment is proposed to illustrate how creative methods using mirrors might continue to shed light on the issue of self-awareness.

A three-part procedure is required. First, members of a group of monkeys should be trained on a match-to-sample task in which the match concerns pictures of non-overlapping body parts belonging to familiar group-members (presented in the form of photographs, slides, or digitalised images). For example, the stimulus might be individual A's face, with the alternatives being individual A's leg (the match) and individual B's leg. This would be a replication of Dasser's (1987) demonstration of the perceptual "completion" of pictures of familiar group-members by a longtail macaque. This finding is interesting from the points of view of monkeys' perception of pictures as representations of conspecifics and their individual recognition abilities. Confirmation of Dasser's (1987) finding would be welcome in its own right, but for the purpose of the proposed experiment this matching-to-sample phase is only a preliminary.

Next, the monkeys would be presented with one or more mirrors fixed vertically to the wall(s) of their enclosure. Each mirror should be big enough to permit a monkey to see its own face, but small enough and located in such a way as to prevent the monkey seeing its full-length reflection, especially its tail. (The tail will be a critical body region in this experiment, and I suggest that at some point, possibly before the start of the experiment, every monkey's tail be made easily distinguishable by dyeing the tip or shaving it in a distinctive way. Since tail grooming is a common social and self-directed behaviour, the monkeys will soon learn about the new appearance of all tails in the group, including their own.) Mirror-image reactions should be recorded as in previous studies. Although it is unlikely that anything particularly new will arise from this phase, it is possible that what happens in the following, critical phase will be related to mirror viewing responses.

Phase 3 consists of retesting the monkeys on matching-to-sample of non-overlapping body parts. The critical trials, to be interspersed among others, will involve presenting the monkey's own face as a sample along with a photograph of its own tail as one of the alternatives (or vice-versa). If my reasoning is correct, if the monkey knows that the owner of the face is the same as the owner of the tail (which is its own), then it should correctly match the alternative to the sample, thereby demonstrating visual self-recognition of its own face (and tail, of course). Remember that the monkey has never seen its entire reflection including the tail, so it cannot simply base a correct matching response on familiarity. Instead, it must make the inference of common ownership of face and tail, which can only be done with the aid of an integrated internal representation of its own physical appearance.

The above-described experiment would not only circumvent the major objections that are sometimes raised to mirror self-recognition experiments with monkeys, such as interference from aggressive stare-out, or insufficient ability to deal with mirrored visual feedback, it would also provide support for evolutionary continuity in self-awareness, as opposed to the discontinuous process which the evidence reviewed in this chapter appears to indicate. Gallup (1991) has argued that self-recognition applies not only to facial features but to other body parts as well. This view leads to the prediction that monkeys should fail the matching-to-sample test outlined above, which would further reinforce the discontinuity view of the distribution of self-awareness among primate species.

Future approaches to the primates' understanding of "self" may also focus on the individual's social interactions and relationships, or on the relative roles of vision, proprioception, and the sense of "agency" when responding to and controlling aspects of the environment (see Rochat, 1995, for an interesting collection of papers dealing with such issues). We await the answers to many outstanding questions concerning primates' sense of themselves, but I hope to have made a good case for the continued importance of the comparative study of self-awareness; new information about how other species deal with external representations of themselves will continue to enrich our understanding of those species' selves, as well as our own.

ACKNOWLEDGEMENT

This paper was written while the author was Invited Professor in the Psychology Department, Faculty of Letters, Kyoto University. I would like to thank Prof. K. Fujita and other colleagues and students for their hospitality and stimulation.

REFERENCES

Amsterdam, B., & Greenberg, L. M. (1977). Self-conscious behavior of infants: A videotape study. *Developmental Psychobiology, 10,* 1-6.

Anderson, J. R. (1984a). Monkeys with mirrors: Some questions for primate psychology. *International Journal of Primatology, 5,* 81-98.

Anderson, J. R. (1984b). The development of self-recognition: A review. *Developmental Psychobiology, 17,* 35-49.

Anderson, J. R. (1986). Mirror-mediated finding of hidden food by monkeys (*Macaca tonkeana* and *M. fascicularis*). *Journal of Comparative Psychology, 100,* 237-242.

Anderson, J. R. (1994a). The monkey in the mirror: A strange conspecific. In S. T. Parker, R. Mitchell, & M. Boccia (Eds.), *Self-awareness in animals and humans: Developmental perspectives* (pp. 315-329). New York: Cambridge University Press.

Anderson, J. R. (1994b). Valeur éthologique des visages et des mimiques chez les primates non humains. *Psychologie Française, 39,* 345-355.

Anderson, J. R. (1996). Chimpanzees and capuchin monkeys: Comparative cognition. In A. F. Russon, K. A. Bard, & S. T. Parker (Eds.), *Reaching into thought: The minds of the great apes* (pp. 23-56). Cambridge: Cambridge University Press.

Anderson, J. R. (1997). *Self-recognition in primates: Experiments with mirrors* (16 mm film and VHS videotape, 35 min). Göttingen: Institut für den Wissenschaftlichen Film.

Anderson, J. R. (1998). Social cues and social rewards in primate learning and cognition. *Behavioural Processes, 42,* 159-175.

Anderson, J. R., & Gallup, G. G., Jr. (1997). Self-recognition in *Saguinus?* A critical essay. *Animal Behaviour, 54,* 1563-1567.

Anderson, J. R., & Gallup, G. G., Jr. (1999). Self-recognition in primates: Past and future challenges. In M. Haug & R. F. Whalen (Eds.), *Animal models of human emotion and cognition.* Washington, DC: American Psychological Association.

Anderson, J. R., & Roeder, J.-J. (1989). Responses of capuchin monkeys (*Cebus apella*) to different conditions of mirror-image stimulation. *Primates, 30,* 581-587.

Bahrick, L. F., & Watson, J. S. (1985). Detection of intermodal proprioceptive-visual contingency as a potential basis of self-perception in infancy. *Developmental Psychology, 21,* 963-973.

Benchley, B. J. (1947). *My friends, the apes.* London: Purnell & Sons.

Beninger, R. J., Kendall, S. B., & Vanderwoff, C. H. (1974). The ability of rats to discriminate their own behavior. *Canadian Journal of Psychology, 28,* 79-91.

Bigelow, A. F. (1981). The correspondence between self- and image movement as a cue to self-recognition for young children. *Journal of Genetic Psychology, 139,* 11-26.

Boccia, M. L. (1994). Mirror behavior in macaques. in S. T. Parker, R. W. Mitchell & M. L. Boccia (Eds.), *Self-awareness in animals and humans: Developmental perspectives* (pp. 350-360). New York: Cambridge University Press.

Boysen, S. T., Bryan, K. M., & Shreyer, T. A. (1994). Shadows and mirrors: Alternative avenues to the development of self-recognition in chimpanzees. In S. T. Parker, R. W. Mitchell, & M. L. Boccia (Eds.), *Self-awareness in animals and humans: Developmental perspectives* (pp. 227-240). New York: Cambridge University Press.

Cameron, P. A., & Gallup, G. G., Jr. (1988). Shadow self-recognition in human infants. *Infant Behavior and Development, 11,* 465-471.

Cavalieri, P., & Singer, P. (Eds.) (1993). *The Great Ape Project.* London: Fourth Estate.

Dasser, V. (1987). Slides of group members as representations of the real animals (*Macaca fascicularis*). *Ethology, 76,* 65-73.

Eddy, T. J., Gallup, G. G., Jr., & Povinelli, D. J. (1996). Age differences in the ability of chimpanzees to distinguish mirror-images of self from video images of others. *Journal of Comparative Psychology, 110,* 38-44.

Fouts, R. (1997). *Next of kin.* London: Michael Joseph.

Gallese, V., Fadiga, L., Fogassi, L., & Rizzolatti, G. (1996). Action recognition in the premotor cortex. *Brain, 119,* 593-609.

Gallup, G. G., Jr. (1968). Mirror-image stimulation. *Psychological Bulletin, 70,* 782-793.

Gallup, G. G., Jr. (1970). Chimpanzees: Self-recognition. *Science, 167,* 86-87.

Gallup, G. G., Jr. (1975). Towards an operational definition of self-awareness. In R. H. Tuttle (Ed.), *Socioecology and psychology of primates* (pp. 309-341). The Hague: Mouton.

Gallup, G. G., Jr. (1982). Self-awareness and the emergence of mind in primates. *American Journal of Primatology, 2,* 237-248.

Gallup, G. G., Jr. (1987). Self-awareness. In G. Mitchell & J. Erwin (Eds.), *Comparative primate biology, Vol. 2B: Behavior, cognition, and motivation* (pp. 3-16). New York: Liss.

Gallup, G. G., Jr. (1991). Toward a comparative psychology of self-awareness: Species limitations and cognitive consequences. In G. R. Goethals & J. Strauss (Eds.), *The self: An interdisciplinary approach* (pp. 121-135). New York: Springer-Verlag.

Gallup, G. G., Jr. (1994). Self-recognition: Research strategies and experimental design. In S. T. Parker, R. W. Mitchell & M. L. Boccia (Eds.), *Self-awareness in animals and humans: Developmental perspectives* (pp. 35-50). New York: Cambridge University Press.

Gallup, G. G., Jr. (1997). On the rise and fall of self-conception in primates. *Annals of the New York Academy of Sciences, 818,* 73-82.

Gallup, G. G., Jr., McClure, M. K., Hill, S. D., & Bundy, R. A. (1971). Capacity for self-recogntion in differentially reared chimpanzees. *Psychological Record, 21,* 69-74.

Gallup, G. G., Jr., Povinelli, D. J., Suarez, S. D., Anderson, J. R., Lethmate, J., & Menzel, E. W., Jr. (1995). Further reflections on self-recognition in primates. *Animal Behaviour, 50,* 1525-1532.

Hart, D., & Fegley, S. (1994). Social imitation and the emergence of a mental model of self. In S. T. Parker, R. W. Mitchell, & M. L. Boccia (Eds.), *Self-awareness in animals and humans: Developmental perspectives* (pp. 149-165). New York: Cambridge University Press.

Hart, D., & Karmel, M. P. (1996). Self-awareness and self-knowledge in humans, apes, and monkeys. In A. E. Russon, K. A. Bard, & S. T. Parker (Eds.), *Reaching into thought* (pp. 325-347). Cambridge: Cambridge University Press.

Hauser, M. D., Kralik, J., Botto-Mahan, C., Garrett, M., & Oser, J. (1995). Self-recognition in primates: Phylogeny and the salience of species-typical features. *Proceedings of the National Academy of Sciences, USA, 92,* 10811-10814.

Hayes, C., & Nissen, C. H. (1971). Higher mental functions of a home-raised chimpanzee. In A. M. Schrier & F. Stollnitz (Eds.), *Behavior of nonhuman primates* (Vol. 4, pp. 59-115). New York: Academic Press.

Heyes, C. M. (1994). Reflections on self-recognition in primates. *Animal Behaviour, 47,* 909-919.

Heyes, C. M. (1998). Theory of mind in nonhuman primates. *Behavioral and Brain Sciences, 21,* 101-148.

Itakura, S. (1987). Mirror guided behavior in Japanese monkeys (*Macaca fuscata fuscata*). *Primates, 28,* 149-161.

Itakura, S. (1992). A chimpanzee with the ability to learn the use of personal pronouns. *Psychological Record, 42,* 157-172.

Iversen, I. H., Ragnarsdottir, G. A., & Randrup, K. I. (1984). Operant conditioning of autogrooming in vervet monkeys (*Cercopithecus aethiops*). *Journal of the Experimental Analysis of Behavior, 42,* 171-189.

Joergensen, M. J., Suomi, S. J., & Hopkins, W. D. (1995). Using a computerized testing system to investigate the preconceptual self in nonhuman primates. In P. Rochat (Ed.), *The self in infancy: Theory and research* (pp. 243-256). Amsterdam: Elsevier.

Law, L. E., & Lock, A. J. (1994). Do gorillas recognize themselves on television? In S. T. Parker, R. W. Mitchell, & M. L. Boccia (Eds.), *Self-awareness in animals and humans: Developmental perspectives* (pp. 308-312). New York: Cambridge University Press.

Ledbetter, D. H., & Basen, J. (1982). Failure to demonstrate self-recognition in gorillas. *American Journal of Primatology, 2,* 307-310.

Legerstee, M., Anderson, D., & Schaffer, A. (1998). Five- and eight-month-old infants recognize their faces and voices as familiar and social stimuli. *Child Development, 69,* 37-50..

Lethmate, J., & Dücker, G. (1973). Untersuchungen zum Selbsterkennen im Spiegel bei Orang-utans und einigen anderen Affenarten. *Zeitschrift für Tierpsychologie, 33,* 248-269.

Lewis, M., & Brooks-Gunn, J. (1979). *Social cognition and the acquisition of self.* New York: Plenum.

Lin, A. C., Bard, K. A., & Anderson, J. R. (1992). Development of self-recognition in chimpanzees (*Pan troglodytes*). *Journal of Comparative Psychology, 106,* 120-127.

Louboungou, M., & Anderson, J. R. (1987). Yawning, scratching, and protruded lips: Differential conditionability of natural acts in pigtail monkeys (*Macaca nemestrina*). *Primates, 28,* 367-375.

Marchal, P., & Anderson, J. R. (1993). Mirror-image responses in capuchin monkeys (*Cebus capucinus*): Social responses and use of reflected environmental information. *Folia Primatologica, 61,* 165-173.

Marten, K., & Psakaros, S. (1995). Using self-view television to distinguish between self-examination and social behavior in the bottlenose dolphin (*Tursiops truncatus*). *Consciousness and Cognition, 4,* 205-224.

Menzel, E. W., Jr., Savage-Rumbaugh, E. S., & Lawson, J. (1985). Chimpanzee *(Pan troglodytes)* spatial problem solving with the use of mirrors and televised equivalents of mirrors. *Journal of Comparative Psychology, 99,* 211-217.

Mercado, E., III, Murray, S. O., Uyeyama, R. K., Pack, A. A., & Herman, L. M. (1998). Memory for recent actions in the bottlenosed dolphin *(Tursiops truncatus)*: Repetition of arbitrary behaviors using an abstract rule. *Animal Learning and Behavior, 26,* 210-218.

Miles, H. L. W. (1994). Me Chantek: The development of self-awareness in a signing orangutan. In S. T. Parker, R. W. Mitchell, & M. L. Boccia (Eds.), *Self-awareness in animals and humans: Developmental perspectives* (pp. 254-272). New York: Cambridge University Press.

Mitchell, R. W. (1993). Mental models of self-recognition: Two theories. *New Ideas in Psychology, 11,* 295-325.

Mitchell, R. W. (1994). Multiplicities of self. In S. T. Parker, R. W. Mitchell, & M. L. Boccia (Eds.), *Self-awareness in animals and humans: Developmental perspectives* (pp. 81-107). New York: Cambridge University Press.

Mitchell, R. W. (1997). A comparative-developmental approach to understanding imitation. In P. P. G. Bateson & P. H. Klopfer (Eds.), *Perspectives in ethology, Vol. 7: Alternatives* (pp. 183-215). London: Plenum Press.

Mitchell, R. W. (1999). Scientific and popular conceptions of the psychology of great apes from the 1790s to the 1970s: Déjà vu all over again. *Primate Report, 53,* 3-118.

Mitchell, R. W., & Anderson, J. R. (1993). Discrimination learning of scratching, but failure to obtain imitation and self-recognition in a long-tailed macaque. *Primates, 34,* 301-309.

Neisser, U. (1988). Five kinds of self-knowledge. *Philosophical Psychology, 1,* 35-59.

Papousek, H., & Papousek, M. (1974). Mirror image and self-recognition in young human infants: I. A new method of experimental analysis. *Developmental Psychobiology, 7,* 149-157.

Parker, S. T., Mitchell, R. W., & Boccia, M. L. (Eds.) (1994). *Self-awareness in animals and humans: Developmental perspectives.* New York: Cambridge University Press.

Patterson, F. G. (1978). Conversations with a gorilla. *National Geographic, 154,* 438-465.

Patterson, F. G. P., & Cohn, R. H. (1994). Self-recognition and self-awareness in lowland gorillas. In S. T. Parker, R. W. Mitchell, & M. L. Boccia (Eds.), *Self-awareness in animals and humans: Developmental perspectives* (pp. 273-290). New York: Cambridge University Press.

Perrett, D. I., Harries, M. H., Mistlin, A. J., Hietanen, J. K., et al. (1990). Social signals analyzed at the single cell level: Someone is looking at me, something touched me, something moved! *International Journal of Comparative Psychology, 4,* 25-55.

Petit, O., & Thierry, B. (1994). Responses to shadows in a group of Guinea baboons. *Human Evolution, 9,* 257-260.

Povinelli, D. J. (1994). How to create self-recognizing gorillas (but don't try it on macaques). In S. T. Parker, R. W. Mitchell, & M. L. Boccia (Eds.), *Self-awareness in animals and humans: Developmental perspectives* (pp. 291-300). New York: Cambridge University Press.

Povinelli, D. J., & Cant, J. G. H. (1995). Arboreal clambering and the evolution of self-conception. *Quarterly Review of Biology, 70,* 393-421.

Povinelli, D. J., Gallup, G. G., Jr., Eddy, T. J., Bierschwale, D. T., Engstrom, M. C., Perilloux, H. K., & Toxopeus, I. B. (1997). Chimpanzees recognize themselves in mirrors. *Animal Behaviour, 53,* 1083-1088.

Povinelli, D. J., Rulf, A. B., Landau, K. R., & Bierschwale, D. T. (1993). Self-recognition in chimpanzees (*Pan troglodytes*): Distribution, ontogeny, and patterns of emergence. *Journal of Comparative Psychology, 107,* 347-372.

Pryor, K., Haag, R., & O'Reilly, J. (1969). The creative porpoise: Training for novel behavior. *Journal of the Experimental Analysis of Behavior, 12,* 653-661.

Rizzolatti, G., Fadiga, L., Gallese, V., & Fogassi, L. (1996). Premotor cortex and the recognition of motor actions. *Cognitive Brain Research, 3,* 131-141.

Rochat, P., & Morgan, R. (1995). The function and determinants of early self-exploration. In P. Rochat (Ed.), *The self in infancy: Theory and research* (pp. 395-415). Amsterdam: Elsevier Science B.V.

Rogers, L. J. (1997). *Minds of their own.* St Leonards, NSW: Allen & Unwin.

Rumbaugh, D. M., Richardson, W. K., & Washburn, D. A. (1989). Rhesus monkeys (*Macaca mulatta*), video-tasks, and implications for stimulus-response spatial contiguity. *Journal of Comparative Psychology, 103,* 32-38.

Savage-Rumbaugh, E. S., & Rubert, E. (1986). Video representations of reality. In E. S. Savage-Rumbaugh (Ed.), *Ape language: From conditioned response to symbol* (pp. 299-323). New York: Columbia University Press.

Savage-Rumbaugh, E. S., Shanker, S. G., & Taylor, T. J. (1998). *Apes, language, and the human mind.* New York: Oxford University Press.

Serre, D., & Anderson, J. R. (1995). *The face in the mirror* (VHS videotape, 25 min). Paris: Leo Productions.

Shillito, D. J., Gallup, G. G., Jr., & Beck, B. B. (1999). Factors affecting mirror behaviour in western lowland gorillas, *Gorilla gorilla. Animal Behaviour, 57,* 999-1004.

Shimp, C. P. (1982). On metaknowledge in the pigeon: An organism's knowledge about its own behavior. *Animal Learning and Behavior, 10,* 358-364.

Suarez, S. D., & Gallup, G. G., Jr. (1981). Self-recognition in chimpanzees and orangutans, but not gorillas. *Journal of Human Evolution, 10,* 157-188.

Swartz, K. B., & Evans, S. (1994). Social and cognitive factors in chimpanzee and gorilla mirror behavior and self-recognition. In S. T. Parker, R. W.

Mitchell, & M. L. Boccia (Eds.), *Self-awareness in animals and humans: Developmental perspectives* (pp. 189-206). New York: Cambridge University Press.

Thompson, R. L., & Boatwright-Horowitz, S. L. (1994). The question of mirror-mediated self-recognition in apes and monkeys: Some new results and reservations. In S. T. Parker, R. W. Mitchell, & M. L. Boccia (Eds.), *Self-awareness in animals and humans: Developmental perspectives* (pp. 330-349). New York: Cambridge University Press.

Tobach, E., Skolnick, A. J., Klein, I., & Greenberg, G. (1997). Viewing of self and nonself images in a group of captive orangutans (*Pongo pygmaeus abelhi*). *Perceptual and Motor Skills, 84,* 355-370.

Tomasello, M. (1996). Do apes ape? In C. M. Heyes & B. G. Galef, Jr. (Eds.), *Social learning in animals: The roots of culture* (pp. 319-346). New York: Academic Press.

Vauclair, J. (1996). *Animal cognition: An introduction to modern comparative psychology.* Cambridge, MA: Harvard University Press.

Vauclair, J., & Fagot, J. (1993). Manual and hemispheric specialization in the manipulation of a joystick by baboons. *Behavioral Neuroscience, 107,* 210-214.

Visalberghi, E. (1997). Success and understanding in cognitive tasks: A comparison between *Cebus apella* and *Pan troglodytes. International Journal of Primatology, 18,* 811-830.

Visalberghi, E., & Fragaszy, D. (1990). Do monkeys ape? In S. T. Parker & K. R. Gibson (Eds.), *"Language" and intelligence in monkeys and apes* (pp. 247-273). Cambridge: Cambridge University Press.

Walraven, V., van Elsacker, L., & Verheyen, R. (1995). Reactions of a group of pygmy chimpanzees (*Pan paniscus*) to their mirror-images: Evidence of self-recognition. *Primates, 36,* 145-150.

Washburn, D. A., Gulledge, J. P., & Rumbaugh, D. M. (1997). The heuristic and motivational value of video reinforcement. *Learning and Motivation, 28,* 510-520.

Westergaard, G. C., & Hyatt, C. W. (1994). The responses of bonobos (*Pan paniscus*) to their mirror images: Evidence of self-recognition. *Human Evolution, 9,* 273-279.

Whiten, A., & Custance, D. (1996). Studies of imitation in chimpanzees and children. In C. M. Heyes & B. G. Galef, Jr. (Eds.), *Social learning in animals: The roots of culture* (pp. 291-318). New York: Academic Press.

Wilcoxon, H. C., Meier, G. W., Orlando, R., & Paulson, D. G. (1969). Visual self-stimulation in socially-living rhesus monkeys. In *Proceedings of the 2nd International Congress of Primatolology, Atlanta, GA, 1968* (pp. 261-266). Basel: Karger.

Pictorial perception: individual and group differences within the human species

J. B. Deręgowski

University of Aberdeen, Scotland

Abstract

This paper examines empirical evidence pertaining to perception of pictures by human beings. It is particularly concerned with the evidence that within the species differences are found between culturally disparate groups; and within such groups between subgroups differing in age and between men and women. It is stressed that whether a stimulus can be regarded as a picture depends on both the nature of the stimulus and the nature of the observer; in addition the task which a subject is requested to perform is a crucial determinant in any assessment of pictorial perception. In consequence stimuli which are seen as pictures by some observers may appear to other observers as mere meaningless lines and blotches or may evoke responses which would be appropriate if the stimulus were the depicted object or scene but not a picture; an infinity of intermediate responses is also available. Two characteristics of pictures, their ability to evoke perception of depth where none is present (eidolicity) and their ability to represent objects (epitomy) are described and their relationship to the skill of pictorial perception is briefly discussed.

Key words: Perception, pictures, culture, development, sex.

Correspondence should be sent to J. B. Deręgowski, University of Aberdeen, Department of Psychology, William Guild Building, Old Aberdeen, AB24 2UB, Scotland (e-mail: psy022@mailserv.abdn.ac.uk).

INTRODUCTION

This paper is concerned with difficulties of pictorial perception, with the consequent differences in perception of pictures said to prevail among distinct human groups, and with the significance of such differences as indices of cognitive functioning. It is not primarily concerned with the art of picture making. (It must be stressed also that concern here is with perception and not with the symbolic significance of depicted objects. A depicted lily is merely a lily. The fact that it may symbolise martyrdom is of no relevance to the thesis). By a picture is meant any pattern on a flat surface which by means of optical similarity to an object evokes a response which the depicted object could evoke.

Pliny the Elder in *Historia Naturalis* (Book 35), describes a contest between two Greek painters in the fifth century B.C. Parrahasius was competing with Zeuxis. Zeuxis painted a picture of a table with clusters of grapes upon it, so cunningly that birds flocked to peck at the fruit. In response Parrahasius brought out a picture and Zeuxis requested that it be uncovered only to find that it was a depiction of a linen sheet. Zeuxis handsomely yielded the victory saying that his picture beguiled only birds but the picture of Parrahasius beguiled him, a master painter. Later, we are told, Zeuxis painted a picture of a boy carrying bunches of grapes in a dish. Again the birds flocked. "I have painted the grapes better than the boy!" he concluded, "if it were not so the birds would have been too frightened to approach the grapes". These ancient observations are of immediate relevance to the subject of pictorial recognition and concern the matter of acceptability and evidence that pictorial recognition has occurred.

At the contest both the birds and Zeuxis responded to the pictorial stimuli; the birds pecked and Zeuxis requested that the linen cover be lifted. This does not mean that they necessarily identified the depicted objects in equal measure; that the birds saw the grapes as vividly as Zeuxis saw the cloth. It is possible that the birds did not see grapes, that they only saw peckable things, just as birds frightened by a butterfly's eye spots do not see, for they cannot possibly see, a large animal looking at them but merely a frightening signal (Hinton, 1973). The behaviour of the birds when the second of Zeuxis's pictures was displayed strengthens this caveat; depicted grapes evoke pecking; depicted boy, unlike depicted eyes on the wings of a butterfly, does not evoke fear. Classifications of depicted grapes by the birds and Zeuxis differ radically. Birds see them as one of peckable objects belonging to the same category as, say, aluminium milk bottle tops; Zeuxis sees them as a kind of fruit and could, if requested, say more about them indicating other categories to which they belong and which are not immediately apparent but are evoked by the picture through the picture's association with depicted objects, categories such as a "juice-yielding fruit", "fruit cultivated on trimmed bushes", "fruit which grows on bushes with tendrils", "fruit which is used for wine making", etc. In short, Zeuxis could define the depicted object in terms which would make its identification possible; whereas the response of the birds, precise as it is, does not lead to such an identification. However, verbal identification of a depicted object, although it implies recognition of its various attributes, does not necessarily mean that the picture is a perfect substitute for an object in circumstances when such substitution is entirely feasible.

The verisimilitude of Parrahasius's picture causes Zeuxis to make a perceptual error seemingly similar to that made by the birds. This does not usually happen. He does not normally mistake depiction of an object for an object. He does not fail to perceive the dual perceptual characteristics of a picture: a picture as a depiction of an object and a picture as an entirely different physical entity. Unlike Zeuxis's response, the response of the birds is not erroneous. They see peckable things and they peck them.

The adopted definition implies that pictures of objects can be created unintentionally. The best known instance of this are probably inkblots used for diagnostic purposes in personality tests. The subject undergoing the test is set to look for a picture, and generally finds within the inkblot a variety of depictions with remarkable ease.

But there are also pictures, products of an artist's consummate skill, which approximate closely to the views which would strike an eye but which yet are difficult to apprehend. M. Jakimowicz's chiaroscuro painting shown in Figure 1 is an example of this genre. Those viewing it generally apprehend, without any difficulty, the pair of entwined hands, but many of them find it difficult to see more. Even when they are given the picture's title "A Kiss" some still flounder. The scene which the picture correctly portrays is this: A man whose entwined hands are clearly visible is seated in an armchair and faces the viewer. He has black hair and a small triangle of his white forehead is just visible. A woman, whose white neck is also visible, leans over his left shoulder and kisses him. A tangled mass of her hair obscures his face, one strand shaped

like a musical clef hangs down and touches the front of his white shirt.
The difficulty, of seeing this immediately, demonstrates that even the
relatively pictorially sophisticated may not readily perceive some pictures. Pictures are not therefore a perceptually homogenous category; an
object which is clearly a picture to one viewer may be less of a picture
to another and not a picture at all to a third. This being so, group differences in pictorial perception should not cause surprise.

Before discussing these differences, it is apposite to recall the conversation with Mein Herr as reported by Lewis Carroll (1889). "What
do you consider the largest map that would be useful?" asks Mein Herr.
"About six inches to the mile." "Only six inches!" exclaimed Mein
Herr. "We very soon got to six yards to the mile, then we tried a hundred yards to the mile. And then came the grandest idea of all! We actually made a map of the country, on the scale of a mile to the mile!"
"Have you used it much?" I enquired. "It has never been spread out,
yet," said Mein Herr, "the farmers objected: they said it would cover

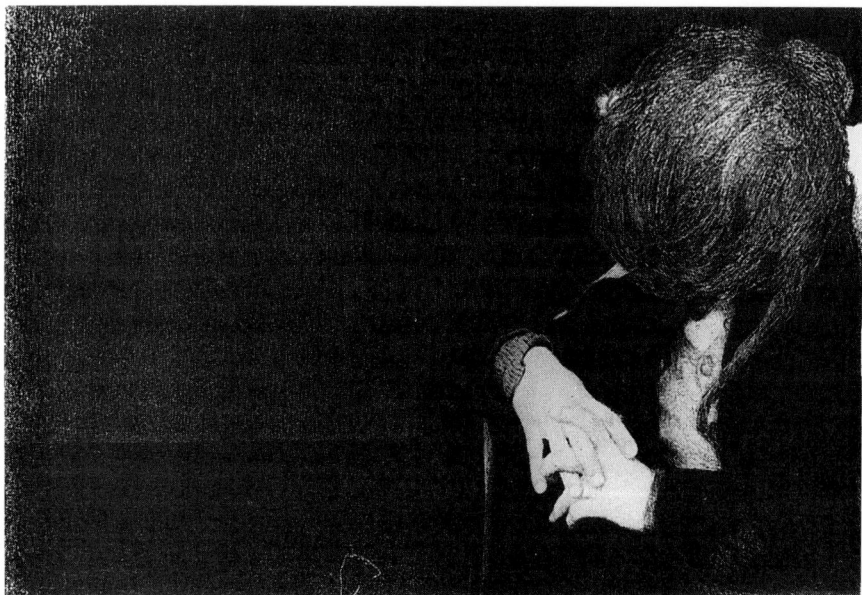

*Figure 1. "'A Kiss" by M. Jakimowicz (original in Muzeum Narodowe,
Warsaw).*

the whole country, and shut out the sunlight! So we now use the country itself, as its own map, and I assure you it does nearly as well." This solution may, indeed, be efficacious but it is not likely to help in understanding of the skills of map readers. As with maps, so with pictures. Pictures too form a continuum extending from pictures whose perceptual meaning is obscure to trompe l'oeil pictures which are readily mistaken for the depicted objects.

Each act of pictorial perception occurs therefore at an intersection of two continua, that of the pictorial attributes of a surface and that of pictorial sophistication of the observer; and the assessment of such an act depends greatly on the measures used, for the picture need not be apprehended fully to be recognised as a picture; recognition of the hands in Jakimowicz's picture is an act of pictorial perception but so is recognition of the picture as depicting a kissing. It matters therefore how pictorial perception is tested. The same subjects tested by means of the same pictures may on one set of criteria be classified as "competent pictorial perceivers" and yet another may show their competence to be questionable. A picture, therefore, can be considered as an act of either accidental or deliberately caused misperception. It is a result of a combination of the two vectors, the state of the perceiver and the inflow of information that an erroneous conclusion is reached and instead of a blotchy piece of canvas one sees, say, a flower. A change in either of the vectors may destroy the illusion, that is, it may oblige the observer to abandon the hypothesis which he/she has entertained in favour of another apparently more plausible hypothesis. The process of generating perceptual hypotheses, the importance of which Gregory (1968, 1973) has repeatedly stressed, is not confined to pictures. It is the normal process of perception which permits the organism to adapt to changing circumstances.

SOME EMPIRICAL OBSERVATIONS

Consider the traditional Piagetian sorting task. A child is given a number of stimuli in the form of toys or photographs of these toys. The toys are either motor cars or plastic animals. The cars are either passenger cars or lorries and the animals are either domestic or wild. Further, each toy is either yellow or red. In the sorting task the subjects are repeatedly required to subdivide the jumble of toys placed in front of them into as many categories as they can. Let us assume that on first sorting a subject divides the toys into two groups: cars and animals. Such a subject is then presented one by one with the groups he/she has created and asked whether he/she can categorise it further. On being presented with the "animals" the subject may categorise them, say, as red animals and yellow animals, thus still treating the wild animals and domestic animals as falling into the same category, the divisibility of which needs to be investigated. This process is followed until the subject indicates that he/she cannot create further categories. The ease of categorisation which this task measures will, not unexpectedly, vary among subjects. Some, relatively few, will be able to create immediately the eight perceptual categories, others may require to progress through a number of steps to reach this goal yet others may fail to reach it altogether by implying, say, that whilst yellow animals differ from red animals, wild animals and domestic animals are of the same category. Further the subjects' performance may differ depending on whether toys or photographs of the toys are used as stimuli, as shown by Derȩgowski and Serpell (1971) in their study comparing Scottish and Zambian children. They found that whilst the performance of the two groups on toys was about equal, their performance on coloured photographs differed. Such variations in categorisation occur among subjects who respond identically when requested to name individual photographs or individual toys, and have no difficulty in naming their colours nor of deciding, say, whether a particular animal is domestic or wild. Thus on a test of labelling no inter-group differences may be found although on the tests of categorisation they may prevail. Since children's ability to see pictures is generally informally assessed merely by asking children to name depicted objects, this discrepancy normally escapes notice, as Sigel's (1978) seminal work, from which Derȩgowski and Serpell's experiment was derived, shows. The effect described is not to be observed only in children; Aberdonian women learn to allocate objects to arbitrarily designated spaces on a table significantly faster than they learn to allocate pictures of these objects, although they readily label both objects and their depictions (Derȩgowski & Jahoda, 1975).

There are, therefore, three variables involved in the subjects' pictorial response:

    1. the nature of the picture,
    2. the level of the subject's pictorial sophistication, and
    3. the nature of the response sought by the experimenters.

The above considerations show that the nature of the response has to be particularly carefully considered when evaluating the observations; the slippery slope of over-interpretation is ever present.

Reports of unusual responses to pictures by members of non-pictorial cultures are dramatic and polarised. There occurs, we are told, either a total failure to comprehend that a pattern shown depicts anything or such a vigorous reaction as to suggest that the picture is mistaken for the depicted object or scene. Instances of failure to recognise pictures are reported by Laws (see Beach, 1901), Herskovits (1948), Kidd (1905), Barley (1986) and others (see Deręgowski 1980b). Laws wrote from Nyasaland (now Malawi) as follows:

"Take a picture in black and white, and the natives cannot see it. You may tell the native: 'This is a picture of an ox and a dog'; and the people will look at it and look at you and that look says that they consider you a liar ... If there are boys about, you say: 'This is really a picture of an ox and a dog. Look at the horn of the ox, and there is his tail!' and the boy will say: 'Oh! yes and there is the dog's nose and eyes and ears!' Then the old people will look again and clap their hands and say, 'Oh! yes, it is a dog!'." (Beach, 1901, p. 468.)

Kidd (1905) agreed with Laws:

"The natives are frequently quite incapable of seeing pictures at first and wonder what the smudge on the paper is there for. When they see that it represents something, they are very excited. Some see a picture instantly, while old men frequently fail to see anything at all, no matter how long and patiently one tries to explain the matter to them; occasionally they become quite irritable because others say they can see the picture."

The reports describe the difficulty but they also suggest that the initially severe difficulty is not insurmountable; it seems that, at least in younger observers, it can be overcome by simple instruction. It seems likely that after such instruction the youth will find the inability of their elders as puzzling as did the pictorially sophisticated instructors.

Instances of exaggerated reactions to pictures are reported by Livingstone (1857), Fraser (1923), and Thompson (1885). Livingstone and Fraser describe how pictures cast upon an improvised screen horrified the viewers, who fled. Thompson states that European women depicted on photographs were thought to be real, but asleep. Livingstone's magic lantern show given to Shinte and his court was a particularly exciting event:

"Shinte was most anxious to see the pictures of the magic lantern ... he had his principal men and the same crowd of court beauties near him as at the reception. The first picture exhibited was Abraham about to slaughter his son Isaac; it was shown as large as life, and the uplifted knife was in the act of striking the lad; the Balonda men remarked that the picture was much more like a god than the things of wood or clay they worshipped ... The ladies listened with silent awe; but, when I moved the slide, the uplifted dagger moving towards them, they thought it was to be sheathed in their bodies instead of Isaac's. 'Mother! Mother!' all shouted at once, and off they rushed helter-skelter, tumbling pell-mell over each other, and over the little idol-huts and tobacco-bushes: we could not get one of them back again."

The bipolarity of the reported responses: "they see nothing/they think it is real", need not occasion surprise. Such unexpected responses are likely to be noticed and thought to be of sufficient interest to merit recording. The veracity of these reports is not questionable and the most plausible explanation for those observations remains that recognition of a picture depends greatly, as one would expect, on the nature of the picture. A picture cast by a magic lantern in darkness, suspended as if it were vertically in mid-air (as was the case in both Livingstone's and Fraser's observations) provides visual cues of different quality than does a picture which is presented on a clearly apprehensible background as, say, a glossy photograph (Herskovits, 1948) which often is smaller than the depicted object and palpably flat.

A confirmation of the importance of the material on which a picture is made and of the manner in which it is presented is provided by a study carried out by the Muldrows (Deręgowski, Muldrow, & Muldrow, 1972) in Ethiopia. The Mekan (Me'en), members of a remote population which had no pictorial art and little contact with such art of other cultures, responded to pictures drawn on paper by crumpling the paper and listening to the noise, by sniffing this unfamiliar substance and even by tasting it. They entirely ignored the pictures. However, when pictures were presented on coarse cloth, a material with which the Mekan were familiar, a remarkable change occurred. Most subjects, albeit slowly and with the experimenter's assistance (the experimenter pointing to the features of a large bold figure laid on the ground), recognised the depicted, familiar animals. It would seem therefore that when the attention of the observers was not distracted by an unfamiliar material on which pictures were presented (paper), they found the task to be easier, or rather, they understood the demands of the task to be different and responded differently, paying attention to the surface markings in accord with the expectations of a typical "western" observer. Similar observations were made by Nadel (1939), who reported that when testing Yoruba boys in Northern Nigeria "they could not identify outline drawings on paper of a man, or even of such common objects as a hut, a crocodile, or a pot, although exactly the same outline figures were at once identified and described when they appeared in carvings or on native leather work, i.e., in their familiar, established cultural context." (p. 190). Some of the Mekan, when looking at the picture flat on the ground and asked what was the depicted animal which they had just identified doing, responded: "It is lying down". When the cloth was then lifted so that it hung vertically they said: "Now, it is standing up". Such orientation effect is not normally encountered in more pictorial cultures; one would see such an animal as upright whether its picture appeared in a book laid flat on the desk or held in hand. In view of the evidence it is difficult to sustain the claim that members of remote, pictorially naive populations fail as a rule to see pictures. It seems more likely that they fail to see particular kinds of pictures presented in particular circumstances.

RECOGNITION OF DEPICTIONS - EPITOMY

The difficulties experienced by some when viewing Jakimowicz's *The Kiss* on the one hand, and the ease with which silhouettes are recognised on the other, suggest that certain representations of objects are more easily recognised than others, notwithstanding the fact that they are optically equally legitimate, and therefore that the essence of the artist's skill resides in his ability to abstract the signal characteristics from objects and to depict them. The characteristic that is of particular concern here is the object's shape. Parsimony implies that it is unlikely that such skill was evolved solely in order to enable the Artist to flourish. It is more likely that the skill is that involved in recognition, and in mnemonic encoding of all objects, and that depiction of the characteristics of the shape of all objects, animate or not, is governed by the same rules.

Examination of Palaeolithic rock paintings offers a hint as to the most important of these rules. The majority of animals depicted are shown as seen from the side. The depictions are therefore those of the animal form as contained within the pronounced contour – a ridge – of the animal's body. Several studies demonstrate the importance of such ridges for classification of objects (Deręgowski, Parker, & Dziurawiec, 1996; Deręgowski & McGeorge, 1998), and for recognition and depiction (Dziurawiec & Deręgowski, 1992; Deręgowski & Dziurawiec, 1996) of geometric solids as well as animal models. They show that such contours have particular perceptual cogency and that their non-transformed depiction (that is, depiction as if they were in the observer's fronto-parallel plane) provides a very strong cue for recognition of the depicted object.

Reported failures of some of the informants to recognise familiar depicted objects might have been the consequence of the use of non-typical contours in depictions. This speculation is supported by Forge's (1970) observations of the Abelam of New Guinea. He recorded that "… the Abelam's lack of understanding of photographs … remains almost absolute, and provides possible support for my hypothesis that they have very definite and limited expectations about what they will see on any two dimensional surface made to be looked at …" (p. 287). Their difficulties were however, as Forge further observes, related to the poses of the portrayed people. On traditional photographs to which the Abelam are used, "… the subjects stand rigidly at attention facing the camera, against a background of either a white sheet or a wall. No Abelam have any difficulty today in 'seeing' such a photograph and in recognising and naming the individual concerned if they know him. But when shown photographs of themselves in action, or of any pose other than face or full figure looking directly at the camera, they cease to be able to 'see' the photograph at all. Even people from other villages who came specially because they knew I had taken a photograph of a relative who had subsequently died, and were often pathetically keen to see his features, were initially unable to see him at all, turning the photograph in all directions." (p. 287). Since the other poses, which the Abelam find difficult, do not exhibit forcefully the typical contours, the implication of these observations is obvious. It is noteworthy too that people do not have as readily observable immutable typical contours as do the quadrupeds most frequently depicted in ancient rock pictures. This makes people difficult to draw whatever their pose and may be the cause of the rarity and, historically, of the late appearance of their portrayals (Deręgowski, 1998).

Ability to see pictures in inkblots and the readiness with which M. Etienne de Silhouette's efforts bore fruit both testify to the fact that a picture need not contain any direct perceptual hints of the third dimension (i.e., of pictorial depth) in order to be recognised as a picture of an object which is known to be three dimensional. Thus a silhouette showing a face in profile is seen as a picture, indeed often as a picture of a particular person, even though it cannot possibly be seen as having a third dimension. There are, at the other perceptual extreme, flat patterns which evoke perception of depth, although they are not recognised as representing anything in particular. Simple forms of such figures are commonly called visual illusions, more complex forms which are perceptually unstable are known, misleadingly, as impossible figures. The Ponzo figure (Figure 2) is an example of the former and the "two pronged trident" (Figure 3) of the latter type. The distinction between two essentially different kinds of representation (those recognisable although seen as flat and those perceptually evoking depth, yet unrecognisable) is important for categorisation of pictures (Deręgowski, 1990a). Pictures which are perceived as depicting objects although they do not evoke the illusion of a third dimension are said to be epitomic, those which evoke the illusion of a third dimension are said to be eidolic.

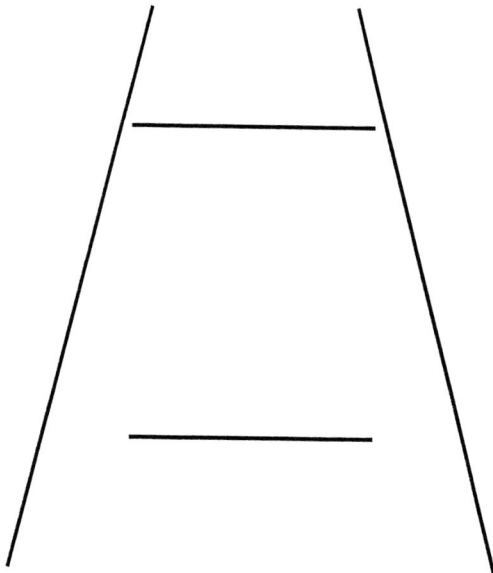

Figure 2. The Ponzo figure.

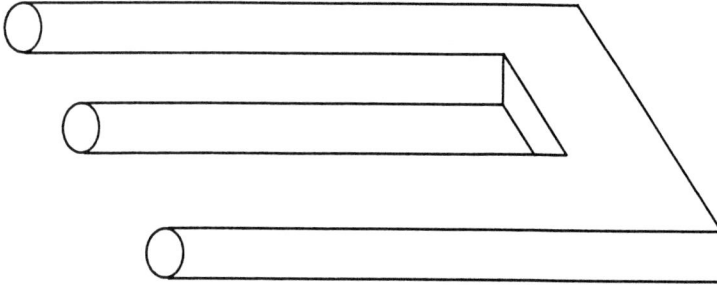

Figure 3. The two-pronged trident.

Hudson (1962) presented a group of African mine labourers with two pictures, shown in Figure 4, and asked each of them which of the two he preferred. There was an overwhelming preference for the spread-eagled elephant, the sole contrary voice (one of 40 subjects tested) being that of a timid soul who preferred the other figure since he did not like elephants which are dangerously prancing about. Hudson's prancing elephant is not stylistically unique. Analogous "distortions" are the characteristic feature of certain artistic styles, notably that of West Canadian Indians (Boas, 1897), and can also be found in other cultures. Consider the portrayal of a cart on an Old Slavonic (5th – 1st B.C.) funerary urn excavated by Łuka, (1968, 1971) on the Polish Baltic Coast (Figure 5). The wheels of the vehicle are drawn as two circles; they are shown in the same manner as are the legs of Hudson's spread-eagled elephant. Such portrayals of wheeled vehicles are frequent and ubiquitous. This fact and their acceptance by the viewers suggest that such representations may be results of the modus operandi of the human visual system. The essence of the effect is simply this: objects are not equally recognisably portrayed from all possible stances, even though resulting depictions may be optically equally justifiable. This principle was clearly demonstrated by Jakimowicz's picture (Figure 1) and is further reinforced by the depictions of wheels as circles and by the fact that a wheel represented as it would appear when its axle is viewed normally would not be recognisable.

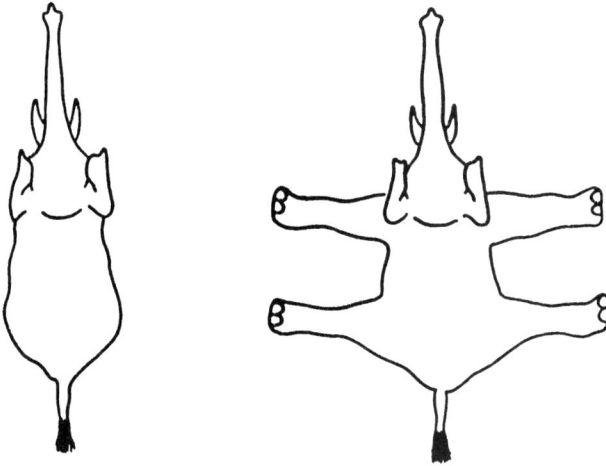

Figure 4. Hudson's two portrayals of an elephant (After W. Hudson, 1962).

*Figure 5. A cart depicted on
a funerary urn excavated on
the Polish Baltic Coast
(Łuka, 1968/1971).*

The difficulty which the Polish potter, and many other artists encounter in depicting a cart is caused by the non-coplanarity of carts' wheels. (A bicycle would present no such problem.) Depiction of the wheels "at their best" leads to figural incoherence. Viewers' tolerance of this incoherence, as demonstrated by the fact that such drawings are readily recognised although they may seem somewhat odd, suggests a considerable perceptual "looseness" of the relationship among the elements of the image. This very effect is probably responsible for some surprising responses to pictures made by the pictorially unsophisticated. Response "elephant" to Figure 6 made by an elderly Kenyan rustic can be explained, as Shaw (1969) observes, as resulting from attending solely to the shape of the animal's feet. The reader can convince him/herself of this by covering the figure so that only the feet are exposed. They do look elephantine. The pars-pro-toto response to a picture encountered in Kenya is clearly related to those reported by Binet (1895) over a century ago: young children confronted with depictions of syncretic animals (body of a dog with cow's horned head and horse's tail, say) did not find these figures confusing and named them simply by giving the name of the animal corresponding to one of the elements. Conceptually the same kind of error is made by a bird which mistakes the eye-spots on a moth's wings for a pair of eyes (Hinton, 1973). Disjointed elements of a picture need not be physically distinct parts of a model. They may indeed constitute a physically cohesive, but perceptually incoherent whole as they do in the case of some animals. The Australian Aboriginal rock pictures bear witness to this (Deręgowski, 1995), as do children's drawings of perceptually incoherent models (Deręgowski, 1990b; Dziurawiec & Deręgowski, 1992).

Not unexpectedly, since interpretations of pictures are affected by individual perceptual inclinations, occasional acrimonious disputes erupt, even among the learned, such as that between Leach (1954, 1958) and Brendt (1958) concerning the significance of a pattern found on Trobriand shields, and shown in Figure 7. Leach maintained that it depicts a witch in the form of a flying fox, as can be clearly seen from an "unfolded" version of the picture shown in Figure 7a. Brendt maintained that the design depicts a sexual act, whilst Tindale (1959) joining the debate said that he saw the design as a conglomeration of small meaningful elements such as local fish. (Deręgowski [1984] questions, on perceptual grounds, the likelihood of the transformation postulated by Leach.)

Figure 6. A tortoise/elephant (After B. Shaw, 1969).

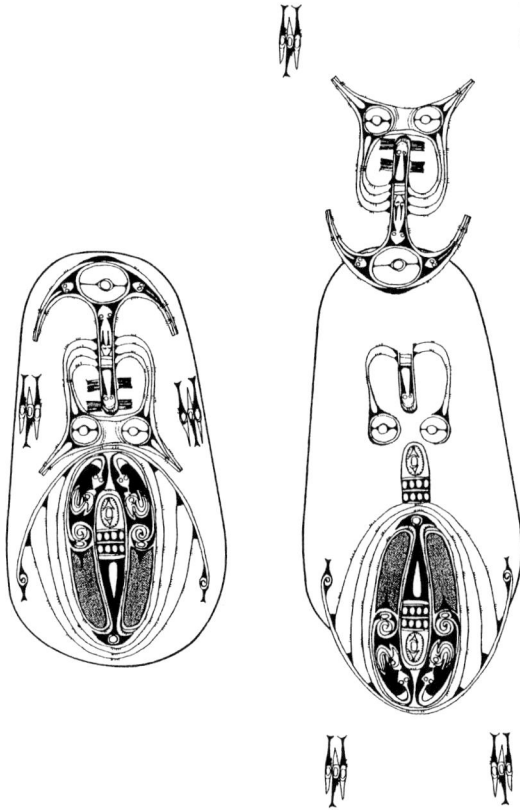

Figure 7. A Trobriand shield pattern.

PERCEPTION OF PICTORIAL DEPTH – EIDOLICITY

The simplest device for measurement of perception of the effect of eidolic cues is probably that called Kwengo callipers. It was used for investigations amongst the Bushmen of the Caprivi Strip (Deręgowski & Bentley, 1986). It consists of two wooden battens, square in section, and hinged together so that they can form a "V" shape, the angle of which is adjustable. When testing, drawings of the callipers are shown to the subject who is required to set a pair of callipers in the hand, just as they are in the drawings. Figure 8 shows a drawing of a pair of callipers so oriented that the 90° angle at which they are set is represented in the plane of the paper by an oblique angle. A subject performing the test can ignore the eidolic cues of the picture entirely and set the angle of the callipers in the hand to correspond exactly to the angle shown in the plane of the picture or he/she can take cognisance of the eidolic cues and set the angle accordingly. Setting the angle at 90° would, in the case now discussed, show that the eidolic cues were taken into account to such an extent that the drawing was treated as if it were another pair of callipers. A setting intermediate between 90° and the angle in the plane of the figure would also indicate that the eidolic cues were attended to and would suggest a perceptual compromise akin to that described by Thouless (1972), when discussing the notion of shape constancy. The Kwengo callipers task was used with two samples of children living in the same rural environment but belonging to different tribes (the Kwengo and the Sekele) and a group of urban Zulu children. Their performance was measured by assessing the angular difference between responses to eidolic and non-eidolic pictures showing the same angle in the plane of the paper. This measure yielded the following proportions of perceivers of the pictorial depth,

    Kwengo: 0.86
    Sekele: 0.60
    Zulu: 0.55

It is apparent that the Kwengo, possibly by reasons of hereditary disposition, showed greater tendency to respond to the pictures' eidolic cues. The likelihood of a hereditary effect is sustained by an earlier study carried out by Coren and Porac (1979), which concerned familial resemblances of responses to Müller-Lyer and Ebbinghaus illusions. The former are of particular interest in the present context since they pertain to an illusion resulting from misperception of eidolic cues (Gregory,

1968; Segall, Campbell, & Herskovits, 1966). The results reported suggest that some of the genetic transmission is likely to be involved in determining susceptibility of individual subjects to Müller-Lyer illusion. It should however be noted that the difference among the three African samples does not mean that the Sekele and the Zulu children are insensitive to pictorial depth cues in general. It merely indicates that they are less sensitive when tested by means of the Kwengo callipers.

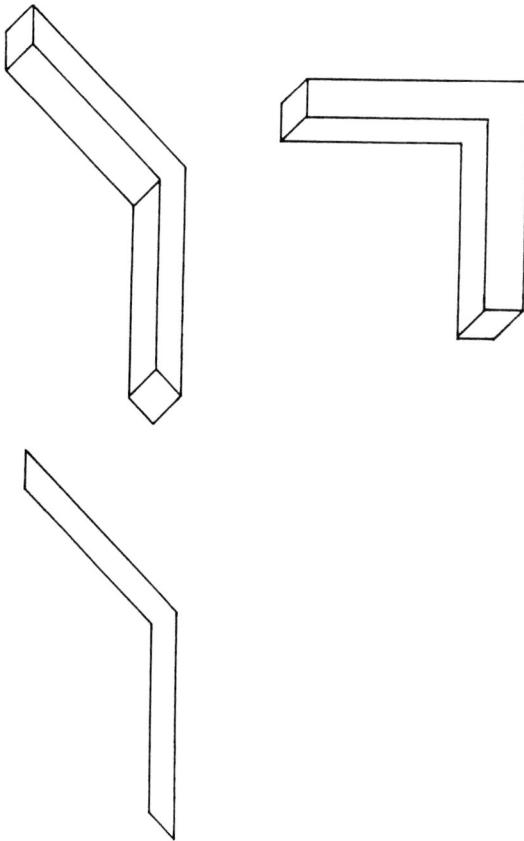

Figure 8. The Kwengo callipers stimuli. Top row: two views of callipers set at right angles. Both pictures are eidolic. Bottom row: depiction of one of the faces of the figure shown immediately above. A non-eidolic drawing.

Inter-population differences on perceptual tasks concerning perception of eidolic patterns are commonly found. The most extensive relevant records derive from the studies of visual illusions extending from Rivers's (1905) pioneering days to the classical work of Segall, Campbell, and Herskovits (1966), and beyond. A variety of tests have been used to assess the difficulties of eidolic perception. Hudson (1960) used specially designed pictures and carefully questioned about the perceived distances between various elements, a pair at a time. The elements were portrayals of a hunter and two animals (a duiker and an elephant) and their correct identification was essential if the correct responses were to be made (an elephant mistaken for a cat reverses the direction of the depth cue provided by the "elephant-duiker" pair). The test therefore relied on correct epitomic responses for assessment of eidolic perception of the picture. Other tasks tackled eidolicity more directly by requesting responses to stimuli which did not call for recognition of elements. Deręgowski (1968) required his subjects to build models of simple depicted structures, using bamboo splints. He also asked (Deręgowski, 1976c) his subjects to draw pictures of regular geometric shapes either with models present or from memory. The models were presented as solids or as pictures of solids. The tendency to introduce distortions into drawings of depicted models done from memory similar to those found in drawings of 3D models, suggested that the drawings were encoded in memory as 3D models. A carefully controlled reconstruction test was used by Jahoda in Ghana (Jahoda & McGurk, 1974a, 1974b); Deręgowski (1980a) evaluated the significance of the results it yielded. An entirely different measure, Gregory's Box (Gregory, 1968) which relies on the interplay between monocular and binocular vision – the distance of a monocularly seen stimulus is assessed by using both eyes – has not unfortunately been used often. Deręgowski and Byth (1970) used it successfully in their investigation of Hudson's stimuli. Copying of impossible figures provides yet another method of assessment. It can be argued that the subject who finds such a figure easy to copy does so because he/she does not perceive the eidolic character of the mutually contradictory elements. (For example the two ends of the two-pronged trident shown in Figure 3 do not appear to the subject to be mutually contradictory because they are seen simply as flat patterns.) This reasoning led Deręgowski (1969) to compare the performance of Zambian children on two tasks, namely, construction of depicted models using plasticine balls and bamboo splints and copying of the two pronged trident (Figure 3).

He found that subjects who built clearly three dimensional models found the copying task more difficult than did subjects whose models did not indicate that pictorial depth was perceived. The data were interpreted as showing that difficulties of perception inherent to the two-pronged trident are related to perception of pictorial depth. This interpretation was later (Young & Deręgowski, 1981) shown to be erroneous. Their finding was that young children's ease of copying such figures was related to a weak tendency to see figures as cohesive. It appears that the difficulties are associated not with perception of pictorial depth but with perception of the relationship between various parts of the figure which are seen as having depth. Observers may perceive elements of the figure as having a third dimension and yet be unconcerned when such three-dimensional elements are spatially mutually contradictory. Young and Deręgowski's finding does not however weaken the support which Deręgowski's earlier data provide for existence of group differences in pictorial perception. Further, if absence of difficulties when interpreting impossible figures is related to lack of concern with integration of the stimuli, then one would expect such failure to occur when dealing with possible figures too. Subjects who fail to integrate would be expected, for example, to build more "incoherent" models when given a picture and asked to construct a model. This is indeed so (Deręgowski & Bentley, 1987). It appears that integration of pictorial stimuli is central to the problem at hand.

The extent of mutual influence of pictorial elements in the eidolic context is demonstrated by the experiments on implicit shape constancy (Deręgowski, 1976b, 1976c). Deręgowski presented his subjects with a drawing of a cube with a simple geometrical figure on one of its faces and with that figure on its own. The subject's task was to choose from a selection of figures, such as shown in Figures 9a and 9b, one that looked most like the stimulus originally briefly presented. There was a significant difference between the responses made to the two types of stimulus. Figures chosen when the initiating stimulus incorporated a drawing of a cube were markedly more similar to the figure which would appear if the cube were presented with the relevant face in the subject's fronto-parallel plane. This "constancy" bias, which is related to perception of pictorial depth as measured by a construction task, was

not equal in all cultures. It was weaker in a sample of African children
than in Scottish children.

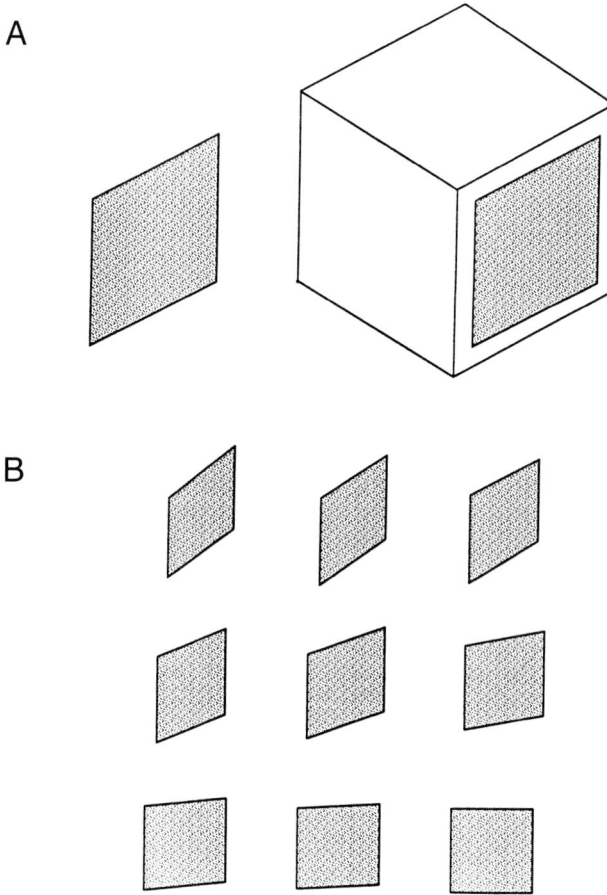

*Figure 9. Stimuli used in the implicit-shape constancy experiment. A: a control
figure and a cube incorporating the control. B: the response matrix.*

The problem of integration of depicted scenes was explored by Nadel
(1937, 1939) in West Africa. He reported marked differences between
the Yoruba and the Nupe, and found that these differences accorded
with the general cultural patterns of the two populations.

"The religion of the Yoruba", Nadel reports, is "characterized by an elaborate and rationalized hierarchical system of deities, each of which has its specific, specialized duty and function. The Nupe have no such system; their religious beliefs centre round a concept of magic of the 'mana' type, i.e., vague, abstract, impersonal power. In the rich, highly developed realistic art of the Yoruba the main *motif* of pictures, plastics and wooden images is the human figure; religious and mythical emblems of this kind play an important part in their life. Again, the Nupe have nothing of the sort, their art is imageless, they have but crude wall paintings, and their strength lies in ornamental, decorative art. Also the Yoruba have a strong sense for pantomime and drama, for which again there is not parallel among the Nupe." (p. 197)

The members of the two tribes differed markedly on description of pictures, a technique inspired by Bartlett (1932), "Among the Yoruba, ... the details ... serve as centres for an interpretation which endeavours to lend a unitary and consistent *meaning* to the whole picture. ... Now among the Nupe there is surprisingly little of such attempts to read a meaning into the picture" (p. 205).

This disparity between the two groups becomes more salient when re-call of previously seen pictures was requested. "Among the Yoruba the proportion of meaning-oriented interpretations increases from descrip-tion to recall, among the Nupe it decreases" (Bartlett, 1932, p. 208). The task is therefore not merely perceptual but more broadly cognitive. This is noteworthy but falls out with the scope of the present review.

It should be noted that the impossible figures themselves are evidence of the importance of the integration process, and that an artist making a picture is prone to the same kinds of errors as its viewer. In conse-quence, impossible figures do occur in works of art long before Reutersvärd and Escher consciously incorporated them into their designs, but they are there as unwitting lapses. An instance of such an occurrence is the depiction of the loom in a French fifteenth century miniature illustrating Boccaccio's *De claris mulieribus*, shown in Figure 10.

Another measure which addresses the problem of the subjects' ability to see a picture as a whole is provided by incomplete pictures: pictures in which certain areas have been deliberately blocked out, such as were used by Gollin (1960, 1961, 1962) and illustrated in Figure 11. It has been shown that when responding to coherent pictures, some subjects treat distinct elements as if they were independent but meaningful enti-

Figure 10. A fifteenth century French miniature.

ties. Incomplete pictures diminish the likelihood of such responses; they do not furnish a scattering of independent elements but of a set of essentially meaningless blotches which have to be integrated to form a meaningful depiction. A conceptually intermediate figure in which individual elements are meaningful and so are their arrangements, can also be designed as Arcimboldo's (1527-1593) faces show. These works of art represent human faces by depicting collages of fruit or animals or other elements, as exemplified by le Petit Larousse (1999), Osborne (1981, p. 71), and Broby-Johansen (1960, p. 158). Such open acknowledgement that a depiction can have several meanings (a cucumber, say, can also be a pendulous nose) has since been made repeatedly by many imitators. Conceptually the notion parallels those of a little boy who uses a carrot to make a snowman's nose and two pieces of charcoal to make his eyes. Developmental studies show that maturation brings about ability to see the significance of the assembly of perceptually independent components in an object and to recognise the picture's dual significance. Such pictures have been used by Elkind (1969) but unfortunately they have not been widely used in cross-cultural investigations. They will not be considered here. Their putative import for understanding of the perceptual mechanism is considered briefly by Deręgowski (1980b). Bentley (1986)

Figure 11. An example of an incomplete figure.

used incomplete pictures to investigate Murray and Szymczyk's (1978) notion that not all elements of a figure were equally weighty so far as perception is concerned, and that deletion of some of them is likely to have much more deleterious effect than deletion of some others. He reports that Zulu children appeared to make use of the distinctive features of depicted objects later in life than do their American counterparts. In an extension of this study (Bentley & Deręgowski, 1987) incorporating other groups (Kxoe Bushmen, White South Africans, and Zulu), further inter-group differences emerge. Those obtained by means of pictures with 80% line deletion are shown in Figure 12. Clearly, and this is borne out by statistical analysis, the outlying group is Kxoe. Kxoe ability to identify depicted objects is superior to those of the Zulus and the Whites, who do not mutually differ.

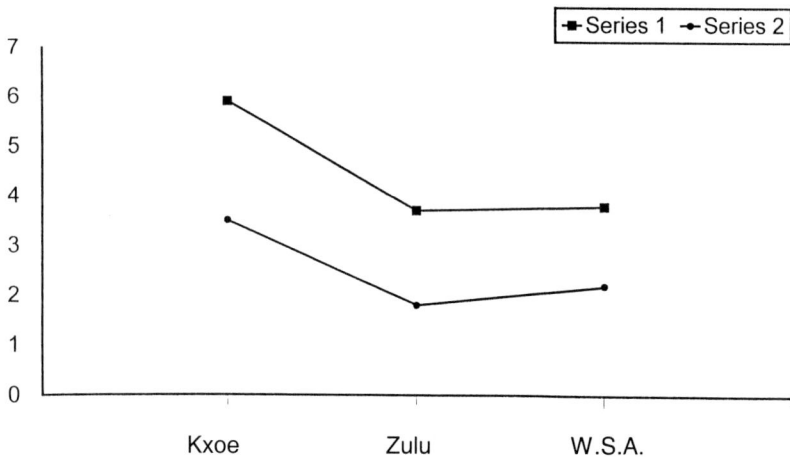

Figure 12. Mean numbers of incomplete figures correctly identified (out of 12) (Bentley & Deręgowski, 1987).

This brief review of empirical evidence shows that differences of pictorial perception prevail:
- among groups differing in age, notably between younger and older children, and
- among groups differing in cultural/genetic endowment (these two characteristics are generally confounded).

They are also present between sexes. The reported differences between the sexes concern, primarily, eidolic characteristics of pictures. A large body of evidence for this has been gathered unintentionally in the course of investigations of inter-sex differences in spatial perception since it is assumed by many, with rather less justification than would ideally be desirable, that the differences in perception of depicted space (eidolic differences) are tantamount to differences in perception of the real space. For a thorough review of these studies and for a meta-analysis of results, see Voyer, Voyer, and Bryden (1995). The evidence gathered shows consistent difference between men and women on certain "spatial" tests. An investigation specifically intended to compare men and women on two tasks, one concerned with real space and another with its depiction, has shown that the sexes differ (Deręgowski, Shepherd, & Slaven, 1997). The task used was devised by Bartel (Bartel, 1960; see also Deręgowski, 1989a; Deręgowski & Parker, 1996). The subject was required to place four "telephone poles" at equal intervals between two "telephone poles" already in position. The task can be presented either in 3D space or on a drawing such as that shown in Figure 13. A replication of Bartel's experiments (in which for the pictorial task a computer display was used and the original figure was therefore simplified), yielded the expected difference between men and women under both 3D and pictorial conditions. Women seemed less influenced by the perspective; they set the intervals between neighbouring poles more nearly objectively equal than did men. Since the effect was observed both in the 3D space and in pictorial space, there appears to be an association between responses in the two kinds of space.

An observer looking at an inkblot can indulge in a perceptual game of trying to see a portrayal in the random trace and does generally succeed in doing so. In these circumstances the pictorial vector of the blot is very weak and the dominant vector is that of the observer's pictorial expertise and the willingness to engage in the game by selectively attending to various features of the pattern.

Seen within this framework, the issues of failure to see a picture when one is intended are essentially those of wrong hypothesis of misplaced attention. The Mekan (Me'en) responses to figures printed on paper, which to them was a new unknown material, provide a particularly telling example of this difficulty as Serpell and Deręgowski (1980) point out. An array of cues is normally available to the observer, who will treat them differently depending on his/her experience and need; he/

she may choose to ignore some whilst regarding others as particularly weighty. The relative weightiness of the cues may not be apparent to an uninitiated observer. It may indeed be a result of intensive training as is often the case with industrial inspectors (Lynn, 1948; Thomas, 1962).

Figure 13. Bartel's stimulus (After K. Bartel, 1960).

Palaeolithic pictures, or rather Palaeolithic patterns which we take to be pictures, inform us of the importance of the typical contours for depiction. These contours, which are perceptually salient features of objects, do, when transferred onto flat surfaces, continue their strong perceptual association with objects, a fact confirmed by the design of the road signs in which typical contour designs dominate (Derȩgowski, 1990a).

Indeed the perceptual system appears to behave as if it were searching for the typical contour and when portrayals do not show this contour as if it were in the plane of the picture, eidolicity often results. This process can be described in terms of Welford's (1968) economy principle, by assuming that integrability of the stimuli is the main factor affecting the operation of that principle. Welford states that a transformation of a flat picture into a three-dimensional percept is governed by the rule of "perceptual economy"; that is, it occurs only when "it is worth it". The effect is easily demonstrable by presenting subjects with figures composed of identical elements but having, when perceived as three-dimensional, markedly different spatial attributes. Thus the solid shown in Figure 14a has only an axis of skew symmetry, but that shown in Figure 14b has a plane of symmetry. Transformation of the latter figure would therefore be more likely. This is indeed the case; only three out of eighteen Zambian children built a three-dimensional structure when asked to build the model shown in Figure 14a but twelve out of eighteen did so when responding to Figure 14b (Deręgowski, 1976d). (It is easy to show that it is the symmetry rather than the mere number of elements that affects the response by adding a member to Figure 14b, thus rendering its three dimensional percept asymmetrical; the resulting figure seems flatter.)

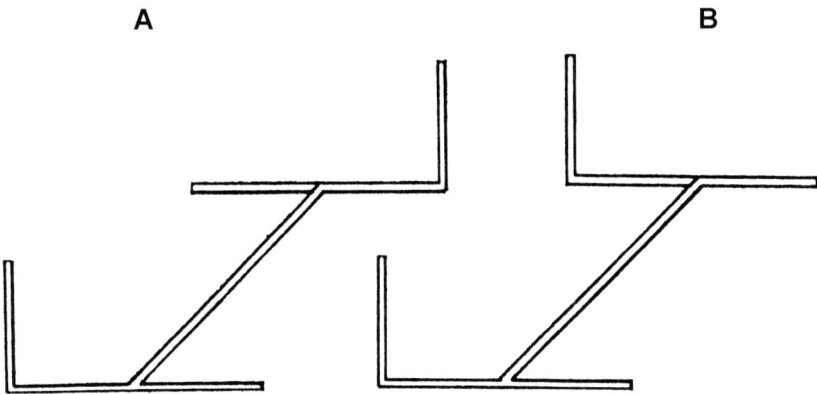

A   B

Figure 14. Stimuli used to verify Welford's (1970) "Economy principle".

The eidolic characteristics of such simple figures are readily perceived and responded to even by relatively unsophisticated subjects.

This need not occasion surprise for the figures in question are akin to the well known illusion figures, and illusions, although subject to inter-population differences, are virtually universal (Segall, Campbell, & Herskovits, 1960), and some of them are not confined to the human species. Thus the Ponzo illusion, a result of misapplication of the scaling mechanism, which treats cues derived from a flat surface as if they were dispersed in space, has been shown to be present in other primates (Benhar & Samuel, 1982; Bayne & Davis, 1983; Fujita, 1996) as well as in horses (Timney & Keil, 1996) and birds (Fujita, Blough, & Blough, 1991). Eidolic cue of convergence which is the essence of the illusion is, therefore, clearly apprehended by lower species. It is not known, however, whether other eidolic cues are equally readily perceived by them, or whether, for example, they would be able to discriminate readily among Perkins's representations of solid figures (Perkins, 1972; Perkins & Deręgowski, 1982), or "possible" and "impossible" figures.

It is evident from the examples of camouflage and mimicry adduced by Hinton (1973) that epitomic pictorial perception is also to be found in lower species. The evidence of butterfly eye spots referred to earlier is a particularly clear instance of this since the eye spots appear on a flat "painter's" surface.

CONCLUDING COMMENTS

In fine, it has to be repeated that a picture cannot be defined only in terms of the physical characteristics of an object. Its description involves the characteristics of the perceiver. This very fact ensures inter-observer differences as to which patterns constitute pictures. This in turn ensures group differences. It does not predict that responses to pictures, or any other pictorial perception phenomena will be uniformly distributed within any group. Nor are they. Within *Homo sapiens* there are clear age differences and sex differences; there are also differences among genetic/cultural groups. The presence of sex differences and the striking difference between the performance of Kxoe Bushmen and that of the Zulu, the Sekele and the South African whites suggest that a genetic element which affects pictorial perception both eidolic and epitomic, but perhaps more markedly the former kind, may be present.

Dramatic responses (e.g., flight or pecking) to pictures (that is, to objects classified as pictures by the presenters but not necessarily seen as pictures by those to whom they are presented) have been reported by observers of human and non-human behaviour. They are seen by some of the latter as evidence that non-human subjects can see pictures; such interpretation does not however fit easily the definition of pictures presented at the beginning of this paper. The responses although dramatic are so narrow in their scope that one is inclined to speculate whether some basic "hard wired" mechanism may be responsible for them. There appears to be no systematic body of investigations of these responses in human beings, although studies of neonates' responses to stimuli resembling faces (e.g., Johnson, Dziurawiec, Ellis, & Morton, 1991) can perhaps be said to fall into this category.

REFERENCES

Barley, N. (1986). *The innocent anthropologist*. London: Penguin Books.

Bartel, K. (1960). *Perspektywa Malarska*. Warsaw: P.W.N.

Bartlett, F. C. (1932). *Remembering: A study in experimental and social psychology*. Cambridge: Cambridge University Press.

Bayne, K. A. L., & Davis, R. J. (1982). Susceptibility of rhesus monkeys (*Macaca mulatta*) to the Ponzo illusion. *Bulletin of the Psychonomic Society, 21,* 476-478.

Beach, H. P. (1901). *Geography and atlas of protestant missions*. New York: Student Volunteer Movement for Foreign Missions.

Benhar, E., & Samuel, D. (1982). Visual illusions in the baboon (*Papio anubis*). *Animal Learning and Behavior, 10,* 115-118.

Bentley, A. M. (1986). Factors influencing identification of incomplete pictures by Zulu children. *International Journal of Psychology, 21,* 733-742.

Bentley, A. M., & Deręgowski, J. B. (1987). Pictorial experience as a factor in the recognition of incomplete pictures. *Applied Cognitive Psychology, 1,* 209-216.

Binet, A. (1895). Perception d'enfant. *Revue Philosophique, 30,* 512-514.

Boas, F. (1897). The decorative art of the Indians of the North Pacific Coast. *Bulletin of the American Museum of Natural History, 9,* 123-176.

Brendt, R. M. (1958). A comment on Dr. Leach's "Trobriand Medusa". *Man, 65,* 65-66.

Broby-Johansen, R. (1960). *Hjemmets Pinakotek*. Copenhagen: Gyldendal.

Carroll, L. (1889). *Sylvie and Bruno concluded*. London: Macmillan.

Coren, S., & Porac, C. (1978). Heritability in visual-geometric illusions: A family study. *Perception, 8,* 303-309.

Deręgowski, J. B. (1968). Difficulties in pictorial depth perception in Africa. *British Journal of Psychology, 59,* 195-204.

Deręgowski, J. B. (1969). Perception of two-pronged trident by two- and three-dimensional perceivers. *Journal of Experimental Psychology, 82,* 9-13.

Deręgowski, J. B. (1976a). Implicit shape constancy as a factor in pictorial perception. *British Journal of Psychology, 67,* 23-29.

Deręgowski, J. B. (1976b). Implicit-shape constancy: A cross-cultural comparison. *Perception, 5,* 343-348.

Deręgowski, J. B. (1976c). Coding and drawing of simple geometric stimuli by Bukusu school-children in Kenya. *Journal of Cross-Cultural Psychology, 7,* 195-208.

Deręgowski, J. B. (1976d). "Principle of Economy" and perception of pictorial depth: A cross-cultural comparison. *International Journal of Psychology, 11,* 15-22.

Deręgowski, J. B. (1980a). *Illusions, patterns and pictures.* London: Academic Press.

Deręgowski, J. B. (1980b). Some aspects of perceptual organisation in the light of cross-cultural evidence. In N. Warren (Ed.), *Studies in cross-cultural psychology.* London: Academic Press.

Deręgowski, J. B. (1984). *Distortion in art, the eye and the mind.* London: Routledge & Kegan Paul.

Deręgowski, J. B. (1989a). Real space and represented space: Cross-cultural perspectives. *Behavioral and Brain Sciences, 12,* 51-74 & 98-119.

Deręgowski, J. B. (1989b). Geometric restitution of perspective: Bartel's method. *Perception, 18,* 595-600.

Deręgowski, J. B. (1990a). On two distinct and quintessential kinds of pictorial representation. In K. Landwehr (Ed.), *Ecological perception research, visual communication, and aesthetics.* Berlin: Springer-Verlag.

Deręgowski, J. B. (1990b). Intercultural search for the origins of perspective. In N. Bleichrodt & J. D. Drenth (Eds.), *Contemporary issues in cross-cultural psychology.* Amsterdam: Swets & Zeitlinger.

Deręgowski, J. B. (1995). Perception - depiction - perception, and communication. *Rock Art Research, 12,* 3-22.

Deręgowski, J. B. (1998). A man is a difficult beast to draw: The neglected determinant in rock art. In S. A. Pager (Ed.), *Rock art research moving into the twenty-first Century.* Occasional SARARA Publication No. 4.

Deręgowski, J. B., & Bentley, A. M. (1986). Perception of pictorial space by Bushmen. *International Journal of Psychology, 21,* 743-752.

Deręgowski, J. B., & Bentley, A. M. (1987). Seeing the impossible and building the likely. *British Journal of Psychology, 78,* 91-97.

Deręgowski, J. B., & Byth, W. (1970). Hudson's pictures in Pandora's Box. *Journal of Cross-Cultural Psychology, 1,* 315-323.

Deręgowski, J. B., & Dziurawiec, S. (1996). The puissance of typical contours and children's drawings. *Australian Journal of Psychology, 48,* 98-103.

Deręgowski, J. B., & Jahoda, G. (1975). Efficacy of objects, pictures and words in a simple learning task. *International Journal of Psychology, 10,* 19-25.

Deręgowski, J. B., & McGeorge, P. (1998). Perceived similarity of shapes is an asymmetrical relationship: a study of typical contours. *Perception, 27,* 35-46.

Deręgowski, J. B, Muldrow, E. S., & Muldrow, W. F. (1972). Pictorial recognition in a remote Ethiopian population. *Perception. 1,* 417-425.

Deręgowski, J. B., & Parker, D. M. (1996). Viewing angle and the perceived orientation of pictorial elements: Geometric or representation effect? *Perception, 25,* 177-185.

Deręgowski, J. B., & Serpell, R. (1971). Performance on sorting task: a cross-cultural experiment. *International Journal of Psychology, 6,* 273-281.

Deręgowski, J. B., & Parker, D. M., & Dziurawiec, S. (1996). The role of typical contours in object processing by children. *British Journal of Developmental Psychology, 14,* 425-440.

Deręgowski, J. B., Shepherd, J. W., & Slaven, G. A. (1997). Sex differences on Bartel's task: An investigation into perception of real and depicted distances. *British Journal of Psychology, 88,* 637-651.

Dziurawiec, S., & Deręgowski, J. B. (1992). Twisted perspective in young children's drawings. *British Journal of Developmental Psychology, 10,* 35-49.

Elkind, D. (1969). Developmental studies of figurative perception. In L. P. Lipsitt & H. W. Reese (Eds.), *Advances in child development and behavior.* New York: Academic Press.

Forge, A. (1970). Learning to see in New Guinea. In P. Mayer (Ed.), *Socialization.* London: Tavistock.

Fraser, A. K. (1923). *Teaching healthcraft to African women.* London: Longmans.

Fujita, K. (1996). Linear perspective and the Ponzo illusion: a comparison between rhesus monkeys and humans. *Japanese Psychological Research, 38,* 136-145.

Fujita, K., Blough, D. S., & Blough, P. M. (1991). Pigeons see Ponzo illusion. *Animal Learning and Behavior, 19,* 283-293.

Gollin, E. S. (1960). Developmental differences in visual recognition under reduced cues. *Perceptual and Motor Skills, 11,* 289-298.

Gollin, E. S. (1961). Further studies of visual recognition of incomplete objects. *Perceptual and Motor Skills, 13,* 307-314.

Gollin, E. S. (1962). Factors affecting the visual recognition of incomplete objects: a comparative investigation of children and adults. *Perceptual and Motor Skills, 15,* 583-590.

Gregory, R. L. (1968). *Eye and brain.* London: Weidenfeld and Nicolson.

Gregory, R. L. (1973). The confounded eye. In R. L. Gregory & E. H. Gombrich (Eds.), *Illusion in nature and art*. London: Duckworth.

Herskovits, M. J. (1948). *Man and his works*. New York: Knopf.

Hinton, H. E. (1973). Natural deception. In R. L. Gregory & E. H. Gombrich (Eds.), *Illusion in nature and art*. London: Duckworth.

Hudson, W. (1960) Pictorial perception in sub-cultural groups in Africa. *Journal of Social Psychology, 52,* 183-208.

Hudson, W. (1962). Pictorial perception and educational adaptation in Africa. *Psychologia Africana, 9,* 226-239.

Jahoda, G., & McGurk, H. (1974a). Pictorial depth perception in Scottish and Ghanaian children: a critique of some findings with Hudson's test. *International Journal of Psychology, 9,* 255-267.

Jahoda, G., & McGurk, H. (1974b). Development of pictorial depth perception in cross-cultural replications. *Child Development, 45,* 1042-1047.

Johnson, M. H., Dziurawiec, S., Ellis, H. D., & Morton, J. (1991). New borns' perceptual tracking of face-like stimuli and its subsequent decline. *Cognition, 40,* 1-19.

Kidd, D. (1905). *The essential Kafir*. London: A.C. Black.

Leach, E. R. (1954). A Trobriand Medusa. *Man, 54,* 103-105.

Leach, E. R. (1958). A Trobriand Medusa? A reply to Brendt. *Man, 58,* 79.

Livingstone, D. (1857). *Missionary travels and researches in South Africa*. London: Murray.

Łuka, L. J. (1968/1971). Obrządek pogrzebowy u plemion kultury wschodniopo-morskiej na pomorzu gdańskim. *Pomorania Antiqua, 2,* 33-73; *3,* 21-100.

Lynn, J. H. (1948). Chick sexing. *American Scientist, 36,* 280-287.

Murray, F. S., & Szymczyk, J. M. (1978). Effects of distinctive features on the recognition of incomplete pictures. *Developmental Psychology, 2,* 356-362.

Nadel, S. F. (1937). A field experiment in racial psychology. *British Journal of Psychology, 28,* 195-211.

Nadel, S. F. (1939). The application of intelligence tests in the anthropological field. In F. C. Bartlett, M. Ginsberg, E. J. Lindgren, & R. H. Thouless (Eds.), *The study of society*. London: Kegan Paul.

Osborne, H. (1981). (Ed.). *The Oxford companion to art*. Oxford: Oxford University Press.

Perkins, D. N. (1972). Visual discrimination between rectangular and non-rectangular parallelepipeds. *Perception and Psychophysics, 12,* 396-400.

Perkins, D. N., & Deręgowski, J. B. (1982). A cross-cultural comparison of the use of a Gestalt perceptual strategy. *Perception, 11,* 279-286.

le Petit Larousse (1999). Paris: Larousse.

Pliny the Elder, *Historia Naturalis Book 35*. (Numerous editions, e.g., (1952), H. Hakham (Ed.), *Pliny natural history with English translation*. London: W. Heinemann.)

Rivers, W. H. R. (1905). Vision. In W. H. R. Rivers (Ed.), *Reports of the Cambridge anthropological expedition to Torres Straits*. Cambridge: Cambridge University Press.

Segall, M. H., Campbell, D. T., & Herskovits, J. M. (1966). *Influence of culture on visual perception*. Indianapolis, IN: Bobbs-Merrill.

Serpell, R., & Deręgowski, J. B. (1980). The skill of pictorial perception: An interpretation of cross-cultural evidence. *International Journal of Psychology, 15,* 145-180.

Shaw, B. (1969). *Visual symbols survey*. London: Centre for Educational Development Overseas.

Sigel, I. E. (1978). The development of pictorial comprehension. In B. S. Randhawa & W. E. Coffman (Eds.), *Visual learning, thinking and communication*. New York: Academic Press.

Thomas, L. T. (1962). Perceptual organisation of industrial inspectors. *Ergonomics, 5,* 429-434.

Thompson, J. (1885). *Through Masailand - a journey of exploration*. London: Sampson Low, Marston Searle and Rivington.

Thouless, R. H. (1972). Perceptual constancy or perceptual compromise. *Australian Journal of Psychology, 24,* 133-140.

Timney, B., & Keil, K. (1996). Horses are sensitive to pictorial depth cues. *Perception, 25,* 1121-1128.

Tindale, N. B. (1959). A Trobriand Medusa? *Man, 66,* 49-50.

Voyer, D., Voyer, S., & Bryden, M. P. (1995). Magnitude of sex differences in spatial abilities: A meta-analysis and consideration of critical variables. *Psychological Bulletin, 117,* 250-270.

Welford, A. T. (1968). *Fundamentals of skill*. London: Methuen.

Young, A. W., & Deręgowski, J. B. (1981). Learning to see the impossible. *Perception, 10,* 91-105.

Author Index

431

Subject Index